13

D0201599

THE MAN WHO BROKE
NAPOLEON'S CODES

THE MAN WHO BROKE
NAPOLEON'S CODES

711. 249. 1076. 718. 320. 1082. 365. 622.
699. 655. 699. 439. 669. 655. 1085. 711.
249. 1076. 718. 320. 1082. 365. 622. 699.
655. 699. 439. 655. 1085. 711. 249. 1076.
718. 320. 1082. 365. 622. 699. 669. 655. 108.

Mark Urban

HarperCollins*Publishers*

THE MAN WHO BROKE NAPOLEON'S CODES. Copyright © 2001 by Mark Urban. All rights reserved. Printed in the United States of America. No part of this book may be used or reproduced in any manner whatsoever without written permission except in the case of brief quotations embodied in critical articles and reviews. For information, address HarperCollins Publishers Inc., 10 East 53rd Street, New York, NY 10022.

HarperCollins books may be purchased for educational, business, or sales promotional use. For information, please write: Special Markets Department, HarperCollins Publishers Inc., 10 East 53rd Street, New York, NY 10022.

First published in Great Britain in 2001 by Faber & Faber Ltd.

FIRST EDITION

Designed by The Book Design Group / Matt Perry Ratto

Printed on acid-free paper

Library of Congress Cataloging-in-Publication Data

Urban, Mark.
    The man who broke Napoleon's codes / Mark Urban.
      p. cm.
    Includes index.
    ISBN 0-06-018891-X
    1. Scovell, George, 19th cent. 2. Cryptographers—Great Britain—Biography. 3. Peninsular War, 1807–1814—Campaigns—Participation, British. 4. Great Britain—History, Military—1789–1820. 5. Great Britain. Army—Officers—Biography. I. Title.

DC232 .U73   2002
940.2'742—dc 21

2001039284

02 03 04 05 06 ❖/RRD 10 9 8 7 6 5 4 3 2 1

For my beloved Madeleine

CONTENTS

PART III: THE CAMPAIGN OF JANUARY TO NOVEMBER 1812

PART IV: WINTER QUARTERS, THE VITORIA CAMPAIGN AND AFTERWARD

PREFACE

*B*etween 1807 and 1814 the Iberian Peninsula (comprising Spain and Portugal) was the scene of a titanic and merciless struggle. It took place on many different planes: between Napoleon's French army and the angry inhabitants; between the British, ever keen to exacerbate the emperor's difficulties, and the marshals sent from Paris to try to keep them in check; between new forces of science and meritocracy and old ones of conservatism and birth. It was also, and this is unknown even to many people well read about the period, a battle between those who made codes and those who broke them.

I first discovered the Napoleonic cryptographic battle a few years ago when I was reading Sir Charles Oman's epic *History of the Peninsular War*. In volume V he had attached an appendix, "The Scovell Ciphers." It listed many documents in code that had been captured from the French army of Spain, and whose secrets had been revealed by the work of one George Scovell, an officer in British headquarters.

Oman rated Scovell's significance highly, but at the same time, the general nature of his *History* meant that he could not analyze carefully what this obscure officer may or may not have contributed to that great struggle between nations or indeed tell us anything much about the man himself. I was keen to read more, but was surprised to find that Oman's appendix, published in 1914, was the only considered thing that had been written about this secret war.

I became convinced that this story was every bit as exciting and significant as that of Enigma and the breaking of German codes in the Second World War. The question was, could it be told?

Studying Scovell's papers at the Public Record Office (in Kew, west London) I found that he had left an extensive journal and copious notes about his work in the peninsula. What was more, many original French dispatches had been preserved in this collection. I realized at once that this was priceless. There may have been many spies and intelligence officers during the Napoleonic Wars, but it is usually extremely difficult to find the material they actually provided or worked on. Furthermore, Scovell's story involved much more than just intelligence work. His status in Lord Wellington's headquarters and the recognition given to him for his work were all bound up with the class politics of the army at the time. His tale of self-improvement and hard work would make a fascinating biography in its own right, but represents something more than that. Just as the code breaking has its wider relevance in the struggle for Spain, so his attempts to make his way up the promotion ladder speak volumes about British society.

The story of Wellington himself also gripped me. Half a century ago his campaigns were considered a central part of the British historical mythology and spoon-fed to schoolboys. More recently this has not been the case, which is a great shame. A generation has grown up without learning about his battles or indeed his mesmerizing and complex historical character. I therefore felt quite unashamed about giving him a central part in this narrative. One cannot think of a person less in tune with the emotional openness and social inclusiveness of our own time, but his results were spectacular: a paradox that fascinates me. He was certainly one of Britain's greatest military leaders, but without doubt one of the most difficult men one could ever have had to work for.

I have written Scovell's saga as a *story*, but the reader should rest assured that nothing significant has been invented to make it a better read. When Scovell is described, for example, as he walks to the top of a lighthouse in Corunna in January 1809 at the very beginning of this book, it's not an invention, but comes from a detailed description in his journal. The notes at the end of the book will hopefully provide the curious with a better idea of where much of the material came from. Journals and letters are the main sources for this text, and I have deliberately adopted a writing style that fits in with those sources, avoiding references to phenomena or people unknown in 1809.

Although this may be narrative history, it is still meant to be history and there were many occasions when I resisted the temptation to put thoughts into his head or those of the others in Wellington's staff. Much of Scovell's emotional life remains a closed book to me. His partnership with his wife was a strong one, but, alas, I have not been able to find letters between them or other documents that would really fill out this aspect of the story. Scovell's journal barely mentioned her since it concentrates solely on his professional concerns. Similarly, he did not leave us an account of his childhood. It was not poor, we know that, but it was not rich either, and it seems that Scovell regarded his life as a struggle to escape his origins and become a financially independent gentleman.

Did he change the face of history? It's up to the reader to decide. What was important to me was that Scovell did extraordinary work but has languished in obscurity for too long.

One word about style. I have used modern spellings in my own text, but often kept period ones in the quotes, notably when transcribing manuscript sources. Thus, most obviously, the modern word *cipher* is frequently rendered *cypher*. While mentioning this frequently used term, it is worth pointing out that the secrets Scovell uncovered were not protected by "codes" in the strictly defined modern sense of the word. The tables used to convert letters or words into digits are properly called ciphers. I hope cryptographers will permit me the liberty of using the two words *codes* and *ciphers* fairly interchangeably in this work: I am doing no more than accepting modern usage. I agreed with the publishers that a book entitled *The Man Who Broke Napoleon's Ciphers* might be misconstrued to be about the humbling of a series of nobodies.

I must of course give thanks to the researchers who assisted me in this substantial task: Helena Braun (for transcribing the journal written in Scovell's often painful hand); Roger Nixon (for certain parts of the Scovell family story); Denise Harman and Ronald Rigby (details of the Clowes family) and Cyril Canet, who delved into the French army archives for me. Martin Scovell, a great-great-great-grandson of George's brother Henry, gave me valuable assistance on their family history.

During my labors the library staff at the Public Record Office, National Army Museum and British Library were indefatigable. Andrew Orgill, librarian at the Royal Military Academy, Sandhurst, was especially helpful. He dug out many interesting items from the papers of Major General John Le Marchant. Mrs. Margaret Richards, the duke of Beaufort's archivist at Badminton in Gloucestershire, rallied to my assistance when I belatedly realized what an important source the letters kept there might be. John Montgomery, at the Royal United Services Institute, was also vital to the project, using RUSI's collection and every interlibrary loan imaginable to help. He is also the custodian of the Challis Index, an almost forgotten attempt (by a long-deceased civil servant) at a complete biographical record of British officers serving in the Peninsular War. As can be imagined, it was most useful for checking details of service, dates, etc.

I must also raise my hat to those established Napoleonic historians who encouraged the amateur: Dr. David Chandler, Rene Chartrand, Paul Britten Austin, and especially Dr. Rory Muir, who checked my manuscript. My editors Julian Loose (Faber and Faber) as well as Dan Conaway and Nikola Scott (HarperCollins) deserve credit for licking into shape my sprawling tract. My editor at Newsnight, Sian Kevill, has my permanent gratitude for allowing me so much book leave. Lastly, I must applaud my beloved wife, Hilary, and daughters, Isabelle and Madeleine, for putting up with me (while writing and in general).

Any mistakes in what follows are mine alone.

THE CHARACTERS

$\mathcal{G}$eneral Arthur Wellesley, duke of Wellington: At the center of this drama is one of the great figures of military history, a man with an uncanny ability to fight on terrain of his own choosing and to understand his opponents' strategies. He was also intensely conservative (after his battlefield triumphs, he became Tory prime minister), defended the established order and believed that officers should rise through "family, money and influence."

Wellington was an utter perfectionist. His dispatches contain brutal criticism of allied commanders and damn his own with faint praise. He was unable to choose his generals—they were sent out by London, often for political reasons. In the face of often breathtaking amateurism by these officers, Wellington tried to exercise total control. He once complained, "I am obliged to be everywhere, and if absent from any operation, something goes wrong."

To insure his instructions were obeyed and incompetents kept under close observation, Wellington used a picked team of officers whose efficiency and objectivity could be relied upon. Men like Scovell and his colleagues on the staff were tools to achieve his ends. Although most respected their general deeply, few expressed any affection for him in their letters and diaries. Even one of those more partial to Wellington noted, "Some complain a little of him at times and are much afraid of him. Going up with my charges and papers for instructions I feel something like a boy going to school." His partisans believed that Wellington's harsh regime was indispensable to victory, one major writing home in 1811, "It is a hard task for a man to teach at once soldiers, officers, commissaries, staff, generals and last of all himself. This, however, he has done."

As an aristocrat and a minister in a Tory government when he assumed command, Wellington distrusted many of those who wanted to modernize the army. He chose as his aides-de-camp dashing young aristocrats, "my boys," who he indulged shamelessly while many of the staff officers who slaved to bring his army to the pitch of perfection he craved went unrecognized.

The Staff: Scovell's friends and workmates had the unenviable task of translating Wellington's impulses into orders, routes of march, and billeting plans. Nothing could happen without their work, but they were rarely taken into their commander's confidence, since he saw them as little more than servants, noting, "The staff officers of the army are attached to me to enable me to communicate my orders to my inferiors, and otherwise to assist me in the performance of my duty."

Wellington's HQ was an unlikely, and often tense, mixture of aristocrats and earnest graduates of the Royal Military College—"scientific soldiers" skilled in preparing orders, mapmaking and languages. Today it is hard to conceive of the subservience expected of these clever, diligent men. One graduate of the Royal Military College, describing in his journal an error of Wellington's that resulted in three thousand soldiers losing their lives through illness, remarked, "One ought not to venture an opinion. Nobody can appreciate all the motives that sway a Commander in Chief but himself."

Even though an appointment to the Staff offered unending toil and little incentive, there was intense pressure to get one. Working directly for a successful general offered desperate officers one of their few chances to come into contact with the great men of the age, be noticed and then promoted. Inevitably there was great rivalry and factionalism in this world, where Scovell was just one of many. A perceptive observer at headquarters noted, "The officers in the lower branches of the staff are sharp-set, hungry, and anxious to get on, and make the most of every thing and have a view even in their civilities . . . there is much obsequious time serving conduct to any one who is on office, or is thought to have a word to say to Lord Wellington."

Three of Scovell's colleagues in particular will feature in the book. Lieutenant Colonel William De Lancey was an American who acted as Scovell's immediate superior during his most tense period of code breaking. The son of a New York loyalist family, De Lancey enjoyed many of the social connections denied to Scovell. Handsome and confident, he was one of the *jeunesse dorée* of Wellington's HQ, since he met the general's exacting criteria of genteel birth combined with professionalism. In the final chapter, De Lancey is killed with Scovell at his side at the Battle of Waterloo.

Henry Hardinge and FitzRoy Somerset both knew Scovell before the Peninsular campaign and remained his friends for life. Hardinge was a classmate of Scovell's at the Royal Military College with a gift for being in the right place at the right time. He had numerous scrapes with death and was also involved with codes. Although the son of a country vicar, Hardinge was able to display the fearless zeal expected by Wellington and so entered his inner circle. This became important after the war, when Hardinge was appointed as a minister in the Tory government headed by the duke. It was Hardinge who saved Scovell from the poverty of half pay when Wellington later forgot his codebreaker.

Somerset benefited from being from one of the great noble families and therefore easily found his way onto the staff without any formal training at the age of twenty-one. Many noticed that Somerset bore a striking physical resemblance to Wellington as a young man, and he soon became one of the commander in chief's intimates. Young FitzRoy was also noted for his kindness and as the general's private secretary proved a well-placed ally for Scovell. Later, as Lord Raglan, Somerset ordered the infamous charge of the Light Brigade during the Crimean War.

Major General John Le Marchant: The guru of "scientific soldiers" like Scovell, Hardinge and several other members of the staff, Le Marchant was the visionary who established the Royal Military College in 1802 and campaigned against the army establishment for the creation of a professional general staff. He believed that Britain had no other choice if it was to stand a chance opposing Napoleon's armies as they swept across Europe. In 1805, after yet another rejection for his staff plans, Le Marchant wrote, "How can we be so absurd as to oppose that, neglecting as we do all instruction and the aid of science in our military enterprises, [if] we are to be victorious over troops that possess those advantages in the highest degree of perfection?"

During the early years of the Peninsular War, Scovell and other Royal Military College graduates wrote many letters to their old teacher, and the Le Marchant papers form one of the fascinating but barely tapped primary sources for this book. As a scientific soldier, Whig and advocate of Catholic emancipation, Le Marchant in many ways stood for everything Wellington opposed. His professionalism was so widely admired, though, that in 1811, to the surprise and delight of his old students, Le Marchant was given command of a heavy cavalry brigade in the peninsula. Scovell's code-breaking breakthrough and Le Marchant's personal moment of triumph came together, at the decisive Battle of Salamanca in July 1812. Tragically, it was at this moment that Le Marchant was killed by a French sharpshooter.

Major General Charles Stewart, Lord Londonderry: The prime minister's half-brother, a reactionary Tory who typified the "gentleman amateur" approach and was a self-appointed scourge of army reformers, Stewart loved to wear extravagant hussar uniforms encrusted with decorations. He served as adjutant general in Wellington's army, but absented himself each winter, when the campaigning slowed down, so that he could attend to business and maintain his social life in England.

Wellington believed that the way to handle men like Stewart, whose appointments he could not prevent but whose presence on campaigns he understood as politically necessary, was to sideline them. Stewart wrote from Portugal to his brother, "the situation and business of the Adjutant General, deprived of close communication with the head of the army, is

reduced to keeping accurately the returns of all descriptions of regiments . . . you will admit it does not carry with it interesting or pleasing
occupation."

When Stewart tried to assert himself, the Commander in Chief
checked him mercilessly. Years later, Wellington described one argument:
"at last I was obliged to say that if he did not at once confess his error
and promise to obey my orders frankly and cordially I would dismiss
him *instanter* and send him to England in arrest. After a great deal of
persuasion he burst out crying and begged my pardon." Early in 1812,
after a number of unpleasant scenes, Stewart went on indefinite leave.

During the long campaigns in Iberia from 1808 to 1814, Wellington
slowly revised his opinion about the desirable qualities for his generals. Le
Marchant and Stewart, at opposite ends of the spectrum, eventually convinced him that professionalism was more important than party allegiance.

Don Julian Sanchez: A Castillian guerrilla leader, Don Julian embodied
the spirit of the anti-French resistance. It was Wellington's good fortune
that the don had grown up in Ciudad Rodrigo, one of the principal
fortresses on the Portuguese-Spanish border and a key area in Britain's
struggle against the French. Sanchez and his *partida* were expert horsemen; before the war they enjoyed nothing more than riding into the oak
forests to hunt wild pigs with *picos,* or lances.

Early in 1810, Don Julian's men wiped out a party of eighty French
dragoons, refusing to take prisoners. The French responded with a
proclamation that Sanchez would be executed as soon as he was caught.
When British forces moved toward Castille, Don Julian's *partida*
applied their pig-hunting skills to the French messengers who tried to
cross the Castillian plain. One of their most celebrated coups was the
capture of the French governor of Ciudad Rodrigo.

Don Julian's dirty war made some British officers most uneasy.
Captain William Bragge described one meeting in his journal: "Don
Julian and Carlos, the great guerrilla leaders, joined our army with
their Myrmidons and a more verminous set of fellows you never
beheld." But such sentiments were a luxury that Wellington could not
afford: the Spaniard provided more of the captured communications
necessary for Scovell's code breaking than any other *guerrillero.*

Marshal Nicolas Jean de Dieu Soult: The son of a small holder and notary in southern France, Soult made his way up the ranks, serving as a sergeant in the Royal Army at the time of the French Revolution. His progress was then swift, rising to divisional general by the time of Napoleon's celbrated 1800 Italian campaign.

Soult was created one of the first batch of marshalls of the empire declared in 1804. His zenith coincided with that of his master, with the glorious victory over Austria and Russia in the 1805 Austerlitz campaign. An able administrator and strategist, Napoleon showered the marshals with titles, honors, and pensions. Having reached his peak influence, Soult became increasingly nervous about his position in later years, taking whatever action he felt was necessary to sustain his wealth and power. Dubbed "the Iron Hand" by his soldiers and "the Sultan of Andalucia" by his rivals in the officer corps, he was a feared opponent on and off the battlefield.

Joseph Bonaparte, King of Spain: Napoleon's older brother was a lawyer by education and would probably have practiced his profession quietly in southern France and his native Corsica had history not placed his sibling on the pedestal of supreme power. After Napoleon crowned himself emperer of France, he sought to secure his hold over the vassal kingdoms he had conquered by placing members of his family on their thrones. For Joseph and his wife, Julie, this initially meant enoblement as the king and queen of Naples.

When the French took over Spain, Joseph accepted its crown (another of Napoleon's brothers wisely refused the same honor) and tried to pacify its rebellious population. Joseph oscillated between a deluded optimism that he could win over his new people, expanding the small pro-French party, and a sense of hopelessness about the scale of his task.

Marshal Auguste Frederic Marmont: When he was sent to Spain, Marmont was the same age as Scovell (thirty-six), but had acquired all of the honors and glory Napoleon's empire could heap upon a man of modest origins who had risen through the technical arms. Marmont was an artillery officer whose early career brought him close to Bonaparte. During the Egyptian campaign, he served as aide-de-camp and was one of the chosen handful who was with Napoleon when he left the army to its fate and returned to Paris to seize power.

Marmont superceded one of the army's greatest heroes in command of the sixty-thousand-strong Army of Portugal. His predecessor, Masséna, had been broken by Wellington, so Marmont went to Spain well aware that it was becoming the graveyard of commanders' reputations. Once in command he was bombarded with often contradictory orders from the emperor and his brother, Joseph, who had been placed on the Spanish throne.

Several times, Marmont outwitted Wellington by skillful maneuver and the use of surprise, but a major victory eluded him as the two men entered the campaign of 1812. Through his captured dispatches Marmont's anxieties emerge as he uses every ounce of his skill and experience to try to avoid defeat in the run up to Salamanca.

PART I

FROM CORUNNA TO TALAVERA,
THE CAMPAIGNS OF 1809

Bay of Biscay

Corunna

ASTURIAS

Bilbao

GALICIA

Cordillera *Cantabrica*

Vitoria

Vigo

Burgos

Braga

Duero

Oporto

Duoro

SPAIN

Tormes

Salamanca

Almeida

Cuidad Rodrigo

Busaco

Frenada

Fuentes d'Oñoro

Fuente Guinaldo

MADRID

Coimbra

PORTUGAL

Tagus

Vimeiro

Abrantes

ESTRAMADURA

Talavera de la Reyna

N

Elvas

Badajoz

Guadiana

LISBON

Albuera

Sierra *Morena*

Seville

ANDALUCIA

0   100   200
kilometres

2000m
1000m
500m
0   Heights in metres

Mediterranean Sea

CHAPTER ONE

*711. 249. 1076. 718. 320. 1082. 365. 622. 699. 655. 699. 439. 669. 655.
1085. 398. 326. 13. 309. 711. 1085. 655. 249. 481. 320. 980. 985. 186. 320.
843. 688. 2. 718. 249. 1297. 536. 174. 1085. 1024 . . . 713. 320. 980. 854.
655. 326. 536. 700. 699. 171. 1015. 1003. 13. 320. 980. 1015. 131. 320.*

RETREAT TO CORUNNA, JANUARY 1809

*G*eorge Scovell brought the glass to his eye and searched the horizon
for sight of sail. The cold blast of an Atlantic westerly buffeted
him this 14 January 1809. He was a little breathless yet again. For a week
he had been climbing the long flights of stone steps to the top of the lighthouse, sometimes several times a day, hoping to glimpse the British Fleet.
With each fruitless visit, he knew the anxiety of the army waiting in
Corunna's hinterland behind him was growing. Where were the ships?

All of Europe knew that Napoleon had perfected the mightiest armament since the legions of ancient Rome. They were steeped in science, they
were daring and cunning too. And now that Corsican Ogre's mighty host
was bearing down on them, weaving its way through the Galician hills. At
any moment the French advance patrols would reach the outposts behind
Corunna and they would have their moment of reckoning. If the ships did
not come soon to take them away from this cursed spot, the British army
would be smashed and its remnants swept into the dustbin of some

hideous prison. Its officers had already begun speculating what the next few years might hold for them as prisoners of war.

Certainly the wind was just right, blowing across the cold gray Atlantic and into Scovell's face. A good wind to carry the fleet into Corunna Bay and set sail again for home. No doubt this was the best vantage point too. The Spanish called it the Tower of Hercules, a great lofty pillar built by the Romans during the time of Trajan, which still served the purpose that those ancient conquerers had intended: as a lighthouse alerting ships to the dangerous rocks off the isthmus that marked this northwestern corner of Spain.

As Scovell glanced through the telescope again, his patience was rewarded. Sails began to blossom on the horizon. First the topgallants, as just the peaks of the first few masts crested into view, then more and more spreads of taut canvas. Admiral Samuel Hood was bringing up a huge squadron: 112 vessels, far more than at Trafalgar four years before. Only this mission was very different, for just 12 belonged to the Royal Navy; the rest were merchantmen chartered cheaply and packed with lubbers under poor captains. Embarking an exhausted army in a crowded harbor, probably under enemy fire, there was much that could go wrong.

Scovell set off, anxious to get the news to headquarters. General Moore's regiments had begun arriving at Corunna four days earlier, after a terrible retreat through the snowcapped Galician mountains. They had been marched beyond the limits of human endurance. Many had dropped dead from exhaustion, thousands more had been left straggling behind. Many of those who fell back froze to death, while others were slaughtered by French cavalry patrols whose energetic pursuit did not allow for prisoners. Those who had cheated a grisly fate had been arriving in small groups for the previous couple of days. Scovell passed many of these wretched soldiers. He had despaired at their condition as they limped toward the sea, some leaving bloody smudges in the snow as they tramped across it, barefoot. They had marched out of Portugal the cream of the British army, mainly first battalions of its finest regiments. Now their scarlet uniforms were stained and patched, bodies crawling with lice, bellies empty and eyes sunk in their sallow faces. Scovell noted in his journal, "Never did so sudden an alteration take place in men, they were now a mere rabble, marching in groups of 20 or 30 each, looking quite broken hearted, and worn out, many without shoes or stockings."

Moore's soldiers had become euphoric at the sight of the sea. It promised deliverance. Their sense of anticipation had soared as they hobbled into the hills just above the port. A few miles before they could see the brine, they had noticed a warming of the temperature and lush vegetation, an abundance of trees bearing lemons, oranges and pomegranates. After the barren wastes they had marched through in Lugo and Astariz, Corunna had seemed like the Garden of Eden. But the relentless threat of the approaching French and the uncertainty about the fleet quickly reminded them of the reality of their situation and the possibility of a fight. As word spread of Hood's imminent arrival, all kinds of rumors coursed through the narrow streets of Corunna.

As Scovell continued by horseback toward the port's hinterland, groups of infantry were being rallied to their different colors. They had to occupy the shoulders of the Corunna peninsula, and in particular the shoulder that commanded the harbor, in order to stop the French from shelling the embarkation. He also saw hundreds of hussars standing next to their mounts, deep in thought. Nobody was quite sure how long their enemy would allow them to perform the delicate operation of lifting off the army, and since there were orders to get the heavy guns and cavalry embarked first, it was clear that not many horses would be loaded onto the transport vessels.

The cavalry knew the army would not surrender thousands of highly trained mounts to Napoleon. In some armies, when capture was inevitable, the horses were hobbled, the tendons on the backs of their legs sliced so the poor animals could barely walk, let alone gallop to the charge. This, however, was not the way that the British cavalry intended to conduct its affairs.

Somehow a rumor began to run through the ranks that the horses were to be killed forthwith—whether they were standing in the cobbled streets of the town or in the fields behind it. None of the cavalry generals would ever own up to having given such a command, but almost immediately an immense slaughter began.

One captain of the 10th Hussars kept a record. He wrote despairingly:

> *"In executing the order for the destruction of these irrational companions of their toils, the hearts of the soldiers were more affected with pity and grief than by*

*all the calamities they had witnessed during the retreat.
On this occasion the town exhibited the appearance of
a vast slaughter house. Wounded horses, mad with
pain, were to be seen running through the streets and
the ground was covered with mangled carcasses."*

At first, it was decided to dispatch the animals with a pistol shot to the
head. However, many of the troopers literally flinched from their duty
as they pulled the triggers of their flintlock pistols, thus either maiming
their chargers or missing them altogether. New orders were barked
above the terrible din of dying animals. "In consequence of their uncertain aim with the pistol," the same hussar officer continued, "the men
were latterly directed to cut the throats of the horses." Corunna's cobblestones were soon running with ruby blood.

Outside the port itself, other regiments set themselves to the same
unpleasant task. Some of the hussars and dragoons wept as they drew
their weapons. Hundreds of horses were shot on the beach, and their
lifeless bodies were soon being dragged back and forth by the waves,
blood bubbling in the surf. On the cliffs just southwest of Corunna, men
of the artillery train, having dispatched their draft animals, pushed their
wagons and caissons over the precipice, watching them smash to pieces
on the rocks below.

Despite the cool of mid-January, the deliberate slaughter of so many
others soon began to create an overwhelming assault on the senses. A
commissary, one of the civilian supply officers accompanying the army,
wrote in his journal:

*"Their putrefying bodies, swollen by the rain and
sun and bursting in places are lying under the colon-
nades in front of the public buildings in the market
place, on the quays of the harbour, and in the streets;
and while they offend the eye, they fill the air with a
pestilential stench of decomposition, that makes one
ill. Over 400 of these wretched animals lie about
here, and the discharge of pistols, which are adding
to their numbers, continues incessantly."*

In fact, when the regiments later accounted for their animals, it became clear that something approaching three thousand horses were killed in and around Corunna.

The sun was sinking over the Atlantic as Scovell left the grisly scenes of Corunna behind him and he reached headquarters up in the hills overlooking the port. Napoleon's wars had transformed Scovell's expectations beyond anything he could have imagined twenty years before when, as an engraver's apprentice, he had seemed destined for a tradesman's life. Instead he had risen to the status of gentleman by the granting of an officer's commission and had even managed to make his way onto the staff of General Moore, one of the most celebrated soldiers of his age.

Captain George Scovell was a deputy assistant quarter master general. Not the deputy, nor one of the several assistants, but a deputy assistant, a title that seemed to say "insignificance" and to say it in a mumble. So did his rank. Scovell was nearing thirty-five years old and running very lamely in the promotion stakes. Certainly he did not look like any young thoroughbred. The hair above his round, benign face had already started receding from the brow. He had overcompensated somewhat by growing his sideburns thick and wide, covering most of the cheek with a ginger brown thatch. It was voguish to sport these, but younger, more handsome types did not cultivate quite such formidable whiskers. On Scovell they seemed to reinforce the impression of a kindly countenance, and of a man who had aged past the point of being a threat in the race for preferment. He wore a red coat with the yellow distinctions of the 57th Foot marking its collar and cuffs, one of the most common combinations in the army. The only striking thing about his appearance were Scovell's eyes. A deep blue, the kind of color the portraitist struggles to capture, they endowed him with the appearance of acute intelligence. But where exactly had favorable impressions gotten him during his thirteen years of soldiering?

Scovell had tried everything from ceaseless labor to the customary sycophancy toward those in authority to the huge expenditure of buying a captaincy in a fashionable cavalry regiment: none of it had worked. In fact, all it had done was bring him to the brink of financial ruin, and, after a series of slights, seen him end up in the 57th. There he bided his time, still cherishing the dream of commanding a cavalry regiment, something most of his colleagues would have regarded as utterly unrealistic.

During these past few months he had worked in the quarter master general's department, under Colonel George Murray. His job was to translate General Moore's orders into reality: to choose the routes of march, find the fodder, chart unknown countryside, locate the billets and, most importantly for what was to happen in later years to Scovell, to gather information. The QMG's labor was vast and unending, for it began all over again each time the army marched into some new place.

Scovell's fellow DAQMGs, also captains, like Warre, were ten years younger. Hardinge, his friend and one of Moore's aides-de-camp,* was a dozen years Scovell's junior. These sharp-set young bloods were running the real race. William Warre, from the family of port shippers who were renowned even in this time, was strikingly handsome. One portrait depicts him in the dashing dark blue uniform of the light dragoons with seductive large eyes, a kiss curl across his forehead and the fur-trimmed hussars jacket, or *pelisse,* thrown over his left shoulder. Another of the young DAQMGs had his own secret weapon in the advancement game: his maiden aunt and her constant companion, Goully, one of the ladies-in-waiting at Windsor. These two formidable spinsters made sure the ambitious officer's name was not forgotten by the duke of York and even the king himself. As for Hardinge, he was in the same lowly regiment as Scovell, the son of a Shropshire clergyman. But Hardinge had two advantages: at twenty-two he benefited from twelve years that Scovell could never regain, and this was an army where the highflyers had to be noticed by twenty-five or twenty-six. Hardinge also possessed that uncanny ability to be at the right place at the right time, something that creates a mystique among soldiers.

Just six months earlier, in the summer of 1808, the British army had set out with bold hopes and noisy public fanfare to aid their Spanish allies in the Iberian Peninsula. All of England had been talking about Spain's heroic struggle against Napoleon. Scovell had joined this expedition a few weeks after it landed in Portugal.

---

* "Field assistants," the junior officers used by a general to communicate orders and act to observe operations on his behalf.

The defeat and capture of a French corps at Bailén in July 1808 had caused a sensation throughout Europe. General Dupont had marched eighteen thousand men into British captivity, a humiliation never inflicted on France by its more powerful enemies Austria and Russia in a dozen years of campaigning. Events in Spain captured the imagination of British society so completely that, for a few months, the usually bitter party game between the Whigs and Tories had given way to consensus. The former were smitten by the romance of Spain's popular rising against the French and the tales of what ordinary folk, animated by patriotism, could achieve. The Tories regarded Napoleon's reverses as the long-awaited evidence that these godless Jacobin regicides would receive their just desserts.

When, the month after the Battle of Bailén, Lieutenant General Sir Arthur Wellesley had defeated a French force at Vimeiro in Portugal, this was all the government needed to send a full-scale expedition to the Iberian Peninsula, under Castlereagh's vague directive to "cooperate with the Spanish armies in the expulsion of the French from that Kingdom."

Late in 1808, however, following the twin humiliations of the French at Bailén and Vimeiro, Napoleon had gone into Iberia to sort out the mess himself, and the Spanish armies there had started collapsing as soon as he struck them. It rapidly became clear that Britain's force of thirty-five thousand was not going to win the war on its own. Retreat was Moore's only option.

While Colonel Murray and the officers struggling to draw up evacuation plans had come under heavy fire for a series of organizational blunders in the course of the campaign, Scovell's duties had actually grown. He had proved himself to Murray as a very capable officer, and the QMG was doubtless impressed by Scovell's thirst for self-improvement and desire to learn as many professional lessons as he could from his first campaign. The captain's habit of sitting down to write in his journal, often after having spent long hours in the saddle in driving rain or snow, was one of his most admirable traits. Whereas other officers might down a few glasses of wine and then lose themselves in the oblivion of sleep, Scovell would find a table and scratch away with a quill, digesting the lessons of the campaign before taking his rest. This diligence led Murray to give Scovell the responsibility for much of the army's communications.

For an army of thirty-five thousand to follow the plans drawn up by Moore and his QMG, a constant stream of messages was needed. In practice this meant orders and reports being scrawled on small bits of paper by a general, often on horseback, and carried away quickly by a courier. If this missive arrived late, in the wrong place, or not at all, the consequences could be catastrophic. Sometimes these dispatches were entrusted to British dragoons. Other times they were carried by a small ad hoc unit under Scovell's personal command, the Corps of Guides. The Guides were an odd assortment, a group of a few dozen men assembled on the cheap, all foreigners hired locally for their knowledge of the countryside and their ability to speak the language. When Scovell was placed in charge of his little band of Italian, Swiss, Portuguese and Spanish deserters and ne'er-do-wells, none of them even knew how to ride a horse, and their commander had been forced to teach them everything on the march. While Scovell resented being worked to the point of exhaustion on a task that would win him few plaudits in the army, he did recognize that it would offer him a good opportunity to display his extraordinary abilities as a linguist, another skill that had already been noticed by Colonel Murray. Scovell's French was fluent, he was picking up Spanish as he went, and he had some grasp of Italian. Using these abilities, he was at least able to teach his men, where most other English officers would have floundered.

Perfecting the army's system of communications was just the type of thankless task eschewed by those members of the staff most obsessed with seeking glory and promotion. Scovell was no less intoxicated by heroic dreams—he clung to his hope that his ultimate destiny lay in leading a regiment of British cavalry, sabers drawn, to some glorious charge—but he was sensible enough to his station in headquarters to know that he could only reach his goal by applying himself diligently to the tasks Murray gave him. Already, Scovell had become fascinated with the workings of secret messages, codes and signals. The navy were the experts in this field, and on his passage down to Portugal months earlier, Scovell had copied dozens of signals into his notebook, filling in the sketched flags with brightly colored inks. It was his attention to the navy's signaling methods that had resulted in Murray delegating him to superintend the vital task that lay in the hours ahead: embarkation at Corunna.

Just as the campaign marked the beginning of Scovell's involvement with trying to organize the army's communications, so it had shown the extraordinary intelligence that could be obtained by intercepting enemy dispatches. One month before, an order from Napoleon's headquarters to one of his marshals, General Soult, had been captured by Spanish guerrillas and sold to the British. From it, Moore had learned that Soult was advancing into northwest Spain with a detached corps small enough for the British to fight successfully. This precious knowledge saved Moore from blundering into the main French army. Later, at the end of December, another vital scrap of intelligence (in the form of a report from a Spanish agent that Napoleon was marching his main force toward the British in an attempt to cut off their retreat) caused Moore to turn his small force around so that it could find a safe place of embarkation.

But now, all hope to expel Napoleon from the Iberian Peninsula seemed extinguished and the British troops were ready to leave the Continent, hopeless and dejected. For just as the army scattered about Corunna had been the best Britain could field, the minds put to the task of directing it had also been top flight. General Sir John Moore was widely acknowledged as the most professional commander in the army. His attention to detail, zeal for the service and active intellect were generally respected. If these men had failed so miserably, what hope was left?

CHAPTER TWO

J. 249. 1076. 718. 320. 1082. 365. 622. 699. 655. 699. 489. 669. 655. 1085. 898. 326. 13. 309. i. 1085. 655. 249. 181. 320. 980. 985. 186. 320. 843. 688. 2. 718. 249. 1297. 536. 174. 1085. 1024 . . . 713. 320. 980. 854. 655. 326. 536. 700. 699. 171. 1015. 1003. 13. 320. 980. 1015. 131. 320.

THE BATTLE OF CORUNNA, JANUARY 1809

*A*t dawn on 15 January the feeble first light revealed a scene of great activity in Corunna Bay. The dismounted cavalry had been embarking throughout the night. Longboats crisscrossed the harbor, carrying the troopers to their cramped berths. They clambered on board with their valises and portmanteaus and into the dirty spaces offered by vessels usually carrying coal or bales of wool. Some of the horses had been saved, generally the officers'. One final moment of anguish awaited one cavalry subaltern who had not had the heart to kill his charger. "One of these poor brutes followed the boat which bore its master—an officer of the 18th Hussars—to the transport," noted the commissary in his journal. The animal's head could be seen straining to stay above the swell, nostrils flared as its legs galloped away underwater, and it "swam like a dog from the shore to the ship; but it could not be taken on board. All who witnessed this incident had tears in their eyes."

Moore's artillery was already largely afloat. Some guns had been hoisted on board the few vessels at anchor in the harbor even before Hood's squadron arrived. By the fifteenth, there were only nine field pieces ashore, and they garnished the infantry's positions on the hills behind the port. Some were apprehensive about this, since they suspected Marshal Soult would bring far more guns to bear, and they were not wrong, for as that dawn broke the first of forty cannon were already being manhandled into range of British positions.

On the heights of Palavea, two of the French field pieces had been dragged up by their gunners and by noon they opened fire. This ominous, unmistakable sound echoed across the bay, shattering the illusions of anybody who might have thought Marshal Soult was going to give up and allow the escape of his quarry. It took no time for the French artillerists to find their range, and many of Moore's troops stood in positions that offered no cover.

Scovell was hard at work down on the quayside. He had his own private worry about the embarkation; namely whether he could honorably discharge his reponsibility to his Guides. Since they were an exotic mix of half a dozen nationalities (none of them English), he was afraid that they would be left behind if the battle was lost and it turned into a pell-mell scramble for the boats. And since many of Scovell's Guides were deserters from the French army, they could expect only one thing if Soult captured them. At this moment, on the afternoon of the fifteenth, however, there was nothing he could do for them. They were still up with their divisions and he had others to embark.

Moore's deputy assistant QMG was unhappy for other reasons too, as he stood watching the bustle in the port. He believed that the order to get so many guns on board was unwise in the extreme. Around fifty pieces had been embarked, turning a British superiority in that arena into a decided weakness. "Knowing that we should be obliged to fight an action to ensure our safety," he asked rhetorically in his journal, "why deprive yourself of so powerful an arm?" He did not take into account, however, something evidently beyond the ken of a frustrated and passed-over captain, that the loss of artillery was a peculiarly political thing, a matter of propaganda. Generals were court-martialed for the loss of guns. Napoleon, an artillery officer by trade, had made a curious fetish of listing with delight the pieces captured during his many victories in his news sheet, the *Moniteur*.

*   *   *

The firing on the morning of the fifteenth had not heralded a general action. The French still had men and equipment they wanted to bring up. Moore's plan of defense, as day turned into evening, was based on a string of hills behind the port, which like two great arms embraced the goings-on in the harbor. The only real weakness in this position was where the arms met, where a small river called the Monelos cut through the massif and ran down to Corunna Bay. If the French could batter their way through this natural opening in the defenses, the withdrawal of much of Moore's infantry would be threatened. Soult could then hope to capture a few thousand of them, and his already considerable prestige in Napoleon's court would be further enhanced. The tactical soundness of the plan was typical of the man, for he had risen by grasping the detail of successful military operations while accepting their overall direction by the emperor. Napoleon himself had broken off the chase when it had become apparent that he and his guard could not catch up with Moore. He did not want the British to have the satisfaction of escaping him in person, so he had ordered Soult, whose troops nicknamed him the Iron Hand, to continue the pursuit.

As Soult surveyed Corunna Bay with his staff, messengers kept arriving and departing with news of his army. Like many of Napoleon's principal lieutenants, Marshal Soult had accumulated wealth and titles during the previous decade's campaigning. He had dressed his young aides-de-camp in a striking uniform of his own design, with blue shakos* and yellow coats. Their outfit was against regulations, but *ma foi!* these ADCs were his personal representatives after all. The marshal himself wore his dark blue general's coat and clad his bow legs with white breeches, and as he gave orders in his strong southern French accent, he cut a fine figure on horseback, his head crowned with black curls and a handsome decoration on his breast. Soult's confidence ran deep. For his generals of brigade and division were similarly experienced in the business of crushing the emperor's enemies. Each knew their place within the Napoleonic system of war and each was the veteran of many battles. These men had beaten the Russians, the Austrians and the Prussians—why should the British worry them unduly?

---

*The shako was a tall cylindrical military hat, usually with a peak and a badge or national emblem on the front.

In the early hours of the sixteenth, the British general was woken by one of his staff with an important dispatch. He still hoped he might not have to fight. "Now, if there's no bungling," said Moore as his assistant went to leave, "I don't see why we should not all be off safely tomorrow."

This was not to be. Under the cover of darkness, the French had been working to prepare an attack on the weak point of the British line. Soult ordered ten cannons to be heaved up the heights of Penasquedo, a ridge overlooking the Monelos gap. The gunners slaved away in the pitch black, using their shoulders, ropes, blocks, tackle and gun spikes to get their pieces into range.

At first light, a young French light infantry officer, rejoicing under the name of Louis-Florimond Fantin des Odoards, looked down from the Penasquedo to the British positions. "As a light fog dispersed, an eminently picturesque view appeared to us," he recalled in his memoirs. "On the opposing heights were English troops, and beyond one could see the city of Corunna, its port and bay crowded with countless ships. A clear sky, brilliant sunshine and all of the warmth of early spring completed the panorama. Nothing broke the complete silence that reigned in the valley between the two armies."

Soult's brushes with Moore's rear guard had taught him that any engagement with the British had to be carefully prepared, and so, even as the hours ticked by on that morning of 16 January, he did not order his assault. The French marshal was bringing up a force of infantry not much larger than the fourteen thousand on the British side. It was in artillery and cavalry that Soult had the decided superiority: more than four times as many guns and a force of three divisions of horses; forty-five hundred fine troops. Soult had a keen military mind, which had led him to the command of that great self-contained military organism that was the French *corps d'armée** at the same age as Scovell, while Scovell, from similarly humble origins, was languishing within his own organization. Since the British only effectively occupied one of the two ridges behind the city (the easternmost, or left from the perspective of the British general looking south), Soult intended to strike in the low ground between them. He would use an initial infantry assault to pin the British

---

*Army corps, an assembly of two or more infantry divisions, light cavalry and artillery—its numbers could vary from 10,000 to 75,000.

down while the cavalry were pushed into the gap made by the Monelos and cut off Moore's line of retreat. All the time, the British battalions, standing in lines two men deep and three hundred to four hundred wide, would be pounded by a hot fire from the Penasquedo ridge.

The French hid their intentions sufficiently well for Moore to resolve on the morning of the sixteenth to begin withdrawing his men in preparation for boarding, starting with Paget's division. They were at the rear of the British position (closest to the port) and were the best placed troops to foil Soult's plan and plug the Monelos gap. It may also be that Soult, lacking decisive infantry superiority and contemplating a difficult assault, was waiting for precisely such a diminution of Moore's troops before ordering the attack. Paget's men had actually been marched to the port when the sound of a heavy cannonade late in the morning caused them to halt.

French guns had opened up from the Penasquedo ridge, sending cannonballs slamming into the British ranks. The standard French field piece was an eight-pounder, firing iron balls about the diameter of a small grapefruit, but the mass of these solid metal spheres was such that if an eight-pound shot hit a file of men standing one behind the other, it could easily kill a dozen before it lost momentum. The range from the Penasquedo heights to the British lines, about five hundred meters, was well within the eight-pounder's effective killing area.

With the cannon dealing death from the ridge, French troops, who had been waiting just out of view, began walking down the Penasquedo in battle formation. Captain Fantin des Odoards's battalion of the 31st Light Infantry was among the leading units, and he noted: "To reach the enemy position, we had to go into a deep gully and climb its other side. At the same time, a powerful battery thundered from the heights we had left toward those of the English; they responded with a hot fire, and it was under a canopy of cannon balls criss-crossing over our heads that we reached the enemy position."

The French veterans were sufficiently used to the demented whiz of cannonballs not to slacken their pace. They kept marching forward. On the British slope, however, soldiers were ducking down as the eight-pound shot began to smack into the bodies and limbs of their comrades. Moore appeared on horseback, apparently oblivious to danger, and tried to reasssure them that the terrifying noise made by a cannonball signified that it had in fact already passed overhead.

At the foot of the British-held slope was the village of Elvina. Soult needed to capture it to secure the flank of his own cavalry force, which was going to rush past it into the Monelos gap. The French succeeded early on in capturing the village and British troops were ordered to counterattack. As they began walking toward Elvina, the 42nd Highlanders (the famous Black Watch) and the 50th Foot had to endure heavy fire from the French battery overlooking them on the Penasquedo. And it was in Elvina that the heaviest fighting of the day raged.

Many officers on the British side had noted the "miraculous transformation" of men they had seen straggling into Corunna a couple of days before. In truth, the redcoat loved a fight. Nothing else compensated for the privations of campaigning in the same way. The marching of the previous two months had worn them out, body and soul. They had seen the French many times, but whenever battle had seemed imminent they had been ordered to resume the trek toward the coast, a retreat that many, officers and men, thought so dishonorable and pointless. Now the echo of cannon was reminding them of their purpose. Even so, Moore must have had his concerns, watching a group of Highlanders recoil in horror as one of their comrades crumpled screaming to the ground, his leg carried off by a cannonball. The general steadied the Scots, calling out to the wounded man, "My good fellow don't make such a noise, we must bear these things better." His troops did not disappoint him.

With each victim the French cannon claimed, the advancing men shuffled toward the colors flying at the center of their battalion, closing ranks. In that way, a continuous line of muskets was maintained despite the losses. The weapons they carried were ineffective beyond two hundred yards and could only be used with devastating effect when fired en masse at half or even one quarter of that distance.

When the 42nd and 50th finally took Elvina from the French, they soon received a heavy counterattack. This contest was a savage affair, the village echoing to the shouts of soldiers impaling one another on bayonets. The crackle of musket fire continued, but was soon joined by much louder explosions; the French had moved several guns forward to rake the buildings with grapeshot. These munitions spewed out dozens of smaller balls, multiplying the killing power of each cannon. Each discharge of grape into Elvina sent shards of stone and plaster flying off the buildings, lacerating the British troops with this debris and choking them in dust and smoke. It did not take long to drive Moore's two battalions out of the village again. The Highlanders had 150 men killed and wounded in this action, the 50th, 185 men (casualties of between one in five and one in four of those fighting).

General Moore rode close to the scene of the action to order a brigade of two Guards battalions to counterattack and retake Elvina. He sent Captain Hardinge, his ADC, to bring up one of the Guards units. The young staff officer reported back to his chief on the slope above the village, within full view of the French batteries overlooking the area.

"I was pointing out to the General the situation of the battalion," Hardinge later recorded, "when a shot from the enemy's battery carried off his left shoulder and part of his collar bone. The violence of the shock threw him off his horse; but not a muscle of his face altered, nor did a sigh betray the least sensation of pain. The blood flowed fast, but the attempt to stop it with my sash was useless from the size of the wound."

Carried from the field, Moore remained conscious as the British stubbornly fought their way back into Elvina and the momentum of the French attack slowly died away. Paget's division marched back up from the port to plug the gap in the British defenses at the Monelos river, and the French cavalry sent to break through in this direction came under heavy fire, leaving it with no choice but to retire.

As darkness engulfed the battlefield, fighting ebbed away and Moore lay dying in a Spanish house, attended by a surgeon and some of his staff officers. It had been apparent to everyone, not least the general himself, that it was a mortal wound. He was barely able to speak, but when news was brought to him that the French had been hammered to a standstill, Moore whispered, "I hope the people of England will be satisfied."

With the hills illuminated only by moonlight, General John Hope, who had taken over command, began the difficult task of extricating his troops. He was well aware that the French might attempt further assaults if they detected this movement, so sentries engaged in a charade of noisy calling between posts and stoking of campfires while the bulk of their comrades filed off.

The British soldiers passing through Corunna at dawn on the seventeenth presented a most sorry spectacle. They had looked dreadful even

before the battle. But now, one eyewitness noted : "They were all in tat-
ters, hollow-eyed, covered with blood and filth. They looked so terrible
that the people of Corunna made the sign of the cross as they passed."

Up on the Penasquedo ridge, the French spent a fitful night. The men
of the 31st Light Infantry shared around some rough wine and stale
bread. "[We were] recounting the day's events, and mourning comrades
who had stood on the threshold of their careers," one of their captains
remembered. "Behind the camp, in some ruins, was our dressing station.
The cries of the unfortunates suffering amputation there, carried by the
gusts of a strong wind, did not lighten our insomnia. Toward midnight
the enemy's fires began going out; by day we were surprised to see their
embarkation had been carried out in the darkness."

On the morning of the seventeenth, Soult, seeing the British had abandoned their positions, moved his batteries forward onto a promentory
overlooking the harbor and ordered them to fire.

For an instant it looked as if the worst fears of the officers organizing the embarkation were coming to fruition. Some of the inexperienced
masters of merchantmen panicked, cutting their cables in an attempt to
escape the French cannonballs and make their way out to sea. "Everybody commanded, everybody fired, everybody hallooed, everybody
ordered silence, everybody forbade the fire," one officer later wrote. In
this chaos, four of the small transports ran aground. Sailors were dispatched in longboats to rescue the crews and passengers of these
stricken vessels. Some of the Royal Navy escorts began responding with
broadsides toward the French batteries. As the grounded merchantmen
were cleared of passengers they were set on fire to prevent them from
becoming prizes of the French. Soon the bay was full of smoke, the
thundering of heavy guns and the cries of men in longboats trying to
find space on board the few ships not full or getting under way.

The moment of Scovell's private anxiety had arrived and he rapidly
assembled his Guides near the waiting boats. He had been ordered not
to take the dozen or so Spaniards home, although some of them pleaded
to be allowed to go with the army. Instead they were each paid a bounty
of fourteen Spanish dollars; they signed for their money and disappeared into the streets of Corunna. But the others, Italians and Swiss

who had deserted the French and given good service to the British army, had to be gotten on board quickly. Scovell calmed them as the bay thundered with the echo of French guns.

With the harbor itself becoming unsafe, the staff decided to switch the embarkation to the other side of the Corunna isthmus. This was risky, since there was no quay there and the rocks that were to be used as a makeshift jetty would answer for this purpose for just a few hours at high tide. Scovell moved his anxious Guides across to this new place, where, to his immense relief, they were taken off on the evening of 17 January.

Scovell himself left it as late as he safely could, when all but a couple of thousand British troops were afloat, taking a longboat out to *Implacable*, an impressive seventy-four-gun line of battleship of the Royal Navy squadron. Early on the eighteenth the last British troops embarked. Later, several officers (including the dashing Captain Warre) claimed in their journals and letters home the honor of being the last man to leave. For these ambitious young bloods, it was important that their patrons learn of their gallant act as quickly as possible, and circulate the story in the salons. Alas it was to be Hardinge, eyewitness to Moore's death, who would be in demand at many a general's table on their return, to tell his melancholy tale.

What could have been on Scovell's mind as he sat down later to an unpalatable meal in *Implacable's* wardroom, exhausted from forty-eight hours without sleep and the strain of organizing the safe retreat? Relief at the imminent return home to his wife, Mary? General Moore, his admired superior, was dead. The British expedition into the Iberian Peninsula had been a failure, vitiated only by the heroic performance of the British infantry behind Corunna and the hussars during the retreat. Many of the regimental officers were whispering about the staff's incompetence. Scovell's own role was known to a few, Murray among them, but hardly glorious enough to bring promotion. Scovell's personal fortunes were as low as they had ever been.

It can be safely assumed that sitting in the dark gun deck of the *Implacable* as it rolled in a heavy Bay of Biscay swell, he was not in high spirits at the prospects opening up before him. He could not have known that his stay in England would last only a few weeks and that he would then join a new expedition that would give him one more chance to distinguish himself.

CHAPTER THREE

9. 249. 1076. 718. t. 1082. 365. 622. 699. 655. 699. 439. 669. 655. 1085. 398. 326. 13. 309. i. 1085. 655. 249. 481. t. 980. 985. 186. t. 843. 688. 2. 718. 249. 1297. 536. 174. 1085. 1024 . . . 713. t. 980. 854. 655. 326. 536. 700. 699. 171. 1015. 1003. 13. t. 980. 1015. 131. t.

INTERLUDE IN ENGLAND, JANUARY TO MARCH 1809

*J*ust a few days after the Corunna embarkation, British ships started appearing in ports along the southern coast. Many commanding officers would not let their men off until they had been cleaned up and dressed in new uniforms. But in some places the remnants, as barefoot ragamuffins of Moore's army, were marched past shocked townsfolk. If the Spanish had been moved to make the sign of the cross, it can be imagined what an impression they made in the prosperous lanes of southern England.

From Falmouth to the Solent, the fleet disgorged the consequences of another ill-conceived foreign expedition in numerous bays and harbors, reminding many of previous disastrous campaigns where the Royal Navy had come to the rescue: in Flanders, the River Plate, Dardanelles and the second Egyptian campaign. One observer wrote in the *Times*, "the fact must not be disguised that we have suffered a shameful disaster."

The *Implacable's* passage took just three days from northwest Spain to Torbay. The ship was a prize of Trafalgar, one of twenty vessels taken when the French sailors had finally surrendered by striking their colors. Three and a half years later, this trophy of the nation's most sublime victory at sea was bearing back the lice-infested survivors of yet another ill-considered adventure on land.

Scovell left the *Implacable* in Torbay and made his way to Portsmouth, where his two horses, servant and the remnants of his Corps of Guides had been disembarked. He returned to a land buzzing with rumor and speculation, one in which the name of Sir John Moore was already being murmured with the reverence befitting a martyr of the long struggle against the French.

It was a sign of those factious times that those who exalted the late general's memory soon found themselves trying to counter a whispering campaign against the fallen commander in Parliament and Horse Guards. Major General Charles Stewart, who had served in the Corunna campaign, was one such malcontent. Stewart damned Moore several years later in one of the first histories of these events: "He wanted confidence in himself—he was afraid of responsibility—he underrated the qualities of his own troops and greatly overrated those of his adversary." The argument over Moore's legacy was an outburst of London's permanent struggle between Whigs (who revered Moore as a reformer and an enemy of the lash) and reactionary conservatives.

Stewart, a cavalry general, was the brother of Lord Castlereagh, the secretary of war, and as such was influential among the ruling Tory faction in London. Of limited brain and boundless confidence, Stewart had risen through influence and was Scovell's polar opposite. Everything about him was show. He loved his hussar's uniform with its rows of rich lace weaving back and forth across the chest, connecting shiny buttons. The ensemble was crowned with a furry busby towering eighteen inches on his head. Stewart was also fond of wearing his decorations, great crusty chunks of enamel and jewels, in the field, seeing himself as the dashing light cavalry officer, a *beau sabreur** par excellence. Moore on the other hand saw him as "a very silly fellow." If only it could have been that harmless. As a member of Parliament serving in the field,

---

*Literally a "handsome swordsman."

something not uncommon, he had no understanding of the dangers of mixing party politics with military duty. Since political influence counted for so much in the army hierarchy, however, he was a fool who had to be suffered gladly by various generals.

Stewart was not the only critic, but others were a little more delicate. A few weeks after the Corunna embarkation, Captain William Warre, for example, wrote in a letter to his father, "Everything I hear confirms my opinion that our retreat from Spain, etc etc etc was inconsiderate, and I fear will place us in rather a disgraceful light. This *entre nous.*"

Word about the Corunna campaign was slowly filtering around the country. London newspapers carried both the French accounts of these events as well as Castlereagh's version. Some carried verbatim translations of French army reports: "The English retreated in confusion and consternation . . . the English have lost everything that constitutes an army; generals, horses, baggage, ammunition, magazines," the *Gentleman's Magazine* reported. And the truth was that eight thousand of Moore's thirty-five thousand had not come home. Perhaps only one-tenth of these had been lost at the Battle of Corunna itself, while the remainder had expired or fallen behind on the dreadful retreat.

For the architects of this expedition, it was important to quash these criticisms by declaring a glorious victory as quickly as possible. Lord Castlereagh went to Parliament on 25 January and paid tribute to Moore, who, he said, could not be blamed for following his difficult orders from London and, "fell deeply lamented, on the 16th January at Corunna, where he defeated a very superior French army and established the glory of the British military character."   ·

Swiftly he moved on to more palatable business. Two days later, with recriminations about Corunna still echoing in the lobbies of Parliament, Castlereagh felt it an auspicious moment to remind everyone of the victory of Vimeiro six months earlier. There, Lieutenant General Sir Arthur Wellesley had defeated the French army sent to occupy Portugal.

On 27 January, Lieutenant General Wellesley entered the chamber to receive the vote of thanks in person. Wellesley looked around, acknowledging the approbation of his fellow MPs. He wore his full dress uniform: red coat, with cuffs, collar and lapels of royal blue, chevrons of gold lace marking his rank on the sleeves. In the field, he preferred a plain blue coat, but Wellesley was a man of finely honed

political instincts and he knew that in this particular arena he must look
the part of the conquering hero. As he listened to the panegyrics, many
members no doubt took the opportunity to study him. Wellesley's
hooked nose and hawklike gaze were often remarked upon. Goya
sketched him a couple of years later with his close-cropped hair brushed
forward across the brow, enhancing the impression of an intense,
brooding intellect. His wiry frame and precise manner of speech suggested an active, zealous personality. Sir Arthur had shown great merit
in his military service in Flanders, Ireland and India. His rise within the
army, though, was due in large measure to political patronage.

Having grown up in one of the great Anglo-Irish political families,
Wellesley understood how to speak to this audience. He may have privately considered many members of the Commons to be little more than
upstarts and blackguards, but Wellesley knew well that they saw themselves as the defenders of England's ancient liberties. Exploiting these
sentiments would consolidate his good standing. In replying to the vote
of thanks, he thus told them:

> No man can value more highly than I do the hon-
> ourable distinction which has been conferred on me; a
> distinction which it is in the power of the representa-
> tives of a free People alone to bestow, and which it is
> the peculiar advantage of officers and soldiers in the
> service of His Majesty to have held out to them as the
> object of their ambition.

While the Corunna affair may have cooled some of the patriotic excitement of the previous summer, the performance of the British troops in
Elvina or of the cavalry in its rear-guard actions had convinced many
members of Parliament that the game in the Iberian Peninsula was still
worth pursuing. Others also believed the nation wanted to see Sir John
Moore avenged, and, finally and most pressingly, there were rumors
that Austria was about to launch a new war against France. The expediency of organizing a further expedition to stir up the Iberian hornet's
nest was clear to most members of Parliament. If anyone was favorite to
lead such a new enterprise it was Arthur Wellesley. In the Commons
they knew he had won victories in India, but what they really cared

about was that he had made such a good showing against the French at Vimeiro (never mind that the odds were stacked in his favor) and that he had the complete confidence of the ministry.

Scovell did not allow himself time to weigh up the events of Corunna for some months. He attended to business in Portsmouth as best he could and then set out at the end of January to find Mary. He had not seen her for six months and the time Scovell spent with his wife in February 1809 was an idyll that would sustain him through untold hardship in later months.

Mary had retreated to Yorkshire, to be with friends and family, and Scovell found her at Sprotborough Hall, a huge mansion with elaborate gardens and great fountain, where she was staying as a guest.

George and Mary had grown up in rather different worlds. She was the eldest daughter of the Clowes family, Lancashire landowners. Her family were not hugely wealthy during her childhood, but by 1809 the expectations of the Clowes clan were looking more promising with each day. Twenty years before, when her grandfather had made a will, their scattered holdings around Salford and Manchester had given him a worth of £5,000—certainly no great sum. The Clowes patriarch, however, had lived on (surviving his son, Mary's father) to see his holdings increase in value several fold as their city became one of the throbbing hearts of England's industrial revolution.

Scovell on the other hand had come from humbler origins. He was "the son of very respectable parents, though not independent gentlefolks," in the tactful words of a family servant. His parents (also George and Mary) had married at St. Martins in the Fields church in Westminster, London, in 1770. Young George, born in the capital in 1774, was the oldest of five siblings. Scovell, it seems—for he was reticent about revealing details of his early life—grew up in the great metropolis of his birth. He had excelled at school, particularly in languages, mastering Latin, Greek and French. As a teenager, George's father had propelled him toward a trade, for the Scovell family could not afford to carry passengers, and George found himself apprenticed to an engraver, an occupation in which his patience and methodical approach to problems could be applied to some profit.

It was the mayhem across the channel, and Napoleon Bonaparte's emergence from it as emperor, that transformed Scovell's prospects. The triumph of France's revolutionaries had touched off a series of invasion scares in Britain. The army needed to be expanded rapidly and vast reserves of militias, yeomanry and fencibles assembled in case Bonaparte's hordes crossed the channel. It was this mobilization that allowed Scovell to escape his destiny hunched over an engraver's table and become a gentleman. When the Warwickshire Fencibles, a regiment of cavalry for home defense, was raised, his intelligence and literacy singled him out for commissioning as an officer in 1798.

When, in 1800, the Fencibles were disbanded, Scovell was offered the chance of converting into a regular cavalry regiment, the 4th Dragoons, with the rank of lieutenant—a transition from a band of county amateurs to one of Britain's best-trained bodies of heavy cavalry. By this stroke of luck, he had taken another step up the ladder of gentility and done so for no outlay whatsoever, for those seeking advancement in a regiment as fashionable as the 4th Dragoons often paid large sums of money to jump the promotion queue.

Scovell loved his new life in the 4th. He took on extra duties as the colonel's adjutant, helping to administer the regiment, while applying himself earnestly to training. His desire to make his way in this new military family was so intense that late in 1803 he paid a vast sum, £3150, to buy a captain's commission in the 4th Dragoons. Since he had netted just £262 from the sale of his lieutenancy, he had to draw on his family for the difference, almost £2900. This high figure (almost as much as the purchase of a commission in the Household Cavalry) reflected the 4th's status as a fashionable regiment.

For Captain Scovell this purchase strained every financial sinew. One year later, in 1804, Scovell's regiment found itself posted to the south coast in response to renewed hostilities with France. But it was not their military duties that were to prove the ultimate cause of his crisis. The 4th found itself in Brighton and Lewes and its officers were soon doing long hours in the salons and assembly rooms adorning the fashionable set surrounding the prince of Wales. There were numerous functions requiring full dress uniform, royal reviews of the regiment, and much granting of reciprocal hospitality.

Finally, the expense of holding his own on the regimental scene exceeded by three- or fourfold his captain's yearly pay of about £270; Scovell had no choice but to give up the game. The bitter remedy for his financial malady involved increasing his income and lowering his outgoings. He accepted the advice of those who told him that the best way for a man of his talents and limited means to make his way in the army was by joining the staff. Late in 1804, a few months after the 4th went to the south coast, Scovell transferred to Derby in the Midlands. There, he received extra pay while working at the local headquarters as one of the new breed of officers being established by Horse Guards. His duties as a "major of brigade" (confusingly, he remained a captain) involved assisting the major general in command of this army district. The tasks of staff officers were many and varied, from helping the general in disseminating his orders to preparing the regiments garrisoned in the district for deployment overseas.

Despite overreaching himself financially, Scovell had still benefited enormously from being in the army. It took him to the centers of fashionable society—to Bath and Brighton, where he could observe the greatest men of his age and believe that he had ventured far from his origins—and it had also transformed the onetime apprenticed engraver into a worthy match for a grander family connection. Scovell's friendship with Captain Leigh Clowes of the 3rd Dragoons (another heavy cavalry regiment), who also lived in Derby, led to an introduction to his sister Mary, most likely at one of the many dances or assemblies attended by the eligible people of the county.

The union between George and Mary had been one of love, as their later adventures would demonstrate, but also one of carefully matched pragmatism. Though she was the eldest child, Mary stood to inherit very little: an allowance of little over £200 per year, in fact. Marrying at the age of thirty in an epoch when a young woman of good family usually made her alliance between twenty and twenty-five, she was also most unlikely to be deluged by rival suitors. By the rates of exchange of the Georgian marriage market, Mary's various liabilities equaled Scovell's one great one: his obscure birth.

For Mary, her brother's officer friend offered a way to escape the tedium of family life in Lancashire and to travel more widely. Her brother John was a clergyman, but although this must have brought many respectable men of the cloth into her social orbit, the prospect of sharing her life with them was evidently unenticing. Mary, it seems, shared Jane Austen's view that marrying into the army was an altogether more exciting proposition than the clergy: "It has everything in its favour; heroism, danger, bustle, fashion. Soldiers and sailors are always acceptable in society."

George and Mary were married in May 1805 in Manchester Cathedral. Soon after their union, Scovell applied to study at the Royal Military College in Wycombe. It was there that he could learn the business of a staff officer and in particular of the quarter master general's branch. His sights were set not just on scholarly edification but on the extra pay received by a deputy assistant quarter master general, just over £172 per annum. An ambitious Wycombe graduate hoped, once qualified, to be sent overseas on some expedition that might bring distinction and the notice of a general who could further his interests.

In 1806, the couple left Derby and took up residence near the college, where Scovell began life as a student. It is evident, though, that for all the happiness of his new life with Mary, Scovell was still in great financial difficulty. Although he avoided the conventional dangers awaiting cavalry captains off the battlefield (gambling, dueling or too much whoring), his life as an officer in the 4th Dragoons was still proving to be far beyond his means.

The promise of extra pay once he left Wycombe was not enough to save him now, so Scovell had to swallow an even more bitter pill. While still at the college, he transferred from the 4th Dragoons into the 57th Foot.

The cavalry carried a greater cachet than a marching regiment of foot, and the difference between being a captain in one regiment and another was a good deal of money: £1650 to be precise. So on 27 February 1807 Scovell signed a deed exchanging his cavalry commission with the less valuable one of Captain Oliver in the 57th. Henry Hardinge, a fellow student at Wycombe (and the same Hardinge who would later witness General Moore's death at Corunna) was also an officer in the 57th Foot, and he helped his friend Scovell arrange the deal. Scovell may have restored his finances with the £1650 gained from the swap, enough to secure his immediate future with Mary, but it also meant that in his early thirties, he had actually gone backward in the promotion stakes.

Prior to his first campaign in the Iberian Peninsula he spent the best part of two years working away at Wycombe on French, German, mathematics, trigonometry, topographical drawing, fortification and siege-craft. But although Scovell's brain propelled him into the ranks of Britain's most diligent and professional soldiers, he found it very hard to accept he had lost the status he had enjoyed for twelve years as a cavalry officer.

Now, in February 1809, following Scovell's return from Corunna, there was some time for reflection as George and Mary walked arm in arm around Sprotborough Hall's formal gardens, wrapped up against the February chill. He was losing hope of ever getting promotion, and his will to carry on working twice as hard as the officers with greater means and better connections was faltering. And did they talk about whether they might still be blessed with children? Or had Mary given up hope, for she was just a few months younger than George and many considered it unhealthy, even dangerous, for a woman of thirty-four to give birth.

While the captain on leave pondered whether he had any future in the army, events in London had taken a dramatic and unexpected turn. The whole system of military promotion and patronage had been blown open by a scandal. It involved sex, corruption and the Royal family. Since the hallowed traditions of Britain's press run as deep as those of its army, details were published extensively in the newspapers.

Days after Parliament had voted its thanks for the Battle of Vimeiro, a member of the Commons, one Colonel Wardle, had leveled a series of damaging charges against the duke of York.

The duke had for years kept a courtesan by the name of Mary Anne Clarke. He had broken off the affair in 1806, but she had continued to spend lavishly on fine clothes and high living, exploiting her connection with royalty to run up huge bills with London tradesmen. When the duke had told her to live within the means of the annual pension he was giving her, she had threatened to go public with accusations that she had been earning money by trafficking in army commissions. Not only had she been paid to bring the names of young officers to the duke's attention for promotion, but she had also been able to fake his signature on letters of recommendation. The commander in chief refused to pay her more hush money, so she had gone to Colonel Wardle with her allegations.

The ironies of the Clarke affair were rich. The duke of York himself often grumbled that the commission system was allowing wealth alone to determine the prospects of officers. The system of purchase, and the setting of higher prices for commissions in certain prestigious regiments, meant that these parts of the army were packed with the sons of rich tradesmen, "nabobs" who had made their fortunes trading Indian spices, or the new industrial barons of Derbyshire or Lancashire. Even the Life Guards, the most prestigious of regiments, had been nicknamed the Cheesemongers in the army a few years before and dismissed by the duke of York as "nothing but a collection of London tradespeople." But Mrs. Clarke had been pushing forward the sons of those very tradesmen the duke so despised, in lieu of settling her debts.

The episode left a bitter taste in many mouths and focused everyone's concern on the injustices and confusion of the system for advancement. Officers could make each step by a variety of means: simply being the most senior in their rank when a vacancy at the next rank came up; jumping the queue by buying that commission; or getting the recommendation of a senior figure like the duke of York.

So serious were these accusations that they resulted in the suspension of the king's son from his role as commander in chief of the army. The Clarke scandal left Parliament with a desire to find a fairer promotion system. Some changes were made. The practice used by many aristocratic families of getting a son commissioned early in his teens and while still at school so he could rise up the seniority ladder was ended. There were also new regulations to ensure that more senior ranks would be promoted strictly by seniority. Attempts would also be made to prevent officers from buying their way rapidly up toward the rank of lieutenant colonel (a method employed by Lieutenant General Wellesley, among others). Nevertheless, the sale of commissions went on, since a thing that miraculously transformed the sons of upstart tradesmen into gentlemen was too lucrative a scheme for the exchequer to quash. The changes in the promotion system were limited, but still angered many conservatives in the army who believed promotion should be based on breeding, connections and money.

On 19 February, a messenger brought the post to the low-bred captain on leave at Sprotborough Hall. Scovell broke the seal on the back of the folded paper packet and opened it. Perhaps the scandal playing itself out in London, and the promise of reform that it seemed to bring, led him to look more favorably on the letter's contents. He was appointed as a deputy assistant quarter master general on the staff of a new expedition to Portugal and directed to make his way to Cork Harbor for embarkation. His orders were signed in person by Lieutenant General Brownrigg, the quarter master general at army headquarters in Horse Guards. A few weeks later, Sir Arthur Wellesley was appointed to command the new venture.

Scovell had another ten days with Mary before he had to gather his portmanteaus, trunk and other effects. He had been with her for three weeks, and it was to be more than three years before they would see one another again. Britain was to try its luck once more in the peninsula. Scovell was chancing his with one more campaign. He was heading back to war.

CHAPTER FOUR

T. 249. 1076. n. t. 1082. 363. 622. 699. 655. 699. 489. 669. 655. 1085. 898. 326. 13. 809. i. 1085. 655. 249. 481. t. 980. 985. 186. t. 843. 688. 2. 718. 249. 1297. 536. 174. 1085. 1024 . . . 713. t. 980. 854. 655. 326. 536. 700. 699. 171. 1015. 1003. 13. t. 980. 1015. 131. t.

NORTHERN PORTUGAL, MAY 1809

*I*t was about 10 A.M. on a typically sleepy May morning as Scovell and some of the other officers on Sir Arthur Wellesley's staff dismounted in the narrow streets of Vila Nova. Oporto, that great city of northern Portugal, had burst out of the natural confines of the plateau overlooking the Douro gorge and the Vila Nova had been created as the New Town, a suburb on its southern bank. Their chief had already gone ahead of them, on the terrace of the Serra monasetry, formulating a plan of battle. As the men found their way through the quarter, the curious peeked from their windows at the red-coated officers. Many started bundling their families down into cellars, anticipating trouble with the British entering one part of their city while the French remained in the other. As Scovell and the others emerged from the huddle of Vila Nova's cheap little houses to join their chief beside the Serra monastery, a steep slope dropped away in front of them and a quite breathtaking vista presented itself. From their vantage points the British could look across the

Douro, deep in its channel. The curves of the river and the depth of its course opened Portugal's second city to them like a ripe fruit: the spires of the Se cathedral and the Tower of Clerigos marking its tempting center. Wellesley intended to make a sensational start to his second Portuguese campaign by delivering Oporto from French occupation.

The Serra occupied a point on the southern side of the river that was singularly suited to the British general's purpose. It was virtually the only one close enough to the heights opposite for cannon to rake them with fire. Looking down to the quayside on the northern bank, the occasional sentry making his rounds marked the only French presence. To the foreigner, there seemed an air of normality in the city. A local would have expected to see more bargemen and fishermen moving about on the quay, but the French sentries had told them to stay indoors. Smoke snaked lazily into the sky from the homes in the city above and behind them.

Wellesley and his men knew that the next few hours were going to determine whether their plan would secure them a famous victory or end in ignominy. So far, their presence in Vila Nova and that of thousands of troops filing through its little streets had gone undetected.

Oporto's heart, that morning of 12 May 1809, remained under the hand of Marshal Soult, and with him the same force that had driven the British into the sea at Corunna less than four months before. Despite the hour, Soult was still asleep after a night of dictating orders, while his staff was settling down to a leisurely breakfast. On the northern outskirts, General Mermet was gathering a convoy of wounded, wagons and artillery, getting ready to evacuate the city.

Soult had pulled back into Oporto when the British had come up from Lisbon, a movement Wellesley began in April. In order to improve the strength of his river line, the French commander had blown up a bridge that connected Vila Nova to the rest of the city. Upstream, he had scuttled the ferry boats. Downstream, he had posted dozens of lookouts from Franceschi's cavalry. The marshal thought Wellesley more likely to attack downstream, between the city and the Douro's exit into the Atlantic, since it was natural for the English to exploit the sea, where they would enjoy so many advantages. For all the marshal knew, the British might use naval transports to sail past the river's mouth and land troops on the coast north of it, so turning his flank. The French cavalry had been deployed to give early warning of any such project. The marshal understood his force was smaller than that of the redcoats and their Portuguese allies, but he relied on the deep dark waters of the Douro to protect him. If things went well, he would catch his enemies in the act of landing and crush them before they had achieved a critical mass. And if things went badly? The river would ensure that he still had a couple of days for a smooth evacuation.

Wellesley's staff was deeply nervous as they watched a small party of soldiers and locals bringing four barges from the northern quay to where British troops were waiting, still apparently undetected by the French. Their general, they were discovering, was as good at hiding his emotions as any man could be: he wore the mask of command, possessing that inscrutibility so vital for a leader in war. But they, who had so much to gain or lose from their master's good opinion, chatted nervously, lit the long brown cigarettes smoked by so many of the local people, and waited for Wellesley's audacious orders to unfold. There was probably much conversation about the previous day's affair at Grijó a few miles away. A squadron of the 16th Light Dragoons had been ordered to charge the French as they fell back to Oporto. The ground, studded with trees and divided by stone walls, was most unsuitable for cavalry. But a figure familiar to Scovell and the other staff veterans of Corunna had then become part of the equation. Major General Charles Stewart, who had used his influence to secure the post of Wellesley's adjutant general, had insisted that they charge, even though he was not in command of the cavalry and had not seen the difficult ground in question. The 16th had gone in and lost many men while the French had retired in good order. Things would have to go better today.

Down on the bank, men of the 3rd Foot, the Buffs, were climbing into the barges. They were usually used for ferrying port wine, that ruby red commodity that lubricated the Anglo-Portuguese relationship. But the barges that carried casks of the stuff down the Douro toward John Bull's table were being pressed into service ferrying troops—thirty men in each. The first wave set off at about 11 A.M. This was the moment of maximum danger, for if the French shot at them in the boats they would be almost defenseless. The Portuguese bargemen skillfully sailed them over, set them down and turned back to the south bank for the next wave.

Until this moment, the British might as well have been invisible, but crossing the Douro in broad daylight they had to be spotted, and they were. Reports began to arrive at French headquarters. Troops in red were crossing the river barely one mile away. Were they Swiss? The Swiss troops under French command also wore red coats. Perhaps some of the sentries were panicky too. Marshal Soult was woken.

As the Buffs formed up on the quay, the few French troops in the area ran to sound the alarm. The British quickly found a steep road that runs up the side of the northern bank. Almost on all fours, weighed down by their equipment, they ran up the flagstones, struggling against the steepness of the gradient. A hail of musketry might engulf them at any moment, so the Buffs' commander raised his men's spirits by getting them to give three cheers as they went. At the top of the slope, the Buffs burst into the Bishop's Seminary, a complex of buildings with the heavy construction of a fortress, and began barricading themselves. At last the French realized what was happening. The seminary was a critical place, since it guarded the landing point down on the quayside where further waves of troops were starting to arrive in rapid succession.

The man responsible for defending this sector of Oporto was General Maximilien Foy, a gifted artillery officer whose career was to become intertwined with that of the British, and he would be present at almost as many of Wellesley's battles as men like George Scovell himself. Foy was sharp enough to know that disaster could only be avoided by swift action. He ordered three battalions into attack formation and sent them forward at about 11:30.

Foy's advance was precisely the counter-stroke anticipated by Wellesley. In the gardens beside the Serra monastery on the other side of the river, three batteries of artillery—eighteen pieces—had been wheeled into position. The gun captains bent down and squinted along their barrels, calling final adjustments to the men with spikes levering away at the rear, so the cannons' mouths would be in perfect position to hurl death across the gorge. At the back of each British cannon, one man stood holding the linstock, a smoldering porte-fire that, when the order was given, would be touched to the hole at the rear of the gun to ignite the powder and begin the barrage. The gunners' eyes followed the columns of Frenchmen they could clearly see moving toward the seminary four hundred to five hundred yards to their front. They could hear them as well—gruff voices echoing across the Douro gorge *"en avant!,"* *"à l'attaque!,"* * the familiar cries of the emperor's victorious legions.

A crackle of musketry opened from within the seminary, puffs of smoke drifting from the firing points. The French, too, wanted to bring artillery to bear and were wheeling guns down by the riverbank on the northern quay. If they could cannonade the British as their barges came ashore, they could do great slaughter, for the redcoats would be caught packed together as they disembarked. Wellesley, though, had no intention of allowing them to give the first blow.

One of the British pieces, a howitzer, fired at the French guns on the quayside, hurling one of the new exploding shells designed by Major Shrapnel. It was not solid, like the six-pound shot fired by most of this battery, but packed with explosive powder that would send shards of its metal casing in all directions. Its target was a team of French gunners who were trying to unhitch their cannon from the horse-drawn limber used to tow it into position. As the British shell went off, it cut down every single one of them, perhaps a dozen men. This was not the first time that the Shrapnel shells had been used in battle, but it was the most dramatic effect many of the Royal Artillery officers had ever seen. The other guns began hitting the French attack columns on the ridge above.

At Marshal Soult's headquarters, the cacophony indicated that a serious battle had been joined in the heart of the city. Reinforcements were ordered up to join Foy's brigade. The evacuation of French stores and guns assumed a desperate speed. Orderlies were stuffing papers into trunks, wagons loaded with spoils, waiting to leave.

As the guns were thundering overhead, many more boatloads of redcoats had crossed the Douro. Men of the 48th and 66th had joined the Buffs up in the seminary. The French withdrew their last men from the quayside to reinforce those fighting on the heights above. As this happened, dozens of Portuguese emerged from their houses to launch fishing boats and more port barges into the river. The trickle of British troops crossing was soon a flood.

After three failed attempts to break into the seminary, the morale of the French troops was beginning to falter. Reports that another Anglo-Portuguese force was about to assault them in the flank were making the

---

*Forward! Attack!

French officers jittery; Foy broke off the attack. By midafternoon a general evacuation of Oporto was under way, with French troops pressing quickly along the roads.

A cavalry attack on the rear of a broken force could yield devastating results, but the ground to the north and east of the city was just as unfavorable as that in Grijó had been the day before. Major General Stewart once again took personal command of a squadron of light dragoons and ordered a charge. Once again, it was carried out with some losses and little positive effect.

Stewart's charge, though, did not spoil the positive results of the day's action. For trifling casualties (125 killed, wounded and missing), Wellesley's force had killed about 300 French, captured about 1,700 prisoners, many of whom had been abandoned in hospitals during the French retreat, and six cannon. The British army had seen its new commander in action and could not fail to be impressed. Wellesley took over Soult's fine headquarters to discover that the Portuguese servants had prepared a dinner, expecting their French guests to return that evening. Instead, the victor savored his culinary spoils.

Breathless at this success, Scovell penned a letter to Colonel John Le Marchant, his old teacher at the Royal Military College: "I must give you a line if it only shows how delighted I am at having been able to pay off my old friend Soult a few of the old scores we were in his debt at Corunna. He certainly never bargained to have them returned so soon and with such good interest." The staff officer had clearly been impressed with May twelfth's operation, telling Le Marchant "the passage of the Douro was certainly as gallant a thing as ever man did." As for the French, "they appear to have been so taken by surprise at the boldness of the attempt as to have completely lost their *brain work*" (underlining in original).

The verdict of some of Soult's officers was not that different. Captain Fantin des Odoards, the light infantry officer who had also been present at Corunna, decided "Marshal Soult allowed himself to be surprised because of an overconfidence that only the French are capable of." For Soult, the evacuation of Oporto had saved most of his troops, but it was the beginning of a greater crisis. He and his men (around twenty thousand) were on their own, with no other French troops to support them within one hundred or perhaps even two hundred miles. There were two main routes back to the comparative safety of Spain.

One ran north, close to the sea, but Soult did not want to use it, fearing that British naval superiority might endanger his withdrawal. The other road ran east, further inland, before turning north. This was his favored line of withdrawal, so Soult had already positioned one of his divisions, under General Loison, on this second route to protect it. After quitting Oporto, Soult therefore marched east to make his first night's bivouac. He needed to put some distance between himself and the English and that meant he could only allow his men a few hours' sleep.

Luckily for Soult, there was to be no British pursuit on the next day, the thirteenth, either. Wellesley had decided to give his men one day's rest after the hard marching of the preceding days, and to allow supply wagons to catch up. This failure to follow hard on Soult's heels immediately would have earned him the scorn of many a French commander. What Soult did not know, however, was that the British general had no intention of letting his enemy get away. Four days before, he had sent a column further inland under William Beresford, a British general who had been given the command of Portugal's army with the very grand (and rather French) sounding rank of Marshal. Beresford was a big, powerfully built man known in the army for his energy and intelligence. His career as a soldier had not always been a happy one, as three years earlier he had taken part in the disastrous expedition to the River Plate in South America and had been wounded, leaving his face badly scarred. Wellesley felt that the newly appointed commander of Portuguese troops was one of his more able generals and selected him for the vital task of cutting the very line of retreat that Soult hoped to take and had so prudently sent General Loison to secure.

In the early hours of 13 May, a messenger arrived at Soult's encampment. He bore a dispatch from General Loison announcing that he had been fighting some of Marshal Beresford's Portuguese, had failed to break through on the road toward Spain and was therefore marching back toward the main French body. It is not hard to imagine Soult's cold shudder on hearing that his line of withdrawal was cut off. He could not turn around and march back toward the sea, since the road through Oporto was in British hands. He was cornered, just like Dupont had been cornered at Bailén by the Spanish the previous year.

Everything Soult had earned by fifteen summers of hard soldiering was in jeopardy. It did not matter that he had shared in the glory of Napoleon's 1800 campaign in Italy, or led the key attack at Austerlitz.

Nor did it matter that France's conquering leader had created him duke of Dalmatia, endowed him with generous estates and substantial pensions. Dupont had been one of the favored too, but after Bailen the emperor had dubbed him *"le capitulard"* and stripped him of every honor and bauble. Napoleon even toyed with the idea of having this "capitulator," this loser Dupont executed, but imprisoned him instead.

Soult understood that there was only one way to avoid this fate. If both of his two possible roads back into Spain were blocked, he would have to cross the land in between them, which consisted of inhospitable mountains. Three chains of high ground, like three giant hurdles, ran east to west, separating him from the Spanish province of Galicia. This was barren ground too, often sodden with water, particularly in May, but supporting little more by way of vegetation than pines, ferns and scrub. There were no proper roads across these mountains, but Soult had been at war long enough to know that there are always paths of some kind, even if they are no more than those tracks used by local herdsmen.

If he was to save his army and himself, Marshal Soult knew he had to sacrifice the accompanying *bordel** of wagons containing booty, supplies and such that restricted his corps to the roads. More importantly, he would have to sacrifice his artillery, since it would not make it along shepherds' paths either. Rising to the crisis he had found himself in, the French commander spent no time bemoaning his fate, but immediately formed a new plan of action.

After sunrise on 13 May, Marshal Soult gathered his commanders together to outline the desperate steps that this desperate situation dictated. Captain Fantin des Odoards left a vivid account:

> The soldiers were ordered to keep only what was indespensable in their rucksacks so as to make room for cartridges. One saw piles of clothes everywhere, booty being consigned to flames; the larger baggage was destroyed, the artillery made unserviceable as far as possible; wagons were jettisoned, even the Marshal's, everything was sacrificed. These extreme measures told us enough about

---

*Literally a brothel, but the term has been used by French military men through the ages to describe the unmilitary gaggle of women and beasts following their troops.

the crisis our little army had found itself in. Anxiety and
pain showed on every face, and it was in a doleful silence
that we passed the scene of the destruction.

Wagons carrying £50,000 worth of silver coin also had to be abandoned.
Soult ordered them broken open, and allowed the passing men to scoop
handfuls of money. Such was the trepidation with which they now
looked at the mountain barrier ahead of them that many of the French
foot soldiers either declined this heaven-sent opportunity or dumped the
heavy coin as the marching became harder. The cannon were parked
with one muzzle aimed at another and fired, rendering them useless.

On 14 May, Captain Scovell set out with a small reconnaissance
force up the coastal route north. Since landing in Portugal for the second time, he had been assigned as the deputy assistant quarter master
general to a brigade of light cavalry. Scovell was not in command of
these troops, nor indeed was he the principal officer of Wellesley's
staff to ride with them. This honor fell to Lieutenant Colonel William
De Lancey, the deputy quarter master general, an officer from a well-
to-do American family whose loyalty to George III during the revolution had cost it much of its wealth and resulted in exile. Wellesley had
known De Lancey since he was a boy, and with his handsome looks,
an impeccable Tory bloodline and a generous ration of self-confidence
the American-born DQMG seemed like an almost perfect embodiment
of the young military gentleman. Even on the march up toward
Oporto, Wellesley had started using De Lancey as his personal execu-
tor with one wing of the army, making sure that orders were carried
out promptly and effectively.

The post with the light cavalry was much more to Scovell's liking than
his previous one. For one thing, it did not involve trying to teach deserters
to ride cheap nags in the Corps of Guides. Another advantage was that the
society among the hussar and light dragoon officers was much more amusing and closer to the ideal of gentleman cavalry officer that he aspired to,
despite his wearing the regimentals of the 57th Foot and the fact that his
company counted for little in the eyes of these rich young men. His new
position also offered plenty of possibilities for a keen soldier to find distinction. And their mission north to help find the French was an ideal
opportunity to bring himself to the notice of General Wellesley.

*   *   *

By the next day, 15 May, Soult's men had cleared the first of their three mountain hurdles, the Serra de Santa Catalina. A heavy rainfall had set in, drenching the French infantry and liberating all the evil smells that a season's campaigning had locked into their woollen greatcoats. Hours of struggling along slippery paths with waterlogged feet were followed by fitful sleep under sodden mantles. Those downpours soaked the British too, waterlogging the roads and splattering their white trousers in mud. The foot soldiers, cursing their prey, quickly nicknamed Soult the duke of "damnation" instead of Dalmatia.

On the evening of the fifteenth, the regiments Scovell was with were joined by Wellesley, Murray and several battalions of infantry in Braga, about thirty miles north of Oporto. Braga, a cathedral town considered Portugal's Canterbury, stands at the mouth of the Cavado Valley, which flows between the second and last of the three mountain barriers of the Minho country that Soult would have to cross. Even though communications with him were proving extremely difficult, Wellesley was hopeful that Marshal Beresford's force would be blocking the other end, the eastern end, of this valley, to block the French from leaving. Late that evening, the Portuguese military commandant of Braga came to the headquarters asking to see Wellesley. He knew the Minho ranges well and wanted to tell the British general about an old Roman road that would allow Soult to escape the Cavado Valley directly to the north, cutting straight across the Serra da Geres—the last of Soult's great hurdles—without running into either the British or the Portuguese forces at either end. Wellesley would not consent to speak to the Portuguese officer, who took it as a snub resulting from his low social and military rank.

By the morning of the sixteenth, Soult's bedraggled column had cleared its second hurdle, had turned east and was marching on top of a sort of shelf along the steep southern side of the Cavado Valley. Using the same route, Wellesley's troops moved swiftly from Braga in the same direction and that afternoon caught up with the French rear guard at a village called Salamonde.

Wellesley had shown daring in Oporto, but here he approached the new situation with the greatest caution. The nature of the terrain made an immediate charge with cavalry impossible. Scovell, De Lancey and some light infantry were sent exploring farther up the steep side of the valley to see if there was an easy way to bypass Soult's blocking force—probably about two thousand men. Wellesley meanwhile ordered up the Guards Brigade to assault the Salamonde position frontally. The British general's caution allowed Soult several hours in which to keep the head of his column marching, taking his corps down the side of the valley to the first of two bridges at its bottom. These spans would have to be crossed before Soult's corps could scale the final ridge and make its way back into Spain.

It was at this point that the advanced elements of Marshal Beresford's Portuguese column came into play. Guided by Portuguese staff, Beresford had the local knowledge that Wellesley lacked: the key importance of the two bridges. The old Roman road from Braga to Galicia in Spain descended the steep valley below Salamonde, crossed the two bridges deep in this natural trough before climbing up the other side, across the Serra da Geres mountains. Quickly, Beresford sent Captain William Warre,* the same officer who had been a fellow DAQMG of Scovell's at Corunna, ahead of the regular troops. He rode ahead of Beresford's regular troops, and using his fluent Portuguese placed himself at the head of the local armed citizenry. The bridge in Ponte Nova was built of wood and, under Warre's directions, they started pulling up the planks that formed its surface. This debris was thrown into a barricade on the northern bridgehead. It was not possible however for the militia to shift the big beams that formed the bridge's skeleton. These remained in place, challenging the daring or desperate to take their chances on narrow, slippery timbers.

Soult's men were not to be deterred. The marshal called for a major of the light infantry by the name of Dulong, who picked a force of hardy stormers and prepared for an assault that very evening. In a hail of musketry, Dulong's men ran across the bridge's slippery skeleton. Some slid off and disappeared into the foaming waters below, but the momentum of Dulong's charge succeeded in driving the Portuguese militia into the hills.

At the same time, around dusk, Wellesley struck the French rear guard at Salamonde. It crumbled immediately, finally showing the British staff how low their foe's morale had sunk on the march from Oporto. "The enemy hardly waited to receive their fire, but fled precipi-

---

*As the son of the celebrated port-shipping family, Warre fit naturally into Beresford's Anglo-Portuguese command.

tately," Scovell noted curtly in his journal. A more shocking account was penned by Fantin des Odoards, who recorded, "When toward evening, an English party attacked our rear guard, a few shots were enough to throw it into unbelievable disorder. Frenchmen are hopeless in retreat, and there we saw the proof of that old axiom of war . . . The confusion resulting from this panic was explosive."

As the French troops began streaming away from Salamonde in what was by then a black night, the head of their column was making its way across the half-demolished Ponte Nova bridge, cleared just moments before by Dulong's stormers. The Roman road in this part of the valley is little more than four feet wide. In the dark, the men struggled not to lose their purchase on its smooth flagstones, which had become slippery from the persistent rain. More and more, Soult's men were losing their discipline, cursing their individual struggle to survive, longing to go home and see their mothers or friends again in the Auvergne, Normandy or Paris. "Infantrymen and horsemen pressed against one another," Fantin des Odoards wrote, "throwing down their weapons and trying to outrun one another." Despairingly he described the crossing of the Ponte Nova, where thousands of frightened French soldiers were trying to make their way along the treacherous remnants of the bridge: "So many crowded on that numerous men were thrown off and drowned in the torrent or were trampled under the horses' feet. If the English had taken advantage of this rout, I don't know what would have become of us, the fear was so contagious, even among the bravest soldiers."

The English, however, were not taking advantage. The road down to the Ponte Nova was not the main route running up the valley, but on a turning off it. It was precisely this misconception that the Portuguese officer had wanted to alert the British to in Braga the night before. So instead of following the French, Wellesley had pressed along the main route east and realized only after a few hours that something was badly wrong—Soult's force had disappeared. Scovell and Colonel George Murray (quarter master general to Wellesley, just as he had been a few months earlier to Moore) were sent galloping into the night, trying to find a peasant who knew where the French might have gone.

By morning Scovell and Murray had discovered the scene at the Ponte Nova so vividly described by Captain Fantin des Odoards. The rear of the French column had already passed over the half-demolished bridge and the Portuguese peasantry had emerged to wreak vengeance on the invaders. Scovell wrote, "Nothing could exceed the horrid scenes I witnessed this morning. The road was literally strewed with dead and dying, and the Portuguese inhumanely murdering and stripping those who otherwise might have recovered. We saved several and took about 30 Prisoners." Scovell galloped back to Wellesley to report that they had found the trail of Soult's column again.

At the front of that mass of confused, tired, soaked Frenchmen, one step ahead of the murderous Portuguese villagers, Soult's advanced scouts had pressed up the Roman road, and on rounding a corner stumbled upon the second bridge. It remains there to this day, an elegant span across a gorge and above a foaming tributary of the Cavado, the Misarella. It seems to leap upward from one rocky promontory and drop downward to the other, which gives rise to its local nickname, the *saltador*, or jumper. Here Captain Warre and the armed locals had prepared another barricade, but without being able to pull up the surface, since this time the Romans had built it with massive flagstones.

Warre's flimsy defenses were all that stood between the French and safety, between these thousands of exhausted young men and their families, between Marshal Soult and disgrace. Looking up at the bridge from the spot Soult and his men would have occupied, the Serra da Geres rises up behind like a great wall. The French knew this was their last obstacle. Once more, Major Dulong was sent for and a team of grenadiers and other volunteers demanded. The columns of troops packed onto this narrow track, with steep drops below in many places, would have had to step aside gingerly as the stormers pushed their way toward the front and the bridge.

At a run, the *saltador* is about thirty paces long. Thirty steps for Dulong and his stormers upon which the whole survival of Soult's army depended. Doubtless many of those at the front of Dulong's little column carried axes or other means of breaking down the barricades placed across the bridge by the few dozen Portuguese and the lone Englishman defending it.

When the signal was given, the French stormers launched their attack under the fire of the Portuguese and, supported by musketry from their own comrades, crouched beside the track leading up to the *saltador*. It was over in moments. The Portuguese farmers could not withstand the charge of those desperate men, skilled in close combat. They were scattered and the last impediment was gone. The legions marching under Bonaparte's eagles were taking the same path out of Lusitania as those under the eagles of Rome. Britain's chance of a second Bailén, the capture or annihilation of an entire corps of twenty thousand Frenchmen, was gone and, though he did not know it then, it was to be Wellesley's only opportunity of this kind in seven years of Peninsular campaigning.

Soult's escape had only been possible at considerable cost, as the commander of British forces was quick to point out to the government, lest there be disappointment in Whitehall. Wellesley wrote to Lord Castlereagh on 18 May, "It is obvious that if an army throws away all its cannon, equipment, and baggage, and everything that can strengthen it and enable it to act together as a body . . . it must be able to march over roads on which it cannot be followed with any prospect of being overtaken by an army which has not made the same sacrifices." His argument had some validity: Soult had lost four thousand men in Oporto and the subsequent retreat. He had left behind dozens of cannon too, leaving his army without any artillery, unfit to take to the field except perhaps against guerrillas.

The British general was not going to dwell on the near miss with Soult at the foot of the Serra da Geres in his letters home. In particular, he was not going to reveal the extent to which Soult's escape had been due to his own miscalculations, caution or failure of intelligence in his HQ. Instead, he made the most of his daring assault of the Douro at Oporto, an action that announced his return to Iberia with the necessary éclat.* It would lift spirits in London. By liberating that part of the country it also cemented the Anglo-Portuguese alliance against the French. Wellesley's official dispatch presented the events in northern Portugal in a suitably triumphant way, but there was little room for real candor since these accounts were published in the newspapers. For Napoleon devoured British news sheets with relish, and they sometimes found their

---

*There is frequent mention in the Napoleonic period to "coups d'éclat," or "actions d'éclat," meaning brilliant feats. France being the world leader in military science at the time, the term was one of many widely borrowed in British military parlance.

way to his Paris *cabinet* within three or four days of publication. So instead of conveying the confused realities, Wellesley soothed the ministry with comforting sentences. In a General Order to the troops on 12 May, the general also singled out the secretary of war's brother, Major General Stewart, for praise in directing the cavalry on 11 and 12 May. The second charge, Wellesley claimed, "obtained the victory, which has contributed so much to the honor of the troops on this day."

Among the ambitious young officers, Warre aside, who had not found the glory they were looking for, Wellesley's politically colored account touched off much frustration. Captain Edward Cocks of the 16th Light Dragoons, an aristocrat but also a fiercely dedicated young officer, wrote to his brother correcting the official version of events and damning the meddling adjutant general: "Depend on it from me, whatever Sir A. Wellesley may choose to say, [Major General Stewart's] only merit on either day was being Lord Castlereagh's brother. On both occasions when he came within sight of the enemy he said, 'there's your enemy, charge them,' and *went* back." (emphasis in original).

Captain Cocks was soon to become involved in intelligence work and to gain Wellesley's unqualified respect, but at this early stage of the campaign he echoed the anger of many in the army that Soult had been allowed to escape. "Why," Cocks demanded in his journal, "was Colonel Murray as QMG so ignorant of the road beyond Salamonde that he could give no directions to the Guards when General Beresford was so well acquainted with the country and when a few questions directed at any Portuguese peasant would probably have given sufficient explanation?"

As a member of Wellesley's staff, Scovell could have answered these questions only too well. Communication with Beresford, whose people knew about the old Roman route, was too difficult, and General Wellesley had refused to see the Portuguese officer who could have imparted the same knowledge. A couple of days after his commander gave up pursuing the French, Scovell noted angrily in his journal, "We have now seen what it is to neglect the advice of an individual, especially one who knew the Country so well as the Commandant of Braga."

Early on in his relationship with his new commander, Scovell had detected the general's aristocratic hauteur,* and witnessed the costs of

---

*Sense of one's own superiority.

maintaining a strict hierarchy at headquarters. It was simply not done for
deputy assistants of the quarter master general's branch to tell the general
he *had* to see someone, or indeed even to say the same to Colonel Murray.
One officer of the QMG department summed up the prevailing relations
among these officers: "One ought not however to venture an opinion . . .
nobody can appreciate all the motives that sway a Commander in Chief
but himself." This attitude was not shared by Scovell. Indeed, in his
account of the Oporto operations sent to Colonel Le Marchant, he made
a number of criticisms of their conduct and of the rigid way that business
had been conducted at headquarters, reasoning: "I think it by far the most
instructive part of a campaign to know why we fail; success is in the
mouth of everyone to account for." At Wycombe, the colonel's former
pupil had evidently perfected the philosophy that no general was beyond
criticism, but that any remarks of this kind must stem from a desire to perfect the army rather than to villify some particular person.

Le Marchant had helped found the Royal Military College in 1799,
and its graduates had come to form a body of professional officers often
referred to as "Wycombites" or, later, as "scientific soldiers." The education of the officer corps was just one plank in the raft of reforms that Le
Marchant and a few like-minded officers wanted to introduce. Their
other ideas extended to the formation of a professional general staff to
plan and oversee operations; reforms of the system of promotion and
patronage, leading to advancement strictly on the grounds of professional competence; and the grouping of troops into divisions of all arms
(infantry, cavalry and artillery) so that they could operate more effectively in battle. The army hierarchy, notably the duke of York, had initially responded favorably to these ideas, accepting that change of some
sort was necessary if Britain were to withstand the mighty French, who
had defeated every major European power. The colonel's most ambitious
proposals submitted in 1802, however, were soon suppressed by generals
who felt that while copying the French army might possibly improve military efficiency, it was too dangerous to Britain's social order. They saw
any argument for reform, be it of promotion or perhaps the granting of
important posts on the staff on the basis of ability rather than patronage,
as a dangerous drift toward ruin, rebellion and Jacobin excess.

In 1806, Le Marchant wrote despairingly:

It is well understood by the Government of the Country that intelligent officers are necessary to an efficient army, and that it is alone a well organised État Major [General Staff] who can lead large bodies of troops to victory. How can we be so absurd as to oppose that, neglecting as we do all instruction and the aid of science in our military enterprises, we are to be victorious over troops that possess those advantages in the highest degree of perfection?

Wycombe men were taught that science and brain power were more important to victory than noble birth or the maintenance of patronage. Not all of those who passed through the college adopted these arguments uncritically; William Warre, for example, seems to have emerged from his studies with his conservative views intact. As for Scovell, it had taken the experience of the Corunna campaign to convince him finally of the army's desperate need for reform. Once he had accepted this creed, Scovell applied his mind devotedly to schemes for tackling the army's myriad faults. He had taken to scribbling away in his journals and notebooks until late into the night, even after a hard day's march. Scovell hoped that one day he might impart the many lessons he was learning on campaign to a new generation of officers, perhaps as a teacher at the Royal Military College. The need to perfect the army was so important and so urgent that he did not feel that his commander or any other senior officer should be placed above scrutiny.

This attitude was precisely the kind of thing that irritated Wellesley, a strict believer in hierarchy. If a captain on the staff had something of benefit to say, doubtless Colonel Murray could say it for him. The general had both personal and philosophical reasons to distrust these self-appointed reformers.

He was a younger son of one of the great Anglo-Irish landed families. He had grown up amid a deafening chorus of panegyrics sung to the intelligence of his older brother Richard, and early on seems to have developed an instinctive dislike of those with too great a measure of intellectual self-confidence. Those with an exaggerated view of their own brain power could go to hell as far as he was concerned.

As a colonel in the army, Wellesley had spent several years attached to headquarters in Ireland, at Dublin Castle. These were times of revolutionary ferment in Ireland (and indeed in 1798, after he had left, of a French-supported rebellion), from which Wellesley emerged with a conviction that land owners were the key to social order and patronage was the best mechanism of keeping them happy.

Events in France and Ireland had persuaded him that the dangers of revolution in Britain were also very real. Wellesley believed it highly significant that Bonaparte had emerged from an artillery academy, and he saw the sons of France's new professional class, the bourgeoisie, as the force that had forged that country's Jacobin mobs into mighty legions threatening the established order of all Europe. British officers who came from a similar background might be just as dangerous. "These are in fact the description of officers who have revolutionised other armies," Wellesley would later write. "Having no connection with the property and rank of the country, they are the more easily disposed to destroy its institutions."

In May 1809, when Scovell wrote to Le Marchant that the most instructive part of a campaign consisted of being frank about its failures, he had set himself entirely at odds with Wellesley. It was one thing to have toyed with such ideas under a forward-thinking commander like the late Sir John Moore, but under the new circumstances of serving a reactionary Tory general, they were close to sedition. And if Wellesley naturally distrusted the reformers, Scovell repaid the compliment. The general's refusal to receive the Portuguese commandant of Braga had been taken by the deputy assistant QMG as snobbery and it clearly rankled. In seven years of keeping his journal, Scovell did not pen one word of affection toward Wellesley. Equally, though, despite the many occasions where he questioned the way operations had been carried out, Scovell never attacked his commander in personal terms either. This was not only the best professional attitude to take, but it was also vital for self-preservation, since he was writing a journal that might, in the event of his injury, be taken from his baggage and read by rivals at headquarters.

Scovell's private criticisms of Wellesley's professional conduct had to be subsumed in public, however, for he understood only too well the reality of relations between the aristocratic general and his lowly DAQMG. Wellesley was the key to everything Scovell wanted in life—

for as long as he remained in the army, in any case. It fell to Colonel George Murray, the QMG, to use his considerable charms to soothe the discord between his reactionary master and a staff that contained quite a few reform-minded Wycombites. As a former teacher at the Royal Military College who hailed from a landed Scottish family, Murray was better suited than anyone for this task.

The tensions were deeply felt in the days after Soult's escape, but with an added sense of foreboding for Scovell. Murray had decided that Scovell himself would play an important part in the prevention of any repetition of these events. Scovell knew what Murray had in mind and it troubled him deeply.

The army retired from the Geres mountains, heading south back to Oporto. Scovell rode with Major General Payne, the commander of the light cavalry brigade. Doubtless he was deep in thought, for Murray and De Lancey had already expressed their desires. But what was it that *he* wanted and how could he get it when he held so few cards? While riding with Moore's headquarters the previous summer, Scovell had formed a scheme and lobbied for it, even though Murray had little time to listen or to read the captain's memorandum on the subject. Scovell wanted to lead cavalry again and saw the opportunity to build a new corps around himself. He had realized that Wellesley, like Moore before him, was working with a limited cavalry force: six regiments, or about 4,000 men. In the coming months Horse Guards was most reluctant to send more regiments of these troops: there was still a threat of invasion to the British Isles, Ireland rumbled away, and the ministry was also assembling a major military expedition to northern Europe. What little cavalry the British commander had was constantly being reduced by detachments: eight dragoons to carry letters here; a troop of cavalry to guard an important convoy there; a squadron to explore uncharted territory somewhere else. Scovell understood that if Britain were to maintain its army in the Iberian Peninsula for the foreseeable future, it would need more cavalry, and that some would need to be locally raised. There were plenty of precedents for this in the American war, and in Egypt nine years before when the British had been accompanied by a mongrel band of emigres, deserters and adventurers called Hompeshe's Hussars.

The auxilliary cavalry raised in these previous campaigns had been trained to ride to the charge and formed into squadrons large

enough to give battle. The Mounted Guides he had organized for
General Moore, on the other hand, were only ever errand boys for
headquarters, and there had been only a few dozen of them. If it was
not possible to place himself at the head of a larger body of fighting
horse, then Scovell would happily remain Major General Payne's
DAQMG for the time being and consider whether he really had a
future in the army.

On 24 May, the major general and his pensive companion reached
the bustle and gaiety of Oporto, a world away from the scenes of the
Ponte Nova bridge, of torched villages, wounded French conscripts
being impaled on the pitchforks of locals and of smashed equipment
strewn across the savage mountains.

Next morning Scovell stepped into the bright light and incessant
noise of the city's streets. He had been invited to see Colonel Murray at
HQ. The captain had washed and donned the smartest coat he could
find in his baggage. He had made the best of his appearance and was
now ready to make the best of his arguments .

Murray did not waste time with preliminaries. It was necessary to
raise the Corps of Mounted Guides again urgently. The Guides' skills
were needed if there was to be no repetition of episodes like Soult's
escape. Wellesley's intention to do this had already been announced two
days earlier in a General Order to the army. The commander of the
forces saw a wider role for them than they had previously had. He was
most anxious that the army obtain the best possible intelligence and he
knew that few men could be trusted with the delicate task. Murray
spoke in his mild Perthshire brogue, fixed Scovell in his gray-blue eyes
and asked him whether he was ready to take on this task.

It would be with the utmost reluctance, Scovell replied. The captain
knew he could not refuse an order, but Murray's request had not yet
been couched in those terms and this was as close as the deputy assistant
QMG could go. Disillusion with the army had finally reached its limit
for Scovell. He had taken on untold extra duties as an adjutant in the
4th Dragoons, his old cavalry regiment, without extra pay. He had
applied himself with complete dedication at Wycombe. He had penned
any number of schemes and plans to try to unite his interests and those
of the service, all without success.

Anxiously, Scovell went on to explain himself. The current situation with General Payne's cavalry brigade was most agreeable to him and offered every opportunity for distinction. The colonel surely remembered that the formation of the Corps of Guides the previous summer had been attended by every conceivable difficulty. He had been presented with a pack of deserters from the French infantry, a few dozen nags bought cheaply in the Portuguese markets and told to turn them into a force of mounted soldiers. There had been no junior officers to assist him. He had devoted himself to this unenviable task while trying to fulfill all of the other duties of a deputy assistant at headquarters.

Murray perhaps realized that the moment when a man as bereft of interest and wealth as Scovell declined a request, it was time for delicate proceedings. The quarter master general also knew that Scovell had shown unique linguistic skill in dealing with his polyglot horde during the last campaign and that he brought abilities to the task that many other officers did not have. Murray was aware that none of the DAQMGs with better connections would regard the job of controlling the Guides as a desirable one. There were no real alternatives.

The Scottish colonel reassured his captain. Murray was capable of great charm, which had won him Moore's respect in Egypt nine years before and Wellesley's on the Copenhagen expedition in 1807. If great captains of such strong will and differing temperaments as Moore and Wellesley had been seduced, then what chance did Scovell have? There was no question of the Guides being established on anything other than the most formal basis, as General Wellesley's General Order had made clear. It would be a much larger unit this time, at least one hundred men, with four lieutenants and four cornets as commissioned officers to carry out Scovell's orders. Couldn't he see that this was the very cavalry that he himself had advocated in his memorandum? Their duties would be extensive, and the enterprise was one that Sir Arthur would overlook with the closest personal interest.

Scovell had made his protest. The conversation was moving to its climax. The general and he himself, Colonel Murray said, understood that such a large task could not be superintended by a humble captain. The QMG made clear that if his deputy assistant accepted the command, it would be rewarded by a recommendation of promotion to major. Scovell knew very well that the step from captain to major was about the most difficult to make. The simple mathematics of the army establishment did not allow any but the most determined or best connected to manage it: there could be a dozen captains in a regiment but only two majors. The promotion would also carry with it one from deputy assistant to assistant quarter master general, which meant greater status and a further increase in pay.

Scovell finally agreed to Colonel Murray's proposal. The die was cast. Captain Scovell was on his way to becoming the man in charge of Wellesley's communications and a vital part of his intelligence apparatus.

CHAPTER FIVE

*9. 249. 1076. n. t. 1082. 365. 622. 699. 655. 699. 439. 669. 655.
1085. 398. 326. 13. 309. i. 1085. 655. 249. 481. t. 980. 985. 186. t.
843. 688. 2. 718. 249. 1297. 536. 174. 1085. 1021 . . . 713. t. 980. 854.
655. 326. 536. 700. 699. 171. 1015. 1003. 13. t. 980. 1015. 131. t.*

From Oporto to Abrantes, June to July 1809

*I*t was still dark on 4 June 1809 when the soldiers of the Guards, the Buffs and numerous other regiments were woken by the reveille of drums and bugles. Men picked themselves up, stretched their stiff limbs, rolled blankets, groped around in the darkness for their coats and slung their muskets. In dozens of places around the south of Oporto the bleary-eyed bloody backs of Wellesley's army fell in, the men forming themselves into files. They gathered at company alarm posts, some simple landmark near the bivouac where the captain in command checked the names of his men against his roll, ready to send the word "all present." And then the tramping of feet would begin, punctuated by the occasional cursing growl of a sergeant and tapping of drums keeping time. It was still early when the companies had been sorted into their battalions, aligning themselves and ready to march in a preordained sequence. Companies*

---

*The strength of a company during this period ranged from forty to one hundred or even more soldiers. Sickness and battle made it hard to maintain such units at full strength.

assembled, ten at a time, into battalions. When each battalion was complete, they sent word to their major of brigade that they were ready to march. Once more, in that murkiness of dawn in the Douro country, the army began composing itself from the bottom up.

The business with Marshal Soult was rapidly slipping into history and the British general was setting his armament on a new trajectory: south. The task of letting each brigade commander know his place in the order of march and how far away the next night's resting place would be was that of the quarter master general's department. For far from being just a matter of improvisation for Colonel Murray, there were rules and conventions he had to observe; the order of brigades on the line of march preserved the hierarchy of George III's army. The Guards went first and the other brigades followed in order of their commanders' seniority. Some newly made up major general, or a colonel acting the part, formed up at the back. Within each brigade the senior battalion, the one with the lowest regimental number, generally led off. In this way even the daily routine of campaigning reminded the officers and men of their places in the greater scheme of things. This sense of order was profoundly comforting to someone like Sir Arthur Wellesley.

Colonel Murray and his acolytes had drawn up plans to move the army down to Abrantes in central Portugal, where they would encamp pending further orders. General Wellesley had freed the north of the country, but he knew that several French *corps d'armée* (under Marshals Victor and Ney, as well as General Sebastiani) lurked somewhere in Spain.* At any time, they could combine to form a much larger force than Marshal Soult's and fall upon the British or Spanish. The next stage of the campaign had to be planned with great caution, for Wellesley knew that Britain's army was small, fragile and, in spite of its success at Oporto, still showing every sign of being unprepared for a general action. Any severe upset at the hands of the French would result in the end of the Peninsular mission.

A wise general measured the marching of his troops carefully. March them too far, too fast, and you wore out the soles of their boots. March them farther still and you started to wear out the men themselves and they would begin falling by the wayside. For this reason, Wellesley and

*That under Victor did briefly enter Portugal.

Murray tried to maintain a reasonable pace as they redeployed, with stages of three leagues, or ten to eleven miles, each day. During each day's tramping along the dusty tracks that passed for Portuguese roads, there would be three or four rest stops. But even this slow deployment was sufficient to bring every kind of problem seeping to the surface.

Boots made cheaply by the contractors who clipped the taxpayer started falling apart. Uniforms had split at the seams and torn, and had to be patched with local gray or brown cloth, for red could not be found. Some soldiers had replaced their boots with the espadrille sandals made by the locals, others had paid the cobblers found within their ranks to patch up and mend their footwear.

Many men began straggling, weary of stumbling along under sixty pounds of equipment. Others fell into despair, wracked with regret at having taken the king's shilling at some county fair or inn back in England only to find themselves awaiting their fate as food for cannon. It wasn't just the feeble and the dejected, however, that lagged behind. The heat of an Iberian summer brought down even stouthearted men, who sometimes fainted trying not to fall behind their mates, or, sometimes for the same honorable aspiration, simply dropped dead of heat exhaustion.

As the troops marched down through Coimbra toward Abrantes, the same daily routine of mustering, marching, halts and bivouac was repeated. Wellesley, Murray and the other staff officers watched their men closely. Much sloppiness was laid bare. Too many officers had no idea of their duties. One captain in the Buffs, for example, confessed in his journal that he knew nothing of the military profession despite having been in the army for two years. Each night's bivouac was accompanied by scenes of disorder. Supplies were sporadic, and often enough the men went hungry for want of organization rather than lack of food. Sentries were improperly placed, allowing soldiers to go off and plunder the local Portuguese. Sergeant Cooper of the 7th Fusiliers described it all vividly:

> No sooner was the day's march ended than men turned
> out to steal pigs, poultry, wine, etc. One evening, after
> halting, a wine store was broken open and much was carried
> off. The owner, finding this out, ran and brought an
> officer of the 53rd, who caught one of our company,
> named Brown, in the act of handing out the wine in camp

kettles. Seizing Brown by the collar, the officer shouted,
"Come out you rascal and give me your name." Brown
came out, gave his name Brennan, then knocking the officer down, made his escape and was not found out.

Brown was a lucky man, for if caught, he certainly would have been
hanged for striking the officer. Evidently, the threat of flogging or even
the gallows had not yet become effective enough to deter those who
went looting.

With each episode of plunder the anger of the peasantry grew, and
with it the chances of confrontation. One officer of the 14th Light Dragoons described an incident in which he and some troopers were stoned
by Portuguese peasants who thought the soldiers were about to steal
from their orchard. The cavalrymen gave chase and administered a
"sound thrashing" to the locals.

As the march went on, Wellesley became more and more vexed by
these incidents and their impact on his campaign. If the rabble under his
command carried on in this way, the peasantry might become as hostile
toward them as they had been to the French. Many on the staff had
been shocked by the brutality toward the enemy wounded they had witnessed during the pursuit of Marshal Soult in the north. And indeed,
lone British soldiers threatening the Portuguese began to fall victim to
the farmers' knives and staves; at least three were killed, presumably
while looting, on the march to Abrantes.

The British commander issued a General Order denouncing "the
conduct of the troops; not only have outrages been committed by whole
corps, but there is no description of property of which the unfortunate
inhabitants of Portugal have not been plundered." As the army
approached its temporary resting place in the center of the country,
Wellesley, Murray and the rest of the staff busied themselves trying to
solve the many problems they had noticed during their brief campaign
in the north and march down. Orders had been fired off as they went:
on 31 May for six thousand pairs of shoes to be distributed to those
who had worn them out on the march; on 1 June concerning the use of
mules to carry stores with the regiments; on 2 June regarding the need to
supervise those left behind sick; and on 3 June requiring units to carry
three days of rations with them on the march.

In the fields outside Abrantes, the troops set to the local pines with axes and billhooks, lopping off branches to make huts for themselves. Far from a perfect shelter, this was their best refuge for the foreseeable future, since it took the administrators in London three years to send tents to the Peninsular army.

While the army gathered its strength in this new cantonment, battalions were drilled and supplies brought up, their commander contemplated a move into Spain. He used this interval in operations to begin tightening his grip on this lax army. He formed the brigades under his command into four divisions, larger bodies that could combine infantry and guns in self-contained elements that trained, marched and fought together. The adoption of divisions was, incidentally, a measure recommended to the duke of York by Colonel Le Marchant eight years earlier and one that had long been in use in the French army.

At the same time that his reorganization was under way, General Wellesley turned his mind to the large strategic picture, seeking political authority from London to enter Spain. With the eruption of war between Austria and France that spring, the British commander believed that a window of opportunity had opened: Napoleon's forces were divided and circumstances ripe for cooperation with the Spanish in seeking to bring to battle some part of the French force. Although British enthusiasm for the Spanish patriotic cause had lessened somewhat after the Corunna expedition, the ministry in London still sensed a popular desire among the English to help this nation in its heroic struggle against Bonaparte's legions. The commander of forces in the peninsula considered that Napoleon's other difficulties in Europe would not go on forever; it was time to seize his chance. In truth, Wellesley's enthusiasm for striking across the border was based on false assumptions about the degree to which the French emperor had reduced his Iberian garrison. Just like John Moore the previous autumn, Wellesley's lack of good intelligence was about to endanger the whole army.

This was now going to change. The memory of the Corunna campaign and their failure to trap Soult in May left Colonel Murray in no doubt that he must improve his knowledge of the situation in the countryside through which they intended to advance. Sir Arthur had made it clear that he expected such an improvement. Scovell's Guides were central to this, but since the QMG needed much more information than they alone could provide, he dispatched his assistants and deputy assistants to all points of the compass, exploring. This did not mean recruiting some spy in the French court; it meant knowing how many horses might graze in a particular valley, or where the bridges were located on the Guadiana River. Even in 1809, Spain and Portugal were very imperfectly surveyed, and the best maps available to headquarters were fifty-year-old inaccuracies. Murray's envoys were to make sketch maps wherever they went, detailing the distances between villages, how many men might be quartered in each, the state of the rivers and their bridges and so on. This information was vital to understanding the enemy's plans and in planning the movement of British forces. When Murray had run out of members of his own staff, he started sending regimental officers.

The Royal Military College graduates had been schooled in military drawing and thought themselves the masters of this art. But Murray did not have time for perfection in this mapmaking. One of Colonel Le Marchant's correspondents in the peninsula wrote back rather tetchily to him in Wycombe, "Colonel Murray, with all his knowledge of ground on the spot, understands very little of it from a military plan and De Lancey privately told me he was most completely ignorant of what a military plan should be . . . the great object with him is to gain an accurate report of a country, its roads, soil, rivers etc and the means it possesses of affording shelter for the army. He employs everybody at this."

As commander of the Guides, Scovell was sent on these missions too. His engraver's craft had been further improved at Wycombe so his maps were pictures of neatness and precision. There was a spareness to his mapmaking too: no unwanted contours or detail, just the pattern of settlements and the roads connecting them. Above each route, the distance to the next village was noted, below it the number of hours required to march it: "3 Leagues, 4 Hours," and so on.

Scovell's opportunities for exploration, however, were short-lived, for, as the army lay in encampments around Abrantes, Murray had other work in mind for him. On 15 June, under the QMG's orders, the captain made his way down to the quayside on Abrantes' River Tagus. He picked up one of the riverboats that plied Portugal's great river which, for half a dollar, would convey you to Lisbon comfortably seated, under the shade of a canopy.

Scovell's Guides were to be formed with the help of the Portuguese army as well as the British. He needed the assistance of the ministry of war in Lisbon, a task he approached with a grim realism. "Colonel Murray has pursuaded me again to take the Corps of Guides, with a promise of endeavouring to procure me promotion," Scovell wrote to Le Marchant at the end of May. "I give you my word I do it with great reluctance . . . if I get disappointed this time I think I shall give over soldiering and come home."

Certainly the challenge facing Scovell might have seemed suited only to an incurable optimist or a fool. The Italian and Swiss remnants of his previous Guides were back in Portugal and were being joined by some Portuguese smugglers, Spanish ne'er-do-wells and Irish soldiers of fortune. Murray had made much of the fact that Scovell would have the assistance of eight junior officers in this new endeavor. But the lieutenants and cornets promised to supervise this polyglot parcel of rogues turned out to be a team of callow youths from Coimbra University. They were men of good Portuguese and Spanish families, no doubt about it. They could speak French fluently and most had some English too. But they did not have the slightest idea of soldiering, and it would fall to Scovell to educate them.

Scovell's reformed Guides were to be entrusted with tasks of the highest sensitivity: guiding the army through unfamiliar territory and carrying the commander's dispatches. Wellesley understood there were risks in entrusting his sensitive communications to the Guides. Colonel Murray had already made clear in writing the previous summer that "the officers are to be *very particular* as to the character of the men" (emphasis in original). Wellesley refused a French émigré a commission in the Corps on the grounds that he might be a double agent and "would have opportunities of acquiring and conveying to the enemy much useful information." Ultimately, general Wellesley and the QMG believed that the loyalty of their messengers was best bought with silver coin, promptly paid and in good quantity. It was a mercenary troop and the General was under no illusion about the type of men who formed it, listing the qualities required of its officers as "intelligence, some honesty, and a knowledge of the Spanish and Portuguese languages and English or French."

Scovell was now responsible for transforming these men of "some honesty" into a reliable, smart, self-confident corps as fast as possible. This would require training, uniforms and weaponry, in search of which he was traveling to Lisbon. Just one month after writing to Le Marchant in despair, Scovell was throwing himself into his new project with vigor. There had been years of fruitless graft in the garrisons of Lewes, Derby and Wycombe, so he was thrilled to begin overcoming the many practical difficulties that faced his Corps. Reclining in his packet boat, he gazed at the lush countryside of the Tagus littoral and his spirits lifted. Even if Captain Scovell believed his new task was his last hope of ever achieving something in the profession of arms, he relished it, particularly as it simultaneously satisfied his passions for travel and culture. He described the passage to Lisbon as "a most delightful voyage."

His riverboat looked much the same as they had in Roman times, a great lateen sail hung from the mast, just like that used by the Phoenician galleys. A flat bottom ensured the craft had the shallow draft needed to clear the river's sandbars and banks. It was an ancient rig, but it answered well enough for navigation of the Tagus. It sped Scovell the eighty miles downstream in just nineteen hours. He disembarked from this shady boat into the radiant light and pungent stench of an early June morning on the Lisbon quayside, ready to execute his mission.

While Scovell was in Lisbon, on 25 June, three French officers were embarking on an infinitely less pleasant odyssey not far across the Spanish border near Tordesillas. Accompanied by his two aides-de-camp, General Jean-Baptiste Franceschi rode toward a river ferry carrying vital dispatches from Marshal Soult to Joseph, king of Spain. Far from being a mere messenger though, Franceschi had commanded Soult's light cavalry division throughout the pursuit of John Moore to Corunna as well as during the previous month's near-disastrous campaign in northern Portugal.

In many ways, Franceschi personified the unusual qualities of Napoleon's officer corps. As a young man, he had never wanted to be in the army: quite the opposite, he had been an artist, a sculptor. When thousands of patriotic French had answered the cry of "*la patrie en danger*"* just after the revolution, Franceschi had volunteered for the Paris "Artists' Company" and had gone to the front. Bobbing along in a sea of revolutionary ferment, he had progressed from infantry soldier to

---

*The homeland in danger.

artillery lieutenant, hussar officer and then aide to Soult in just five tumultuous campaigns.

Franceschi's flamboyant temperament made him well suited to the French cavalry. Among these men, the hardships of campaign or the possibility of death were born with humor, fatalism and a sense of honor. He had evidently considered that he was safe enough riding with an escort across this rebellious land. Marshal Soult was anxious, in any case, that King Joseph learn as quickly as possible of the terrible state of the army that had escaped the British in northern Portugal and crossed the Serra da Geres. It was probably a Spaniard who had seen Franceschi during a stopover that passed on word of the important traveler.

When the general and his two companions neared the river, they were ambushed. The guerrilla party reponsible was not large—some accounts say just eight men—led by a local tough nick-named *El Capucino*, the Friar. Any struggle was short-lived; perhaps the guerrillas succeeded in dismounting their victims before offering the choice of death or captivity. This offer of quarter was rare during such an attack, but *El Capucino* must have realized that this senior officer was a considerable prize.

Franceschi was initially taken to Zarza la Mayor, close to the Portuguese frontier. Several days after this capture, Major General Charles Stewart arrived in Zarza with a small escort. The adjutant general was charged with handling prisoners and, in Stewart's view, tapping them for intelligence. Since Franceschi was a Spanish prize, formalities had to be observed. Stewart could not remove the general from their custody, although he left this account of their interview:

> "He appeared dreadfully out of fortune with his evil
> humour, repeatedly ejaculating, 'Oh! how sad it is for a
> general of hussars to be taken by a Friar! Yet French-
> man-like he met all our advances with the greatest
> frankness and candour."

Stewart remarked in his later history of the war that the French captive had been carrying important dispatches. Whether he discovered this at the time of their melancholy conversation but could not induce the Spanish to part with them, or whether he did not even think to ask, is unclear. What is certain is that he returned to Wellesley's camp in possession of nothing other than his insights into the French national character. The two long letters to King Joseph that had been in Franceschi's care were sent to the Spanish war ministry in the south. Protocol being what it was, these messages had to be copied before they could be handed to the British minister there. The Anglo-Spanish alliance was still tinged with mutual suspicion, for the two countries were old enemies that had been fighting as recently as 1807, and it was only Napoleon's invasion of Iberia that had led them to set aside their differences in the face of a common foe. The British representative relayed the copies of Soult's letters to Wellesley on 9 July, describing them as "infinitely curious in various respects," and the commander of British forces finally received them several days later, almost three weeks after they were written.

Marshal Soult's dispatches to Napoleon's brother, King Joseph, ran to dozens of pages and were indeed packed with information. One painted the bleakest picture of his operations in northwest Spain, noting the many factors that led to "an increase day by day in the number of our enemies, and make the war in this country most murderous, infinitely unpleasant, and without any end in sight." Soult needed huge sums of money to provision his army and cover the many expenses of occupation. He also told the king that he was moving southeast, closer to Wellesley's next intended area of operations. Even so, the time it had taken to get hold of the dispatches and the limits of Soult's own knowledge about wider French deployments meant that this "infinitely curious" mail could not dictate Wellesley's next strategic moves.

The British commander shared Stewart's sympathy with the plight of the captured French general, but there was nothing they could do to prevent his maltreatment by the Spanish. Animated by patriotic fervor, Britain's allies had treated their prisoners lamentably, if indeed they had consented to take them at all. The Spanish had broken an agreement to send home the corps captured at Bailén the previous year, confining the unfortunate French troops to prison hulks or barren islands in the Bay of Cadiz where epidemics carried them off in the thousands. Wellesley believed that the rules of war and civilized behavior should have dictated a different attitude, particularly toward Franceschi, and tried by various methods to arrange his exchange, send him money and alleviate his situation. The Spanish, however, kept him in a series of dark dungeons, subjected him to regular beatings and provided only measly rations. The following year Franceschi became ill with yellow fever and died in captivity. This kind of event contributed to the increasingly grim reputation of Spain among French troops. In other campaigns they had marched across Italy or Austria to be greeted by deputations of local worthies who, anxious to avoid too much unpleasantness, even presented them with the keys to their towns. In Spain and Portugal, on the other hand, they had found that many townspeople would rather fight to the death than yield to the invaders, and the countryside was awash with bands of murderous brigands. One French general wrote, "I shall always remember how I was afflicted with great anxieties; every day saw the murder of several Frenchmen, and I travelled over this assassin's countryside as warily as if it were a volcano."

It had not taken long for the French footsloggers to begin repaying brutality in kind. Punitive missions against villages where there had been attacks on imperial columns soon assumed a vicious character. One Frenchman conscripted in the summer of 1809 and bound for Spain noted this reception from veterans at his military depot in Angouleme:

> They painted a picture of Spain in such sombre colours
> and spoke of the excesses committed by the two sides
> in such a grave tone that we became deeply sad. Unable
> to believe in such barbarism, I thought the speaker was
> acting the poet, in fact, as I was soon to discover, he
> was nothing but an accurate historian . . . even then,
> Spain was called the tomb of the French.

The poisonous character of the conflict between the Iberians and their invaders was firmly established, even as early as 1809, and defined the battle for information for both the French and the British. Messengers, as Franceschi's saga demonstrated, could not move unescorted without the risk of becoming targets for popular wrath. Rapidly, the situation became so acute that Madrid or Paris might hear nothing from an expeditionary corps in some corner of the peninsula for four, five, even six weeks at a stretch. Under these circumstances, it was increasingly difficult to coordinate the operations of different corps around Spain. Although the French discovered some sympathizers in the towns among the poorer sort of professionals or artisans, the peasants in the countryside were generally unwilling to provide King Joseph's scouting parties with information on the whereabouts of their enemies. The guerrillas, or British, on the other hand, usually found plenty of willing collaborators.

Franceschi was not the first French messenger to be taken, of course, but his capture did galvanize the court of Napoleon's brother in Madrid to think more seriously about its difficulties of communication.

Small detachments of troops were positioned in fortified blockhouses at regular intervals along main routes like the one from Madrid to the French frontier at Bayonne. In this way, messengers could spend the night in safety and would never be too far from help if ambushed. Inevitably, this level of security could only be provided on a small number of routes, since it consumed troops by the thousands. Unfortunately for the French, similar factors prevented them from using one of the most revolutionary inventions of the country's brilliant military science. In France itself, high-level messages were regularly carried along optical telegraph relays. Chains of telegraph stations (each one had to be visible to the next) were used to send messages from Paris to the eastern frontier or the south at previously unthinkable speeds. In Iberia, however, the vicious enmity between French troops and locals would have meant a constant risk to the security of communications. Setting up telegraphs to link Madrid with the provinces would have required scores of stations, exposing the operators to the constant risk of guerrilla attack. And any successful assault on one of the relay stations might have delivered the code of signals into enemy hands, compromising the secrecy of the entire system.

Instead the tried and tested method of pen and paper had to suffice. Where the safety of an urgent communication was in doubt, two or more copies were sent. Increasingly dispatches would arrive bearing the words "*Duplicato*" or "*Triplicato*" at the top. During the latter part of 1809, the French were not quite ready to move to protection of the actual contents of their military messages, even though in sensitive diplomatic correspondence the emperor did employ secret ciphers, using code tables that converted words, letters or phases into numbers. One hundred years earlier, under Louis XIV, France had been the masters of this kind of secret writing, and, during the century leading up to the rev-olution, French diplomats had perfected ciphers of ever-increasing com-plexity. An early cipher of Louis XIV's day, for example, might allow the transcription of a message into numbers from one to six hundred. By

1750, though, French ministers were being equipped with an enciphering table of twelve thousand numbers. With each development of this kind, the complexity of the transcription grew and the task facing any would-be decipherer was made yet more difficult.

The French Revolution had created much turmoil in the diplomatic service, stocked as it was with gouty aristocrats, but it didn't endanger the knowledge of codes and ciphers—this kind of esoteric know-how had always been the preserve of a certain type of petit bourgeois* administrator who came through the revolution unscathed. In drawers of the foreign ministry there were still copies of the 1750 ciphering table, as well as other more exotic codes involving hieroglyphs. All were intended for use by ambassadors, ministers and secret informants, people whose situations made it imperative that they take the time to encipher and decipher messages.

As for Napoleon's army, it had tried using codes in some of its campaigns but they were quite simple, usually termed *petits chiffres,* or small ciphers, that might just transpose letters into numbers from one to fifty. While this was fast, it was also so easily broken that it could only protect the message for a few hours. Such codes might suffice if the letter in question was an urgent order for the movement of some body of troops. Napoleon and his staff knew that things had to be kept simple in the heat of battle. How complex could something be if it had to be used by some general's aide-de-camp while perched on the back of a horse, perhaps with the whiz of cannonballs overhead? A great table of the type used in the foreign ministry was the size of a large map, so its physical dimensions alone posed difficulties on campaign. There were other, more basic problems too. What was the point of enciphering your dispatch if you had no knowledge that the recipient could decipher it? The French armies in Spain had been continuously in motion since the summer of 1808, with no time to send each commander a set of code tables. Attempts to pass such a sensitive package through the bandit-infested countryside carried unthinkable risks. What if the British ended up in possession of one of the secret charts, or worse still were able to copy it without the French being aware it was compromised?

---

*A minor professional, a clerk or such like; what we might today term lower middle class.

After Franceschi's abduction, Joseph would have known that it would be quite impossible to send out copies of code tables quickly and safely. Speed was of the essence, because the French had learned of the advance of Wellesley's army into eastern Spain. On 3 July 1809 the British army had entered his kingdom in the mountainous central sector of the frontier. Joseph and his military advisers knew that there was a Spanish corps under General Cuesta also lurking somewhere in this region. The combined Anglo-Spanish force might then move on Madrid. If Sebastiani and Victor were brought together, they could block the Allied advance, and once Soult and Ney were also brought into action, the French would have a hefty preponderance of force over the British and Spanish. But everything depended on a swift concentration of troops.

Despite all the difficulties, the king was resolved to do something about the security of his dispatches. Franceschi had, after all, fallen into enemy hands because he was wearing the uniform of a French cavalry general and was accompanied by two finely appointed ADCs. Perhaps the answer lay in greater stealth. There were so many possibilities. Why not make use of the *afrancesados**, the natives who had welcomed the arrival of the French? If a Spanish spy could be given a message, he might make his way dressed as a shepherd or some itinerant pilgrim. Joseph resolved to use any means necessary to get a message through to Marshal Soult in time to tip the balance in the imminent battle against the British.

---

*Derived from the Spanish for French, *frances*, this might be loosely defined as "the French party" or "French lovers."

CHAPTER SIX

T. 249. 1076. n. t. 1082. 365. 622. w. 655. w. 439. 669. 655. 1085. 898. 326. 13. 809. i. 1085. 655. 249. 481. t. 980. 985. 186. t. 843. 688. 2. 718. 249. 1297. 536. 174. 1085. 1024 . . . 713. t. 980. 854. 655. 326. 536. 700. w. 171. 1015. 1003. 13. t. 980. 1015. 131. t.

From Talavera to the End Campaign, July to October 1809

*S*covell's stay in Lisbon had proven a fruitful and agreeable interlude. His business was transacted as swiftly as was possible with the Portuguese war ministry, but it nonetheless required him to remain there twelve days, time that Scovell spent exploring the city's streets. In 1809 Lisbon was a place of considerable bustle, color and adventure, with palaces, fine avenues and many narrow backstreets. A good number of the public buildings dating from the wealthy days of the previous century had been built in a Portuguese baroque style, with their impressive soaring colonnaded facades. Away from the pungent aromas of the river quay, visitors found themselves seduced by the more pleasant smells of strong coffee and fresh pastries.

One morning Scovell walked up into the Bairro Alto, the city's high quarter, and found his way to the church of Sao Roque. Its nondescript exterior concealed a magnificent interior adorned with mosaic works of such astonishing intricacy that they defied the observer's attempts to distinguish them from paintings. Sao Roque's baroque altar is a master-piece of decoration and proportion. "Nothing can be more beautiful or wonderful," Scovell declared, marveling that the French had not pillaged the artworks during their brief occupation of Lisbon the previous summer.

Scovell was not the only red-coated captain to be found on the streets of Lisbon that June. During the past year the city had become used to the perambulations of visiting British officers: many were passing through on their way to or from the fighting, others belonged to that habitual class of shirkers to be found to the rear of any army engaged in operations. Captain Moyle Sherer of the 34th Foot had disembarked with his regiment, preparing to move toward the Spanish border, and like Scovell walked up to see Sao Roque, being struck not just by the beauty of the art but by the flirtatious glances of young Portuguese women peering out from their mantillas as they left the church followed by their Brazilian maids.

Men like Sherer and Scovell, who wanted to drink in the culture, sights and language of the Portuguese, were in a distinct minority. Sherer recorded returning to dinner that day with his brother officers, where he found that "some of our party had been very differently impressed with the morning's ramble to what I had been. They drew comparisons between London and Lisbon exultingly . . . they had only seen the heaps of dirt . . . a squalid beggar . . . or been saluted by some unfortunate puff of air, impregnated with garlic."

One of the principal distractions for bachelor British officers, often raucously drunk, were nights at the opera. The Sao Carlos had been modeled on Milan's La Scala, and its program was mainly of Italian light opera. Although the air may have been close in this packed auditorium on a midsummer's night, the audience's behavior was anything but stuffy. The British officers made eyes at the Portuguese maidens up in their family boxes, tried to force their way into the stars' dressing rooms after the entertainments and were even sometimes to be seen caterwauling on stage. When he received repeated reports of misbehavior, Wellesley became so exasperated that he wrote with his distinctive blend of caustic disapproval and mordant wit to the senior officer in Lisbon:

> *"It has been mentioned to me that the British officers*
> *who are in Lisbon are in the habit of going to the the-*

atres, where some of them conduct themselves in a very improper manner, much to the annoyance of the public and to the injury of the proprietors and performers. . . . The officers of the army can have nothing to do behind the scenes and it is very improper that they should appear upon stage during the performance. They must be aware that the British public would not bear either the one or the other, and I see no reason why the Portuguese public should be worse treated. *

After this letter, its recipient, Colonel Peacock, posted armed sentries at the stage door of the Sao Carlos. If this episode reflects something deeper than the perennial struggle to limit the discord between soldiers and civilians, it is the British commander's fear that many of his officers were as much of a liability in their dealings with the Portuguese or Spanish as the private soldiers who plundered the countryside. Wellesley was already quite familiar with the figure of the Briton abroad trying to make himself understood by repeating the same English phrase louder and louder until his perspiring face turned the same color as his regimental coat. He would later write to Colonel Peacock: "I am sorry to say that our officers are too much disposed to treat with contempt all foreigners." When this subsequent row (concerning the use of a Portuguese barracks building) occurred, Wellesley recommended officers of the QMG's department as the only ones who could be relied upon to deal with the Iberian allies in a professional manner.

By late June 1809, George Scovell completed his mission to Lisbon. He had arranged uniforms for his men: brown jackets (like those worn by the Portuguese light infantry) with red collars and cuffs, trimmed with black lace, as well as leather helmets crested with a comb of fur like those of the British light dragoons. It was not as splendid as some of the getups of the French *guides* and *eclaireurs*,* who had a truly elite status in the some of the generals HQs, but it was distinctive enough. The mixture of

---

*The general added, "I have been concerned to see officers in uniform, with their hats on, upon the stage during the performance." I find the implication that this behavior might have been more acceptable if hats were removed both hilarious and perplexing.

*From *eclairer*, which meant "to enlighten or explore."

clothing demonstrated the Anglo-Portuguese parentage of the corps, underlining the common anti-French cause that united the two nations.

Throughout the first half of July, Scovell stayed behind with his men at the camp of Abrantes while Wellesley and the main army struck out toward the Spanish general Cuesta, intent on joining the two armies prior to bringing the French to a general action. Scovell's task in the meantime was to teach his Guides the basics of mounted soldiering, even if they were destined to be posted in small packets around the army and unlikely would ever act as a united force on the battlefield. Many, no doubt, had to be taught even how to stay on the horses that Scovell had bought them. There was sword drill and some basic instruction in maneuvering. Some of the training must have been designed with the very specific tasks of the Guides in mind. Officers had to be taught how to prepare reconnaissance reports for the British generals they were to be attached to, and all of the men had to learn how the British system of military communications would work. Relays were to be used to carry orders across long distances. They would be positioned at particular inns or farmhouses and each packet of dispatches was to have a ticket on which its progress along this chain would be noted. This way Scovell, Murray and even Wellesley would be able to monitor the men's activities and, in the event of mail going missing, could detect fairly precisely where and at what time it happened.

On 19 July, Scovell and the Anglo-Portuguese army's latest squadron set off in Wellesley's tracks into New Castille along the higher Tagus valley, fairly much along the shortest line between Lisbon and Madrid. This was difficult country of many hills carved about by deep river courses.

It must have been with great pride that the commandant of the Corps of Guides led his hundred or so troopers through spectacular scenery toward their rendezvous with headquarters. There were familiar faces in the ranks, some of the Italians that had endured those nerve-wracking hours on the quayside of Corunna, and there were new ones. All had been united in the brown uniform of his new command. A clatter of hooves and jingling of the men's accoutrements announced their progress. During a journey that took more than one week, the main army had once again moved farther forward into Spain.

Since leaving Abrantes, Wellesley had marched his twenty-one thousand troops toward the Army of Estremadura, one of the Spanish forces that had survived the first two years of campaigning and was lurking in corners of the country unconquered by the French. The British general wanted to join them and move toward Madrid. This threat to King Joseph's seat of government would then force the French to unite forces in defense of their capital, thus easing the pressure on those areas that had still not fallen under French control. This strategy was similar to General Sir John Moore's advance at the end of 1808, a sally into northern Spain that many said bought southern Iberia another year's freedom from invasion. Wellesley's thrust, seven months later, took advantage of a more favorable strategic climate. Napoleon had left Spain early in 1809, with thousands of picked troops of his old guard and much heavy cavalry, leaving his forces in Spain without a dominating leader and scattered more thinly. However, Wellesley's relations with Britain's supposed allies were to prove as poor as Moore's.

On 10 July the British commander had set out to meet the leader of this Army of Estremadura, General Cuesta, only to get lost on the way, a mishap Scovell must surely have thanked the heavens that neither he nor his Guides had anything to do with. Once he had met the Spanish general, Wellesley was exasperated to find him choleric, obstinate and apparently determined to assert his independence from British orders at all times. The only immediate benefit from the junction with Cuesta's army was that it provided Wellesley with a healthier flow of intelligence. He was now able to appreciate they were about to take on a French army of around forty-five thousand men. Faced with the problems of coordinating his troops, King Joseph had gone forward from Madrid to take personal command. It is a measure of the success of Wellesley's gamble that his Anglo-Spanish force had covered two-thirds of the distance between the Portuguese border and Madrid by the time the French had to assemble their forces at Talavera de la Reyna in mid-July.

Much to Scovell's regret, his Mounted Guides did not reach the army until the general action sought by Wellesley was almost over on 28 July. The British commander had deployed his forces in a defensive line three miles long running north from Talavera to the Sierra de Segurilla. Geography made it very hard for the French to go around either end of this line. Wellesley's northern flank was protected by the rocky hills of the sierra, and its southern end was anchored on the city of Talavera astride the great River Tagus. Even the central section of his line afforded some advantages to the defender, for there was a little brook running north to south that was difficult to cross in parts. Where the British and Spanish armies met (about one mile north of the city), Wellesley had strengthened this formidable natural position by ordering the construction of an earthen redoubt containing several cannon.

The French had assaulted the Anglo-Spanish defenses during the twenty-eighth and been driven off. Both sides had been almost too eager to fight, for despite the passing of sixteen years in which the British had been the leading light in orchestrating and subsidizing Europe's anti-French coalitions, the two antongonists' armies had come face-to-face only on a handful of previous occasions. One French corps had attacked precipitately on the evening of the twenty-seventh, and the British First Division had mounted an attack at one moment on the twenty-eighth. Without having been ordered to do so, they rushed across the brook that marked the front of Wellesley's position and received a bloody check. The price for this almost savage determination to lock horns with the old enemy had been heavy casualties on both sides: 7,268 French and 5,365 British.

Despite the losses, in his dispatch to London Wellesley promptly declared a victory, reasoning that the Anglo-Spanish force had with-stood a determined assault by the conquerers of Europe. They had also inflicted greater casualties upon the French. But it was the kind of tri-umph that Wellesley had no desire to repeat: it was too costly for too lit-tle strategic gain.

The army's officers knew that the butcher's bill Wellesley paid at Talavera had resulted in part from the amateurishness already detected in the Oporto campaign. In addition to the heavy losses taken as a result of the 1st Division's unauthorized advance (including the Guards) on the twenty-eighth, there had been incidents of British units opening fire on one another by mistake on the twenty-seventh, and of the army's follow-ers having fled the battlefield, joining several thousand scattering Spanish troops. The principal lesson Wellesley drew from Talavera was that there was absolutely no point in cooperating further with the Spanish.

As he pulled back from the battlefield, Wellesley saw an opportu-nity to seek a smaller battle, at much more favorable odds: a way to cap the campaign with something altogether more clear-cut than Talavera's messy outcome. He knew from Marshal Soult's letters captured with General Franceschi that this body had begun moving southeast from its position on Portugal's northern border toward his own area of operations. Subsequent reports from the Spanish peasantry had confirmed the arrival of French troops just a couple of marches distant from the line of British communications back into Portugal. General Wellesley assumed that Soult's corps (the 2nd, which had survived May's campaign in northern Portugal) would still be in a parlous state after its narrow escape across the mountains. But just a few days into his march, on 3 August, Wellesley had to abandon his plan.

A couple of days earlier, some Spanish guerrillas in Avila had detained a monk traveling by one of the dusty roads in that corner of the country. What had aroused their suspicions? An implausible manner? Perhaps a spoken Castillian that showed a little too much education, or was it an unlikely traveling itinerary? With drawn weapons they searched the man thoroughly and found that he was carrying a message from King Joseph to Marshal Soult. It may safely be assumed that the messenger, an *afrancesado* or Spanish collaborator, was swiftly put to death and his precious package sent to General Cuesta without delay. Fortunately for Wellesley, relations between the two men had not yet deteriorated to the point that Cuesta did not realize the import of this windfall and inform the British commander of it immediately.

Joseph's message urged Soult to move rapidly to cut off Wellesley's line of withdrawal. The arrival of this intercepted letter caused consternation at British headquarters because it blew apart their earlier assumptions about French deployments. It revealed that Soult was not just in command of his own battered corps of eighteen thousand, but also of Marshal Ney's—a combined strength of thirty-thousand men. There were only eighteen thousand British under Wellesley's command, so it was only by the capture of Joseph's secret messenger that a disaster had been averted.

Scovell was back at headquarters by the time this dramatic intelligence effectively ended the British campaign of 1809. He resumed his many duties mapping, exploring and generally involving himself in the business of communications. His Guides were scattered in their small packets across the army, in fours or fives to each division, and then on to the wayhouses and stopping points on the stages that connected these forces.

By 3rd September, British headquarters had been established at Badajoz, a fortified Spanish town close to the border with Portugal, and the army was withdrawing itself from active operations for the remainder of the campaigning season. Even in August the army found itself facing considerable supply difficulties in Spain, which would only intensify with the onset of autumn as the fields became bare. Wellesley knew that if he was to feed his troops and their horses he would have to take them back, closer to the Portuguese harbors through which they would be sustained for the winter.

As for the headquarters itself, its arrival at each new location during the dying months of 1809 followed a familiar ritual. Firstly an AQMG or a deputy assistant, accompanied by a Guide, the mayor or some other worthy, would locate suitable premises. Large farms, convents, or the mayor's own residence might all answer for the purpose. The staff officer would then go around the new HQ and its surrounding buildings, chalking the names of particular officers or staff on the doors. When the headquarter's baggage arrived on its carts and beasts of burden, the servants would then begin to unload effects into their preassigned quarters. There was not a vast disparity between the retinues of the highest and lowest in this entourage. Scovell traveled with his servant, Healey, and two horses. His commanding general eschewed grandeur in the field, making do usually with half a dozen servants of the human species and seven or eight of the equine.

The day after his arrival at Badajoz, Wellesley was created Viscount Wellington in honor of Talavera. This transformation from a vaguely familiar to a household name happened at an appropriate time, since it was during these last months of 1809 that his decisions about the future of the army under his command would ensure his entry into the pantheon of great military leaders.

When granted his peerage, Wellington had been campaigning for five months, enough time for the army and the general to know one another better. In action on the Douro or Talavera, many regimental officers had noted the general's superb grip of his men as well as his air of calm even at times of crisis.

"I was particularly struck by the style of [his] order, so decided, so manly, and breathing no doubt as to the repulse of any attack; it confirmed confidence . . . he has nothing of the truncheon about him; nothing full-mouthed, important, or fussy: his orders on the field are all short, quick, clear, and to the purpose," one young captain wrote.

Wellington had also cast his merciless gaze on the army and spotted many of his generals for the plodders or incompetents that they were. Perhaps it is unsurprising that in the case of the army's adjutant general, Major General Charles Stewart, five months had sufficed to convince Wellington of his failings. In addition to being an overdressed buffoon, Stewart's desire to question prisoners was too important a matter to be overlooked, particularly since episodes like his interview with General Franceschi. Lord Wellington later gave this account of a furious row:

> "I found him full of the pretensions of this Department of his, although he and it and all of them were under my orders and at my disposal. . . . At last I was obliged to say that if he did not at once confess his error and promise to obey my orders frankly and cordially I would dismiss him *instanter* and send him to England in arrest. After a great deal of persuasion he burst out crying and begged my pardon."

Wellington had gambled correctly in thinking that Stewart would do almost anything to avoid being sent home in disgrace, and rather than simply dismissing him—Stewart was Lord Castlereagh's brother, after all—Wellington tried to sideline him from any significant military business. Stewart may not have been bright, but by September 1809 even he realized that his commander was not interested in seeking his opinion or even talking to him very much. The exacting task Wellington had in mind for him was the weekly adding up of soldiers in the Army, based on returns from the different regiments. Stewart wrote from Badajoz to his brother, Lord Castlereagh, complaining:

> *The Adjutant General, deprived of close communica-*
> *tion with the head of the army, is reduced to keeping*

> *accurately the returns of all descriptions of regiments*
> *... you will admit it does not carry with it interesting*
> *or pleasing occupation.*

Wellington's "Stewart method" was copied in various departments of headquarters and divisions of the army. In most cases, though, it seems to have been achieved without reducing the generals in question to tears. The general quickly spotted the talentless officers, but rather than risk scandal, Wellington allowed them to serve on in some posts, and simply made sure that underneath this titular commander there was someone he could rely upon.

Affairs were happy enough in the quarter master general's branch. Both George Murray, its head, and William De Lancey, his deputy, fitted Wellington's bill down to the ground: they were active, handsome men of good family. The QMG branch thereby became his principal organization for getting things done.

While Wellington used his more zealous assistant or deputy assistant QMGs ceaselessly, and understood their professional merits, he could not necessarily conceive of them as the best company at mealtimes, or indeed as the stuff of which future generals were made. Those who wished to climb in the army hierarchy required both a modicum of military competence and breeding, in his view. "If there is to be any influence in the disposal of military patronage, in aid of military merits," Wellington asked rhetorically of one of his correspondents in London, "can there be any in our army so legitimate as that of family connection, fortune and influence in the country?" By these criteria, Murray and De Lancey were sitting pretty. There were also the young men sent out to learn generalship at his feet, the aides-de-camp. Their numbers included sons of several of the greatest Tory landowning families of the day. As for someone like Scovell, his only "family connection" was with the Lancashire property of his wife Mary's clan. Only through ceaseless dedication to the organization of headquarters and perhaps valor on the battlefield might he be able to bridge the chasm between his actual social position and the kind Wellington thought desirable for promotion.

Mealtimes were the main ritual of the day at headquarters and revealed much about the staff's internal relations. The staff officer sent

ahead to find quarters always had to make sure that there was somewhere suitable for the general's table.

The mood of the assembly varied according to the news he had read
in the London newspapers and the general state of the war. Earlier that
summer, he had been in high spirits as the Austrians battered Napoleon
at the Battle of Aspern-Essling. By September, though, Napoleon had
turned the tables on the Hapsburgs, who had been forced to accept an
unfavorable peace. The long-awaited British military expedition in
northern Europe, a landing in Holland, had turned into the usual fiasco.
They had failed to cause any noticeable diversion in support of the Austrians and the navy had returned the army to southern England with
thousands of its men dying of malaria. In London, the prime minister
had suffered a stroke and the government was in imminent danger of
collapse.

The usual coterie around at dinner was drawn largely from his
aides-de-camp although others, including Scovell, were often present.
Those who received these dining-table morsels of bad news from their
general were most often the ruddy-cheeked young scions of Britain's
great political and aristocratic families serving as his ADCs. Wellington
sometimes called them "my boys," and like all proud fathers looked to
them for a reflection of his own youthful perfection. He was already
becoming estranged from his wife, Kitty, and his own children seemed
to fascinate him less than those of his military family.

FitzRoy Somerset, the youngest son of the duke of Beaufort,
became his firm favorite. When headquarters reached Badajoz the
twenty-one-year-old captain still had little idea of campaigning and no
formal military education. He owed everything to birth and interest. His
position on the staff had been obtained on the recommendation of the
duke of Richmond, who wrote to Wellington that Somerset was "an
active and intelligent fellow and is anxious to go on service." The commander of forces could hardly refuse, since he had been working for the
duke, who was Ireland secretary, until shortly before the campaign.
Although Somerset had been commissioned into the army five years
before, he had been on almost continuous leave, precisely the kind of
practice that fed the calls for reform of the officer corps.

Although dilatory about his military duties prior to arriving in the peninsula, Somerset had acquired the engaging manner and ready humor indispensable for survival as the youngest of nine brothers. His family regarded him as nice but somewhat hopeless, a background similar to Wellington's, who had also been eclipsed for years by his older brothers and whose mother had written dismissively, "Anyone can see he has not the cut of a soldier." There was another similarity more obvious to those dining around the commander's table. Somerset's hooked nose and arresting eyes suggested a young Wellington. His thick, tousled hair and good nature readily aroused a paternal love.

Like his new patron, Somerset was no fool either. He was kind, considerate, good at languages and very discreet. He was soon acting as private secretary to the general in numerous delicate matters of politics and intelligence. Somerset's charm won over even those whom he had eclipsed. FitzRoy's original commission had been into the 4th Dragoons, Scovell's old regiment, which was commanded by his older brother Lord Edward Somerset. While serving as adjutant of the 4th, Scovell had gotten to know Edward and the Somerset family. He and FitzRoy were already corresponding during the captain's studies at Wycombe. The young Somerset seems to have aroused some sort of paternal love in Scovell too. It was becoming clear by this time that he and Mary could only ever have children of their own by some miracle. Young FitzRoy's perfect manners and his evident rapport with Lord Wellington allowed him to become the vehicle for a sort of vicarious ambition on Scovell's part.

So the man who apparently had nothing in the race for advancement now had a precious thing in the young FitzRoy Somerset, a connection who was becoming privy to the commander's great secrets and had his complete confidence. The wheel of fortune was beginning to turn and Scovell's vast investment in a cavalry commission years earlier was beginning to pay dividends. Young Somerset may have had every advantage in life, but he had evidently seen Scovell's talents for what they were and, when the time came, would be ready to share with him the toughest intelligence problem facing his commander.

As these relationships moved into alignment, the greater scheme of military operations that Wellington would pursue for the next two years also became clearer, at least to those in the know.

In Badajoz, Wellington had time to take stock of his army's situation. Since news had reached him of Austria's defeat by Napoleon, it was clear that in 1810 the entire weight of the French military machine could once again be turned against him. Britain could not afford an army capable of meeting 100,000 Frenchmen in open battle. The Spanish army could not be relied upon in any way at all. The French, he deduced, could soon sweep aside the Spanish regular armies and fall upon him with considerable strength. Since he had no intention of engaging such a superior enemy force, he would probably have to withdraw to Lisbon and embark the British army. Probably. As he considered the ignominy of a second Corunna, alternative strategies formed in his mind.

If Spanish cooperation was of dubious value, a quite different picture had emerged with the Portuguese. Since July, Marshal William Beresford had been retraining these forces with the help of dozens of seconded British officers. Scovell's classmate from the Royal Military College, Henry Hardinge, had joined this effort. He was serving as deputy to the quarter master general of the Portuguese army, Lieutenant Colonel Benjamin D'Urban,* another Wycombite. Their reports to Wellington were sufficiently encouraging that Wellington decided (early in 1810) to incorporate a Portuguese brigade into each division of British infantry.

On 20 October 1809 Wellington gave secret orders to his chief engineer, Colonel Fletcher, to begin the construction of a series of defensive lines just behind Lisbon. Fletcher was to be given enormous resources of labor, materials and cash to create a system of forts, ditches, inundations and other obstacles, the lines of Torres Vedras. Wellington reasoned that the farther the French advanced into Portugal, the longer their lines of supply would be and the shorter his own. If he combined these defenses with guerrilla action and devastation of what was already a very poor countryside, the French would be starving by the time they reached the Torres Vedras defenses. Their logistic predicament would either force them into a precipitate and extremely costly assault or leave them melting away.

In order to delay the French entry into Portugal, and make the stakes as high as possible, Wellington needed to defend the two natural gateways into the country. The northern one led from Castille across a barren

---

*No relation to the author.

heathland in the Portuguese Beira down, southwest, through hills to Lisbon. The southern route went from Badajoz in Spanish Estremadura, across the Alemtejo plain to the mouth of the Tagus just south of Lisbon. Each of these gateways to Portugal was guarded by a powerful fortress: Almeida in the north and Elvas in the south. Laid out according to eighteenth-century principles, these places had been surrounded by deep ditches and armed with numerous walled bastions bristling with heavy guns, making the capture a major undertaking. Almeida and Elvas each had its twin on the Spanish side of the frontier, namely Ciudad Rodrigo and Badajoz. Each of these places was somewhat less strong than its Portuguese counterpart. At the end of 1809, all four fortresses were still in the hands of their Portuguese and Spanish masters. Wellington had greater confidence about the survival of those on the western side of the frontier, since their Portuguese defenders had been stiffened with British officers and were under his control. While he hoped the Spanish could hold up the French for a while at Ciudad Rodrigo and Badajoz, he was less inclined to make any great effort to assist in their defense.

As he prepared his defense in depth at Torres Vedras (about one year before he would use it), Wellington also had to give urgent consideration to the issue of early warning for the border fortresses. If he knew sufficiently far in advance of an imminent French offensive and which of the two major invasion routes the French were taking, he would enjoy enormous advantages. However, during the recriminations that had followed Talavera, he reported, "At present I have no intelligence whatsoever . . . as the Spaniards have defeated all my attempts to obtain any by stopping those who I send out to make enquiries." The British commander knew he must develop his own network of spies and other methods for obtaining information.

In the autumn of 1809 and the following winter, he therefore sent out several British "exploring officers" who scouted no-man's-land in uniform alone or with one or two orderlies. They ingratiated themselves with the Spanish authorities in the border region, observed what was going on and gathered reports of French movements. Brave as they were, their grasp of languages was generally no greater than the average officer of their island race. Locals were needed to recruit and operate a spy network. Contact was made with Spanish civilians willing to relay reports and generous sums were promised: 100 dollars per month in one case (with supplementary payments of four dollars for each report received); £500 being assigned to the establishment of a circle of spies in another province.

While committing bags of silver to this goal, Wellington and the staff were predisposed to view any intelligence it produced through spectacles tinted by their unfortunate experience with Spanish and Portuguese reports. "Spaniards more frequently report what they wish than what is true, as we all know to our cost," Major William Warre told his father in a letter, and Wellington himself noted: "It is most difficult to form any judgement from the Spanish and Portuguese accounts of the strength of any French corps; and I generally form my estimates of their strength, not only from these accounts, but from intercepted letters."

Access to his enemy's mail was critical. Wellington was beginning to realize that it presented him with the most valuable form of intelligence. Not only were these missives penned by the enemy's commanders themselves and therefore free of Iberian exaggeration, but they also might give warning of a French action *before* it happened. The great majority of his spies and indeed his own observation officers, on the other hand, could only report the march of a French division once it had begun.

The first task therefore was to get the guerrillas to hand over captured French dispatches to agents of the Anglo-Portuguese army rather than to the Spanish, thereby speeding up the whole process and keeping it free from Allied interference. In part, this could be achieved simply by circulating the word that handsome amounts of silver would be placed in the hands of anyone providing such trophies, but it would also require the British to form close relationships with some of the guerrilla commanders. As 1809 slipped into 1810, all of this work was under way. The staff in Portugal soon enjoyed a good flow of intelligence since its native officers could pass easily in the border area, and some of Scovell's Guides could also be sent to meet agents or their messengers and convey their information directly to headquarters.

It was in winter quarters 1809–1810 that Wellington laid the foundations of his intelligence network and, more importantly, the strategy it was designed to serve. During the next two years events would reveal the wisdom of his calculations.

PART II

The Campaign of 1811, and Evolution of French Codes

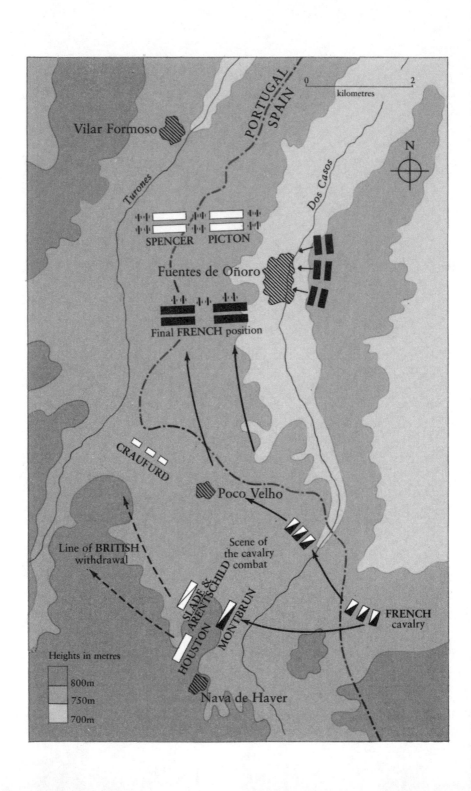

PORTUGAL

SPAIN

0   2
kilometres

Vilar Formoso

Turones

Dos Casos

N

SPENCER   PICTON

Fuentes de Oñoro

Final FRENCH position

CRAUFURD

Poco Velho

Line of BRITISH
withdrawal

Scene of
the cavalry
combat

FRENCH
cavalry

SLADE &
ARENTSCHILD

HOUSTON

MONTBRUN

Heights in metres

800m

750m

700m

Nava de Haver

CHAPTER SEVEN

S. 249. 1076. n. t. 1082. 365. 622. w. 655. w. 439. 669. 655. 1085. 398. 326. 13. 309. i. 1085. 655. 249. 181. t. 980. 985. 186. t. 843. 688. 2. 718. 249. 1297. 536. 174. 1085. 1024 . . . 713. t. 980. 854. 655. 326. 536. 700. w. 171. 1015. 1008. 13. t. 980. 1015. 131. t.

THE BATTLE OF FUENTES DE OÑORO,
MAY 1811—THE ARMY OF PORTUGAL CIPHER

*B*efore the first light of dawn, 5 May 1811, Captain Brotherton rode out with the guerrilla commander Don Julian to the farthest outpost, a couple of miles south of Fuentes de Oñoro, where some Spanish irregulars had been posted at this vantage point the previous night. His short trip took him eastward, through a copse of pygmy oaks and dense brush, across the stream that the locals called the *ribiera del campo,* and then atop the little tor that stood just to the east of it. There was patchy mist in the hollows, and as Brotherton arrived with the celebrated guerrilla at his side a nighttime chorus of bull frogs was giving way to the avian one of dawn. The small Spanish camp was already stirring into life that morning. While maintaining professional courtesies, Brotherton didn't entirely trust Don Julian, and the mission he had been assigned, manning the forward outposts of the army's right, was too important to be left to chance.

A couple of hundred yards behind the outpost, Brotherton and his companion passed two squadrons of British light cavalrymen already sitting in their saddles, awaiting the sun's warmth on their stiff bodies. Their supports, two more squadrons from Brotherton's regiment, the 14th Light Dragoons, were also saddling their mounts nearby, readying themselves for whatever the day might bring.

As the gray gloom of the Castillian horizon began to brighten, Brotherton saw movement in the trees below their vantage point.

Don Julian, are those men yours? he asked.

Most certainly, Captain Brotherton, our forward pickets coming back from their patrol.

Are you sure, sir, they seem too numerous?

You may rely upon it, they are ours.

To Brotherton the silhouetted figures who appeared fleetingly between the branches seemed too many altogether for pickets. A few more minutes passed. The sun had crowned the horizon and was shining straight into their eyes, making it difficult for Brotherton to discern movement elsewhere in the copse. Men were leading their horses through the trees to their left as well as ahead of them. Familiar noises were beginning to surround them—the tapping of sword scabbards on men's hips, the jingling of horses' bits as the beasts swayed their heads from one side to another.

Captain Badcock, commanding one of the squadrons to Brotherton's rear, could hear the sounds too. And then the more ominous noises—men shouting in Spanish, the crack of a pistol shot. Badcock's troopers scanned the tree line ahead of them. Their squadron was drawn up in line, ready to receive whatever issued from the woods; since they knew the Spanish irregulars were ahead of them they could not just charge the first troops who appeared in front.

Then at last men began appearing from the trees a couple of hundred yards ahead of them. Were they French or were they Spanish, the men forming in clumps and then mounting their horses? Nobody knew. The shape of the shakos on the heads of these horsemen told the light dragoons nothing, since Don Julian's men were clad in the stuff they had stripped from the corpses of Frenchmen.

Eventually the squadrons ahead of Badcock's men began moving toward them at a gentle trot. It did not have the appearance of a charge, to be sure. The British troopers strained their eyes, scanning the faces of the men moving toward them to see if they recognized any of Don Julian's scouts. Captain Badcock's horse stood alone, several yards ahead of the squadron, and he saw that the officer approaching them was ahead of his troops too. Badcock was at a loss: should he greet him cordially or draw his sword? As the other officer was closing in on him with just seconds to go, the unknown man suddenly drew his sword, stood in his stirrups and swung it with the practiced motion of a seasoned cavalry officer. It hit Badcock on the side of the face, slicing it open and breaking several of his teeth. His mouth was filling with blood—perhaps only the brass scales of his chin strap and a slight error in the Frenchman's aim had prevented Badcock's head from being taken off in one terrible motion. No doubts remained: the 14th Light Dragoons and the French sabered one another like possessed men.

Meanwhile, Brotherton and Don Julian were galloping through the copse, ducking branches and swerving around the trees with the skill of accomplished huntsmen. The Spanish troops around them had scattered through the undergrowth hallooing, firing and trying to grab a few scattered possessions. The English and Spanish officers galloped past two squadrons of British light cavalry drawn up on the French side of the campo stream. As hundreds of enemy horsemen emerged into the clearing the British officer commanding these 110-odd cavalry had the choice of fighting or fleeing. Since there was a stream and boggy ground to their rear and trees behind the Frenchmen, the losers would have their formation broken, and once cavalry became disordered there was every chance of a slaughter.

The British commander ordered his trumpeter to sound the charge. One officer of the 16th Light Dragoons related, "This is the only instance I ever met with of two bodies of cavalry coming in opposition, and both standing, as invariably, as I have observed it, one or the other runs away. Our men rode up and began sabring, but were so out-numbered that they could do nothing and were obliged to retire across the defile in confusion, the enemy having brought up more troops to that point." Dozens of the British cavalry were hacked down.

Brotherton and Don Julian galloped two miles to Poco Velho, with scores of French cavalry at their heels. "As I approached," wrote Brotherton, "I saw [Poco Velho] occupied by redcoats and began to breathe and feel secure." For some reason, however, the infantry were not opening fire. "I rode up to the first officer I could approach and asked him why he did not fire and stop the progress of the enemy. He replied with astonishment, 'Are those the French?'"

The right of Wellington's line had been completely surprised. Between Poco Velho and Nava de Haver, a village almost two miles south, around thirty-five hundred French cavalry had erupted from the tree line. The British general had stretched his men over a dangerously long distance and now his light cavalry and the 7th Division, holding Poco Velho, were paying a very heavy price. A cry of "No quarter!" was going around the British cavalry, in truth more an attempt to give them courage than a reflection of who might really be taking whom prisoner, as a couple of hundred troopers tried desperately to stem the flow.

Among Wellington's staff, about two miles away near the center of the Allied position, initial reports of these events caused deep alarm. "The consequence [of the French attack] was that there was a general, I might say, flight, but the disorder was really terrible," Major FitzRoy Somerset wrote home with a candor that would be absent from the official account, "and it was at one time to be decided that during this disorder the enemy cavalry might advance and not only destroy ours but put our infantry out of a situation to resist them." With the survival of Wellington's right wing in question, some members of the staff set spurs to their horses and galloped across to Poco Velho to try to save the situation.

Captain George Scovell was one of the first to appear, trying to rally the cavalry who had been broken by the initial French onslaught. Don Julian Sanchez's guerrillas were attached to Scovell's Corps of Guides, in any case, so he had every reason to be there. He rallied some troopers around him and led them back into the hand-to-hand fighting. "It was," wrote Edward Cocks, captain of the 16th Light Dragoons and sometime intelligence officer, "complete confusion: Spaniards, French and British all mixed together hacking and sabring." Many of those fighting were soon drenched with blood, for they delivered and received wound after wound without the death blow being given. Scovell noted in his journal later, "I saw several men receive 5 or 6 cuts fall on the arms and shoulders without any impression." Many a British horseman was learning belatedly that only a razor-sharp weapon could disable another rider swiftly.

Brotherton meanwhile had joined his own squadron of the 14th in time to witness an untimely order from another member of the staff who had just arrived on the scene. Major General Charles Stewart had ridden up and directed Brotherton's little squadron to attack the French. It was, the junior officer wrote, "an injudicious order . . . a dangerous step," since the tide could only be turned by using the few remaining British squadrons in concert, not committing them piecemeal. Brotherton, however, had no choice but to obey the adjutant general, a senior cavalry officer who should have known his business, and order his men forward "at a brisk trot; for, in action, the least hesitation or slowness in executing an order is inexcusable in an inferior officer." His squadron had only covered one hundred yards when Wellington himself "rode up to me and asked me where I was going. I told him of the orders I had received from [Major General Stewart]. He made no further observation than 'Go Back!'"

With Wellington's arrival, Stewart's irresponsible intervention was at an end. The British commander quickly assessed the situation. The 7th Division, securing the southern, or right, end of the line was too far from the main group of his forces, farther north along the same ridge. French cavalry was swarming around the open plain between Nava de Haver and Poco Velho. Wellington needed to rally his cavalry and bring back the infantry of the 7th Division north, closer to his main position. This would be a delicate operation; any unsteadiness during these maneuvers and the French horsemen would pounce. Wellington ordered forward his crack troops of the Light Division to cover the withdrawal of the 7th. As the light troops came up, the French would be distracted from pressing home their attacks on the battalions abandoning Poco Velho.

Fortune at last began to smile on the British. The French horsemen had been charging about and slashing away for an hour or so. Their sword arms were leaden, their horses gasping for breath and lathered in sweat. Some troopers had become faint from the saber wounds that had drenched their uniforms in blood. They needed immediate support from infantry and guns if they were to maintain their pressure on the British. When these reinforcements did not appear quickly enough, however, the 7th Division began making its escape through the squadrons of exhausted enemy horsemen.

The Light Division, meanwhile, having drawn off much of the

pressure, were ordered to turn around and return to the safety of the main British position. If the French cavalry wanted to pursue them there, right to the mouths of several batteries of British cannon, they were welcome to try. Before the light troops could reach this haven, though, they would have to march one and a half miles across an open plain with swarms of French horse milling about them. When faced with the prospect of a charge, the infantry's best defense was to form a square, the troops facing outward with fixed bayonets, so defending themselves from assault on any side. Since a square was an immovable thing (soldiers could not walk backward or sideways in this formation), the Light Division had to move its men toward the main position in battalion boxes with all soldiers facing the direction of march. Whenever the enemy threatened a charge, the light infantry, who were the most highly trained foot soldiers of Wellington's army, would stop, face outward with their bayonets pointing at the enemy, and deter any further onslaught. When the cavalry moved away, they would once again turn to face the direction of march, and continue onward while maintaining themselves in a square. This feat of drill and steadiness won the Light Division the admiration of many spectators.

The crisis of the Battle of Fuentes de Oñoro having passed, the French restricted themselves to a costly but fruitless frontal assault on the village of that name. Wellington had beaten off the French attack. Captain Cocks later wrote in his journal, "I heard Lord Wellington say afterwards at his table he thought he had never been in a worse scrape." The British general was grateful to those who had saved the day, most obviously Major General Robert Craufurd, commanding the Light Division, a man whose allegiance to the principles of scientific soldiering and Whig politics might have made him very suspect to Wellington two or three summers before. The general was also sufficiently relieved to bear no grudge against Don Julian. He knew that this Spaniard and his band were as excellent at gathering intelligence as they had been execrable at the business of regular soldiering. Perhaps there was also a mite of gratitude for Captain Scovell.

It was still "captain," two years after the interview in Oporto when Colonel George Murray had promised Scovell promotion in return for his taking command of the Guides. Murray was always such a charming fellow, but where was this blessed step of rank? Might this battle produce his majority, which he had waited so long for? Wellington appreciated physical courage, even if he had little time for men like Scovell under any other circumstances, and there was no doubt that his commandant of Guides had exposed himself to considerable danger on 5 May. A successful general could bring distinguished officers to the notice of Horse Guards in his victory dispatch. But when Wellington drafted it on 14 May, Scovell's name was not among the eighteen listed for promotion. There were eight officers from the cavalry regiments involved in the butchery near Poco Velho. Tomkinson of the 16th Light Dragoons obtained his captaincy. Badcock of the 14th had gotten his step to major, lucky fellow, but Scovell was disappointed yet again.

Between the end of 1809 and May 1811 the campaign had followed precisely the pattern predicted by Wellington back in those autumn days after the battle of Talavera. The French had indeed invaded Portugal and marched right up to the lines of Torres Vedras. On the way, Wellington had administered a heavy defeat to Marshal Masséna, one of Napoleon's most talented subordinates, at Busaco, and then watched his myrmidons starve at the gates of Lisbon. Early in 1811, the British had followed them out of Portugal and Wellington knew that the fighting for the next year would center around the border fortresses. Three of those four key fortified places—Ciudad Rodrigo, Badajoz and Almeida—had fallen into enemy hands.

The French had left a garrison in Almeida, and Wellington surrounded it before pushing beyond it to the Spanish frontier. Realizing that the British could starve the Almeida garrison at their leisure, Masséna had attempted to fight his way back toward those stranded troops. Wellington had anticipated this, and had chosen a strong position to block him, producing the battle of Fuentes de Oñoro. After his failure on 5 May, Masséna had no choice but to send word to the Almeida garrison under General Brenier that they would have to fight their way out. Masséna's headquarters found three soldiers who were willing to run the risks of trying to penetrate British lines and get the message to Brenier.

Two of the French messengers, leaving shortly after the battle, disguised themselves as peddlers and tried to make their way through.

Apparently they were intercepted and executed as spies, although it is not clear what became of their secret messages. The third soldier, Andre Tillet of the 6th Light Infantry, made his way in uniform, often crawling through the fields close to the Spanish border and up to the French outposts at the fortress.

Brenier signaled his receipt of the message by firing heavy guns at a prearranged time. He prepared the fortress for demolition and on the night of 10 May his men moved out of Almeida. The British pickets left surrounding the fort were too few in number and too dozy to stop Brenier's battalions from brushing them aside. Most of Wellington's army had its backs toward Almeida anyway, since it was facing eastward on the frontier. Brenier escaped the few miles through British outposts to French lines to the delight of Napoleon, who promoted him and gave Private Tillet the Legion of Honor and a pension of six thousand francs. Wellington was furious, for the escape had nullified the heroic defense at Fuentes de Oñoro. "The most disgraceful military event that has yet occurred to us," he wrote to Earl Liverpool, venting on the inadequacies of his senior officer corps. "I am obliged to be everywhere, and if absent from any operation, something goes wrong . . . it is to be hoped that the General and other officers of the Army will at last acquire that experience which will teach them that success can be attained only by attention to the most minute details." Any fair-minded observer in the army would have said that it had already been thoroughly reformed since 1809, but in his quest to turn the armament at his disposal into the most perfect engine for driving out the French, Wellington could see only imperfections in its organization and imbecility in many of its officers.

The French army, too, took stock after its retreat from Portugal. Napoleon wanted changes in its command and in the field, and many staff officers felt that communications had become impossibly difficult. In the spring of 1811, secret writing was blossoming in the French army. Staff officers in different places finally began doing something to protect the contents of their messages.

During Masséna's campaign against Lisbon, guerrilla activity had been so heavy that his Army of Portugal had been out of contact with Madrid and Paris for six weeks at one point. Portuguese partisans had swarmed about the countryside, cutting the throat of any French foot-slogger who fell behind his column and arresting any suspicious-looking person who might be carrying a message. Masséna's attempt to emulate Joseph's tactic of sending out a local collaborator in civilian clothes proved unsuccessful. A Portuguese sympathizer, Lieutenant Mascaren-has, had been arrested while carrying dispatches in the disguise of a shepherd. Pathetically, Mascarenhas's idealized notion of peasant dress (he had equipped himself with a puppy in a wicker basket) and refined speech gave him away to the locals and he was later executed. In the end, Masséna had to send General Foy with an escort of an infantry battalion and a squadron of cavalry to fight their way through the guerrillas and act as his personal emissary to Napoleon. Foy had traveled all the way to Paris in search of pearls of strategic wisdom from their imperial master. The cycle of violence between the Iberian peasantry and French army had brought matters to a head, where now the dispatch of sensitive communications by mail was impossible.

Change, however, was afoot, as the British would soon realize. In April, the Anglo-Portuguese force operating to the south near Badajoz under Beresford's command had picked up a most interesting dispatch. Its message had been translated into a stream of symbols. Lieutenant Colonel Benjamin D'Urban, quarter master general to Marshal Beresford, commanding this Anglo-Portuguese force, had noted in his journal the capture of a ciphered letter from General Latour Maubourg.*

It translated letters of the alphabet into random symbols: for example, A was ., B was 1, all the way down to +, - and = for x, y and z. To anyone with an understanding of deciphering, such a simple code was not hard to crack. Since the most commonly used letters, like the vowels e and a, were only represented by a single symbol in the cipher, it was just a matter of using the known patterns of spelling to break it. Indeed when Latour-Maubourg's message was brought into Beresford's HQ, D'Urban and his deputy, Major Henry Hardinge had little difficulty deciphering it. Hardinge, like his Wycombe classmate Scovell, had learned a little about codes at the college and had a particular interest in

---

*Latour-Maubourg was an aristocrat who personified the sangfroid and gallows humor of the French cavalry. On losing a foot at the Battle of Leipzig in 1813, he cursed his sobbing manservant with the words, "Stop snivelling, you fool, that's one less boot for you to polish."

them. He and D'Urban discovered the meaning of the captured message on the same day they received it. A large French army was building up to challenge the Allies on the plains of Estremadura. Beresford, who had two British divisions with him, was also cooperating with Spanish troops, with the aim of besieging the fortified town of Badajoz.

Intelligence led British headquarters to suspect that Marshal Soult, the old enemy of Corunna and Oporto, had put himself at the head of French forces in Estremadura. With the disastrous business of Almeida still souring Wellington's mood, he resolved to move south quickly to reinforce Beresford.

Wellington sent two divisions off on 15 May and followed them with a small suite of staff officers, including Scovell, on the next day. But as they rode down in hard stages through the hilly countryside, ominous news reached them. Soult had already attacked Beresford at Albuera on the sixteenth and it had been a most sanguinary affair.

On the afternoon of 19 May, Wellington rode through the *place d'armes** and into the center of Elvas, the greatest Portuguese fortress. The town sat in a place of exceptional natural strength, its whitewashed buildings occupying the crown of a hill. To Wellington's party, riding down to Elvas from the north, one of the most striking things about the town was the vast three-tiered aqueduct built into it in the sixteenth century. Each of the natural routes around the town were in turn dominated by two great outworks. Its defenses were so strong that Marshal Soult never felt the confidence to put them to the test.

Wellington's party clattered through the narrow streets and established a headquarters in the town center. There he received reports of what had happened a couple of marches across the border on the sixteenth. At about 4 P.M., he jotted a note to Lieutenant General Brent Spencer, who was in command of the divisions left behind to guard the natural gateway into northern Portugal. "I do not yet know the particulars of the action, nor the extent of the loss; but it is certainly very severe." He then began to compose a letter to Beresford. He had driven Soult off all right, for the reports were clear about that. The British infantry had fought with magnificent determination, but their ardor had carried one brigade into disaster. It had been caught in the flank by

---

*The open ground near the entrance to a fortress where troops assembled.

French cavalry and in five ghastly minutes 1,250 out of its 1,570 men had been killed, captured or wounded. The other British brigades had taken a heavy pounding too. Perhaps four in every ten redcoats in Beresford's army were dead or wounded.

Wellington knew that when word reached England about the scale of this loss, it might look very bad. All those carping Whigs and Radicals would be on their hind legs in the Commons denouncing the ministry's war policy yet again. With these concerns swirling around his head, Wellington jotted a sympathetic note to Beresford: "You could not be successful in such an action without a large loss; and we must make up our minds to affairs of this kind sometimes, or give up the game." The next day, Wellington fired off orders, telling the hospitals in Lisbon to prepare for two thousand wounded and ordering up more gunners. The attempt on Badajoz had cost the British dear at Albuera, but it had cost Soult dearer still and his army was withdrawing, leaving the French garrison inside that fortress to face the inevitable siege. Having just paid this awful price, Wellington was determined to continue his attempt on the city and was ordering heavy guns and supplies forward.

On the twenty-first, Wellington left Elvas and rode a dozen miles across the plain of the Guadiana River to direct operations himself. He decided to look over the battlefield of Albuera and Scovell followed in his suite. They found the ground strewn with thousands of corpses. Wild dogs and carrion birds were already making a meal of them. Here and there, remarkably five days after the slaughter, plaintive voices cried out for mercy or deliverance. The Allied medical services had broken down completely. In some places, Wellington could see an orderly helping a canteen to the blood-caked face of some French hussar or Portuguese chasseur. Wellington wrote to Beresford, "I don't know what to do about the French wounded at Albuera. We must remove our own in the first instance."

For Scovell, the field held its own particular horror. One of the four battalions in the brigade that had been ridden down was his own, the 57th Foot. After touring the battlefield with Lord Wellington, Scovell noted in his journal, "Our people had buried till they could work no longer, and there still lay an immense number that never could be interred. Of about 7000 British not one half remained fit for duty, and only two officers of my Regiment the 57th came out of the field unhurt. The left Centre Company had only two men left." The colonel of the

57th had told his men to "Die Hard!" as the Polish Lancers and 2nd
Hussars rode down on them. The moment entered army mythology, and
the CO's order the English language.

Wellington returned to Elvas, where he reviewed Beresford's official
account of the battle, a document that had been tainted by Beresford's
terrible state of mind: he had gone to pieces after Albuera and sunk into
a deep depression. "This will not do," Wellington remarked as he read
the dispatch, "write me down a victory." The document was redrafted
to be more upbeat. To ram the point home, the commander of British
forces added in his covering note to the secretary of war in London, Earl
Liverpool, "After a most severe engagement, in which all the troops
conducted themselves in the most gallant manner, Sir W. Beresford
gained the victory." In letters to London and to the political authorities
in the peninsula, he blamed the Spanish troops at Albuera for being
incapable of maneuvering to defend themselves.

Among the staff officers milling about outside headquarters in Elvas
the affair of the sixteenth generated much gossip. Wellington's aristocratic young military secretary, FitzRoy Somerset, wrote home telling his
brother that he would not find the truth about Albuera in the official dispatch, confiding, "Beresford does not appear to have managed the battle
with much skill." Apparently Beresford had fallen into indecision *during*
the battle itself. At one point, the marshal had fought for his life with a
Polish lancer and clearly been shaken by the experience. Shortly afterward, Beresford had lost all hope and ordered a general retreat. The victory, if it could really be called one, had been won only when one of his
staff officers had galloped forward on his own initiative and ordered forward the reserve, a brigade of fusiliers, to attack the faltering French. The
word was that Hardinge had saved the day. A twenty-six-year-old staff
officer had shown the character and presence of mind that Beresford
lacked. Anxious lest he be eclipsed, Hardinge's superior, D'Urban, let it
be known through his own partisans that he had given the fateful order
to bring up the reserves and that Hardinge had been merely his errand
boy. Preferring not to choose between them, both, it would later become
clear, earned Wellington's gratitude for their presence of mind.

If Hardinge and D'Urban were to profit personally from the car-
nage of Albuera, so too was Scovell. He may have been disappointed
after the Battle of Fuentes de Oñoro, but on 24 May, his friend FitzRoy

Somerset set pen to paper with good tidings. Scovell was promoted at last to major. The slaughter of the 57th at Albuera had left most of the regiment's commissions vacant. After years of trying to impress generals with his enthusiasm, plans and extra labors, Scovell had gotten his step the traditional way in war: into a dead man's shoes.

"The Commander in Chief having been pleased to direct Lord Wellington to recommend such officers for brevet rank as may have particularly merited his notice and approbation," Somerset's letter to Scovell began, "I have much pleasure in being the channel of communicating to you that his Lordship has taken the opportunity of recommending you for the rank of Major and I beg you to accept my congratulations on an occasion naturally gratifying to your feelings."

If the losses of the 57th had created vacancies, those who worked most closely with Wellington—Murray, De Lancey and Somerset—must also have impressed him of the candidate's virtues. The staff had come to know Scovell's restless energy well, for they had observed time and again that while he might lack the laconic wit of a Warre or Somerset, he was utterly tireless in his dedication to the task of improving the army. However keenly they had started their campaigning, most of the officers around Wellington could not sustain their professional zeal after months of riding about, getting shot at and sleeping badly. A good number of them, including FitzRoy Somerset, had already enjoyed leave in London. Scovell, on the other hand, had stayed put, always jotting observations about the campaign in his journal, darting about on his beloved horses, comparing notes with others before sitting down again at some rough-hewn peasants' table to make further scribblings.

During the winter inside the lines of Torres Vedras, finding that his occupation with communications was taking up too little of his time, Scovell set his mind to inventing something. He had seen that every cavalry regiment in the army had trouble with the carts used by its blacksmiths. The animals used to draw these wagons had frequently been worked to death on the Portuguese roads that were little better than tracks. Scovell therefore designed a portable forge that could be broken down and packed on two mules who might walk anywhere a regiment's horses could. In time, this invention would be credited with saving dozens of horses.

The importance of the Corps of Guides had increased greatly once the army had emerged from the lines of Torres Vedras, early in 1811, and gone out to the open border country again. The general's scheme of operations for taking Ciudad Rodrigo and Badajoz involved dividing the army, and this meant successful operations were vitally dependent on timely communications between these two wings.

Wellington had seen Scovell's Corps of Guides at work and had been impressed, believing that they were better at their job than British soldiers ever could be. "Our English non-commissioned officers and soldiers are not very fit to be trusted alone, and out of view of their officers, in detached stations at a distance from the Army, as the soldiers of the Guides are for months together, without occasioning any complaint," he subsequently explained to London.

Later that summer, Scovell and the Guides were given the task of establishing a daily post between the two halves of the Anglo-Portuguese force. It soon became a service that Wellington almost literally set his watch by. The journey between the two headquarters was completed in stages of ten to twelve miles, with the progress of each packet recorded on its accompanying ticket. The messengers "rode post," picking up a fresh horse at each of the wayside halts and leaving their tired mount to recover. Scovell later said, with evident pride, "There was no instance of any of these orderlies betraying his trust."

By August 1811, Scovell was fulfilling his duties so effectively that Wellington considered putting the entire civilian and military post of Portugal under his control. If the job of postmaster seemed a rather long way from Scovell's early ambition to lead a regiment of cavalry, the newly made major understood very well that dreams of glory do not satisfy one's creditors. The myriad tasks he took on in Wellington's HQ each carried its own pay or allowances; by accepting them he was making himself a most prosperous officer. While in the end the reform of the entire Portuguese postal service did not fall to Scovell personally, Wellington nevertheless announced by General Order:

> Major Scovell is appointed to superintend all the communications of the army; and the post master sergeants, at headquarters and at Lisbon, will place themselves under his orders, as likewise Senhor Oliveira, the Director of the Portuguese posts. The messengers, likewise, will receive their orders from Major Scovell.

These many tasks also included supervision of the telegraph system in the country. Prior to Masséna's invasion, the Portuguese had maintained links of signaling stations up to Elvas and Almeida on the frontier. These had been destroyed by the Allies as they fell back to Torres Vedras. By the summer of 1811, Scovell was trying to reconstitute some of these links, although they never attained the same strategic importance as his daily post between Wellington and the officer in command of the Allies' southern wing, Lieutenant General Rowland Hill.

With these duties, Scovell more than doubled his earlier pay. The promotion from captain to major was worth almost five shillings more each day. He had also moved from deputy assistant QMG to assistant, which also carried a raise in pay of several shillings each day. Once he became superintendent of military communications he was given extra pay of £50 per annum, which was soon increased to £80.

To Scovell's satisfaction, the extra money also came attached to the responsibility for, among other things, codes and ciphers. Major Scovell was handed a small notebook containing a handwritten copy of a most unusual text: *Cryptographia or The Art of Decyphering* by David Arnold Conradus. The origins of this tract are obscure. It is possible that Conradus may have been a monk, for men of the cloth were preeminent among the secret servants who made or deciphered codes for the princes and great captains of Europe during the seventeenth and eighteenth centuries.

Anyone in possession of Conradus, a detailed knowledge of French and a good brain could attack the kind of simple ciphers that had appeared that summer in Spain and do so with a good chance of obtaining results, which was exactly what Hardinge and D'Urban had done with Latour-Maubourg's letter before the Battle of Albuera. Conradus had evidently spent many years studying the principal languages of Europe and his little book consisted of propositions and rules. The first section, headed "General Theory," began:

> Proposition 1: The art of decyphering is the explanation of secret characters by certain rules.
>
> Prop. 2: Every language has, besides the form of characters, something peculiar in the place, order, continuation, frequency and number of the letters.

Rule 1: In decyphering regard is to be had to the place, order, combination, frequency and number of letters.

Rule 2: In decyphering nothing is to be left to conjecture, where the art shews the way of proceeding with certainty.

Prop. 3: In a writing of any length, the same letters recur several times.

Rule 3: Writings of any length are most easy to decypher from the frequent recurrence and combination of the same letters."

Conradus then explained the peculiarities of the main European languages that might show themselves in ciphers. Chapter V concerned French and contained many vital pointers: that *e* was the most commonly used letter; that words ending in double letters most likely ended in *ee*; that *et* meaning *and* was the most common word; that there were only thirty-nine two-letter words in French (which he helpfully listed); and that a single letter on its own was an *a*, *y* or a consonant with an apostrophe.

If one counted up the code numbers in any given message, the most frequently occurring was likely to be *e*, the second most frequent was *i* and so on.

The approach contained in *The Art of Decyphering* was, long before 1811, clearly understood by those who made codes. Among diplomats and royal princes ciphers had been growing in size and complexity: the Spanish had introduced a five-hundred-character cipher in the late sixteenth century; King Charles I had used one of eight hundred characters during the English Civil War; Louis XIV had a *Grand Chiffre,* or Great Cipher, of six hundred, but distributed several different sheets to his ministers overseas, allowing choices as to which particular coding table had been used. All of these steps were designed to defeat the basic approach contained in Conradus, which was to draw conclusions from the frequency of different code numbers. In the summer of 1811, such Great Ciphers had not appeared in the French Peninsular army, which fortunately for Scovell gave him time to cut his teeth on simpler codes. Change, however, was afoot.

*   *   *

On 7 May, two days after Fuentes de Oñoro, Marshal Masséna had been superceded in command of the Army of Portugal. His replacement was Marshal Auguste Frederic Marmont, duke of Ragusa. Masséna had embodied the swashbuckling verve of the revolutionary armies; he was a man who believed in himself so completely and was so comfortable with risk that he had many a time clinched victory in an apparently hopeless situation. Marmont on the other hand was altogether more methodical, more scientific, an artillery officer who knew back to front the business of tangents and trajectories. Marmont had shown himself an able administrator, reorganizing the artillery throughout the army. Whereas Masséna cursed in his Piedmontese dialect, the duke of Ragusa was a cultivated man, *un savant*, someone who knew about science, art and philosophy. And while Masséna had kept his mistress at headquarters during the Portuguese campaign, Marmont, although reputedly one of the most handsome men in Paris, brought no Venus to the field of Mars.

Marmont was a man of energy too; thirty-six when he took over the Army of Portugal, he was fifteen years younger than the marshal he replaced. It was the kind of radical change the emperor wanted, and Marmont reveled in his reputation as one of Bonaparte's closest confidants during his epic campaigns in Egypt and Italy. It was only natural, though, that arriving with such a reputation, Marmont should excite jealousy in some quarters.

Although Masséna had coaxed it into battle on 5 May, the Army of Portugal was still utterly exhausted by its expedition across scorched earth to Lisbon and back. Upon assuming control, Marmont began a thorough reorganization.

Napoleon had grown sick of the constant bickering between Masséna and the commander of his three *corps d'armée*; Marmont disposed of this layer of command and consolidated his troops in six strong divisions, all under his own hand. Napoleon thought it absurd that 100,000 French troops in western Spain could be kept in check by 40,000 British, and Marmont understood that the solution lay in close cooperation with his neighbors, the Army of the North and Soult's Army of the South. In order to do this, prompt and effective communication would be needed. The marshal knew enough about codes to be sure that the kind of simple ciphers appearing in his own and Soult's armies were inadequate, and Marmont had one advantage over the others. He had used ciphers in the Balkans while in command of Napoleon's Army of Dalmatia in 1807. That code had been a hieroglyphic form of *petit chiffre*, or small cipher. It was not very strong, however, and its complex symbols made it hard to use in the heat of battle.

If any further incentive was needed finally to make the move toward communicating in code, it may well have come from an incident involving General Maximilien Foy, who, while traveling back to Spain in March 1811, after briefing the emperor, had narrowly escaped capture during a guerrilla ambush. One of the first things Marmont did in his new post was to elevate Foy to the command of one of his divisions. The two men had been in the same class at artillery academy in 1792, campaigned together in 1805 and trusted one another completely. Foy had fought the British more times than almost any other commander in the French army. He had been at Vimeiro, Wellington's Peninsular debut in 1808, had placed himself at the head of troops trying to storm the seminary in Oporto following the crossing of the Douro in 1809, and had been seriously wounded leading his men into action at Busaco in 1810.

Before his own departure from Paris, Marmont had already discussed the possible introduction of a *Grand Chiffre* for use in high-level communication with Paris and Madrid with Marshal Berthier, Napoleon's chief of staff. While this question was being considered, he got his staff to prepare a new code table for use between himself and the Army of Portugal's six divisional commanders. This fell in complexity somewhere between the simple ciphers of thirty or fifty numbers and the 1750 pattern *grand chiffre* with its printed tables of twelve hundred. It would come in its own standard table of 150 characters. Marmont and his chief of staff had grasped two important points: a cipher for use by the Army of Portugal would be much easier to distribute in his own area of operations than one for use by the senior commanders right across Spain, and since he only had to get copies of the cipher to his own commanders, its security could be maintained by occasional changes of code table.

In the meantime, Marmont took the field with his reorganized army and prepared it to march shortly before the end of May. Wellington had been busy trying to find a way to continue besieging the French garrison of Badajoz. When Don Julian's scouts near Salamanca detected the French preparation to go south, Wellington did not believe that Marmont's exhausted host could possibly be ready to march. But he knew that his siege of Badajoz would have to be abandoned if he was wrong and Marmont did march south to join Soult.

Uncertain of the value of the intercepted dispatches he continued to receive, Wellington relied heavily at this moment on his exploring officers. In particular, Colquhoun Grant, a young captain of the 11th Foot, who sent in valuable reports based on reconnaissance he carried out inside the French lines. Grant had begun this secret work a few months earlier, while the army was still inside the Torres Vedras lines. He operated in uniform, alone or with one or two comrades, and relied on the speed of his hunter to gallop clear of any pursuing enemy. Like Scovell, Grant loved Spanish culture and language, using his excellent grasp of it to win the confidence of locals up and down the frontier. "His knowledge of the enemy's army was exact," wrote one officer at headquarters, "he knew not only the regiments, but the character of every superior officer."

The presence of men like Grant deeply unsettled the French. Sometimes a column of infantry marching across a dusty Estremaduran plain would see the glint of a telescope on a nearby hillside and then catch sight of a silhouetted figure on horseback. One Army of Portugal staff officer recorded:

> We frequently saw observers of this kind flitting round us. It was vain to give chase to them, even with the best-mounted horsemen. The moment the English officer saw any such approach he would set spurs to his steed, and nimbly clearing ditches, hedges, even brooks, he would make off at such speed that our men soon lost sight of him, and perhaps saw him soon after a league further on, note-book in hand, at the top of some hillock, continuing his observations.

Although many French felt powerless to stop Wellington's exploring officers, their trade was in fact a most hazardous one. Lieutenant Colonel Waters, an officer who had played a vital part in the Douro crossing two years earlier, was captured in April 1811. Another lieutenant colonel, confusingly also called Grant (first name John), disappeared in Estremadura while observing Marmont's advance.

On 10 June 1811, Wellington was finally in possession of enough

reports from his exploring officers and spies to realize that the Army of
Portugal was moving south and that his plans to take Badajoz would
have to be abandoned. In any case, the artillery's attempts to batter
breaches in the town's defenses had achieved only limited success. There
was no time for further attempts; Wellington ordered his army to retire
behind the Guadiana River, on the Portuguese frontier.

Ten days later, Marmont and Soult's united force of sixty thousand
men stood opposite Wellington's army, consisting of forty-six thousand
troops, of whom only twenty-nine thousand were British. These were
odds that the British general would be most reluctant to fight with,
although he had posted his troops in strong positions. And this was not
all, for Wellington was becoming apprehensive for the safety of Badajoz's
Portuguese counterpart, Elvas. A series of tetchy orders were fired off,
ordering supplies thrown into the place and the governor told to put it in
a state of defense. For Wellington was anticipating that he might have to
fall back across the Alemtejo plain and leave the Elvas garrison under an
enemy siege. This was a tense period, during which Wellington outwardly
displayed his usual sangfroid and businesslike calm to his staff and soldiers. But his anxiety that an onslaught by Soult and Marmont's combined forces might force him all the way back to Lisbon was very real,
revealing itself in a letter to his brother on 21 June: "Matters are in a very
critical state just now; but I think I shall carry them through."

Charting the campaign's progress, Wellington had learned a worthwhile lesson during those summer months of 1811. He could not be in
two places at once and he could not rely on others to act according to
the letter of his orders. Moreover, if French generals cooperated rather
than bickered, as they had on the plain of the Guadiana, his calculations
would all be ruined.

He knew that for as long as he was one man trying to guard two
routes into Portugal from invasion by two or three French armies, communications would be paramount. His would have to be impeccable
and those of the enemy needed to be harassed, intercepted and their
secrets revealed. The success of all future operations depended upon this
and his superintendent of communications, George Scovell.

Top: Wellington as field marshal and duke at the end of the Peninsular Campaign in 1814. *(Credit: The V & A Picture Library, London)*

Bottom: King Joseph, Napoleon's brother, sent to rule Spain. Despite the artist's attempt to present Joseph as a military leader, Joseph did not share his younger sibling's genius for war. *(Credit: The V & A Picture Library, London)*

The somewhat romanticized image of a French general on campaign conveys the vital importance of the written dispatch in military operations and the expectation triggered by a messenger's arrival. *(Credit: The V & A Picture Library, London)*

A section of King Joseph's deciphering table. The gender or case of many code numbers was dependent on context, hence the alternatives listed in some places. *(Credit: The Trustees of The Wallace Collection, London)*

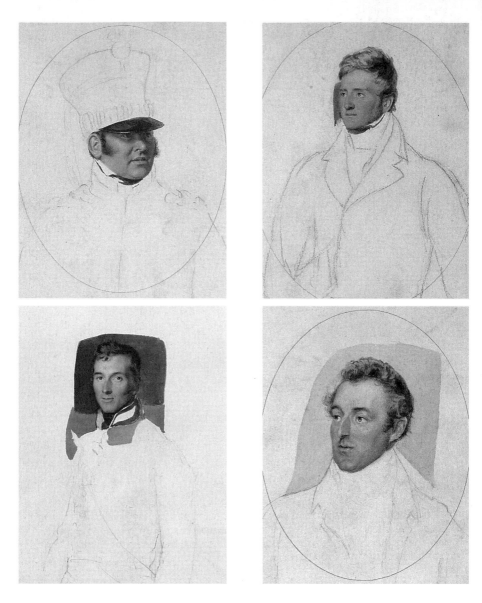

Top left: George Scovell sketched on campaign in 1813 by Thomas Heaphy. The distinctive headgear belongs to the Staff Cavalry Corps.

Top right: FitzRoy Somerset, Wellington's military secretary for much of the Peninsular War and a friend of Scovell's for life.

Bottom left: Sir George Murray, quarter master general of the Peninsular Army. Diligent, persuasive, and highly effective, he was Wellington's "chief of staff" long before the British army officially recognized that term.

Bottom right: Wellington, also drawn in the summer of 1813, in a study that captures his intense, sometimes intimidating presence and does not flatter him in the manner of later heroic pictures.

Top left: Marshal Nicolas Soult, duke of Dalmatia. He was capable of great general-ship but put self-interest first during the campaign of 1812.

Top right: Marshal Auguste Marmont, duke of Ragusa. A favorite of Napoleon's, he showed great skill in keeping Wellington in check during 1811, but was later humiliated by the British at Salamanca.

Bottom left: General Maximilien Foy met the British on a dozen battlefields between 1808 and 1815. His personal papers survived, providing precious insight into the dilemmas facing the French in Iberia.

Bottom right: Marshal Jean-Baptiste Jourdan. His appointment early in 1812 as chief of staff to King Joseph caused much resentment among other officers, and despite his sound diagnoses about French problems in Spain, he achieved little.

(All courtesy of the National Portrait Gallery, London)

The Battle of Vitoria, 21 June 1813. This watercolor by Atkinson shows the birth of a more propagandistic style among British artists in the immediate aftermath of the wars. British troops are depicted capturing a French eagle (in fact, it was a less significant standard), while a genuine trophy taken in this rout of the French army, Jourdan's marshal's baton, awaits Wellington. *(By courtesy of the National Portrait Gallery, London)*

Wellington and his staff at Waterloo. The British commander saw several Peninsular colleagues killed or maimed during this final confrontation of the Napoleonic era. *(By courtesy of the National Portrait Gallery, London)*

George Scovell, aged eighty-five or eighty-six. His longevity guaranteed that he would be one of the select band of Peninsular veterans to be photographed. Scovell reached the rank of full general and was granted the Grand Cross of the Bath, worn proudly on his coat. *(By courtesy of the National Portrait Gallery, London)*

CHAPTER EIGHT

*S. 249. 1076. nt. 1082. 365. 622. we. w. 489. 669. e. 1085. 898.
326. 13. 309. i. 1085. e. 249. 181. t. 980. 985. 186. t. 843. 688.
2. n. 249. 1297. 536. 174. 1085. 1024... 713. t. 980. 854. e. 326.
536. 700. w. 171. 1015. 1003. 13. t. 980. 1015. 131. t.*

THE BLOCKADE OF CIUDAD RODRIGO,

JUNE TO NOVEMBER 1811—THE GREAT CIPHER

*T*he carriage carrying Joseph sped through the gates of Rambouillet's palace and clattered out onto the cobblestones. A handsome team pulled the vehicle and coachmen dressed in the king of Spain's livery rode postillion. Hidden behind the coach's windows, Napoleon's brother was deep in thought as he left the Gothic spires and turrets of the palace behind him.

For two days he had laid before the emperor every vexatious fact, every tedious detail of his life as the embattled sovereign. This farce in which he must play the role of "His Catholic Majesty" was unsupportable. He begged to be allowed to end it, to abdicate.

Before Joseph even started the long journey from Madrid, the emperor had done everything he could to avoid this scene and had seen to it that Joseph was virtually held prisoner in his Iberian kingdom. But knowing that he would never get past the frontier if he actually sought permission, his brother had simply traveled into France on 10 May

without it, ignoring an order delivered by one of the imperial *estafettes**
on the wayside in Gascony to turn around and go back to Madrid.

On the fifteenth he had arrived not in Paris but at the Bourbon's old
hunting domain south of the capital, where Napoleon preferred to conduct the interview. In latter years Marie Antoinette had made Rambouillet the royal dairy, her *ferme ornée,*† where manicured sheep
grazed the park and the queen conducted experiments in scientific husbandry. It was as good a place as any to soothe his irksome brother.

Joseph complained that he had no authority or respect. The marshals
ignored him and conducted the war as they saw fit. There was no proper
system of taxation, and money raised was often sent back to France or
disappeared into the pockets of military commanders. Starved of revenue,
the court had become an impoverished affair lacking in majesty and spectacle; moreover, there was nothing to fund the changes that would draw
the Spanish bourgeois to the bosom of Napoleon's cause. And while
Joseph entertained some hopes of winning more converts among the professional classes, almost everywhere in the countryside the grim business
of violence and retribution had alienated the population.

After they had talked for two days in the salons of the chateau and
walked in its ornate corridors, Napoleon reminded his brother that he
was no general: it would be impossible to nominate him actually in
command of the French armies in Iberia. Why then, asked Joseph, not
appoint a marshal to act on my behalf? This was not a question
Napoleon could answer easily. He knew better than anybody that his
marshals were guilty of every kind of absurd pretension and petty
rivalry once they strayed from his sight, but he knew that trying to place
one of them above his peers would produce all sorts of new problems.

In theory Marshal Louis Berthier, prince of Neufchatel and his formidable administrator, still held the title Major General de l'Armée
d'Espagne, or chief of staff of the Army of Spain. In fact, as the emperor
knew only too well from the experiences of Masséna's campaign in Portugal, news from the field commanders often took weeks to reach
Berthier in his office in Paris.

---

*A courier of the imperial service.

†"Gilded farm"; it was a fashion in the eighteenth century for aristocrats to
turn the soil with silver trowels and generally affect an interest in agriculture.

Joseph appreciated soon enough that his brother was loath to lessen his personal control over the French armies that garrisoned Spain's northern and Catalan coasts. These troops, the Army of the North and the Army of Catalonia, had direct contact with France through the frontier. The emperor inisted that these two armies must continue to operate under direct orders from Paris.

However, Napoleon did recognize the justice of some of his brother's complaints and knew that it was vital to have him on his way back to Madrid as quickly as possible, lest some of the accompanying Spanish courtiers with him write home with damaging details about the gravity of this crisis.

When Joseph finally left Rambouillet in his carriage, he had been promised that the French exchequer would fund the expenses of his court to the tune of 500,000 francs each month. Furthermore, he carried a note dated 17 May summarizing their agreement in the military sphere. Before setting off for Madrid, Joseph went to see his wife, Julie, at their estate in Mortefontaine, were she spent most of her time to avoid the looking-glass world of her husband's court and its empty flattery. She thought Joseph much changed and could not understand his euphoria about the meetings with Bonaparte. Joseph's "frivolity was inconceivable and his self-confidence was equally inexplicable," she wrote, "he was surprised that we did not look at him with great admiration, so convinced was he that he had performed great deeds." Queen Julie, it seems, was a better judge both of her husband's impossible situation and of the emptiness of the promises made at Rambouillet, and with each league of his journey back to Spain, Joseph should have seen himself that the 17 May memorandum was worthless.

It began promisingly enough from Joseph's point of view: "The King of Spain, as the Emperor's lieutenant, commands the French armies of Spain and Portugal in accordance with the direction he receives from the Emperor, through the Chief of Staff the Prince of Neufchatel." Joseph would be assisted in these duties by a military figure, "responsible for the details of the overall direction of troops garrisoned in the provinces."

But just a few paragraphs on, the body of this Rambouillet accord then proceeded to undermine line by line all that had been so confidently stated at the beginning. Marmont's Army of Portugal and Soult's Army of the South would "correspond" with Madrid, a clause which those two commanders took to mean keeping the king informed rather than accepting any commands from him. The armies of the North and Catalonia would be run under different arrangements: military governors appointed by Napoleon ran administrative matters, and he also supplied their operational orders. A small Army of the Center, operating around Madrid itself, would be the only corps directly controlled by the king.

One week after their meetings at Rambouillet, Napoleon began to rethink even his limited concessions. Above all, the emperor was loath to appoint a single marshal as *primus inter pares** directing operations from Madrid. However logical that might be militarily, it carried all sorts of risks to the emperor's personal authority. Writing to Berthier on 27 May from Normandy, Napoleon revealed the extraordinary depth of his own egotism: "I cannot give away that supreme command, because I do not see any man capable of managing the troops . . . it is in the nature of things that if one Marshal were placed in Madrid, and directed all operations, he would want to have all of the glory along with all of the responsibility." The emperor added lamely, "I want to do all that I can to give the King a new prestige on his return to Spain."

Berthier, as chief of staff, had to make sense of this sibling rivalry and emotional insecurity masquerading as military directive. As Napoleon's right-hand man for more than a decade, Berthier was propelled by nervous energy. When contemplating some conundrum of army administration, he paced up and down in his office and gnawed at his fingers until they bled. This situation was a dilemma to really make his digits suffer. The emperor wanted to dictate the overall direction of the war, that was clear. These gentlemen, Marmont, Soult and the like, wanted to decide the actual details, and Berthier knew what difficult customers they could be. Now, on top of all this, he needed to make Joseph feel important, when in fact he had been given almost nothing. The king of Spain must be kept informed, that was vital, because the note agreed to at Rambouillet would lead Joseph to expect a constant flow of letters from the provinces. Berthier understood that this increased communication carried great risks. If Marmont and Soult were writing to Madrid as well as to him in Paris, there would be sensitive bits of parchment flying all over the Iberian Peninsula. How could Joseph be satisfied while protecting the Army of Spain's secrets? A

---

*First among equals.

Grand Chiffre, that was the answer. That was prestige, all right, a Great Cipher for a Great Monarch.

Restored to his palace in Madrid, Joseph resumed his courtly life. He had vented his frustrations at Rambouillet and, for the moment, felt better for it. A military chief of staff was to join him soon. Reports began to arrive from the far-flung armies. There appeared to be some hope of concerting military operations with his plans for the edification of the Spanish nation. Once he could dedicate more lycees, eradicate the superstitious influence of the Church in matters of law and trounce a few of those guerrillas, then things would begin to turn.

On 12 July, Berthier wrote to Joseph, briefing him on the latest military developments. The letter was in a *Grand Chiffre*. Not the sort of thing the army had played about with in Italy or the Balkans, this was a complex code, a proper diplomatic cipher, that Berthier had obtained from Hugues Maret, the secretary of state, and his civilian opposite in matters of both routine and sensitive imperial administration.

The arrival of Berthier's missive caused consternation at Joseph's palace. Nobody could decipher it. The king's secretary, seeing the cipher for the diplomatic one that it was, sent for the *Comte* de Laforest, the French ambassador in Madrid. A few days later the reply came back that the embassy had no knowledge of this particular *Grand Chiffre*. On 27 July, Joseph had to write back to Berthier, "We are not in possession of this cipher." Could the prince possibly send his message again, only this time "in the French ambassador's actual cipher, and send me one that can be used by the two of us in particular." A couple of days after he wrote to the chief of staff in Paris, the thought seems to have occurred to Joseph that perhaps Berthier had slipped up in his dispatch of 12 July and accidentally revealed a cipher that Paris shared with the other army commanders but not with Madrid. Was this code, far from being a tool for his authority, something that was being used to circumvent it?

On 5 August, Joseph sent a messenger to the commander of the Army of the North with a letter about various administrative matters, which included, "Mr. Frochot will inform you about a mishap that prevents me understanding a dispatch that must be most important, judging by the means in which it is ciphered. If you are able to let me know any more about it, you would give me pleasure."

Five days later, abandoning his earlier coyness about the sender of the 12 July letter, the king wrote to Marshal Marmont, asking for enlightenment "on the contents of a ciphered dispatch that I cannot read." On the same day, Soult was sent a letter also containing a copy of Berthier's original message and "hoping you might be able to shed light on the contents."

By now, the arrival of the *Grand Chiffre* in Spain, despite Berthier's hopes, had become a farcical episode. By failing to ascertain exactly which deciphering tables were in the possession of the king or French ambassador, Berthier had simply compounded Joseph's insecurity rather than contributing to his confidence. Further months in which French military secrets might have been properly protected had been lost and Wellington had continued to receive intercepted high-level dispatches *en clair*,* revealing much about the state of the French armies and their operations. The British staff had also learned something of the king's unhappiness over his powerlessness and his visit to Paris. "[We] greatly pity the poor King Joseph for I am convinced nothing but force could have made him return to this country," wrote Wellington's military secretary.

As the delicate issues of granting Joseph a semblance of power and the introduction of a Great Cipher played themselves out, Marshal Marmont found himself operating once more in the plains of Leon and Castille, close to northern Portugal. Having returned from helping Marshal Soult in Estremadura, he put into effect his earlier plans to improve the security of his communications, something that had become all the more important as he faced new threats from the British and their allies. It was during the late summer of 1811 that Marmont's generals began cloaking their orders in the Army of Portugal cipher.

Ciudad Rodrigo, the fortified town on the River Agueda, had become the subject of Wellington's attentions. French troops still held this strongpoint, which was in the border highlands, sparsely inhabited and studded with forests of black and pygmy oak. Around Rodrigo itself, to a radius of a couple of miles, was a verdant pasture, which allowed sufficient cultiva-

---

* "In clear," i.e., uncoded, a term still commonly used by today's codebreakers.

tion and husbandry to feed the people of the town but could not sustain invading armies. A siege, or indeed a defense, of this place thus posed considerable difficulties of supply. Wellington understood that if an army of twenty thousand or thirty thousand troops was to canton the area around it for weeks while the engineers conducted their regular approaches, large amounts of food and ammunition would have to be brought up to them.

Marmont, on the other hand, was obliged by considerations of supply to keep his army in an arc that stretched down from the northern part of the province of Leon, through Salamanca, about forty miles to the northeast of Rodrigo and southward, toward the River Tagus (most of the way to Badajoz). Although the Salamanca plain had once been an area of agricultural abundance, the war had ravaged its farms, and the Army of Portugal had been left chronically short of the supply wagons. All the same, forces in Salamanca were still close enough to Ciudad Rodrigo for a movement of three or four marches to allow them to drive off any British force blockading it. Marmont had resupplied the fortress in July, but by August it was clear to him that Wellington was preparing to attack it.

The British general's plan involved a blockade by Spanish irregulars, British cavalry and light troops while heavy guns were moved slowly up to the frontier. If this cordon could be maintained the garrison might be starved out, or at least reduced in numbers and spirit. It was in the struggle to seal off Ciudad Rodrigo from resupply or information that the guerrilla chief Don Julian Sanchez came into his own.

Don Julian was a native of the lands between Rodrigo and Salamanca. He and many of his horsemen had grown up riding the borderlands, hunting in its forests. Their favorite chase involved the pursuit of *jabalies*, wild pigs, much enjoyed roasted as a local delicacy. These animals shot through the trees at a fearful pace, defying their pursuers to skewer them with their lances, or *picos*. In August 1811, the don's quarry was human, but his hunt was pursued with the same tactics and often with just as little mercy.

In the summer of 1810 his men surprised a company of about one hundred French dragoons. Eighty had been killed, the few survivors testifying to an attack of merciless ferocity. After this, one British officer noted in his journal, "the French promise to hang him and he in return gives them no quarter." Sanchez had served as a noncommissioned officer in the Spanish army until the death of his father in 1803 forced him into civilian life. He had reenlisted in a volunteer cavalry regiment in

1808 following the outbreak of what the Spanish called their War of
Independence against the French. He had then risen swiftly through the
ranks. The don and his men sported curled mustachios, carried fearsome lances, tucked pistols into their gaudy red sashes and in general
resembled the worst nightmare of every French convoy commander.

As a former soldier, the don was keener than many other guerrillas
to give his men some semblance of uniform and order, but even so, one
British officer drew this memorable pen portrait:

> *"A more verminous set of fellows you never beheld.
> The infantry in English clothing and the cavalry, both
> horse and man, completely armed and equipped in
> the spoils of the enemy, so that it is next to impossible
> to distinguish friend from foe. The Don himself wears
> a pelisse like the 16th Dragoons with an immense
> hussar cap and the Eagle of Napoleon reversed. In
> this dress, [he is] accompanied by two aides-de-camp
> equally genteel in appearance, twelve lancers, a trum-
> peter on a grey horse."*

Sanchez had been brought under British pay in October 1810, receiving
silver coin and weaponry from swords to light cannon. The following
year his troops (perhaps 250 cavalry and twice as many on foot) had
been attached to Scovell's Corps of Guides. They were vital as scouts
and in collecting the secret intelligence scrawled on scraps of paper by
agents in Ciudad Rodrigo or Salamanca.

In August and early September 1811 several dispatches were brought
in by Don Julian and some other guerrillas in the peculiar new cipher of
the Army of Portugal employed by Marmont and his staff. Wellington
and Somerset looked them over, noting immediately that they were not
the simple codes that had been used earlier in the summer. Scovell was
brought in to help.

Marmont's code consisted of numbers from 1 to 150. An example from
one of the messages sent by Marmont's principal aides-de-camp shows how
it defeated the simple analysis prescribed by Conradus in Scovell's notebook.

A portion is written out in 711 code numbers. The great majority of these figures represent a single letter, although with the 150 possibilities in this cipher some whole words like *Marmont* or *the enemy* could be written as a single coded number. The rules of French composition described by Conradus hold true to the original text, but the cipher succesfully hides them. Fully 131 of those 711 code numbers stand for *e*, the most frequently used letter in French, because the cipher allocates nine different code numbers to the writing of this most common letter. Other vowels each have several alternatives, obscure consonants only one or two. In this way the cipher balances out the patterns detected by earlier decipherers and conceals them.

Looking more closely at this particular letter, Scovell would have seen that the most common code was 14, which had been written thirty-five times in the 711 characters. Needless to say, it does not stand for a common vowel but for *r*. Little wonder that Scovell wrote on one of the facing pages of his decipherer's notebook, "The art of writing in cypher is so much improved since Conradus wrote as to render it next to impossible (when knowing the language made use of) to unravel what it conceals without being in possession of the key."

He was not a defeatist, though, and what may be "next to impossible" may certainly just be possible. Scovell believed the cipher could be broken by two principal methods: the writers usually mixed code with clear text to save time, so clearly the context could tell you much. Moreover, once more messages had been brought in, the small fissures opened up by examining the context could be widened into great cracks by comparing the messages.

A message from General Montbrun, commanding Marmont's cavalry division, to the governor of Ciudad Rodrigo provides a good sense of how Scovell attacked the cipher as he sat at his table in Fuente Guinaldo, surrounded by the scraps of paper that were brought in by the guerrillas. In its first paragraph, Montbrun acknowledged the previous communication from the besieged town and went on:

> "I am making haste to pass on the contents to 25.
> 13. 8. 9. 38. 19. 18. 37. 14. 10. 33. 28. 17. 34. 17. 26.
> 5. 19. 21. 23. 31. 32. who has ordered me to open
> communications with you."

This was a very good passage to attack the code, since it had been enciphered somewhat stupidly by Montbrun or, more likely, one of his ADCs: it was a good bet that the general was referring to orders from his chief, Marmont. It was then a matter of trying every possible way that the marshal might be referred to in French and seeing whether it had the right number of letters: "*M le Marechal Marmont*," not long enough; "*M Le Marechal, Duc de Raguse*," one letter too short. Perhaps "*S.E. Le Marechal, Duc de Raguse*" (the S.E standing for His Excellency)—that was the right number of letters. It was correct, too, since the two code numbers that occur twice (19 and 17 for *a* and *d*) fit exactly. With this partial knowledge of the cipher revealing the meaning of twenty-one of the coding numbers, the decipherer could continue into the text with his attack. The last paragraph contained a long body of code, running across several lines. But how did its beginning, where it switched from *clair* to code in full flow look with the knowledge of those characters used before to make up Marmont's name?

> "*It would seem that there are not many people you can count on there. 30. r. 15. 30. 15. s. 55. 33. L. h 15. m. m. e. 27. u. 49. 47. e. u. 15. u. s. e. 16. u. 29. e.*"

It was evident to any decipherer that he still had to find two vowels, since he had only discovered *a*, *e* and *u*. In any case there were various ways of writing vowels, so perhaps it was not the best way to proceed. What about consonants, since some of those might only have a single code number and several (like *b*, *d*, *f*, *j*, *k*, *n*, *p*, *q*, *t*, *v*, *x*, *y* and *z*) were unknown to him. Knowing that the second letter of the first word is *r*, it is then a matter of methodical puzzle solving. The repetition of the codes 30 and 15 eventually suggests *proposez* to the patient decipherer. With each stage of the deduction, for example, does the code number 15 signify *o*? Comparison with other places later in the text quickly allows some sense of whether the supposition is right once the letters derived from higher up in the message had been added in. For this particular passage, the decipherer will eventually discover a peculiarity of Marmont's cipher: that *u* and *v* are interchangeable; and that where he has assumed a *u* occurs in this later portion, the code reveals a peculiarity, namely that numbers 23 and 34 can represent *u or v* depending upon the context.

After long hours of meticulous study then, the last paragraph reveals itself as: "It would seem that there are not many people you can count on there. *Proposez à l'homme que je vous envoie . . .*" Translating the whole of this last paragraph from French into English:

> "*It would seem that there are not many people you can count on there. Suggest to the man I am sending you that he should search out the English in Gallegos and Fuente Guinaldo, and come back through El Bodon, and you will send him back to me forthwith. Tell him I will pay him well if he wants to make this trip, but if he refuses, I ask you not to force him.*"

This was a most interesting item in the battle for information, for it gave clues about the French intelligence network on the frontier. The fate of Montbrun's unnamed spy is not known. Being locals, Don Julian's men were able to sniff out fairly quickly anyone who did not belong in the area. A thorough search would be conducted of his clothing and possessions. Since the discovery of some ciphered scrap of paper usually meant death for the collaborator, some of these terrified messengers declared themselves to the guerrillas as soon as they met them, in order to save their lives. This set Scovell thinking about the uses such a man might be put to, since an *afrancesado* arriving with a correctly coded message would immediately gain the trust of its recipient.

The only real problem in deciphering the French general's text was with numbers. Once the message was decoded, five digits remained, and it was not possible to deduce what those code numbers stood for. Montbrun's message also revealed that a large convoy of supplies was being collected in Salamanca in readiness to throw into the fortress. In this way, a critical sentence about the date when the supply convoy might set out for Ciudad Rodrigo could not be deciphered. More messages in the same code would be needed before these numbers could be made out. On 18 September, Wellington wrote to the secretary of war in London:

> "*I enclose the deciphered copy of a letter in cipher, from Gen. Montbrun to the Govenor of Ciudad*

Rodrigo, from which it appears that it is the enemy's intention to endeavor to introduce large supplies of provisions into that place from the side of Plasencia, as well as from that of Salamanca. The dates being all in cipher, and not having been able to discover that part of the key, we don't know exactly on what day the operation is to commence, but I should imagine about the 20th or 21st."

Wellington's supposition, filling in the last piece of the jigsaw, was exactly right. Marmont's operation began on 21 September. The British commander already knew from other deciphered messages and scouts' reports that the Army of Portugal had been joined by a strong force from the Army of the North, so his position was precarious. Estimates suggested that the combined French armies would outnumber the Allied troops in the area by fifteen thousand or so. In September, as in June 1811 at Badajoz, successful French cooperation forced Wellington to withdraw. He would have to abandon the siege of Ciudad Rodrigo. Wellington's frustrations burst out as he wrote to Beresford, "The devil is in the French for numbers."

On the twenty-fourth, the British fell back in front of Ciudad Rodrigo, allowing the French to enter the town. Since he had no intention of offering battle in the plain beside it and Marmont had achieved his limited objective of breaking the Rodrigo blockade, Wellington assumed the danger was over.

The following day Montbrun, with a strong force of twenty-five hundred cavalry, pushed down the road from Rodrigo to Fuente Guinaldo, where Wellington's headquarters was located. They caught several British battalions about halfway up this route at El Bodon unprepared for a serious defense. For a couple of hours, the fate of these British troops hung in the balance as they fell back under heavy pressure from the French cavalry.

Despite this small success, Marmont could not, however, move his infantry forward fast enough to capitalize on Wellington's mistake and bring on a general engagement while the British were still at a decided disadvantage. Still, the French commander had learned a great deal from El Bodon. Wellington made mistakes, just like any other general, and the key to future French success would be in exploiting such an error more quickly.

The day after this engagement at El Bodon, both generals brought up reinforcements. In Marmont's case this included regiments of the Imperial Guard belonging to the Army of the North. Scovell and other members of the staff took position on a hillside and watched as these picked men marched into view. The French army formed up in front of them and troops were drawn up in lines for review.

The Guard infantry were altogether smarter in appearance than the footsloggers who normally stood against Wellington. They marched with precision and their shakoes were decorated with tall plumes. The Guard cavalry also made a fine spectacle. The horse grenadiers, resplendent in bearskin hats, sat atop magnificent chargers while the *chasseurs à cheval,* on smaller mounts, wore a gaudy uniform of green and red draped with lace and aiguillettes. The Guard's bands starting playing their old favorites, the thumping of drums echoing around the hills, and the French marshal rode along the lines, cheered by the troops. Scovell wrote in his journal, "Marmont passed down the line in great state. Not a shot was fired on either side." The marshal had only been in command for four months, but the British staff had been most impressed. One of them noted they had formed "an extremely favorable notion of the judgement and good sense" of Marmont.

Wellington had chosen not to fight following this display of power because it was already apparent to him that he could not defend the Fuente Guinaldo area against such numbers. Resigning any designs on Ciudad Rodrigo for the time being, he ordered his men back into Portugal, daring Marmont to follow.

Wellington was certain that Marmont would be most reluctant to pursue him onto the barren border plateau, and within a few days headquarters had settled down in Frenada, a grindingly poor Portuguese village a little to the east of the Coa gorge, just a mile or two behind the spot where Scovell had fought for his life against the French cavalry on 5 May. With the seasons turning, this countryside reminded many a British officer of Dartmoor or the west of Ireland. The leaves on the oaks browned, Frenada's chimneys sent zigzags of smoke into the gray sky and the dry stone walls around the village were dusted each morning with a coating of frost. The air on this upland plateau is intoxicatingly pure and riders going to and from Frenada were charmed to see all forms of game scampering between the big boulders and ferns that carpeted the landscape.

For Major Scovell, arriving in Frenada allowed him a moment for reflection on family matters. It was the first time in months that he had broken the continual ritual of moving from one barn or bivouac to another. His billet in one of the village's low-roofed farmhouses was a spartan one and most likely it was here that he began wondering whether Mary might join him in Portugal. A few weeks before he had received the sad news that his wife's brother Samuel Clowes had died.

The death of Samuel threw Clowes family affairs into some turmoil. Mary's grandfather was still alive but he had buried a son (Mary's father) and now a grandson both of whom were heirs to the dynasty's newfound wealth. The succession had devolved upon another of her brothers, the vicar John Clowes. He was forty-four years old, and childless like his sister. If he remained so, then the fortune would go to the next brother in line, Leigh Clowes, who incidentally had arrived in Portugal in August of 1811 as a major, second in command of the 3rd Dragoons.

The loss of Samuel must have been difficult for Mary to bear. It was made all the more so by Major Clowes's emergence as the likely heir to the family fortune at precisely the moment that he had placed himself in the midst of a dangerous campaign. George wanted to be with Mary at this difficult time. There was no question of his taking leave just as he was becoming indispensable in headquarters. What was more, Wellington's refusal to grant leave to his low-born officers while sending the aristocrats home to winter in London was already the subject of muttering and resentment in the staff. Scovell did not even dare ask; instead he began thinking about a different project.

Some officers in the army had brought their wives with them. His old friend Lieutenant Colonel Dalbiac of the 4th Dragoons, or rather Dalbiac's wife, Susannah, was the talk of many a mess. Riding with her husband at the head of the regiment, she shared every hardship of campaigning, and when the 4th were sent to Estremadura earlier that summer, she had slept under the stars like a common trooper.

If Scovell could not comfort Mary at home, why not bring her to Portugal? After all, she would not be leaving any children behind if she did come.

Leigh Clowes was not the only relation to join Scovell in Portugal that autumn. George's brother Henry, aged twenty, had come out to fill a lowly civilian post, as a deputy assistant paymaster general. Major Scovell, it seems, had already begun to use his influence, slim as it was, at headquarters to the benefit of his family.

And the war itself? Wellington did not rule out another attempt on Ciudad Rodrigo as the forces concentrated by Marmont began to disperse again, but the moment would have to be chosen most carefully. In the meantime information would be accumulated, so Don Julian continued to seize the enemy's messages and to bring reports from Wellington's spies.

In Ciudad Rodrigo, the principal agent was a former member of the town *junta*, a committed and brave man who had remained within the walls incognito. Of course, many people knew who he was as he went about gathering information on the state of the garrison's supplies, but he relied on their hatred of the French to protect his secret. When the town gates were opened at daybreak, some small report would be handed to a farmer going outside the walls to work, who would then hand the spy's report to one of Don Julian's scouts.

In Salamanca, Wellington's principal correspondent was an Irish priest, Father Patrick Curtis. Already seventy-odd years old, this gray-haired little man moved about the streets of the university town in his black habit, acknowledging the respectful greetings of its citizens and observing the comings and goings of the French army.

Wellington could not have been more fortunate as to Curtis's location, geographic and social. Salamanca was the ideal place to gain warning of any great project of Marmont's three or four days before it might bear fruit on the border. Being professor of astronomy and natural history at the university, as well as rector of the Irish College, Curtis also had an entrée into the higher level of society. When Marmont was in Salamanca, he frequently entertained the town's grandees at his table. From some of these contacts, Curtis might learn something about the marshal's plans.

These agents' reports, combined with those of exploring officers and deciphered letters, were consumed voraciously by Wellington in his Frenada headquarters. Scovell worked away on his deciphering, and Somerset received some of the agent reports from a Guide coming to the door, but only the commander himself obtained the intelligence picture in its entirety. He guarded this prerogative jealously, and by the autumn of 1811 was becoming quite nervous about sharing his knowledge with others, lest it lead the French to find his agents. The commandant of northern Portugal, one General Silveira, needed to be kept in the picture about French movements but, as Wellington noted in a letter to Beresford, the Portuguese officer had aroused his anger because "the intelligence received from Salamanca by General Silveira, and forwarded by him to the Portuguese government, from which papers it is copied in the English papers. Our correspondents there will certainly be discovered if this practice is continued."

On 15 October, Wellington and his staff momentarily forgot any anxieties they may have had when Frenada's little central square echoed English voices bearing some unexpected and quite remarkable news. General Regnaud, the governor of Ciudad Rodrigo, had been captured by Don Julian Sanchez.

The day before, Regnaud had ridden out of the fort with a small escort of cavalry. The tedium of his situation was such that he had wanted to take some exercise riding around the little plain of Rodrigo. A party of guerrillas was lurking in the trees not five hundred yards from the gate. They had gone there to carry off as many of the garrison's cattle as they could find, a brigandry that had assumed a patriotic legitimacy, since it was designed to reduce the supplies available to the French. Seeing the governor's party make its way down the steep slope from the city walls to the river and then cross the Roman bridge over the Agueda, the guerrillas had decided that the odds were favorable for combat. Regnaud, two of his staff and a good many cows were taken.

Regnaud must have thought himself a lost man when he was bound and carried off by the guerrillas. Who indeed would not have wondered whether they would torture him, whether they would finish him off with a knife or a shot to the head? He had been delivered first to the HQ of General Carlos D'Espagne, commander of a small Spanish force attached to Wellington's army. This release from the custody of the guerrillas brought no relief—far from it—for D'Espagne had first wanted to shoot Regnaud. The British, however, prevailed upon D'Espagne to hand over his prize, and Wellington thought it only right that Regnaud should receive decent hospitality at Frenada. The governor, after all, had

become a British prisoner, unlike the poor General Franceschi. The captured Frenchman was invited to dinner.

Wellington's table in the Frenada headquarters was not a large one,
so Regnaud joined about a dozen British officers as they sat down for
their meal at five in the evening. Major General Charles Stewart was
there, as was Scovell, Somerset and several of the commander's young
ADCs. Stewart commiserated with their guest for his bad luck. The
adjutant general noted "his misfortunes were borne with the utmost
philosophy and good humor," and there was every reason why they
should be.

There must have been several times between his capture and this
meal when Regnaud feared immediate execution, yet here he was in the
warmth of Wellington's headquarters consuming a tasty roast and feeling the inner warmth of the fine claret. Finding himself in such elevated
and civilized company, relieved beyond measure, the governor became
most talkative. Scovell's presence at the table was assured by his superb
grasp of French and his need to learn as much as possible about the hidden world of the enemy camp. Any detail Regnaud let slip about the
name of some brigade commander or the jealousies between two generals might prove significant in the deciphering of dispatches. One of the
keys to breaking strong ciphers, Scovell had scribbled in his Conradus
notebook, is "knowing *well* what is going on" (emphasis in original).

Wellington naturally led this gentle cross-examination; it was his
table, after all, and his own French, polished decades before at a military school in Anger, was extremely good. After several meals in this
company, Scovell had learned much. He summarized it in his journal:

> "He assured us that all was silence and distrust in
> French society and that no man thought himself
> secure with his friend where there was a third person.
> He instanced the table of Dorsenne, and compared it
> with ours where every man spoke what he thought.
> The different Armies in Spain are all independent and
> only acknowledge the Emperor's order."

The ebullience at headquarters resulting from Regnaud's capture brought
its own bitter aftertaste two days later. The French had launched a hunt

for spies, with exactly the consequence that Wellington had feared. Father Curtis had been arrested in Salamanca. Eventually he obtained his release, but he remained under suspicion by the French for the rest of the campaign, having to rely on ever more elaborate methods to get his messages out. Wellington's spy in Ciudad Rodrigo immediately fled the city, fearing an imminent arrest.

Just before the end of that month, however, a happy equilibrium was restored at headquarters. Lieutenant Colonel John Grant, who had disappeared while on exploring duties in Estremadura some weeks before, presented himself. He had been taken by the French, but was rescued by a guerrilla commander called Temprano while taking exercise outside his prison in Talavera. It was precisely the kind of guerrilla daring that made the French look flat-footed and cheered the company around Wellington's dinner table greatly. News from Lieutenant General Rowland Hill, commanding Anglo-Portuguese forces to the south, was also most encouraging. He had attacked and routed a French division at Arroyo de Molinos, leading Napoleon to recall its commander in disgrace.

At the end of October a ciphered message from Marmont to General Foy was captured and brought in to Frenada that proved particularly interesting in light of Regnaud's table talk.

Marmont and King Joseph had fallen into dispute. Foraging closer and closer to Madrid in search of supplies, the Army of Portugal had incurred the king's displeasure by raiding storehouses earmarked for other troops. Marmont wrote to Foy, "As a general principle you must not obey any order given to you in the name of the King, if it runs counter to my stated aims." The marshal added, "I am going to Madrid and will spend two days there in the hope of enlightening the King on the conduct his true interest dictates he should display toward the French army."

Wellington was evidently thrilled at receiving this deciphered message. It gave some inkling that the cooperation between Marmont and his fellow generals that had thwarted British plans since June was not necessarily going to remain a fact of life. It was also the kind of high-level gossip that he loved. Writing to the secretary of war in London on 13 November, he enclosed a copy of Marmont's letter, "which shows how these gentry are going on; in fact each Marshal is the natural enemy of the King and of his neighboring Marshal." Mindful of the risks to his sources of intelligence, Wellington added, "Pray take care that this letter is not made public, as it would disclose that we have the key of the cipher."

The key, in fact, was already changing. Ever careful, Marmont's staff made sure that new cipher tables were circulated whenever possible. When Regnaud's successor as governor of Ciudad Rodrigo arrived on 30 October (escorted by an entire division of infantry), he most likely brought new codes with him, for when the Allies captured a message bound for the fortress a couple of weeks later, it could not be deciphered from the existing Army of Portugal key. The changed cipher was based on the same 150-character table, but the meanings of each number had been rearranged.

For weeks, a small number of officers had been setting their brains to the methodical elimination of possibilities required to make out each letter, word and then sentence in code. Scovell had been doing it, but so had Somerset, and even Wellington himself, all of them trying to solve the puzzle together. By November, with changes being made to the Army of Portugal cipher, Scovell found himself increasingly responsible for the effort. The duties of the army commander and his military secretary were too varied and too consuming to allow much time for chasing after these riddles. Scovell had shown great aptitude and more and more he became the master of this work. Wellington increasingly looked to him for prompt solutions to these vital puzzles. Scovell relished his new-found position.

Deciphered by Scovell, the message brought in mid-November produced intelligence of another mission to replenish the fortress. Wellington prepared a military response, a kind of ambush in which the Light Division would be used to surprise the relief, but the French were becoming cannier. When they had escorted the new governor into Ciudad Rodrigo at the end of October, they made sure nobody was allowed to leave Salamanca for forty-eight hours before the column departed, barring the way to any tinker or muleteer concealing a scribbled warning to Wellington from Father Curtis. Marmont's staff also had its own spies (usually itinerant Spaniards) and they seem to have detected British preparations. On 27 November, Wellington abandoned his mission, noting in a letter to London, "I think it probable that they will have heard of our movements; and if they entertained the intention of moving a convoy to Ciudad Rodrigo, they will now abandon it."

Scovell however was thinking of ways to turn the French army's secret writing to British advantage. He was in possession of the new cipher. What if they also obtained the services of one of the captured *afrancesados* and used him and the code to get a false message into Ciudad Rodrigo? He noted in his journal, "The French figured Cipher is a very mean one. I have suggested that it might be employed by us with effect against the Garrison."

The idea was certainly ingenious: a fake letter in the Army of Portugal cipher might be used in conjunction with some *ruse de guerre*, such as sending troops dressed as Frenchmen to one of the gates at a predesignated time, so penetrating the defenses without a costly siege. Ingenious, but not to Lord Wellington's taste. That type of trick was the sort of thing the French and Spanish got up to, but it would not answer for him. He was already meditating plans for a new attack on the fortress with his powerful siege guns and several divisions of infantry.

As the temperatures dropped and November became December, the army was put into winter quarters. Divisions and brigades were broken down and sent to the little villages of the Beira Baixa hill country. There the men and horses could sleep in barns or farmhouses while their chief considered his plan of war for 1812.

PART III

THE CAMPAIGN OF JANUARY TO
NOVEMBER 1812

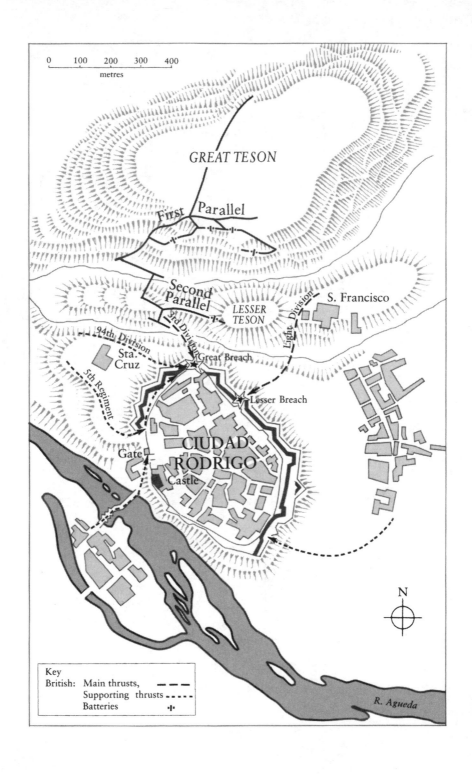

0   100   200   300   400
metres

GREAT TESON

First Parallel

Second Parallel

LESSER TESON

3rd Division

Light Division

S. Francisco

94th Division

Sta. Cruz

Great Breach

Lesser Breach

5th Regiment

CIUDAD RODRIGO

Gate

Castle

N

Key
British: Main thrusts,   — — —
           Supporting thrusts · · · · ·
           Batteries   ·|·

R. Agueda

CHAPTER NINE

S. d. 1076. nt. 1082. 365. 622. we. w. 439. 669. e. 1085. 398. 326. 13. 309. i. 1085. ed. 481. t. 980. 985. 186. t. 843. 688. 2. n. d. 1297. 536. 174. 1085. 1024. . . 713. t. 980. 854. e. 326. 536. 700. w. 171. 1015. 1003. 13. t. 980. 1015. 131. t.

THE ATTACK ON CIUDAD RODRIGO, JANUARY 1812

*D*uring the dying days of 1811, Wellington's officers were making the most of the lull in military activities. On many a December's morning they could be seen setting off from Frenada or Almeida in their undress coats and fur-lined caps. They slung fowling pieces over their shoulders and bounced along to the pleasing rhythm of cantering hooves and panting dogs, searching out the hares, foxes and any number of game birds to be found in the quieter folds of this wilderness. A gentleman could hardly hope for better sport. Wellington, who liked nothing more than a hard ride of twenty miles on a bracing December's day, himself hunted the Portuguese foxes in the traditional English manner, with hounds baying and horns blaring.

Since the long evenings in familiar company dragged, there was much reciprocal entertaining, the officers riding from one smokey little Portuguese village to its neighbor, where some rough-hewn peasant's table groaned under all manner of delicacies procured by generous payments

of silver dollars. To help fill the nights they got up to the sort of entertainments that recalled the country houses of their youth. A wrecked
chapel on the outskirts of Fuente Guinaldo was fitted with painted
scenery and soon echoed to Shakespeare's words as the young officers of
the Light Division put on their production of *Henry IV*.

While daily sport and leisure continued, Wellington was already
considering his next campaign, and he kept a small number of officers
on the staff busy compiling every scrap of information they received
about the dispositions of the French army. Colonel George Murray had
become the general's right hand in these and other matters. Early criticism of him during the 1809 operations in northern Portugal had given
way to a much more positive impression. One of Colonel Le Marchant's
correspondents in the peninsula informed those back at Wycombe,
"Nothing can be more gentlemanlike in every instance than Colonel M.:
I find that whole Army giving him credit for ability."

Captain Edward Cocks, one of those quick to judge Murray, had
been able to remove himself from staff duties and expressed the customary disdain of fighting soldiers for those who remained in such appointments: "A Staff man is not much with secret till he gets pretty high in his
department. Colonel Murray may have the key to the great strategic
movement of the campaign but your Deputy Assistants have little more
to do than to look out for encampments with regard to water and forage
and chalk doors for General officers."

Notwithstanding these views, by the end of 1811 it had become
clear to many an ambitious officer that an attachment to Lord Wellington's staff could be most advantageous. No less a personage than
William, the prince of Orange, had appeared in the late summer to boost
the bloodline of the general's corps of ADCs. On hearing of Orange's
imminent arrival, FitzRoy Somerset had written home, "We understand
that a great many amateurs intend to favor us with their company." The
duke of Richmond's son, Lord March, who had been an ADC for more
than one year, became the prince of Orange's firm friend. Both of these
handsome youngsters loomed large in Wellington's affections, eclipsed
only by Somerset. Even a bad cold on Lord March's part caused
Wellington to set pen to paper, telling the young peer's mother, the
duchess of Richmond, "He is really a fine fellow; and you may depend
upon my taking as much care of him . . . as if he were my own son."

Wellington's solicitude in the case of this particular ADC was doubtless connected with his desire to treat the duchess as he would have done his own son's mother.*

Some on the staff believed Wellington's favoritism toward aristo-crats stemmed from boundless personal ambition rather than disinter-ested affection. "You may suppose the Puff is not without its object," Lieutenant Colonel Alexander Gordon wrote home, explaining a favor-able mention given to the callow prince of Orange in Wellington's dis-patches. That must be so, Gordon reasoned, since Wellington "has no idea of gratitude, favor, or affection, and cares not for anyone however much he may owe to him or find him useful." This brutal verdict on the general's "private character" was given by an officer who described himself in the same paragraph as someone who "could not desire to be on a better footing with Lord W. in every sense of the word."

For someone like Henry Hardinge, whose daring exploits had attracted the commander's notice, it became vital to remain in Portugal at all hazards, ignoring any chance of leave as this influx of aristocratic "amateurs" meant new competition for Wellington's attention. As someone whose prospects were far less rosy than these handsome young gents', the same lesson clearly applied to Scovell.

Those who were latecomers to this military ensemble found that only virtuoso performance would get them heard by Wellington or Mur-ray. One acute observer noted: "The officers in the lower branches of the Staff are sharp-set, hungry, and anxious to get on, and make the most of every thing and have a view even in their civilities . . . there is much obsequious time serving conduct to any one who is on office, or is thought to have a word to say to Lord Wellington." Scovell, at least, could rise a little above this, for he was now the veteran of several cam-paigns and being entrusted with secret work by the general.

His spirits were further lifted by the appearance at Frenada of John Le Marchant. He was newly promoted to major general and was going to take over command of a brigade of Wellington's heavy cavalry. Having left the classrooms of the Royal Military College behind, Le Marchant wasted no time applying his ideas in the field. Soon after his arrival, Le Marchant

*This lady being the same duchess of Richmond who threw a ball in Brussels in 1815 the night before the Battle of Waterloo. She and Wellington were later rumored to have become lovers.

learned that his beloved wife, Mary, had died while delivering their eighth child. The general's family and friends stepped in, urging him not to return from service since the opportunity in Iberia could be the making of him. Le Marchant resolved to stay with his brigade despite this terrible family news, thus displaying the kind of professional zeal that overcame any prejudice Wellington may have had against such a reformer.

Wellington had to think carefully over his next gambit in Frenada. He knew that there was little point launching a siege of Ciudad Rodrigo while Marmont or Dorsenne could come to the garrison's relief, and the British would find themselves witnessing a repeat of September's French concentration. He needed to know where each division of these armies was and how long it would take them to march toward Rodrigo. From this he could calculate when his enemies could achieve the kind of concentration needed to drive him off.

Meanwhile, everything had to be readied so that he could launch his strike without a moment's hesitation before the united French forces could intervene. The British siege train of powerful battering guns had been parked inside the walls of Almeida (just two or three marches from their target), awaiting the general's word of command. Other supplies too had been gathered: powder and shot to fuel these monstrous cannon; gabbions, great baskets that could be filled with earth to form protective cover for a besieging force; fascines, the bundles of brushwood that would be thrown down into the deep ditches around Ciudad Rodrigo's defenses; and a train of pontoons that would be used to bridge the Agueda upstream of the fort, allowing the British guns to be brought to the best place of attack.

Winter, in Napoleon's mind, was a time to take advantage of British lethargy. Autumn had already shown the emperor what kind of general this Wellington was: evidently not a man with great belief in himself, since he would never run the slightest risk. His army seemed to be full of sick men too, as far as the British newspapers and spies' reports went. The emperor felt it was ridiculous that affairs in the peninsula should consume so many troops and be such a source of vexation, and all just as he was contemplating a great military expedition against Russia. It was time to knock his marshals' heads together and put some order in the Spanish house.

On 19 November, Napoleon started dictating a series of terse orders.

The commander in the southeast was to hurry up and finish the siege of Valencia. The Spanish defenders of this great southern city had been struggling on for months and its continued resistance was an affront to the power of French arms. Marmont was to send him six thousand troops to settle this interminable affair. The emperor knew this would prompt some carping from the Army of Portugal, so he told Berthier to make it clear to Marmont: "the English have 18,000 sick in Portugal and are unable to undertake anything."

And Dorsenne, what was he playing at? Why were these two infamous thieves, the guerrillas Mina and Longa, still raiding the Bayonne road at will? He was to set about those *banditti* and liquidate them. If he needed Bonnet's division, the northernmost of the Army of Portugal, to help, so be it. Berthier: tell Dorsenne one more thing. He must understand, "the great object is to take Valencia."

As for Soult, he should know better. Lieutenant General Hill's victory in October smashing a French division at Arroyo de Molinos had been a disgrace. Tell him, Berthier, "it is unfortunate that, with an army of 80,000 men, they could not make the dispositions which prudence demanded to avoid being beaten by a troop of 6,000 English." And lastly: "the great object at this juncture is to take Valencia."

Having set his schemes in train in mid-November, the emperor didn't let his brother Joseph know about them until 13 December. He too would probably be worrying about the effect all this might have on the Portuguese frontier. So Berthier informed Joseph, "it is probable that the English will not undertake anything from now until the month of February, and there is reason to believe they will remain on the defensive." The emperor had become fixated with Valencia and he was confident that the English would not emerge early from their winter quarters.

What did Joseph make of all this? Once again, he had taken offense at his brother's high-handedness. Now, however, he had a confidant in the palace to commiserate with—one detail of May's Rambouillet agreement that had at least been honored. Marshal Jean-Baptiste Jourdan had arrived in Madrid in September. Initially he was simply the governor of that Iberian city, but had also been sent out to act as the king's military adviser. This Jourdan was no youngster. He had already been a soldier when Marmont was born, even fighting in far-off America back in 1781. As the commander of the army that saved the country from being overrun by invaders in 1794 at the Battle of Fleurus, he had earned the lasting gratitude of many in revolutionary France.

He may have looked old and tired, but Jourdan, a small, rotund cannonball of a man, still had a wise head on his shoulders. He had also, during his previous service in Spain, learned how to give Joseph military advice in a tactful and friendly manner. The news of his arrival in Madrid excited all kinds of resentment in the headquarters of those commanding armies in the various corners of Spain. Men like Soult, Marmont, Dorsenne and Suchet viewed one another with suspicion at the best of times, feelings that had already emerged in General Regnaud's table talk (at Frenada) and in the letter from Marmont to Foy that had been deciphered at Wellington's HQ. While somehow, during the second half of 1811, they had managed to sublimate these feelings in the common good, Jourdan's arrival seemed to turn this volatile assembly of ambitious men more and more into open rivals, an effect that had been compounded by the angry tone of Napoleon's orders of late November and early December. Every field commander aspired only to remain high in the esteem of his imperial master in Paris, but they knew that Joseph had not only been militating for a greater role but that the emperor was likely to launch his Russian campaign soon, so removing himself from day-to-day superintendence of Iberian matters. For a Soult or Marmont, anxious to increase his wealth or perhaps even secure the throne of some vassal kingdom, the emergence of this partnership between Jourdan and Joseph in Madrid was most unsettling.

As Jourdan began organizing a proper military headquarters to serve Joseph, the issue of securing his high-level dispatches had at last been settled. The *cabinet* of Hugues Maret, Napoleon's chief administrator in Paris, had at last furnished the king and his marshal with a Great Cipher, which during the last days of 1811 had been circulated to all of the most senior leaders. There would be no repeat of the farcical episode of the previous summer: the field commanders, Joseph in Madrid and Marshal Berthier in Paris would all have the right codes to begin secret communication.

Each user of Joseph's new *Grand Chiffre* would have two tables: one for enciphering, the other for deciphering. The basis of the new code was one of the 1750 ciphering tables printed up by de Puisieulx for the Bourbon foreign ministry. The enciphering table arranged words, syllables, phrases or letters alphabetically. *A* began with four different ways of writing the letter on its own and then continued:

> abs . . . 273
> abaisse, ment . . . 1179
> abandon, ne . . . 1035
> abdique, action . . . 565
> able, s . . . 185, 808
> abord, e, age . . . 316
> absolu, e, ment . . . 1157
> ae . . . 1162

In this way, the ciphering table set out the numbers to be used as the staff officer or confidential secretary turned his master's prose into secret writing. The table used the same coding number for different cases or genders. In addition, it allowed many options for breaking words down into syllables or bigrams (two-letter groups).

At the receiving end, the person deciphering would use the other table, one in which the codes were listed in numeric order, each followed by its meaning. The deciphering table was drawn up with a grid of columns and horizontal lines. Looking from the top left corner, the first column ran from 1 to 100, the second across started at 101 going down to 200, and so on. The horizontal lines separated the code numbers into groups of ten, all of which was meant to aid rapid deciphering.

The code table sent to Madrid had 1,200 code numbers, and these were mostly already filled out. As a ready-to-use diplomatic cipher, it therefore contained many words that were irrelevant to military operations in Spain: 490 stood for Stockholm, 837 for the Crimea, and so on. Additionally, Joseph's officers could soon see that many standard words and phrases needed for waging war in the peninsula were not included in this cipher. Rather than spelling them out laboriously, they decided to add to the standard 1750 table, increasing the coding numbers by 200 to a total of 1,400.

The use of a 1,400 number cipher by the French marked an enormous advance. While Napoleon's army was the best organized and the most scientifically perfected the world had ever known, it had never before used ciphers of more than 200 characters for military operations (imperial diplomacy was another matter). The new cipher would make life much harder for someone who had cracked the Army of Portugal's 150-figure code, especially since the Great Cipher allowed so many permutations in the writing of any simple phrase or even of any single word. Taking the example of *Seville*, it could be encoded as:

> 1359, the single-letter code given to this city in the modified table;

> 173.90.1085.711.1118.521.439, when made up of single-letter codes (and there were many different variations possible using different single-letter codes);

> 189.1071, using the codes for *se* and *ville*;

> 1181.1085.631.929, a mixture of bigrams, or two-letter codes, with a single-letter one—it breaks into 1181 [*se*] 1085 [*v*] 631 [*il*] 929 [*le*].

The different approaches could be combined, and within one and the same dispatch the astute user could encode a recurring word differently each time. In addition, the cipher retained a few vacant numbers that could be put randomly into the middle of a word to make code-breaking guesswork even harder.

In short, the design made it extremely hard to deduce anything from the length of a coded passage or the numbers used to encipher it. *Seville*, as we have seen, could be turned into anything from the single number 1359 to any number of variations up to seven or eight figures. Even if the person using it made a mistake as crass as the one in General Montbrun's letter of August 1811 to the governor of Ciudad Rodrigo (mixing code and *en clair* in an obvious reference to "H.E. Marshal the Duc of Ragusa"), it would be far less damaging in this new cipher than before. For whereas that mistake had revealed 21 code numbers in a 150-figure cipher, the same phrase in Joseph's *Grand Chiffre* would only compromise one or two out of 1,400 numbers. It was a code of such strength that Napoleon considered it safe to send letters about matters of the utmost importance in the hands of some local peasant. Such a messenger would rarely arouse suspicion, and if he proved to be a traitor and delivered his precious missive to the enemy, nothing would be lost.

In sending out the tables, Marshal Berthier urged the recipients to keep the secret tables in their private papers and only allow a trusted individual of their retinue to learn their workings. He also sent instructions together with the ciphering tables adding one or two tricks of the trade to help an inexperienced cipher secretary. The most cunning read, "When finishing the ciphering by the code that marks the end, add a certain number of vacant codes of your choice after it." This anticipated that a decipherer might well attack the end of a letter first, since there were standard forms of signing off, such as "be assured, sir, of my highest esteem and consideration." Clearly, anyone trying to crack the code this way would be wasting their time on meaningless code numbers.

Once put into action, King Joseph's new code marked a great step forward in the security of communications. It applied to the military sphere those lessons that had been learned during the evolution of diplomatic ciphers during the previous two centuries.

Napoleon's orders to Marmont to march his men to the southeast in support of the Valencian operation arrived in several installments in early and mid-December 1811. They were not protected by the Great Cipher, but this did not matter since it seems that none of these critical dispatches were intercepted. One by one, French battalions began breaking camp and forming into their constituent regiments. Then they began tramping down to La Mancha, where a force of two infantry divisions and one of cavalry (nine thousand troops or thereabouts) was being formed.

The French movements were detected by spies. Guides carrying scribbled notes came clattering into Frenada's little square, tethered their exhausted mounts and delivered each morsel of information to the door of Wellington's headquarters. The first really reliable report arrived on 24 December: one of the southernmost divisions of the Army of Portugal had moved out of its usual cantonments and away from the Portuguese frontier.

In Frenada and the other villages of the border country, British troops sat down to their Christmas dinners. For many, the preferred bill of fare was lean roast beef followed by plum pudding. Others opted for a roast goose or game birds. Good claret flowed freely, and the low-ceilinged Portuguese farmhouses were crowded with ruddy-cheeked officers loudly singing festive choruses. Inwardly, many, no doubt, were reflecting on the loved ones they had left behind in Old England. Few had any notion how soon they would be ejected from their warm havens and marched into battle once more. Even Captain Edward Cocks, the dashing but serious-minded officer of the 16th Light Dragoons who occasionally dined at Wellington's table, couldn't foresee anything but boredom when he wrote home to his brother on the last day of 1811, asking for more reading matter to be sent out. Cocks wanted Ferguson's *Lectures*, Rousseau's *Nouvelle Eloise* and some military texts, joking that "if we have a dull campaign next year as we had last I shall have time to read through the Bodleian Library."

It was only in the little two-story house in Frenada, where Wellington and his staff plotted the latest French troop movements, that there were intimations that a great project might soon be afoot. In the last days of December, two most significant bits of intelligence were received: one, on Napoleon's orders, the Army of the North had sent most of its Imperial Guard troops back toward France, preparatory to the Russian campaign; two, the concentration of the Army of Portugal's Valencian expedition was completed and they began marching away from the Portuguese frontier on 29 December. Also in accordance with the emperor's orders, another of Marmont's divisions, under General Bonet, had gone north to assist in the operations against the guerrilla chiefs Mina and Longa.

News of this general eastward movement caused a stir in Frenada, and Wellington conferred with his chief engineer and quarter master general. The view in headquarters was that they needed at least twenty-four days to encircle Ciudad Rodrigo, batter breaches in its walls with heavy guns and storm the place. The British commander knew he could bring most of his troops into action from their cantonments along the border in just two or three days. Leaning across his maps and plotting the marches of Marmont's divisions toward Valencia with a pair of dividers, he waited patiently for them to get far enough away to guarantee him that working time.

At last, on the first day of 1812, Wellington decided that his operation to seize the border fortress was finally feasible. He knew it would be several days before Marmont even realized what was happening, at which point a good portion of his force would have marched too far away to alter the issue. The QMG department drew up detailed orders and dispatch riders flew to the army's divisions to set the great machine he had assembled on the frontier into motion.

The Light Division headed off first, with the mission of putting a close blockade around the fortress. "During this march," one of its young officers recorded, "a tremendous storm of sleet and snow took place. The snow froze and adhered to the horses' hooves, forming balls which raised them several inches from the ground." The soldiers of this force then forded the Agueda in this freezing weather and marched around the town in a great encircling movement. Further upstream, heavy wagons and guns began crossing a specially built bridge, and by 8 January the fortress and its two thousand defenders were surrounded.

Any good engineer could see that the best means to approach Rodrigo was from a hill called the Great Teson, less than half a mile from its defenses. The French had assumed this high ground would not be used by the enemy's heavy guns because of the natural obstacle of the River Agueda, and added further discouragement by placing a small fort on top of the feature. An improvised bridge had taken care of the river, and on 8 January an assault by picked men of the Light Division dealt with the little redoubt atop the Teson. Up there, they could start using their guns and begin working toward the points of the fort's walls they intended to attack.

That night the infantrymen had worked away feverishly in the darkness with picks and shovels; racing against the sinking moon, they knew that at first light their trench would certainly be bombarded by the city's defenders. By the time dawn came this first parallel, six hundred yards long, was completed handsomely, with a four-foot rampart of earth-filled gabbions, and at daybreak, a furious artillery battle was joined. The French tried to knock down the parallel trench and prevent the British from putting their siege artillery into it. The attackers used their guns to try to silence the defenders and then begin the process of battering holes in the defensive walls.

At night, the British troops hacked away once more, advancing a new trench toward the city. Not only was it was it cold, dirty work, with the men often standing up to their knees in muddy water, but it was also extremely dangerous. Aiming into the dark, the French began using two heavy mortars to kill the men digging their way forward. These weapons fired a great explosive shell high into the air, which if its fuse was cut to just the right length, would explode ten or twenty feet above the diggers, cutting them to pieces with shards of metal. The British troops soon christened these mortars Big Tom and Little Tom, and when they heard the distinctive boom of a heavy mortar, a keen-eyed man would scan the night sky for sight of the fizzing fuse burning away on the shell, and his shouted warning would send the others diving into the mud. "Now was a time to cure a skulker or teach a man to work for his life," wrote one private of the 95th Rifles engaged in this grim work. "We stuck to our work like devils, sometimes pitching ourselves on our bellies to avoid . . . being purged with grape or canister."

The British move had come as a grim surprise to the French, and the fort's governor knew it was vital to get word to Marmont that he was under attack. A Spanish collaborator was finally able to slip out of the fortress with an urgent message concealed in his clothing, but patrols of Don Julian's guerrillas were so frequent that it took him days to arrive in Salamanca. It was not until 14 January that word reached Marmont himself in Valladolid. Little did he know it then, but as he issued his orders for an immediate concentration of French forces, matters in the borderlands were already moving toward their critical stage.

The progress of Wellington's excavations was such that one week after operations had begun, on 15 January, a second parallel had been thrown up much closer to the walls; only about two hundred yards away to be exact, on a small ridge called the Lesser Teson. After nights of back-breaking labor, this new trench was finally close enough to allow the battering guns to begin smashing Rodrigo's defenses. With one brigade of guns installed in this position and four more firing from the higher ridge behind them, the town's works began to crumble. All day long the booming report of twenty-six siege guns was followed moments later by the crump of the heavy ball hitting flagstones at the base of the walls. For the unfortunate French conscripts, this hail of roundshot marked a counting of the hours until their situation would become hopeless. They could feel each tremor under their feet as a twenty-four-pound ball struck home and chipped a little more of their security away.

By 19 January the Royal Artillery had opened two breaches in the wall. The larger of the two was a gap about thirty feet wide, two hundred yards from the second parallel. Not only had the topography of the Teson ridges favored this point by allowing the guns to fire down at the base of the wall, but the harsh curve of the walls made it very difficult for the French to enfilade any infantry attacking here. Since it was important to attack such a target at several points at once in order to make sure the defenders would be unable to concentrate effectively at any one point, a lesser breach had been made about two hundred yards to the east of this great gap.

At dusk on the nineteenth, men of five British assault columns moved into position. The air was thick with trepidation, for no task was more dangerous than the storm of a breach. One sergeant watching the stormers walking down toward the second parallel pitied them, knowing their task was "the worst a soldier can undertake, for scarcely anything but death looks him in the face." The defenders would have piles of loaded muskets stacked and ready to fire, as well as grenades, mines and other devices to cut down as many of the stormers as they could. All the same, most of the soldiers embarking on this horrific duty were volunteers driven by a reckless sense of adventure and, in some cases, ambition. In the Light Division, twice as many had offered themselves than were needed. Each man, officer and private alike, sought to beat the odds, and by mounting the breach first, distinguishing himself in the eyes of his generals. Their gamble was a desperate one, but if they succeeded and survived, a mention in dispatches by Wellington would bring promotion to a young captain and perhaps even an officer's commission for a ranker. Watching them shuffling forward, other men shouted encouragement. A ration of spirits was broken out and a band played a tune recognizable to them all as the "Storm of Paris." As they crouched behind gabbions waiting for the signal, musket balls cracking and whining overhead, many offered up a prayer. General Craufurd spoke to his men, exorting them: "Soldiers! the eyes of your country are upon you. Be steady, be cool, be firm in the assault."

Looking up at the defenses, the stormers could see the glow of the French linstocks burning slow matches, ready to be touched to a mine or cannon, showering them with grapeshot. Picked volunteers would be the first over the top of the trench and would lead the way to the base of the breach, a task so dangerous that these groups were called Forlorn Hopes.* At seven, the bell tower atop the cathedral chimed the hour

---

*The volunteers given the most difficult tasks at the beginning of a storm.

and those leading stormers broke cover and began running across the open ground. General Picton's 3rd Division was taking the main breach, Craufurd's Light Division the lesser one and three other columns were heading for other sections of the defenses with scaling ladders.

For the British stormers, their advance caused the whizz and whine of musket balls overhead to intensify into an incessant cacophony. With the first men dropping, the Forlorn Hopes had to negotiate an earthen rampart that went all the way around the town, protecting the walls themselves. The first promotion-hungry man of the 3rd Division to mount this obstacle was, appropriately enough, Major Ridge.* Others followed, and once on top they hurled bags of straw and fascines down into the ditch behind it. Using these objects to break their fall of fifteen or so feet, they jumped in and groped their way toward the breaches. "As we neared the breach, the shot of the enemy swept away our first men. Canister, grape, round-shot and shell, with fireballs to show our ground, and a regular hailstorm of bullets came pouring on and around us," one Light Division soldier later wrote.

The first men looked up into the great breach to see the mouth of a cannon aimed right across the big gap in the wall, its crew waiting to cut them down. But the big gun had been rolled just a little too far forward, so that men hugging the side of the breach were invulnerable to its fire. Soon the first men appeared atop the ramparts, and a great cheer went up from the 3rd Division stormers.

The Light Division meanwhile, assaulting its own, smaller gap in the wall, heard the jubilant shouting of the 3rd and "this had a magical effect; regardless of the enemy's fire and every other impediment, the men dashed over the breach carrying everything before them." It was at this moment of triumph, however, that the Light Division paid a hefty price. Its commander, "Black Bob" Craufurd, was standing atop the rampart, urging on his men, but he had only been there a few moments before he fell in a puff of red mist, mortally wounded by a musket ball. Further to their right, as the 3rd Division soldiers mounted the walls, they came under intense fire from their flanks and

---

*Ridge was not alone. Wellington's army contained an engineer called Lieutenant Trench; a Major Cimetiere (it means cemetery in French) who was put in charge of a hospital; a river-crossing expert named Sturgeon; and Pine Coffin, an officer who went home for health reasons.

from French sharpshooters in the building behind the breach. One after another, soldiers scrambling over the ramparts were cut down. One eyewitness noted the heavy losses suffered by Picton's men at this key moment: "In this small space they suffered a tremendous loss of nearly 500 heroic officers and soldiers. During the fighting, their dead and wounded were piled [one] on top of the other. The wounded cried out in agony as they were trampled upon."

With the two breaches carried and other storming parties scaling the walls elsewhere, resistance crumbled and a group of officers and men made their way quickly into the city's central plaza to plant their regimental colors there. Despite Wellington's orders to the contrary, triumph soon turned to riot as those who had survived the storm sought to profit from it, breaking into houses to loot and drink themselves senseless. Many hours passed before order could be restored.

At Wellington's headquarters there was celebration. The operation had been successfully concluded and not in twenty days but in twelve. The British had suffered about one thousand casualties, the French twice as many (seventeen hundred being taken prisoner). Not only had the battle delivered one of the frontier's key fortified places, but the Army of Portugal's own siege train of heavy guns had been inside Rodrigo when it fell. No less than 153 cannon had been delivered into Wellington's hands and the loss of these would render Marmont powerless to retake the town or pose any serious threat to the security of northern Portugal.

Wellington's victory dispatch to the secretary of war, penned on the twentieth, contained much praise for the officers and men who had taken the city, and the engineers and gunners always so central to such an enterprise were given their due as well. It would not have shown good manners to trumpet his own personal achievement too loudly in the official record, but Wellington made sure that his partisans in London understood what a remarkable feat it had been to seize the fortress in twelve days. In a private letter to the duke of Richmond, he noted, "We proceeded at Ciudad Rodrigo on quite a new principle in sieges. . . . The French, however, who are supposed to know everything, could not take this place in less than forty days after it was completely invested." Not only had Wellington won his prize, but he was delighted to have the

opportunity of denigrating his enemy and their supposedly unchallenge-
able grasp of military science.

The speed of events at Ciudad Rodrigo did indeed cause complete
bewilderment in French headquarters. Marmont had expected to bring
his forces together to relieve the fortress on 29 January, but this plan
was fully nine days too late. Captain Cocks noted in his journal, "Lord
Wellington's correctness in choosing this moment for the siege proves
the exactness of his calculations. I would not be Marmont's aide-de-
camp to report the event for a year's allowance."

And how would Marmont "report the event" to his master in
Paris? It had happened after all because Napoleon had diverted three of
the Army of Portugal's divisions toward Valencia, sent one more northward and insured that the best troops of the Army of the North had
moved away from the frontier too. Marmont's command had been left
too weak and scattered to do anything. He knew that it would be quite
impossible to send a report to Paris along the lines of "Sire, it was all
your fault for trying to direct this war at a distance of 300 leagues."
The marshal himself had erred in thinking he had until late January to
get a relief column up to the border. Despite the repeated reports of
British siege supplies building up in Almeida the month before, Marmont had shared Napoleon's assessment that the enemy were too sick
and lethargic to do anything during the winter months.

French staff officers murmured to one another about the *événement
funeste*, the "disastrous occurrence" at Rodrigo. Marmont had never
experienced a reverse like this. His trajectory through the ranks of the
Grande Armée toward the dukedom of Ragusa and the coveted marshal's baton had been cometlike. Not only did the loss of Rodrigo
undermine his self-confidence, but for the first time he sensed that his
reputation might be buried in the Iberian graveyard, just like that of his
predecessor, Masséna. Count Miot de Melito, one of King Joseph's private secretaries, wrote, "This beginning hardly inspired great confidence
in the military talents of this young marshal who had not, up until that
moment, exercised higher command, and who was not known for any
brilliant act, and owed the post in which he had succeeded one of the
great captains of that period [Masséna] only to the blind favor shown
by the Emperor to one of his old pupils."

Inevitably, the emperor's response to the fall of Rodrigo was what

Marmont would have feared. Napoleon, Marshal Berthier wrote on 6 February, "is not satisfied with your direction of the war; you have a superiority over the enemy, and, instead of taking the initiative, you are always on its receiving end. You march your troops around and tire them out; this is not the Art of War."

Marmont sent his senior aide, one Colonel Jardet, to Paris to pick up what gossip he could about whether the Rodrigo episode had caused lasting damage to his reputation. After a few days in Paris, Jardet wrote a twenty-eight-page letter to his commander in Spain describing the state of affairs with great clarity and candor. Matters of this delicacy naturally needed the protection of a cipher. Since the colonel was not in the possession of the *Grand Chiffre,* and it made sense in any case to encode it in one understood only by the Army of Portugal, he chose one of Marmont's 150-character ciphers. While this step may have secured the contents from the great majority of French officers or indeed Spanish guerrillas, it did not withstand an attack by Major George Scovell, and it was on his desk that Jardet's letter ended up.

After the British triumph at Rodrigo, while Marmont worried about his fall from grace, Wellington considered his next step carefully. The obvious move now was an attack on Badajoz, the last of the four great frontier fortresses still in French hands. Just one week after the fall of Rodrigo, the general had sent off sixteen of the twenty-four-pounder siege guns on their long journey to the southern frontier. Wellington knew that once he had taken Badajoz he could consider Portugal secure and would then be able to launch his army in earnest into the Spanish interior, perhaps even to the gates of Madrid itself. On the other hand, if the move on Badajoz went as badly as Beresford's had in 1811, the end result would be the same: to destroy any hopes of achieving great things in the campaign of 1812.

Wellington had always appreciated that he would have to bide his time until the heavy rains of February and March to nourish the Estremaduran fodder and thus sustain the large force of cavalry needed on the plains around Badajoz. Additionally, if the disappointment of the previous summer was to be avoided, he had to frustrate any concentration of French forces for several weeks while he prosecuted the bloody business of siegecraft. This would require inspiration, since Marshal Suchet had at last successfully concluded the siege of Valencia, freeing thousands of French troops for action elsewhere.

At this stage, every insight into the deliberations of the enemy camp was vital, so Scovell had to attack the cipher used in Jardet's letter with alacrity. The colonel had begun *en clair*, describing his arrival in the metropolis and his interview with Marshal Berthier late at night in his office. Napoleon's chief of staff had evidently been in a generous and self-effacing mood while pacing up and down in his office and holding forth to Jardet. As the letter moved to more serious matters, it switched into streams of digits. Jardet had used the cipher cleverly, inserting many blank codes and using parts of words *en clair* to cause confusion: to take one example, the word *loi* appears at one point bracketed with numbers (25.17.loi.54.43.19.17.me.58.18.2). While this might at first seem like a reference to law, *loi* in French, it was in fact the result of a canny encipherment of a longer word, *l'eloingment*.

Despite Jardet's skills at this craft, the great length of his message and the limits of the Army of Portugal cipher meant there were several good places to start the attack. The colonel noted:

> *"Ah my friend, he could not disguise that he 20.14.59.29 the 36.49.1.12.63.14.17 of 6.28. 27.30. 31.21.17.41.40.30.49.10.41.39.31.43.10."*

The first section, as it switches into code, is vulnerable. Could the first four letters represent *etait, he was*? No, since *etait* is a five-letter word. What about *est,* or *is*? That is one letter too short, but of course blank codes could make coded words longer than the originals. Scovell was also sufficiently versed in this type of cipher to know that higher numbers were often used as vacant codes. If 59 is blank, then 20 is *e*, 14 is *s* and 29 stands for *t*. Moving on to the next coded word or phrase, 36.49.1.12.63.14.17, it is sandwiched between two words *en clair* : "that he is the 36.49.1.12.63.14.17 of." Here again the context reveals something. He is: "the architect of," "the instigator of," "the father of"? There were only so many possibilities, which again had to be tempered by the suspicion that blanks might have been used to increase the length of the coded word. Eventually, Scovell could have tried "the cause of." He suspected in any case that 14 stood for *s*, and if he knocked out the two highest numbers (49 and 63) as blanks, it would fit. This kind of assumption was obviously unscientific until it had been tested in other passages containing the same code numbers, and of course the great length of Jardet's missive gave him many other places to check his solutions. Eventually the passage above emerges as:

> *"Ah my friend, he could not disguise that he is the cause of the capture of Rodrigo."*

The colonel's skill in ciphering was impressive compared to many other staff officers whose efforts reached Scovell, but it could not overcome the basic limitations of the Army of Portugal cipher. In one passage, for example, Jardet wrote that Marmont could not "be responsible for the 36.49.10.50.45.28.18.53.41.20 of the Army of Portugal." The section in code seems too long for the word *command*, but in fact Jardet had padded it out with the blank numbers 49 and 53. While this might seem ingenious, the cipher he was working with contained vacant codes only above 40, so the decipherer would soon be speculating about the relevance of those higher values.

After many hours of work, the product of Berthier and Jardet's lucubrations in Paris revealed itself to Scovell. Marmont's operations, it was clear, were severely hampered by supply problems. Any future mission to assist Soult in defending Badajoz would require the Army of Portugal's commander to stockpile supplies in the Tagus valley so that his men did not starve on the journey south.

The letter, however, did give reason to doubt that Marmont remained committed to helping Soult again as he had been the previous summer, particularly since the Rodrigo business had shown him that all manner of mischief might take place on his own patch if he divided his army to help save Badajoz. Jardet revealed that each marshal was now just looking to save his reputation:

> *"When Badajoz is taken it will not be a great misfortune since Marshal Soult will be obliged to evacuate Andalucia and all of the south and to fall back on Valencia, or to have to go there at another time, when the English go to Madrid. Eh bien! That will doubtless be a disastrous thing, but not as disastrous as you getting beaten."*

Jardet, it is clear, had explained to Berthier that Marmont had no desire to continue in his post under the current circumstances. Berthier, ever the conciliator, had tried to smooth things over. The emperor understood, of course, the rigors of Spanish service and that the duke of Ragusa did not have a magic wand to produce supplies for his hungry men and broken-down horses. Jardet's letter continued:

> *"I saw that the prince was about to end the conversation and I said to him: Mon Prince! the Marshal cannot fulfill his task in the current situation; he receives orders from Paris that arrive, are impractical, because the circumstances are not those really pertaining here and on pain of avoiding a catastrophe the Marshal is obliged not to follow them."*

This finally drew from Berthier what Marmont's shaking confidence had craved: a frank reassurance that the emperor did not bear a lasting grudge for the loss of Rodrigo.

Jardet's deciphered message caused considerable eclat at British headquarters. For one thing, it confirmed the high impression they already had of Marmont's military judgment, for he had successfully forecast the move on Badajoz and even Madrid. But it also showed them that senior officers felt helpless in the face of these impending events. Lieutenant Colonel D'Urban, the Portuguese quarter master general, commented in his journal that Marmont had sent Jardet to Paris "to represent his difficulties, to remonstrate, to solicit supplies and to beg to be relieved from his irksome and disgusting command."

The intercepted letter contained intelligence of the highest grade, but now Wellington had to decide how to exploit this and the other information at his disposal to bring about a swift success at Badajoz. Scovell, together with some of the other scientific soldiers at HQ, regarded this new target with foreboding. The assistant quarter master general could not share the breathless sense of triumph at the storm on the nineteenth, noting somewhat grumpily in his journal, "Cuidad Rodrigo was by no means a strong place." He knew from earlier abortive attempts that to take Badajoz would certainly be another story.

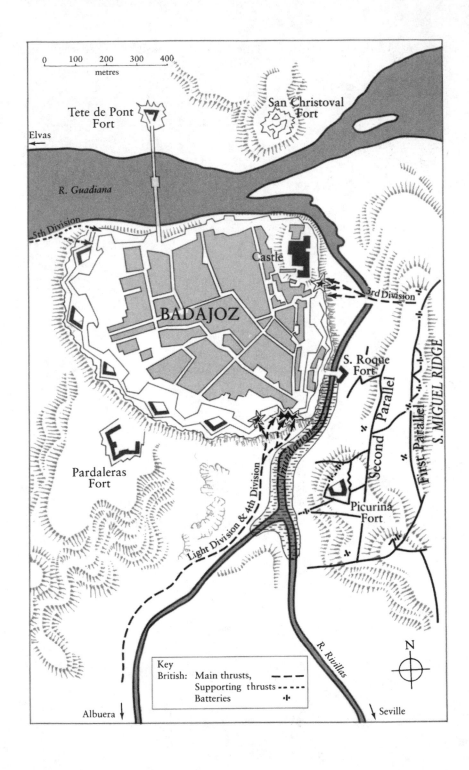

0   100   200   300   400
metres

Tete de Pont
Fort

Elvas

San Christoval
Fort

R. Guadiana

5th Division

Castle

BADAJOZ

3rd Division

S. Roque
Fort

Second Parallel

First Parallel

S. MIGUEL RIDGE

Inundations

Pardaleras
Fort

Light Division & 4th Division

Picurina
Fort

R. Rivillas

N

Key
British: Main thrusts,
        Supporting thrusts
        Batteries

Albuera

Seville

CHAPTER TEN

S. dont. 1082. 365. 622. we. w. 439. 669. e. 1085. 398. 326.
13. 309. i. 1085. ed. 481. t. 980. 985. 186. t. 843. 688. 2.
n.d. 1297. 536. 174. 1085. 1024 . . . 713. t. 980. 854. e. 326.
536. 700. w. 174. 1015. 1003. 13. t. 980. 1015. 131. t.

THE STORM OF BADAJOZ, MARCH 1812

O n 17 March 1812, the bands struck up the tune of "Saint Patrick's Day" and the battalions bivouacing around Elvas began trudging through the murky dawn toward the River Guadiana and the Spanish border. There were thousands of Irishmen in Wellington's army; it was their patron saint's day and the music was intended to cheer them up as they marched toward their rendezvous with Badajoz. By the afternoon, the Light Division was following the 3rd and 4th over a pontoon bridge across the Guadiana, making sure to break step so as not to cause the floating span to bounce up and down too much. One young officer of the 95th Rifles hoped that the Light Division's heroic work at Ciudad Rodrigo in January might mean their regiment would be spared from undertaking a similar mission. "We were soon undeceived. We were destined for duty, to our mortification, for soldiers hate sieges and working parties."

As these men progressed around the fortress—about one and a half miles away from it to remain out of artillery range—they could see a

French tricolor fluttering from the large tower that crowned the city's medieval keep. Every man knew this siege would be a bloody business. There were five thousand defenders for one thing (roughly three thousand more than garrisoned Rodrigo) and the layout of the walls and gun batteries was much stronger. What was more, that main belt of defenses surrounding the city was itself buttressed by strong outlying forts on the only bits of high ground that commanded the works. Only once La Picurina and Pardaleras—satellite positions on the southwestern approaches, Wellington's chosen axis of attack—had been reduced could the serious business of breaching the city's defense belt begin. This would be no twelve-day wonder like January's siege. It might take weeks, during which the French had to be prevented from making mischief.

Just as at Ciudad Rodrigo, the troops moved into position shortly before dusk; a full day's march was followed by a night of backbreaking graft with pick and shovel to throw up the first parallel trench. Their nocturnal labor was followed, as it had been in January's siege, by a furious bombardment from the French garrison the following morning. Once the enemy had seen the great scar on the ridge, they knew their fight to the finish had begun.

Other divisions moved into place to blockade the city and to stand ready to repulse any French attempt to break the stranglehold. Wellington had deployed almost all of his effective forces for the task: eight British infantry divisions, one of Portuguese and several brigades of cavalry. He had brought his main army the 160 miles down from the Almeida/Ciudad Rodrigo area, leaving those two places garrisoned by Spanish and Portuguese brigades. Of his own troops, only a single regiment of hussars, the 1st of the King's German Legion, had been left behind with them to face Marmont's Army of Portugal. While this might seem like a huge risk, everything had in fact been calculated quite precisely using the excellent intelligence at Wellington's disposal.

Wellington's plan at Badajoz could be upset by attacks from either of two directions: one southward by the Army of Portugal, or to the north by Marshal Soult from his bases in Andalucia with a large reinforcement for the corps he already had in Estremadura. Either of these events might be enough to hamper his siege work, since he would have to stop his men digging and unite them on the battlefield to defend themselves. If Marmont and Soult acted together and united anything up to eight thousand men as they had in June 1811, then not only would the siege be over, but Wellington would be forced onto the defensive.

The British commander knew from Colonel Jardet's deciphered letter that Marmont would face severe supply difficulties in coming south and that moreover he was concerned about what might happen in his absence from Leon and Castille. Wellington played on these fears by inciting Spanish forces in Galicia and Asturias, regions north of Marmont's bases around Salamanca, to begin attacking outlying French positions. But if the Army of Portugal remained in the north, might it not instead attack westward into Portugal, threatening all of the gains of the previous year's campaigning? Little did the British know, but this was precisely the course of action that Napoleon had urged upon Marmont.

Although none of the messages from Paris ordering such a diversionary attack by the Army of Portugal had reached Wellington, it had occurred to him that the French might take advantage of his temporary absence from the area around Almeida and Ciudad Rodrigo. If the French attacked across the Beira Baixa upland plateau of the frontier, they would have a march of several days without supplies. Wellington felt confident that if the Army of Portugal undertook such an expedition, its men and horses would soon start dropping from hunger.

The best insights into Marmont's possible strategy that were available to the British general came from Jardet's deciphered letter. The marshal's staff officer had written to him from Paris that the Army of Portugal should "above all" remain on the plains around Salamanca, where they could threaten the British. This vague instruction had been superceded by further orders (those Wellington did not know about) from Napoleon on 18 and 20 February. If Wellington went to Badajoz, Marmont should "no longer think . . . of going south, and march straight into Portugal." The second letter had expanded the emperor's concept: "If Lord Wellington were to march on Badajoz, there would be a certain, prompt, and decisive method of recalling him, by advancing on Ciudad Rodrigo and Almeida."

Napoleon's ideas rested upon the misconstrued notion that northern Portugal was a land of abundance, full of trees groaning with fruit, lush pastures and well-stocked British magazines ready for the plunder, whereas it could not possibly sustain a large army. His belief that Marmont might bring Wellington scurrying back by threatening to ravish the border fortresses of Almeida and Rodrigo was also nonsense, since the loss of the Army of Portugal's entire train of heavy guns in January had nullified this threat. Marmont's men would be able to do nothing more than hungrily wander up and down outside the towns' massive walls, while the well-fed occupants hurled abuse and round shot at them. Marmont knew these ideas dictated in Paris by a master who was spending eighteen hours a day organizing his vast expedition into Russia were half-baked at best. His military instincts told him that if Wellington marched south, he should do the same, but Napoleon's orders had now given him the less risky option of a limited foray into Portugal.

For Marshal Soult and his Army of the South, Wellington had also prepared a diversion. At the end of January, Wellington had written to his brother Henry, Lord Wellesley, the British minister at Cadiz, "It is absolutely necessary that the whole of Soult's force should not be brought upon us with impunity." To this end, he had asked Lord Wellesley to enlist the services of General Ballasteros, the commander of a Spanish flying column in Andalucia, to threaten Soult's base at Seville. Ballasteros was a typical fighting patriot whose faith in his own operations was inexhaustable, despite a catalogue of routs, drubbings and *débandades*. With a few thousand men, he would happily march around the south, causing nervous French governors in their outlying garrisons to panic and raise the alarm left, right, and center.

Wellington's underlying assumption in planning these diversions was that if neither Marshal Marmont nor Marshal Soult wanted to take risks already, a small eruption of Spanish troops would provide them with the perfect excuse for staying put. And if one of them did not march, why should the other try his luck against the British singlehandedly? As Jardet's letter had confirmed, in Marmont's staff the loss of Badajoz was viewed as a lesser evil than their master's defeat and the ruin of his reputation.

Into this psychological equation came a further variable, one that Wellington had not foreseen.

On the very day that Badajoz had been invested, Napoleon had scribbled a most important order to Berthier in Paris:

"Let the King of Spain know, by a special courier tonight, that I confide in him the command of all my armies in Spain, and that Marshal Jourdan will fulfill the functions of Chief of Staff . . . Write to Marshal Suchet, to the Duke of Dalmatia [Soult] and to the Duke of Ragusa [Marmont] that I am confiding the command of my armies in this Kingdom to the King . . . and that they must obey all orders that they receive from the King so that all of the armies pursue the same objectives."

This directive, sent hurrying along the road to Bayonne and thence Madrid with an imperial courier, would seem at first glance to be exactly what Joseph and Jourdan had been praying for. It ended the nonsense that a man should be in command far away who worked with two- or three-week-old intelligence in the Tuileries and whose orders then took a similar time to reach the field commanders. It acknowledged, as the emperor was preparing to head east, that he could not personally control two wars at the same time and that the one against Russia had to take priority.

Although this new order had been dictated by the emperor in a more genuine spirit than the Rambouillet note of May 1811, King Joseph would soon discover that it was not what it seemed either. For one thing, Napoleon had not ordered Berthier to place General Dorsenne and his Army of the North under command of Madrid. He would remain under the direct control of Paris, and that arrangement proved to be a potent source of difficulty for Joseph. Moreover, Napoleon felt that if one of his marshals was to seek the emperor's advice while he was campaigning in Russia, he could not refuse.

Even in the symbolic act of passing the cipher to General Clarke, the duke of Feltre and minister of war, Joseph's new liaison back in Paris revealed Napoleon's desire simultaneously to be rid of Spanish affairs and carry on meddling in them. In his note to Berthier explaining these new arrangements, Clarke's new role is set out in a brief and businesslike manner, to which the emperor could not help but add this postscript: "Don't forget to send [Clarke] all of the ciphers; it might be a good idea for us to keep a copy, in case some letter from the King reaches us when we are with the Army."

Napoleon's directive instituting the change of command, like almost all messages sent out by Paris, took its time getting to Madrid, but when it did, its arrival changed the whole system of communications. Joseph was now to be at the center of the web. The volume of messages passing to and from Paris was to decrease, that going via Madrid to increase correspondingly. In many cases, this exposed the messengers to greater risk. Prior to the change, messages from Marshal Soult, in southern Spain, for example, had often been conveyed by ships sailing out of Malaga or some other safe haven to ports on France's Mediterranean coast. If they were to go to the Spanish capital then they would have to run the guerrilla gauntlet of several groups active on the roads south of this city. Similarly, Joseph's need to bring General Dorsenne's Army of the North under his operational control would also require many couriers and *afrancesados* to take their chances riding through the northern hills. Joseph and Jourdan felt they knew the answer to this problem: plenty of silver dollars to hire the services of cunning couriers; the regular sending of duplicate or triplicate messages; and the use of the *Grand Chiffre* to protect the contents. Thus, even if every other thieving Spaniard who undertook such a mission were to convey his precious cargo to the enemy, it didn't matter, since everyone up to the emperor himself had complete faith in the code.

While imperial edicts on the new command arrangements were filtering through the Iberian Peninsula, the British received an object lesson in the fickle nature of many messengers in French pay. On 20 March, three days after beginning their siege at Badajoz, some redcoats squinting into the driving rain spotted a sodden Spaniard riding toward the British lines. He was duly presented to the staff, where he suggested a business proposition. He told them that he had been paid to take a message from the governor of Badajoz, General Phillipon, to Marshal Soult's headquarters in Seville. The French, he said, had given him the princely sum of 512 dollars to execute this hazardous commission, but if the British matched it, he would extricate the dispatch from its most ingenious hiding place and present it to Phillipon's enemies instead. It does not seem to have crossed the minds of Wellington's staff that they could simply hang this rogue and subject his belongings to the kind of minute examination employed by Don Julian's men. Evidently the war for information had already assumed a more sophisticated character than that. Instead they agreed to his offer and paid him the additional 512 dollars. It was with some difficulty that he then removed the metal top soldered onto his riding crop and drew a thin slither of parchment from within. General Phillipon was not in possession of the *Grand Chiffre*, so the principal difficulty in making out his message consisted of reading its minute letters. The contents were what Wellington would have expected: Phillipon raised the alarm that a British siege had begun and that "within these few days the English works have assumed a formidable appearance." By paying the messenger additional money, Wellington had ensured that he would continue his journey to Seville with every incentive to repeat a most profitable transaction. After all, he had just earned himself 1,024 dollars. Phillipon's appeal for help would still reach Marshal Soult's headquarters, only it would do so with a delay and the Spanish collaborator would retain the trust of the French, perhaps delivering future dispatches into British hands as well.

The rain that had soaked the Spaniard was also making life a misery for the British working parties digging their way toward Badajoz's outlying defenses. One young officer recorded, "It required every man to be actually in the trenches digging for six hours every day and the same length of time every night which, with the time required to march to and from them, through fields more than ankle deep in stiff mud, left us never more than eight hours out of the 24 in camp, and we were never dry the whole time." The endless downpour was hampering operations in various ways, not least in raising the level of the Guadiana and cutting the British pontoon bridge there. This meant that for a couple of days, had the French surprised them, there would have been no line of retreat for the three divisions digging the approaches.

On 25 March, at about 10 A.M., the great sheet of rain that had divided the British parallel on the San Miguel ridge from the main defenses of Badajoz suddenly drew back like the curtain of a vast natural theater. On cue, the demented timpany of twenty-four-pounders began its performance. Most of the British batteries were trying to smash French cannon, a task requiring some marksmanship, since it meant directing fire through the embrasures in the bastions. At their end, the French were desperately trying to beat back the British from positions not two hundred yards from Fort Picurina atop the ridge. Ten of Wellington's siege guns were firing into that small work at point-blank range, with a weight of shot that overwhelmed

the two hundred defenders. Any man who tried to serve one of the Picurina's cannon was soon scrambled by a British twenty-four-pound ball, dis-
integrating into a shower of body parts. By the afternoon, the French
defenders were making no attempt to fire their guns, cowering instead in
the lower part of the work and praying for deliverance.

That evening, Wellington gave the order for Kempt's Brigade of the
3rd Division to storm the Picurina. His engineers had been studying the
battered fort closely and believed that the time was right. Major Henry
Hardinge, the deputy QMG of the Portuguese army and Scovell's friend,
decided to accompany the stormers. As a staff officer, he had no formal
role in the command of troops, but he knew of the opportunities to
enhance one's reputation in such desperate moments.

When the signal was given, the heavy British guns stopped firing and
Kempt's men ran the short distance through the darkness toward the Picurina's slanting walls. Once they were close, the officers leading the storming
parties then made a dreadful discovery: they could see no way into the Picurina. Pallisades of sharpened stakes surrounded it at every point, and even as
they hacked their way through, they could see that the ditch in front of the
work was so deep that their ladders, once placed in this well, would not
reach up to the top of the walls that rose above it. While the redcoats milled
about in confusion, the work's defenders used the respite from British
artillery to come running out onto the Picurina's top with primed muskets
and repay their earlier sufferings. Firing down on the stormers from only
forty feet away, the French quickly slaughtered two hundred men. In this
moment of crisis, one Captain Oates of the 88th was seized by a sudden
inspiration. Seeing a lip at the far side of the ditch, he ordered his men to lay
their ladders across the deep obstacle. They scurried along them, stood on
the ledge hugging the base of the wall, and then raised their ladders in this
new position. They were in. Fort Picurina had fallen.

The charmed Major Hardinge came through the storm just as he
had survived the death of General Moore and the Battle of Albuera.
"Hardinge got shot through his coat at the assault and as usual behaved
with great zeal and courage," William Warre reported to his father.

For the French the fall of Fort Picurina was an ominous event. It
allowed British batteries to be established just four hundred yards from
the Santa Maria and Trinidad bastions on the city's southeast corner.
From here on, it was just a question of how many days it would take

them to silence all the guns in these casements and batter some breaches in the walls that connected them.

From Wellington's perspective, matters looked a little different. The *fausse braie*, the great earthen rampart around the walls themselves, was more massive at Badajoz than it had been at Rodrigo. It would have to be blasted away if the stormers were not to drop twenty feet into the ditch behind it. This ridge also screened some of the main wall, even from batteries on the San Miguel feature, and it would therefore not be possible to cut breaches right down to the base of the walls.

The engineers usually had two ways of dealing with such a problem. They could dig a trench right up to the *fausse braie* and blow it up with a mine, or they could use the exploding shells fired by howitzers for the same purpose. Both methods usually filled the ditch behind it with earth and debris, further reducing its effectiveness as an obstacle. Unfortunately for Wellington, neither technique provided a panacea: the first would subject the sappers to a murderous fire and the latter would take too long. Wellington knew he must press matters forward as quickly as possible. Sooner or later Soult or Marmont, or perhaps both of them, would have to do something to save Badajoz.

For Major Scovell these final days of the siege were a time of high personal expectation. Mary had set sail on the Lisbon packet. His masters in headquarters had agreed that he could have a short leave to go and see her as soon as the business at Badajoz was completed. It is unsurprising then that Scovell did not venture into the breaches in search of glory, like the impatient young bachelors Hardinge, Somerset or Lord March. After all, Scovell had not seen his wife since they had parted at Sprotborough Hall in 1809, and it would be tragic indeed for Mary to endure the journey to Lisbon only to receive the terrible word that she had become a widow.

By the evening of 5 April, Wellington's engineers reported to him that there were three breaches in the main wall practicable for assault, but he was worried that the *fausse braie* in front of them was still too high. He asked for the general's orders.

The general was seized by doubt: what if the ditch behind this obstacle was still so deep that injured stormers would pile into it and then be unable to escape? They would be butchered or taken. He did not have too much time, but he must see the *fausse braie* bombarded for at least another day.

While the British tried to use shells to shift tons of earth, General

Phillipon made every preparation to resist the assault. Each night when
the bombardment had stopped, French troops went into the great ditch
around the walls and scattered every kind of impediment: iron crows'
feet and boards studded with nails to injure the feet of anybody coming
through; explosive mines cleverly sited in those places where the stormers might take cover; and an intimidating array of *chevaux des frises*,
wooden trestles bristling with sharp blades that had been chained to the
top of the breaches themselves. Behind these broken walls, a new parapet had been built, giving the British a second wall to storm.

On 6 April, Wellington was once again asked for his orders. He knew
that the *fausse braie* had hardly been touched in the day's extra battering
and that he was running out of time: Marshal Soult was finally reported to
have left Seville on 1 April, heading for Badajoz with a large column. Marshal Marmont had begun moving toward northern Portugal (as ordered by
Napoleon) and was threatening Almeida. Wellington's earlier confidence
about the security of that fortress began to falter a little. He needed to
bring this Badajoz business to a conclusion quickly, even though it was
going to cost him the lives of many more of his soldiers. At last, the assault
was ordered. The Light and 4th Divisions would attack the breaches. Picton's 3rd Division would make an attempt to mount the walls farther along
with scaling ladders. Two more attacks would go in on the western side of
the fort. There, a more favorable topography had allowed British sappers
to put giant mines under the *fausse braie*, and these would be detonated
prior to the troops attempting their own escalade.*

At lunchtime on the sixth, a heavy pall of apprehension hung over
the staff. As they sat around the table with Marshal William Beresford,
the Portuguese army commander, one diner recalled:

> "There was little conversation . . . but a young man
> inconsiderately said, 'of the number now present, how
> many will be alive and with their limbs whole this time
> tomorrow, or even four hours hence?' A dead silence of
> some continuance followed this observation, and the
> Marshal gave the officer a look of displeasure."

---

*An assault by means of ladders. Like so many terms used in siege warfare, its
origin is French.

That evening, men of the main storming parties marched down toward the breaches. Sergeant William Lawrence of the 40th had volunteered for the 4th Division's Forlorn Hope with his mates Pig Harding and George Bowden. They had been inside Badajoz before, back in 1809, and, as Lawrence noted: "We knew where the shops were located. Having heard a report that, if we succeeded in taking the place, three hours' plunder would be allowed, we arranged to meet at a silversmith's shop." Wellington would not have explicitly encouraged looting at any time, but the young officers who walked forward with Sergeant Lawrence and his friends did nothing to disabuse them. Every man needed to believe that if he survived the hideous business ahead, there would be some reward at the end. It was, after all, entirely in accordance with the Laws of War* that any town that refused the besiegers' summons, as Badajoz had done, forfeited all right to the lives and property of its inhabitants.

Between 8 and 9 P.M., the stormers were paraded, given a lump of bread and a double tot of rum. They continued on their way in the darkness. "Off we went with palpitating hearts," one of them later recalled. "I never feared nor saw danger until this night. As I walked at the head of the column, the thought struck me forcibly—you will be in hell before daylight!"

As they approached the walls illuminated by the moon, some could see the French defenders looking down on them. The British batteries had maintained a fire of blank rounds, trying to lull Phillipon's men into a false sense of security. But they were not deceived in any way. They were just waiting for the stormers to enter their killing ground.

When the first men mounted the *fausse braie*, barrels of burning tar came bouncing down from the ramparts. Their targets thus illuminated, the defenders unleashed a storm of bullets onto them. Rifleman Costello of the 95th was one of a team burdened with scaling steps:

> "Three of the men carrying the ladder with me were shot
> dead in a breath and its weight fell upon me . . . our men

---

*During the previous two centuries a general understanding of elaborate "rules of the game" concerning siege operations had emerged in Europe. Among other things, these said that if a garrison refused the besiegers' summons to capitulate, once there were breaches suitable for storming, then the attacking army could do what they wanted with the inhabitants and their property.

were falling fast. The remainder of the stormers rushed up, disregarding my cries, and those of the wounded men around me. Many were shot and fell upon me so that I was drenched in blood."

With each flash and bang a ghastly new sight of decapitation or evisceration came briefly into view. As the stormers fell into the ditch between the *fausse braie* and the walls, many were hurt and lay helpless as others came piling down on top of them. Rifleman Costello lay under a bank of bodies while "the fire continued to blaze over me in all its horrors, accompanied by screams, groans, and shouts, the crashing of stones and the falling of timbers. For the first time in many years I uttered something like a prayer."

With two bits of shrapnel in his knee and a musket ball lodged in his side, Sergeant Lawrence was also down in the trench. "On the cry of 'come on my lads!' from our commanders, we hastened to the breach." Lawrence scambled up the smashed section of wall only to find the immovable array of blades and spikes on top and spy the further ditch the defenders had dug behind this broken wall. "The *cheval de frise* was a fearful obstacle and although attempts were made to remove it—my left hand was dreadfully cut by one of the blades—we had no success."

The attack was faltering and hundreds of men were dying in the ditch in front of the breaches. While Wellington watched the scene from atop the San Miguel ridge a few hundred yards away, his boyish ADC Lord March was beside him, as was Sir James McGrigor, the army's surgeon. Scovell and other staff officers were scurrying about in the darkness trying to collect reports on the progress of the different columns. Wellington stared grim-faced into the night, wracked with worry as he tried to catch sight of what was happening in the brief glare produced by one explosion after another.

Faint from loss of blood, Sergeant Lawrence staggered out of the trench and back toward the surgeons. His mates were both dead: Pig Harding had been riddled with seven musket balls and George Bowden had both his legs blown off. Lawrence had forsaken any idea of plundering the silversmiths; he was just trying to find some help before he bled to death. Stumbling up the San Miguel ridge, he walked straight into Wellington and his two staff. "He enquired whether any of our troops had got into the town," Lawrence recalled later. "I told him no and that I did not think they ever would because of the *cheval de frise*, the deep entrenchment and the constant and murderous fire of the enemy behind them."

As further news arrived from the breaches, it became clear that the men were losing any hope of breaking in to Badajoz. This moment, one of the greatest crises of Wellington's life as a general, was memorably recorded by Sir James McGrigor:

> "*An officer came up with an unfavorable report of the assault, announcing that Colonel McLeod and several officers were killed, with heaps of men, who choked the breach . . . another officer came with a still more unfavorable report, that no progress was being made and that he feared none could be made; for almost all the officers were killed, and none left to lead on the men, of whom a great many had fallen. At this moment I cast my eyes on the countenance of Lord Wellington, lit up by the glare of the torch held by Lord March; I shall never forget it to the last moment of my existence, and could even now sketch it. The jaw had fallen, and the face was of unusual length, while the torchlight gave his countenance a lurid aspect.*"

At midnight, two hours after the dreadful business had begun, Wellington sent orders for the 4th and Light Divisions to be recalled. Only Picton could now save the affair. Wellington did not know it yet, but Picton had already started on his own initiative to try to escalade the old medieval wall on the eastern side of Badajoz. Wellington sent McGrigor forward to tell the fiery Welsh general that his attack might be their last hope. But before the surgeon had traveled far, news came that Picton's men were already successfully climbing their long ladders and getting into the fortress. Phillipon could not defend every possible point against attack, and indeed at the other end of the fortress, its western point close to the Guadiana, a column of the 5th Division, intending only to deliver a diversionary attack, was also pressing home its unexpected success.

After hours of mayhem Rifleman Costello, still lying in the ditch in front of the great breach, heard "a cry of 'Blood and 'ounds! Where's the

Light Division? The town's ours, hurrah!' It was, no doubt, from some of the 3rd Division." Costello struggled out of the killing ground and found his way into Badajoz, where gangs of soldiers had already begun breaking into houses, smashing them up in search of hidden money or drink and beating any Spaniards who stood in their way. "It has to be considered that men who besiege a town in the face of such dangers generally become desperate from their own privations and sufferings," Costello wrote later of the events during the early hours of 7 April. "Once they get a footing within its walls, they are flushed by victory. Hurried on by the desire for liquor and eventually maddened by drink, they will stop at nothing."

This rioting soon turned to murder and rape and the British officers who tried to restrain their men were among the dead. Major FitzRoy Somerset, Wellington's young military secretary, fought his way through the rampaging mob to save General Phillipon and his daughters. One eyewitness saw:

> "General Philippon, the governor, with his two daughters, holding each by the hand; all three with their hair dishevelled and with them were two British officers, each holding one of the ladies by the arm, and with their swords drawn making thrusts occasionally at soldiers who attempted to drag these ladies away. I am glad to say that these two British officers succeeded in conveying the governor and his daughters safely through the breach, to the camp. With the exception of these ladies, I was told that very few females, old or young, escaped violation by our brutal soldiery, mad with brandy and passion."

It would take many hours before the situation could be brought under control, requiring the hanging of several soldiers in the town's main square to serve as an example. William Warre wrote wearily in a letter home: "It was almost impossible to restrain the avarice and licentiousness of the soldiery, which so greatly sullies the brilliancy of their conduct and victory . . . it is also prudent to hold our tongues and shut our eyes on miseries it is out of our power to prevent, but must deeply feel."

As Wellington surveyed the wreck of the town on the seventh, he began to understand the scale of the butcher's bill he had paid for this victory. There had been forty-six hundred Allied casualties between the investment of the fortress on 17 March and that bleary April morning. More than eighteen hundred of these dead and wounded had belonged to the storming parties of the Light and 4th Divisions.

The official dispatch, as always with a public document, was full of praise for the conduct of the troops: "It is impossible that any expressions of mine can convey to your Lordship the sense which I entertain of the gallantry of the officers and troops on this occasion." There was fulsome thanks to Picton, who was wounded in the fighting, and many other officers. Scovell's friends Somerset and Hardinge were both promoted lieutenant colonel for their parts in events, achieving this lofty step at twenty-three and twenty-seven years old respectively.

In his private correspondence, however, Wellington expressed great anguish and pain at what had happened at Badajoz. Attaching a confidential note to his victory dispatch, he told the secretary of war, "I anxiously hope that I will never again be the instrument of putting [my men] to such a test as that to which they were put last night." He expressed dismay that the British army had no proper corps of engineers for carrying out such operations and that this had forced him to adopt many second-rate improvisations. The inability to demolish the *fausse braie* ramparts in front of the breach and pressure of time had placed him in an impossible position on 5 April: "I was obliged then to storm or give the business up, and when I ordered the assault I was certain that I should lose our best officers and men. It is a cruel situation for any person to be placed in."

Many surviving soldiers and officers profited from the siege in the way they had hoped to, by pocketing cash and jewels or making off with church plate that they cashed in at a later date. Others got the promotions they so earnestly desired. For Scovell, there had been only one thought after the successful conclusion of this sanguinary affair. Bright and early on 8 April, he set off to see his beloved Mary in Lisbon.

CHAPTER ELEVEN

*J. dont. 1082. 365. 622. we. w. 489. 669. e. 1085. 898.
326. 13. cei. 1085. ed. 481. t. 980. 985. 186. t. 843. 688.
2. n. d. 1297. 536. 174. 1085. 1024... 713. t. 980. 854. e.
326. 536. 700. w. 171. 1015. 1003. 18. t. 980. 1015. 131. t.*

From Lisbon to Fuente Guinaldo,
April to June 1812

*W*alking through Lisbon with Mary on that bright spring morning, the hell of Badajoz slowly receded and the promised land of a two-week leave opened up before Scovell. For three years now he had ridden about Iberia, answering the whims of Wellington or the quarter master general, and doing it in double time, sir! For months at a time he had kept his portmanteau packed and his horses ready, and laid his head in a different place every night—usually without removing his clothes. He had endured mortal danger on at least half a dozen occasions and finally achieved his majority.

In Lisbon, he was enfolded in Mary's arms, lay with her between crisp sheets and ate the finest food. He had time to guide her through the narrow streets of the Bairro Alta, sharing his discoveries—the Sao Rocque church or the riot of color in the Chiado fruit market. When Mary tired, there were so many places to find refreshment. The Grotto was a favorite eating house for British travelers, down in the Largo de

Sao Paolo: there they could watch fashionable society drift by while tasting strawberries and delicately flavored sorbets and imbibing coffee or hot chocolate. Having accumulated a good deal of money during his campaigning, George could treat her to the finest.

What must Mary have made of him when she saw him after three years? Like most Iberian campaigners, wind and sun had weathered Scovell's face to a leathery tan. He was probably much thinner than when they had parted, too. His hair had also receded a little farther from his brow and his clothes must have shown every sign of wear and tear. Perhaps Scovell was tempted to blow some cash on a smart new uniform. Certainly the merchants of the city competed to sell their wares to men like him, one officer recalling a similar experience: "The streets of Lisbon glittered with uniforms; the shop windows of all the embroiderers furnished a grand display of military ornaments. The magazines of the gunsmiths and sword cutlers were constantly filled with customers."

Scovell had the option of wearing the Mounted Guides' uniform, with an embroidered brown light cavalry jacket and handsome crested Tarleton helmet, or the new staff outfit. The latter consisted of a red coat with dark blue facings, rank being shown by embroidered white waves on the lapels and cuffs. It was topped off with a cocked hat, trimmed with a broad stripe of gold tape. This outfit was quite splendid, so much so that from a distance, it could easily be mistaken for a general's suit. That was all very well promenading down Horse Guards, but for officers on service it was a distinct liability: "I suppose our good chiefs do not think our Generals or Staff get killed off fast enough that they order them cocked hats with gold binding," William Warre explained in a letter home. "It must only be meant for Wimbledon. There are no *Voltigeurs* [sharpshooters] there, and a gold laced cocked hat, though very ugly is a very harmless thing—not here."

As the Scovells enjoyed the sights of Lisbon, headquarters was in motion again, moving back from Badajoz toward northern Portugal. Major Scovell's leave had only been possible because the main army would take a week or ten days to make its way back to its usual domain on the northern Portuguese frontier. But the commander of forces may well have rued giving even this short furlough to his assistant QMG, because in his absence the British suffered a significant intelligence setback.

❋   ❋   ❋

Marshal Marmont met his dinner guest that evening with some sense of curiosity and excitement. His servants were preparing his meal in unusual surroundings, a large house in Sabugal that had been requisitioned as French HQ. Marmont's incursion into northern Portugal had reached its high water mark and the supply situation being what it was, he would soon have to turn back into Spain. Still, he was not unhappy. He had followed the emperor's instructions while having the satisfaction of being proved right, since "laying waste northern Portugal" had not caused Wellington to adandon the siege of Badajoz. Secondly, he had a most interesting dinner companion, someone who might be useful in penetrating the miasma of uncertainty that enveloped his enemy's operations.

Marmont's guest was none other than Lieutenant Colonel Colquhoun Grant, Wellington's intelligence officer. To say that his presence at the marshal's table was reluctant would have been understating matters. For on 10 April, Grant had been captured. Sent north ahead of the main army to plot French dispositions, he had been caught between two patrols of French cavalry. Realizing they were surrounded, Grant and his Spanish guide, Leon, had dismounted and tried escape through a copse. This final gambit had failed and Leon, who was not wearing any uniform, had been executed on the spot.

As the cutlery clicked on the marshal's porcelain and crystal glasses full of wine were emptied, he had cross-examined Grant. Tell me more about the character of Wellington? Will he try to cut off my withdrawal into Spain? What is the spirit of your army? Marmont, it seemed, viewed his contest with Wellington as an intellectual challenge. He wanted to learn as much as he could about how the British general's mind worked. He wanted his guest to know, as he seemed to want everyone around him to know, that the English were doing battle with one of the finest minds of the French army. Grant met these enquiries with politeness, while concealing whatever knowledge he actually possessed of his master's plans.

As the meal drew to a close, Marmont evidently felt that his hunger for information had not been satisfied. He looked across at Grant and told him, "It is fortunate for you, sir, that you have that bit of red over your shoulders [meaning his uniform]; if you had not, I would have hung you on a gallows twenty feet high." The marshal asked for, and obtained,

Grant's *parole*, his word, that he would not try to escape. Their interview was at an end and the captive was taken back to Salamanca.

While Marmont's army was menacing Almeida and generally driving the Portuguese about the countryside, militiamen and Don Julian Sanchez's guerrillas had swarmed about the French rear. As Wellington brought his HQ back to the north and Marmont began inching back into Spain, a packet of intercepted dispatches was delivered to the British commander. Two, dated from the Portuguese town of Sabugal on 12 April, shortly before he pulled out of that town, gave arrangements to Marmont's divisional commanders for the withdrawal back to the border. Fortunately for Wellington it was in an Army of Portugal *petit chiffre* and it is likely that Somerset was able to discover its details.

Wellington then acquired, in fairly quick succession, four messages in the higher command *Grand Chiffre*, the fourteen-hundred-character cipher circulated to the most senior officers a few months before. Two had come from Marshal Soult in Seville, and were taken from one of his ADCs. The first was long, with dense passages of the strong cipher, but from what they could make out it was evidently an essay of self-justification following the fall of Badajoz, since the fortress was located in his area of responsibility. Soult sought to blame Marmont for those events and displayed his own suspicions about the communications war being waged by Britain and its allies, telling Paris:

> *"The way the English conducted themselves during this action was so well thought out that we may suppose that they intercepted some part of the correspondence which revealed to them the Army of Portugal's system of operations and the irresolution of the Duke of Ragusa [Marmont]."*

Soult's letter may be taken as evidence that the paranoid are not necessarily wrong. But he was not completely right either, since he did not consider that Wellington might already have resolved to finish the siege of Badajoz before intercepted letters from Marmont actually reached him. Marshal Soult had in any case demonstrated his confidence in the Great Cipher in writing his own letters. Shortly after his staff officer was captured, a further letter in this cipher, from Marmont to Berthier and dated 16 April, was taken. Finally, a short message from General Dorsenne, commander of the Army of the North, to Marshal Jourdan in Madrid and also dated 16 April, was seized.

Scovell rode back into headquarters on 25 April after bidding fond farewells to Mary. She was going to stay in Lisbon until they could meet again. Like many an officer who ekes every last moment out of his leave, he was obliged to ride hard when he left the city and it took him just three days to travel from the Portuguese capital to Fuente Guinaldo, a few miles across the Spanish border, where Wellington's staff had once more taken up residence.

From late April through to early June, Wellington remained in the handsome mayor's house in Fuente Guinaldo's plaza. Upon returning north he had been disturbed to find that a Spanish garrison thrown into Ciudad Rodrigo had put down its tools because of arrears of pay, leaving January's breaches in the city's defenses unrepaired. Although he had taken possession of all of the main border fortresses by mid-April, Wellington did not feel free to make his next move until he was confident that Rodrigo would be able to resist a purposeful enemy attack. Once this work had been done, he would be free to launch himself into Spain.

Major Scovell, meanwhile, had returned to HQ and was able for the first time to consider several examples of the *Grand Chiffre*; Wellington had christened it the Great Paris Cipher. If he had expected Scovell to crack it with the celerity he had shown on Marmont's codes, then his lordship would certainly have been disappointed. Scovell looked upon the captured scraps of paper with wonderment. This was something altogether different from the Army of Portugal codes. A solution might be impossible. If this new cipher was changed regularly, as Marmont's had been, then it would certainly be. Can you produce the key or can you not, Major Scovell? He would have to study these messages most carefully before he could say.

None of the messages was entirely in code. That was one distinct advantage. What was not encoded often provided useful context, as he had learned with his earlier deciphering. Further study also allowed certain deductions to be drawn from the way certain passages had been enciphered—in particular, the longest and shortest of them. Soult's weighty catalogue of excuses of 14 April yielded something to the reader, even if the meanings of its long ciphered sections were obscure. It had used hundreds of code numbers ranging from 2 to 1390. Many numbers were not used at all, others only used once or twice. Some, however, did repeat themselves rather a lot: 13 had been used twenty-five times; 210 was repeated thirteen times; 413 appeared in a dozen places and 2 in nine. These most frequent codes (13, 210, 413 and 2): Were they very common words, letters or bigrams? Could one of them be *et*, the most frequently used word in French?

When looking at how these frequently recurring numbers appeared in the other messages that fell into British hands in April and May 1812, some early hypotheses could have been formed. Marmont's message of 22 April, for example, contained the passage, "nothing will stop the Emperor's Army of Portugal 13.70.354 . . . ." In this context 13 might mean *de*, or *from* in this sense. The word *of* seems to come through quite clearly in a wish list (for various supplies) compiled by the duke of Dalmatia that featured the code 13 repeatedly. Elsewhere in Soult's message of 17 April, there is a passage of code ending ". . . 722.1074.13.821 campaign." If 13 means *de*, then 821 must be *la* since the gender of the word campaign is feminine in French, and it finally becomes a fair working hypothesis that "13.821 *campagne*" stands for *de la campagne*. A similar methodology, working across several dispatches, would have suggested that the commonly occuring 210 meant *e*.

The shortest letter, Dorsenne's, was even more interesting. In its entirety it reads:

> *"I received Your Excellency's letter of the 2nd of this month, inviting me to send the King reports of 1238 with the aim 607.73.432.1181.192.1077.600.530. 497.701.711.700 that he considers appropriate.*
>
> *In the letter of 16th March, 1207 announced 516.1264 was giving 703.1328 command of 409.1327.1333.210.249.523, but was making 1165.1060.1238.820. Your Excellency will appreciate then 139.229.531.305.69.862.605 to make the efforts required of me. 187.609 I would humbly assure 73.516.918 will not neglect any opportunity to 605 give a full account of everything*

> *that could interest 240.196 and that requires his attention."*

Dorsenne's dispatch was crassly enciphered, as bad in its way as the General Montbrun letter of August 1811 that had proven vital to the breaking of the Army of Portugal code. Given the much greater size of the *Grand Chiffre*, the damage resulting from this inept staff work was considerably less, but damage there was because this note could be used to begin a substantial attack on the Great Paris Cipher. Mixing in and out of code gives far too much away, an effect that is more pronounced in its original French, since the gender of nouns or form of verbs can reveal much.

Taking the second paragraph, which begins "In the letter of 16th March, 1207 announced 516.1264 was giving. . . ," it is fairly clear that 1207 is a person. The construction "announced 516" is also interesting, since the normal use of language dictated the word *that* must follow. Does 516 mean *that*, or is it just the letter *t*, a bigram for *th* or even a blank, with 1264 meaning *that*?

A little later on, we see "I would humbly assure 73.516.918 will not . . ." The code 516 is repeated. The sense of this second phrase is clearly something like: "I humbly assure you," or HM or the King, whoever, "that . . ." There seems to be a likelihood 516 does indeed mean *that*. This becomes all the clearer with what follows this code number. In French, "918 *ne negligerai aucune occasion,*" the tense and person of the verb *to neglect* makes it apparent that 918 must mean *je*, or *I*. Examining the passage, it is clearly a good working hypothesis that 516 means *that* and 918 *I*.

As he sat struggling with this puzzle, Scovell's superb grasp of French grammar and syntax was his best weapon. His ability to absorb language was quite remarkable. Having landed in Iberia with Latin and some Italian, he had quickly obtained a sophisticated grasp of Spanish, noting in his journal following an evening's entertainment with Spanish hosts just a few months later: "I could easily perceive that the double entendre was the grand substitute for real wit." With French, he had the benefit of having studied the language for twenty years and was therefore able to fill in the blanks in ciphered passages better than almost anyone else at headquarters could have done.

Going back to the first part of the second paragraph of Dorsenne's letter, if 516 on its own means *that*, then 1264 is likely to be another individual. Attacking these passages something begins to emerge: that numbers from 1201 up represent many individuals, names of particular armies and places.

It may be recalled that several months before, when the *Grand Chiffre* arrived at Joseph's headquarters, it had consisted of a 1750-type cipher table of twelve hundred numbers previously filled out in Paris. In expanding the table to include terms used in Peninsular warfare (by simply gluing on two farther columns of one hundred numbers each) the staff officers responsible had made the mistake of adding their new codes entirely in the columns marked 1201 to 1400. So 1201, the first of the coding numbers created by this expedient, stood for Malaga, 1202 for Valladolid, and various other numbers for the commanders and armies found in the Iberian theater of war. Certain military terms were also contained in this appendix of ciphering numbers: 1330, for example, meant *gunpowder*; 1392 was the French National Guard.

It would have made more sense for Joseph's staff to have created a completely new cipher in which these terms were spread throughout the numbering as a whole, rather than being mostly confined to those between 1201 and 1400. Evidently, secret writing was a strange alchemy to the officers of Joseph's staff and they did not feel confident enough to alter the basic table that had been sent to them; it was evidently the fruit of endless cogitation by the savants at the foreign ministry. The effect of all this was that before Major Scovell or Wellington had ever clapped eyes on this Great Cipher, it had been weakened, albeit slightly, by the very people responsible for securing the French army's messages. It was not the case that *all* Peninsular terms and names were confined to that limited range of codes, because the original diplomatic code (sent out from Paris) did have entries for Madrid (it was 505) and a few other relevant places.

Nevertheless, as the first few messages in the new code were being studied at Fuente Guinaldo, a French staff officer's decision to add the extra two columns to the 1750 cipher table was already showing its effects in the similarity of the two names or titles: 1207 and 1264. Looking back to the first paragraph of Dorsenne's message, 1238 appears in a context that strongly suggests it can only mean something like *my command, my corps* or indeed the *Army of the North*.

As Scovell had scribbled in his notebook copy of Conradus, breaking these complex ciphers required the decipherer to know as much as possible about the affairs of the enemy camp. He would soon discover something about Dorsenne's relationship with the authorities in Madrid that would open up more of the meaning of that letter of 16 April. The emergence of a good working theory about common codes (like 13 or 516) or proper nouns and military names (1207, etc.) prompted a few successful guesses but was admittedly a very limited start to breaking the Paris Cipher. Even if deduction or just plain guesswork was to produce the meaning of a long string of code numbers bar one, that single unknown quantity, which might be the destination of a military movement or the date of its arrival, might render the entire work of decipherment worthless.

There was one other, quite unexpected aspect of the messages that was helping the decipherer to expand his knowledge of what was going on in the enemy camp. Since Marmont was assuming many of his messages would fall into British hands, he could use the uncoded passages to say some things directly to his enemy, *en clair*, and others, in code, to his masters. Marmont wanted it clearly understood by *whoever read* his letter of 22 April that Wellington had not intimidated him out of Portugal. At the time the British general had been to the south, some *parlementaires*, Allied officers under flag of truce apparently seeking to exchange prisoners, had ridden out to the French lines and made much of the imminent arrival of Lord Wellington's army. Marmont wrote in his letter, "This news was given affectedly by *parlementaires* and we haven't seen anything other than the single 1st regiment of hussars." Marmont signaled also, to Berthier and the English, that he had not been seeking a general action with the Allies when he crossed into Portugal and did not retreat because he feared one. He also revealed that he considered he had been sent on an ill-conceived mission, writing *en clair*, "Your highness may judge from this that the results of the diversion that I tried to make in support of the Army of the South are more or less nil." Thus, the French commander, unable to sublimate his intellectual pride, began quite deliberately sending interesting pointers to Wellington and Scovell. Had Scovell and Wellington been able to read that clutch of coded dispatches in their entirety, they would have learned much about the alarm of the French command and its fears about where the British might strike next.

After Badajoz, Marshals Soult and Marmont both expressed the same conviction in their letters to Paris and Madrid: I will be the next target of Wellington's attack, the other French army must come to my help. There was hardly a general in Spain who had not reflected on the emperor's imminent departure for Poland, each drawing their conclusions about what it meant for their own expectations. Napoleon and his chosen commanders were embarking on an odyssey that promised easy victories (how could Soult forget his moment of glory pummeling the Austrians and Russians at Austerlitz?), opportunities to enhance their reputations in the eyes of wider society, and abundant plunder. The sense, growing now for some months, that they had missed the Russian boat while being becalmed in this ghastly Spanish war led most of the key protagonists in the Iberian Peninsula to try to resign their commands in late 1811 and early 1812. Marmont had already tried to do so through his ADC Colonel Jardet when he went to see Marshal Berthier in Paris. King Joseph had once again been threatening to abdicate (prior to his receiving the supreme command). While Jourdan could hardly have left so soon after coming out, he had made his extreme reluctance to go there in the first place perfectly clear. Jourdan's appointment as chief of staff had itself brought Soult close to resignation.

The spirit of these officers was summed up well by General Foy, who asked Marmont to relieve him of the command of his division: "I ask to be posted to another army and the greatest favor I can request is to be sent somewhere with greater opportunities for manoeuvre, danger and glory." Although busy preparing his campaign against the Russians the emperor soon detected these signs among the proteges he had abandoned in Spain. Through Berthier he wrote back to Marmont on 16 April, "I have prescribed the specific measures necessary to take the initiative, and give the war a character that conforms to the glory of French arms and ends these meanderings and vicissitudes, that already seem to announce a defeated army." To pep up the forgotten army, Berthier ended his dispatch, "On his return from Poland, His Majesty will go to Spain; he hopes that he will only be able to praise what you have done, and that you will once again merit his approbation."

But by April 1812, those sitting on the Portuguese frontier knew that Wellington had gained the advantage and that, notwithstanding Berthier's flowery prose, the emperor would forget about them for months unless they, perish the thought, fell victim to some disaster. It was time for each army commander to look to his personal interest first.

Wellington himself, sitting at his desk in the mayor of Fuente Guinaldo's house, had not yet decided where he would strike next. In a letter to his brother in Cadiz, the British commander expressed his hopes that the repairs on Ciudad Rodrigo's defenses would soon be complete and added, "I don't yet despair, between ourselves, of being able to undertake the expedition into Andalucia this year." Wellington, like some of the French superior officers, had half expected that the fall of Badajoz might precipitate an evacuation of the south by Marshal Soult. Remaining where he was exposed Napoleon's commander in southern Spain to the risk of having his line of withdrawal on Madrid severed by the British.

Still, Soult, for reasons best known to himself, was staying put. Wellington understood from intercepted letters that the French were so desperate for supplies that the Army of the South would have difficulty resisting any move the Allies made until the Andalucian harvest had been reaped in June or July. Just as he had carefully calculated the positions of French troops before launching his attacks on the border fortresses, so the British general now took his time to consider what he could achieve in the time available before the crops were in and the enemy armies were finally able to combine against him in southern Spain. Should he perhaps forget Soult and attack Marmont directly instead? The harvest came a little later in the north, which bought him a week or two more to fight the Army of Portugal that lurked just inside Spain on more favorable terms. It was also true that if he fell upon Marmont, Soult was less likely to march north, for not only was the man notoriously self-centered but the Army of the South also had many troops tied down preventing revolt in the Spanish localities, and this made it harder for them to assemble a few divisions quickly.

One thing was clear to Wellington. Whether he hit Soult or Marmont first, he needed to stop them helping one another. A French pontoon bridge had been built over the River Tagus at Almaraz, roughly halfway between the two French forces. Some magazines had also been established nearby, as he had learned from captured letters. Demolish the bridge and the French would have to go much farther upstream, most of the way east to Madrid in fact, to help one another. Destroy the magazines and it might even mean any French reinforcements would have to turn back. Already before the siege of Badajoz, Wellington had thought about sending the commander of his detached corps in the south, Lieutenant General Rowland Hill, to attack Almaraz, a raid that could only be launched if the British were sure that the area was weakly garrisoned.

On the last day of April, one of Marmont's messengers was seized by Don Julian's lancers on the road from Salamanca to Madrid. His packet of letters contained a note *en clair* about the imminent dispatch of Lieutenant Colonel Colquhoun Grant to France for imprisonment. Wellington had already received at least one note smuggled out from the prisoner and knew he was being held in Salamanca. The intercepted letter recorded Marmont's lack of interest in a possible prisoner exchange. Seeing that all hope of getting his intelligence officer back by such means was gone, the general sent messages to various guerrilla commanders promising a generous reward to the man who would spring Grant from captivity. None however was able to achieve this, and Colquhoun Grant was soon on his way back to France under heavy escort.

Despite this bad news, it was the other elements of Don Julian's haul that caused Wellington to move into action. A letter to Jourdan, although it had been partially ciphered in the *Grand Chiffre*, gave an indication that Marmont's forces were suffering most serious difficulties of supply.

Marmont's letter had been rather well enciphered, so its transitions in and out of code did not give a huge amount away. Had the British staff been able to read it, they would have learned much about the duke of Ragusa's operational problems. The shortage of rations meant that his army was so dispersed that it would require twenty-five days to concentrate and move to the assistance of Soult in the south, whereas the British could switch their axis of operations in just five days. It was, in effect, a carefully constructed and longer version of a theme that was already becoming familiar to Jourdan from his other correspondents Dorsenne, Marmont, Soult and Suchet: My problems are immense, don't expect me to give any great help to anyone else. While for the moment at least the *Grand Chiffre* was protecting much of that information successfully, the passages *en clair* allowed Wellington to learn something of its import. Revealingly, at one point Marmont had said, "I am staying at Salamanca until I am better instructed as to what 164.516 . . . ," and after the coded passage picked up, "with more considerable forces than those that I have until I am certain that Lord Wellington has established his HQ on this frontier."

It could be deduced from the marshal's letter that he was staying put pending a discussion with Jourdan and Joseph on the next strategic move. Knowing from his other sources of information that the Army of Portugal's southerly deployments were not particularly strong, the British commander saw that the moment had come to strike at the junction of the two main armies opposed to him, on the River Tagus just across the Spanish frontier. On 4 May, he sent orders to General Hill to move quickly to destroy the bridge at Almaraz.

CHAPTER TWELVE

*I. dont. 1082. 365. 622. we. w. 489. 669. e. 1085. 898. 326.
decei. 1085. ed. 481. t. 980. 985. 186. t. 843. 688. and.
1297. 536. 174. 1085. 1024 . . . 713. t. 980. 854. e. 326.
536. 700. w. 171. 1015. 1008. de. t. 980. 1015. 181. t.*

THE SALAMANCA CAMPAIGN OPENS, MAY 1812

*E*arly on the morning of 19 May 1812, soldiers of the 71st and 92nd Highlanders found themselves stumbling about in a steep-sided ravine close to the Tagus. The sun had yet to warm the still air, but the men were clammy from the unfortunate combination of a humid season, a red woolen coat and a heavy burden of impedimenta. The men of this British brigade were carrying heavy scaling ladders to help them enter the small forts that protected the Almaraz bridge. They had tried to move into position before dawn, but the country was so difficult that "when daylight . . . at length showed us to each other, we were scattered all over the foot of the hill like strayed sheep, not more in one place than were held together by a ladder." Amid much whispered Gaelic cursing, the sergeants tried to bring the soldiers together again, fearful that at any moment their presence would be discovered and the morning calm would erupt into gunfire.

Almaraz's bridge was defended by a fort at each end. The larger,

Fort Napoleon, was the first target of the assault. Several miles away, the crossing was overlooked by three smaller posts along the Mirabete ridge. These positions had a breathtaking view over the valley of the Tagus and dominated the pass through which the French army's traffic north and south had to go. As the morning air warmed, eagles began circling around the Mirabete ridge, their great spread of wings banked to keep them inside the rising draft of warm air, their eyes scanning left and right in the perpetual search for prey. Neither the men in the forts on the ridge nor their avian companions would have spotted the High-landers that morning, though. The British raid had been carefully planned, and the soldiers were bypassing the Mirabete behind a small ridge that screened them from its far-off lookouts.

The risks involved in taking this roundabout route through rough country were all part of Rowland Hill's unconventional plan. The sol-diers had nicknamed this ruddy-faced general Farmer or Daddy Hill, friendly sobriquets that arose from Hill's even temperament, diligence and paternal concern for his soldiers' welfare. Notwithstanding his benign reputation, Hill had given orders "that every person in the vil-lage of Almaraz should be put to death, there being none but those belonging to the enemy in it." As the troops neared their target, they received the order "Fix bayonets."

Marching to Almaraz had taken two days, and moving to the assault position a couple of hours, but the Highlanders' rush under the guns of the fort was over in minutes. The French were able to fire once or twice before they could hear the shouting of British soldiers just a few feet away at the base of their ramparts. Heavy stones and grenades were hurled over the parapet. Not for the first time, the stormers found an unexpected problem at this most critical juncture. Their ladders were too short. After a few moments, however, they found a way of lashing them together in pairs and soon were mounting their steps and pouring into the fort.

Seeing the British success, the French on the other side of the bridge turned their ordnance on Fort Napoleon, trying to dislodge the British from their new prize. The French cannon fire failed to turn the tide, however, and General Hill's troops soon set about destroying the pon-toon bridge, torching supplies and breaking up the rest of the stores that the French had gathered there. Most of the defenders, despite Daddy Hill's earlier order, were able to flee into the surrounding hills.

The British would have lingered around the Tagus longer to achieve the secondary objective of destroying stores around the crossing point, but an alarm spread by Major General Lumley, the cavalry screen commander, led them to pull back quickly. Still, Wellington's main task had been performed: any attempt by Soult or Marmont to reinforce one another would now take one week or even ten days longer.

News of the Almaraz operation was greeted with satisfaction in Fuente Guinaldo. The perfectionist Wellington dwelt long on Major General Lumley's panic, "taking alarm at the least movement of the enemy." But Hill, the only man Wellington would place his trust in on an independent mission of that kind, had shown himself worthy of that distinction once more. The news of Almaraz and the general appreciation that some great project was about to be launched created an air of expectation about the headquarters. The comings and goings of messengers and ADCs reached a new level of intensity, and conversation around the commander's table each evening was decidedly animated.

There was so much of import to discuss, after all. The prime minister, Spencer Perceval, had been assassinated in the House of Commons, prompting vivid speculation that the killing might be the work of Radicals or even French agents, until it turned out that the assassin was an insane bankrupt. Nevertheless, this violent act produced a great deal of maneuvering by two of Lord Wellington's correspondents, his brother Lord Wellesley and the secretary of war, Earl Liverpool, to see if they could form a new government. Having been born and bred to this kind of Tory intrigue, Wellington, behind his customary mask of inscrutibility, awaited the outcome of this new campaign at Westminster just as keenly as he did that of Napoleon's expedition to Russia.

Napoleon's Polish war (for the emperor referred to it as such, scarcely imagining he would have to go as far as Russia itself) was an altogether safer topic for table talk than London politics. Major Cocks, who had dropped in for dinner before setting off for Lisbon, felt that the Russians would be able to draw the French deep into their country and do them all sorts of mischief. D'Urban believed the emperor intended "amid the blaze of a successful Russian war to throw the Peninsula and his defeats there into the shade." Wellington, of course, would have had the last word in these ruminations and his view was that whatever the outcome of the eastern campaign, it had precipitated a weakening of forces in Spain, a situation that was to his advantage but could not go on forever. His thinking in 1809, prior to Talavera, had been similar, but this time he had far better intelligence about the numbers and movements of French forces—in particular the withdrawal of two divisions of Imperial Guard from northern Spain, which had left the Army of the North running from one rebellious conflagration to another. This disorder was once again requiring some of Marmont's troops to move up northward, weakening his central deployment in the plains around Salamanca.

More and more it seemed to Wellington that Marmont should be the target of his next operation. There were one or two months in which to take advantage of the fresh fodder in the fields and the drier weather. An attack on Marmont, if successful, would eventually force an evacuation of Andalucia. If he struck Soult first, though, the Army of Portugal might either move down to help him or just remain where it was, keeping its communications with Madrid and France open. On 26 May Wellington sat at his desk in Fuente Guinaldo and drew all of these arguments together in a letter to the secretary of war, which concluded: "I propose, therefore, as soon as ever the magazines of the army are brought forward . . . to endeavor, if possible, to bring Marmont to a general action . . . I am of the opinion also that I shall have the advantage in the action, and that this is the period of all others in which such a measure should be tried." This was a momentous decision. It marked the first time since his return to Portugal three years before that Wellington was going to try his hand at an offensive battle. Waiting for the enemy to come to him, at Talavera, Busaco or Fuentes de Oñoro, had worked very well, because it had always allowed him to choose the ground, a judgment of which he was the master.

There was another reason for striking the Army of Portugal first, and it was based on the information gleaned from intercepted correspondence. A further package of captured letters, dated 1 May, had revealed much about the relations between the senior French commanders. Whoever had prepared these dispatches was guilty of an unpardonable lapse in security. In a letter to Dorsenne, the king's secretary had included a copy of another missive from Marmont to Madrid in April—a copy, however, that was entirely *en clair*. Scovell must have treated the arrival of every subsequent messenger in Guinaldo's little plaza with nervous excitement. Had some guerrilla commander intercepted and sent in an original of that same letter, one in cipher, then the French higher command code would have been blown apart. Unfortunately for Scovell, who was devoting long hours to deciphering, the original never appeared. The cipher therefore remained a puzzle to which he could only find a partial solution.

The *en clair* copy of Marmont's letter did however provide a vital insight into the row that had broken out between Joseph and Dorsenne after Napoleon transferred the command of his armies. Dorsenne was refusing to cooperate with any orders coming from Madrid. Whether by oversight or by some game of *divide et impera*,* Berthier's instructions to the two men had been different. The notice of the transfer of command sent to Joseph had included Dorsenne and his Army of the North, but the general himself had received no such order. Indeed, Napoleon's note to Berthier prompting the change had not mentioned Dorsenne.

This new information would have helped Scovell in opening up much further Dorsenne's sloppily ciphered letter of 16 April. Looking again at its second paragraph:

> "In the letter of 16th March, 1207 announced 516.1264 was giving 703.1328 command of 409. 1327.1333.210.249.523, but was making 1165. 1060.1238.820. Your Excellency will appreciate then 139.229.531.305.69.862.605. to make the efforts required of me. 187.609 I would humbly assure 73.516.918. will not neglect any opportunity to 605 give a full account of everything that could interest 240.196 and that requires his attention."

Looking at the first sentence, early work already suggested two of the codes:

> "In the letter of 16th March, 1207 announced 516 [that]1264 was giving 703.1328 command of

---

*Divide and rule.

409.1327.1333.210 [and]249.523, but was making
1165.1060.1238.820."

Reading the 1 May dispatches, it became fairly obvious that 1207 was Berthier, 1264 the emperor and 1328 seemed to be Joseph. It could then be deduced that 1327 and 1333 were Soult and Marmont's armies (although not which was which: that 1333 was the Army of Portugal became apparent when looking at some of Marmont's letters). The phrase "but was making 1165.1060.1238.820," then appears to be something like "but was making an exception of the Army of the North."

The uncoded copy of Marmont's April letter may not have turned up in its ciphered form, but the others in the 1 May packet reproduced some of its phrases, since some dealt with the same business. The commander of the Army of Portugal had evidently asked Dorsenne to send a division to Valladolid in support of his operations. In a partially encoded 1 May letter from Jourdan to Marmont, the chief of staff in Madrid noted: "The General has just replied to me that this army is not under the King's orders; HM cannot, as you ask, order General Count Dorsenne 13.577.264.90.1282.544.118.1045.514.2.1202." Insert the meanings of 2 and 13 and it reads: ". . . order General Count Dorsenne to 577.264.90.1282.544.118.1045.514 to 1202." In this scheme, 1202, it becomes clear, is Valladolid, 577 is likely to mean *order* or *send* and so on.

The impact of each of these discoveries became magnified when transferred to other contexts in different messages. By the end of May 1812 Scovell was beginning to get a real toehold on the slippery precipice of the code. As he worked away on the letters, Scovell jotted his hypotheses on scraps of paper—envelopes, official forms, whatever came to hand. He drew up a table about two feet wide and eighteen inches high, marked in columns of one hundred numbers, much like the deciphering tables issued to the French marshals themselves. When he had some confidence in the value of a number, it migrated from the bits of paper to his table.

As Major Scovell tried to attack the Paris Cipher, he was still expected to fulfill his other duties as commander of the Guides and as an AQMG on the staff. Wellington might have been most anxious to receive the key, but it was not a reason to upset the regularity of the quarter master general's department and the smooth running of head-quarters. Code breaking was therefore an activity that he had to pursue in spare moments, often by candlelight in his billet in Guinaldo. Bit by bit, though, he was building up the numbers on his table, scrawling them with his scratchy quill. Sometimes, when he saw a hypothesis handsomely confirmed, he would have the satisfaction of underlining the word on his table. This precious piece of paper was folded into his Conradus notebook and kept about his person. And yet, it was still too early to celebrate the breaking of Joseph's code. Although there were scores of entries on Scovell's chart, there was still a great deal of the cipher that remained obscured to him.

These gaps in Scovell's knowledge of the cipher perplexed Wellington. After all, the Army of Portugal codes had been broken in a couple of days. A few good discoveries had usually sufficed to prize the whole thing apart. Yet here was Scovell, still plodding away with more than a dozen specimens of the Great Paris Cipher, unable to provide the key. With the army preparing to march on Marmont, Wellington was impatient; it was imperative that progress be made quickly.

What else could be done? The Spanish had some decipherers at Cadiz, Wellington knew that. There was also the little office in London, off Abchurch Street, where the foreign secretary and prime minister retained a few fellows skilled in the black arts of secret writing. But sending a dispatch to England or Cadiz would take time; heaven knows when it might come back. There was risk, too, for some minister might boast of the discovery and it would end up in the newspapers. Similarly, if the key were intercepted on its return journey by some French privateer, word would soon get back to Madrid and the whole labor of deciphering would be rendered pointless. There were definitely advantages to keeping this work in his own headquarters. He would allow Scovell more time, but his patience had its limits.

In Salamanca, Marmont was learning of Wellington's preparations through his own network of spies. The bringing forward of magazines announced in Wellington's letter to London was becoming visible to the muleteers and intinerant lemonade sellers who journeyed back and forth across the frontier. Great Portuguese mule trains were coming up from

Guarda toward Vila Formosa on the border. Some British battalions were also in motion. On 1 June, Marmont wrote to Jourdan, "Lord Wellington remains at Fuente Guinaldo and the stores he has gathered there are building up in an incredible fashion. It seems certain that the campaign will begin here in ten days and that the enemy will march on Salamanca."

The marshal's intelligence, in both its senses, was most acute. He and Wellington were beginning to understand one another and the potentially decisive nature of the contest that was about to start. Just to make sure that his adversary appreciated this all, Marmont resorted once more to his expedient of leaving those words about Wellington's intentions *en clair*. His message got through, for Marmont followed usual procedures and sent duplicates. One messenger was detained by guerrillas and in less than a week the British general had read it and was soon telling London about his opponent's good judgment.

In Madrid, Joseph and his chief of staff awaited events with a sense of enraged impotence. Jourdan had drawn up a memorandum at the end of May outlining what needed to be done in order to defend French interests in Spain. The document showed that Jourdan remained a sound strategist, even if he had long forfeited the emperor's respect. It went through the different armies under the king's command, noting their poor state and the recalcitrance of their commanders before concluding, "The Imperial armies can undertake nothing other than the occupation of the conquered provinces: one can also see that if Lord Wellington . . . falls on the Army of the South or of Portugal, the army under attack will not be in a state to resist him." Jourdan could see that after the destruction of the Almaraz bridge, these two armies could do little to help one another rapidly. The answer, the king's adviser believed, lay in the creation of a powerful central reserve under his own hand that could move to assist either army on the frontier and help defend the capital itself. This clear-sighted blueprint was sent to the minister of war in Paris, who showed his own powerlessness and intellectual timidity by replying with a restatement of the emperor's beliefs that no territory should be relinquished, that the French should maintain "an imposing attitude" toward Wellington (an empty piece of imperial *bragadoccio* if ever there was one) and that the forces at Joseph's disposal allowed him to do whatever the situation demanded.

For the two men nominally running the war in Madrid, irritation over the minister left to mind the shop in Paris and incapable of understanding the gravity of the Iberian situation was minor compared to that engendered by the different army commanders' plain disobedience. Marshal Soult's letters still placed his own command, in Andalucia, at the center of all of Wellington's designs. Even though, as Jourdan remarked by early June, "it was clear to everybody, except the Duke of Dalmatia, that the danger was to the Army of Portugal." Soult in turn argued that the entire defense of Spain should gravitate southward, even if this meant giving up Madrid and, by implication, any overland connection with France. Soult's letters ran so squarely counter to what all logic in Madrid (or indeed in Wellington's own headquarters) dictated, that they left the king quite puzzled. It was decided to send an emissary to Seville to find out what on earth the duke thought he was doing. The choice fell upon Colonel Francois Desprez, a thirty-four-year-old officer of the engineers from Amiens. As the 1812 campaign progressed, Desprez found himself cast in the unhappy role of sherpa, trekking back and forth between the mountainous egos of the marshallate. Moreover, his mission to Seville required him to travel down some of the most dangerous roads in Spain.

Antoine Fée, the young pharmacist to a dragoon regiment serving in Andalucia's principal city, could have saved Colonel Desprez the journey. He had already become disgusted by Soult's regime:

> "The Marshal, commander of the Army of the South, seemed to be more the King of Andalucia than the Emperor's humble lieutenant. No monarch surrounded himself with greater majesty, no court was more submissive than his. . . . On Sunday, elite troops lined the route to the Cathedral, awaiting their general in chief. He was followed by the civic authorities and a distinguished staff. This whole gilded entourage wore smiles or a certain look; he rewarded one or the other with a cold and mannered dignity."

Soult had not only taken on the affectations of a monarch, but he was also helping himself liberally to the wealth of southern Spain, confiscating treasures such as old master paintings by Murillo and Velasquez that were worth a fortune. He was quite certain that he was not going to relinquish his domains, whatever that old fool Jourdan said in Madrid. Desprez discovered in his meeting that Soult bitterly resented Jourdan's appointment as chief of staff, a job that he felt was his by right, and that he had no intention of sending forces to help Marmont if he came under attack by Wellington.

As for Dorsenne and Suchet, they had already manifested a similar spirit in their letters. The commander of the Army of the North had made clear that he could not support Marmont, and Suchet, in charge on the east coast, had refused a request to provide a division for Jourdan's new central reserve.

Why were Soult or Dorsenne not sacked for insubordination? Jourdan argued in his memoirs: "These chiefs were important personalities, secured in command by the Emperor, who had his confidence and were in correspondence with him and his ministers: the King was reluctant to displease his brother and excite his jealousy or unhappiness by removing them from the army." Little did Joseph appreciate it at the time, but his reluctance to displease was to be his undoing.

At Wellington's headquarters, there was not yet any intimation of the kind of views Soult expressed so bluntly to Colonel Desprez. On the contrary, intercepted letters from the king to the duke of Dalmatia had led the British general to believe that the Army of the South was expected to make a strong detachment to the north once Marmont came under attack. Scovell's grasp of the *Grand Chiffre* had grown sufficiently strong for him to be able to get some sense of these coded orders from Joseph. Unfortunately for Britain's intelligence effort, Soult's replies had not been intercepted.

Wellington found the fragmented knowledge of the contents of these messages unbearable. He had left a strong Allied detachment under Lieutenant General Rowland Hill to guard the southern entry into Portugal. But what if the king's orders had directed Soult to make mischief somewhere between the traditional northern and southern invasion routes? After all, it was through the mountainous country of the central border region that France's first attack on Portugal had taken place in 1807, and indeed the British move toward Madrid in July 1809. The thought of this vexed Wellington considerably. Toward the end of May, Marshal Beresford had been sent out to examine this inhospitable country, accompanied by Scovell and some Mounted Guides. They had found one or two places where an army might be able to pass with its artillery, and this raised the prospect of a French corps appearing in the Allied rear some weeks or even days after he had launched his offensive increased Wellington's concerns.

It was imperative that as much as possible be found out about the contents of the king's coded messages to Soult and to his subordinate commander, the Count D'Erlon, who was closest to this possible route into Portugal. On 7 June, Wellington sent copies of three of the messages to his brother, the British minister at Cadiz. These were to be passed on to the Spanish War Ministry to see if they could shed any further light on the contents. Perhaps their decipherers would succeed more quickly than Scovell.

Meanwhile, the divisions of Wellington's army had broken camp and were building up on the Spanish frontier. His attack force would number about 50,000. The stalwarts of the Light Division would be in the van, backed up by six divisions of infantry. There were also four cavalry brigades, totaling around thirty-five hundred sabers. Half of this mounted force would be used for scouting and light actions. The other portion (Le Marchant's brigade and one under the old German cavalry officer General Bock) were made up of heavy cavalry, a precious reserve that could be used to turn the tide in a crucial moment.

Wellington intended to launch himself forward and smash Marmont's army, ideally on the plain of the River Tormes, before the French would be able to concentrate properly. In planning his move, Wellington had not neglected to summon up all of the alarms and excursions that the guerrillas and Spanish army could provide. General Ballasteros was once again incited to move on Seville, threatening Marshal Soult's base. Others were asked to move forward in Galicia and Asturias to the northwest and north of the intended area of operations. The logic behind these attacks was to be the same as it had been in January 1812: to anchor French detachments to the points where they stood and prevent them from answering any of Marmont's signals for a general concentration.

Marmont gained scraps of intelligence as all this was under way. His analysis of the information at his disposal had been sufficiently good to have expected attack on or around 10 June. He knew better than anyone that it would take him time to concentrate, even without the Spanish diversions. He had therefore already sent word out to some of his outlying garrisons to begin their march.

Despite this, as the British were poised to launch their attack, Marmont's troops were still scattered. His available forces included thirty-six thousand infantry and twenty-eight thousand cavalry. The enemy exceeded this by more than ten thousand, and it was clear he could not face Wellington with these numbers. Once Brenier and Bonnet had come in and joined him with their divisions, as well as men from some other outlying posts, he would have a field force of fifty thousand. Then he could fight if he had to. All the better if he could bring in some more, especially more cavalry and guns, from the Army of the North or Joseph's Army of the Center. These reinforcements were requested urgently.

In the meantime, Marmont knew that once Wellington allowed his juggernaut to begin rolling down from the border highlands it could not be stopped by inferior forces. There was no point seeking an action in front of Salamanca, he would just get crushed. Instead, the marshal resolved just to try to slow the enemy down a little by leaving a couple of strong forts in the center of this city, redoubts skillfully built to dominate the bridges over the River Tormes. It would be very hard for Wellington to use those causeways (necessary for the transit of supplies and heavy guns) under French fire, which would hamper any movement forward and force the British to lose time trying to storm the works. Once the marshal had concentrated fifty thousand or even more men, then he would seek his own battle, giving a forceful demonstration of his powers to the English and those who whispered about him in Madrid.

On the evening of 12 June, the soldiers of Wellington's army rested around their bivouacs. They sat in clumps under the oaks of the border country, pipe-claying the white cross belts that carried their fighting kit, joining in songs and drinking some of the wine that sutlers brought out from Rodrigo or Guinaldo. They all knew what awaited them: some bloody hard marching that required each man to have two or three spare pairs of shoes in his knapsack. As the sun sank on the western horizon, young officers toured about checking that their men had packed only what the regulations allowed. They had enough to carry as it was, sixty or seventy pounds in marching order, so a flask of grog or a bag of potatoes might make the difference between a good marcher and a straggler. In the 4th or Light Divisions, which had suffered most heavily at Badajoz, there were many new drafts, callow youths who sat around and listened to the yarns of old soldiers with patched clothes and scarred bodies. Several hundred convalescents had come up too, men who had been wounded earlier in the campaign but were now fit to march again. Their reunions with those who had survived the horrors of April's siege created a festive atmosphere in the dark forests.

As was customary on the eve of a great movement, there was no rest for the staff. The burden of organizing the army's march had fallen on thirty-one-year-old William De Lancey, the American-born deputy quarter master general. George Murray, formerly his chief, had been summoned back to Britain by Horse Guards, much to Wellington's chagrin. In the headquarters, young deputy assistants scribbled out copies of De Lancey's orders for the dragoons or Guides who kept appearing in the door and were bound for the commander of each division or brigade. "The Light Division and 1st Hussars to form the advanced guard of the Army," De Lancey's instructions began. The march was to be in three columns: Sir Thomas Graham commanding the right, Picton the left, with the center under Wellington's hawklike gaze. Below these introductory remarks, a table had been drawn showing where each of the three columns would bivouac on each of the following three nights. For years, Wellington's strategy had been defensive, aimed above all at preserving the British army's toehold in Iberia: now it was time to go forward.

CHAPTER THIRTEEN

S. dont. 1082. 365. eve. we. w. 439. 669. ev. 898. 326.
deceived. 481. t. 980. 985. 186. t. 843. 688. and.
1297. 536. 174. o. 1024 . . . 713. t. 980. 854. e. 326.
536. 700. w. 171. 1015. 1003. de. t. 980. 1015. 131. t.

The Great Cipher Under Attack,
June and July 1812

*T*he people of Salamanca did not stint as the first British soldiers entered their city on 17 June 1812. Everything flowed in abundance: shouts of *Viva!*; cups of local wine; petals scattered from upstairs windows and kisses to the bronzed cheeks of Wellington's host. The townfolk "were out of their senses at having got rid of the French," wrote one young officer, "and nearly pulled Lord Wellington off his horse." Warre, of Beresford's staff, wrote in a letter to his mother, "It was quite affecting to see the joy of the inhabitants. Many absolutely cried for joy, and we were embraced or had to shake hands with everybody we met. One old woman hugged and kissed [Wellington] to his great annoyance and one man literally kissed my horse as I rode into the town."

It was not just that the British commander disdained such effusions of unbridled emotion; he was trying to concentrate on giving battle. The French had not cleared out of the city entirely; their forts still dominated the old Roman bridge over the Tormes. Although he had learned of their construction from his spies in the city, he did not expect the strength of one work in particular (the San Vicente convent) or the complication of trying to assault it in the midst of some impromptu street fiesta. Battalions of the 6th Division were marched up to the river and stood under arms, ready to receive an order to attack at any moment. They were still being mobbed by the public, while the staff looked on, hoping these citizens would not soon be exposed to a hot fire.

As the hours passed, Wellington realized that the main position, the San Vicente convent, had been barricaded and built into a position of such strength that it could not simply be rushed by his men. It stood on a natural promontory, with sheer faces on two of its sides. Houses had been demolished on the convent's other flanks, giving French gunners a clear field of fire and providing debris to build a considerable *fausse braie*. Battering guns would be needed, and the labors of Wellington's engineers. Scovell, one of the few officers in the army to have been in Salamanca before (while accompanying Moore's expedition in 1808), was most struck by the destruction of buildings in that elegant university city that had been necessary to create these French positions.

Salamanca's strange atmosphere that 17 June, became all the more peculiar when the French defenders started to use their guns. The center of the city echoed their fire and citizens who had one minute been running to greet the British were sent scurrying for their lives the next as projectiles whizzed overhead.

Having put the 6th Division into positions around the forts, Wellington pushed the rest of the army beyond the city, using two fords to cross the Tormes. He knew Marmont was not far away, since he had cleared out just ahead of him during the early hours of the morning.

Wellington had begun calculating the strength of the forces opposed to him with an almost obsessive diligence, knowing that he would not attack if he was outnumbered. On setting out a few days earlier, on 13 June, he had assumed that he would have a comfortable superiority over Marmont. He had been concerned however to receive an intercepted letter the following day that contained, *en clair*, nothing less than the army of Portugal's Morning State for 1 April. This precise listing of every man available for duty in each regiment showed that the duke of Ragusa's army numbered 51,492 in all, made up of 43,396 infantry, 3,204 cavalry and 3,393 artillery. The British commander had written to Lieutenant General Graham, "notwithstanding that the enemy is considerably stronger than I believed he was, I propose to continue our present movement forward."

He had penned that before observing the Salamanca forts. Now that he knew their strength his worries surfaced again. Wellington understood that Marmont had not yet concentrated these 51,492 men and needed time to do so. By placing the Salamanca forts in Wellington's way, he might just delay the British enough to allow him to unite the entire Army of Portugal.

On the day the British entered Salamanca, Wellington calculated that the enemy field army was not more than 47,800 (in fact it was considerably less). But when the British commander totted up how many troops he could bring to the Tormes plains beyond the city, he would have to subtract his own 6th Division, which would have to be left behind to cover the city's forts, and it was possible that the British force might then no longer outnumber Marmont. What was more, Wellington knew from messages intercepted in the Army of Portugal cipher (which was still in use in this area) that the last of Marmont's forces, Bonnet's division, was probably only two or three marches away. Taking a deliberately cautious view, Wellington calculated that by 19 or 20 June his opponent could meet him with a superiority of four thousand to five thousand men. All of this undermined the initial confidence with which the British general had struck into Spain. Wellington did not intend to give battle on inferior terms, unless he was in one of those strong defensive positions that he could choose so well.

Wellington believed that Marmont's sense of honor would require him to do something to save the men in the forts. He therefore decided to search out a strong defensive position where such intentions might cause his enemy to throw the Army of Portugal onto a strong British defense. He found it a few miles northeast of Salamanca where the ridge of San Christoval commands the rolling country of the city's hinterland. There he marched his men into fields of waist-high corn, onto the ridge. Monsieur le Marechal was most welcome to present himself here and learn the same lesson Marshal Masséna, his predecessor, had at Busaco.

*　　　*　　　*

In the duke of Ragusa's camp, the numbers looked a good deal less encouraging even than they did to Wellington. Marmont knew that the force he had concentrated and had immediately available did not much exceed thirty thousand, since they had not been coming together as quickly as he had hoped. The new circumstances would oblige him to move forward and, as the emperor might put it, show an imposing attitude. As for actually giving battle, this could not be considered until he had brought in his last divisions and hopefully some additional reinforcements from the Army of the North. Having seen his troops gathered and in motion across the plains, he had every confidence in their abilities. The men of the Army of Portugal included many veterans, and they were inured to hard marching. Their officers had drilled their men to the point that a sudden change of formation or an order to turn an entire division through right angles and then assume a defensive position could be carried out with swiftness and precision.

Among the rank and file, Marmont was a popular leader. The soldiers sometimes chanted a song from the Austrian campaign three years earlier. One of its verses went:

> La France a nommé MacDonald,
> L'armée a nommé Oudinot,
> L'Amitie a nommé Marmont!

Loosely translated, it meant "France appointed [Marshal] MacDonald, the army appointed Oudinot and friendship appointed Marmont." It celebrated their marshal's march hundreds of miles from the Balkans to join Napoleon on the Danube in 1809. One officer noted that Marmont "was most courageous and very much loved for the care he took of the soldiers." The spirits of the French lower ranks were raised by the idea that they were on their way to an honorable affair with the English, rather than having to put up with more of the bitter counter-guerrilla fight in the Spanish countryside. Just as the British footslogger corrupted the names of his adversaries (the duke of Dalmatia becoming the duke of Damnation), the French infantry, as they marched across the Castillian fields, cursed Wellington as *Vilainjeton*, a phrase that suggested both meanness and duplicity. The senior officers of this force saw matters somewhat differently, and many openly questioned their chief's abilities, but Marmont knew he could rely on them to act with their customary professionalism.

It was this faith in his army's abilities, particularly of maneuver, that conditioned Marmont's approach to his confrontation with Wellington. He would send divisions this way and that, try to outflank the English, conduct night marches, whatever: the aim would be to open a gap between two British corps so that they could not support one another. Or he might disorder some formation by forcing it to turn about in some rough country, perhaps before a river. At this point he would fall upon them, concentrating his own force at a weak point and breaking one or two of Wellington's outlying divisions, just as he had nearly succeeded in doing at El Bodon in September 1811. Marmont summed up this strategy in a letter to King Joseph: "I will maneouvre about Salamanca in such a way as to divide or set in motion the English army and profit from that."

On 20 June, at about 4 P.M., Marmont marched into sight of the San Christoval position. There was a flurry of activity atop the ridge as British officers scrambled for their telescopes. They could see three columns on parallel tracks marching toward them. The sandy soil crumbled under the weight of these tramping feet, sending a cloud of ochre dust into the sky behind each phalanx.

Wellington's staff galloped about, trying to seek a better vantage point, conferring with one another. How many regiments do you make it, Somerset? Do you see that officer, followed by his suite on the left there, is that Marmont?

The British general looked down: battle could now be joined very quickly indeed. Some cannon fire into the heads of the French columns to disorder them, followed by a brisk movement downhill from half a dozen Allied divisions. He might catch the French before they'd even had a chance to deploy from their lines of march, hammering the columns at the front, and sending broken battalions fleeing backward, breaking up the formations behind.

The staff looked to their chief, waiting for him to start scribbling directives and send them galloping to every corner of the army. Wellington kept his counsel. No attack was ordered. Only a very few men, De Lancey, Somerset and Scovell among them, could have guessed the reasons for his hesitation, for only they were versed in the secret business of headquarters. Wellington could not believe that Marmont was offering battle with what seemed to be no more than thirty thousand men. There must be two or three divisions unaccounted for, which, the general knew from intercepted letters, must be with Marmont soon. Even if Bonnet had been delayed by Spanish attacks, Wellington had to assume his and the other missing troops would be up, sooner or later. Might they suddenly appear on one of his flanks, at some point that could even threaten the British line of communications?

As the French began deploying from column of march and taking up positions, in some places no more than five hundred yards in front, their batteries began sending shot into the British lines, sending some dragoons somersaulting backward off their mounts, dead before they'd hit the ground. Another ball whizzed overhead of the 79th Highlanders, causing one ambitious young officer to note dryly, "a round shot, 8lbs, went very near Major Lawrie who stands in my way for promotion!" At the foot of the ridge, a sharp fusillade between skirmishers began; the British were being forced back. Some green troops of the 68th were forced out of a village at the right of the British position. Wellington summoned his generals.

The light faded as the divisional commanders clustered around their chief: Cotton in his outlandish hussar's uniform; Baron Alten, the German commanding the Light Division; Picton (whose disregard of dress regulations meant he usually wore a top hat, civilian coat and carried an umbrella); Leith and Cole. Wellington stood with his map, outlining the enemy dispositions and the action to be taken should Marmont attack at one point or another. Seeing this group, the French gunners could not resist this tempting target. With a bang and a whoosh they started sending cannonballs toward Wellington and his generals with that distinctive ripping sound they all knew only too well. "Very little confusion was occasioned," noted one of those present. "His Lordship moved a few paces and continued his directions."

Coolness under fire was one thing, but did Wellington have the mettle to fall upon the army that Marmont had laid open in front of him?

At dawn on the twenty-first, the artillery fire and skirmishing were rejoined. The British troops had slept on beds of flattened corn, their muskets by their sides, ready for anything that might happen in the night. In the light of day, their officers could see that the French had barricaded two villages at the base of the ridge, turning them into strongpoints.

And still, Wellington was wondering: Is Brennier up? Where is Bonnet? He was also still deeply concerned than the Count D'Erlon, with his corps of fifteen thousand, might appear somewhere in his rear, racing up from positions further south, opposite Lieutenant General Hill in Estremadura.

Later that day, two French deserters were brought in and interrogated. Bonnet was expected at any moment with eight thousand men, they said. With that, the general resolved: He was not going to attack Marmont and would take steps to protect his flanks or rear. He pulled the Light Division back a couple of miles to secure a line of withdrawal, one of the fords over the Tormes.

The reluctance to attack, especially on the twentieth when less than half of Marmont's force had shown itself, disappointed many officers in the army, including Scovell, who wrote, "Had it taken place, I have little doubt of the event, as we have since learnt they had but 15,000 [sic] Bayonets in the Field, nor do I think their Columns could have deployed before we should have been upon them."

As the second day of this impasse ended, Marmont convened a meeting of his own generals. The marshal's old classmate General Foy was among them and recorded this council of war. As Wellington had anticipated, one of the main arguments concerned the need to rescue the Army of Portugal's troops in the Salamanca forts a few miles away. Marmont intimated that they must try to force their way through, but sought the opinions of others. Foy kept his counsel and waited to see what the others would say. Most of them seemed to second their chief's resolution. Then it was Clausel's turn. Anyone who had been at Busaco, where Masséna had come unstuck in 1810, knew the folly of attacking Wellington on such a strong defensive feature, he said. They did not have the numbers to defeat him. They would be exposing themselves to an inglorious defeat. The mention of Busaco was enough to turn the mood of the meeting; Maucune and Foy had both taken bullets there. Foy recorded his own contribution: "I thought that just because we had left a garrison of 400 in the Salamanca Fort, there was no point getting 6,000 killed and hazarding the honor of our arms to get them out . . . the Marshal was unhappy; he thought the generals were conspiring against his plans." Marmont may have been secretly quite pleased, but he had to affect this attitude if for no other reason than it would have seemed callous to abandon the garrison of the fort.

When all was said and done, Marmont, Foy and the other divisional generals knew that a substantial reinforcement was needed to guarantee victory. They understood well enough to expect nothing from the "Sultan of Andalucia," as they disparaged Soult. The Army of the North would have to help, perhaps that of the Center also, although Joseph's force could only deploy a few thousand troops.

Wellington and the staff went back into Salamanca, where heavy guns were set up, and steps were prepared for the siege of the San Vicente fortified convent. For the general, there was an opportunity to receive his secret correspondent, Father Patrick Curtis, and show him the respect due to such an invaluable spy. Some officers questioned the wisdom of this, for once the hysteria of Salamanca's liberation calmed down, it became apparent that a pro-French party still existed among its people and they would surely get to hear of Curtis's visit. Many of the staff simply collapsed into bed after days on the San Christoval position with, as one of them complained, never more than four hours' sleep a night.

While Marmont had come forward to challenge his enemy, Don Julian's guerrillas had once more made their way around the flanks and rear of the French army. More captured messages were brought into town.

A few days in Salamanca had allowed Scovell to push his calculations forward considerably. He was working from dozens of dispatches, some of them up to twenty pages, and it was most likely in some smoky billet in this Spanish university town that he was able to draw together, for the first time, all of the discoveries he had jotted on scraps of paper and the deciphering table.

Records suggest that the assistant quarter master general had entered values for about 450 of the 1,400 cipher numbers by the end of June. Even though a small number of Scovell's suppositions were actually wrong, this was solid progress, and represented rather more than one-third of the code, since there were a few score numbers that had never been filled in by the French on their enciphering tables, particularly in the series 1,201–1,400.

With his knowledge of the earlier ciphers he had worked on, Scovell would have known that a code number that did not appear in any of the messages was not really worth worrying about. There were perhaps one hundred entries in the cipher standing for places or terms irrelevant in Peninsular warfare that fell into this category. Vacant code numbers did find their way into some of the messages, but Scovell would already have spotted many of them.

But viewed from the perspective of someone who was not a specialist decipherer, and who was a perfectionist to boot, Scovell's fold-out crib showing his decoding efforts contained a disturbing number of blank spaces and crossings out. Wellington resolved that he must obtain the services of the best decipherers in Britain to join the attack on the Great Paris Cipher. Wellington felt it was time to share Scovell's early work with London. Accordingly he wrote off to London on 25 June, enclosing Scovell's early results and copies of three letters in the *Grand Chiffre*. The general felt that much of the *Grand Chiffre* still remained a mystery to him and he thought that Whitehall would also find it useful, since "it is the same cipher used by the Emperor's ministers, and the discovery of the key, therefore, may be important for other objects as well as for our operations." In this last suggestion, the general showed his limited knowledge of French secret writing, for the *Grands Chiffres* being used by Napoleon in eastern Europe, for example, were based on sheets of the 1750 diplomatic table and made up with completely different ciphers.

Since the commander of forces had enclosed Scovell's work to date, we have an excellent insight into what the staff were able to make of the dispatches brought into Salamanca at the end of that second week of the campaign. A tiny scrap of paper concealed in the clothing of a Spanish messenger revealed Marmont's thoughts as he marched from the San Christoval position:

> *"I do not believe I should have attacked yesterday without knowing the results and my observations convinced me 145.69.918.718.58.168.713.919. 566.1168.173.58.614.170.402.53.314.58.1185.862 .13.773.713.843.1015.637.1122.64.906.504.62?.530 .521.217.1122.424.402.566.134.212.69.1252.722. 1127.1137.1111.314.164.874.81.74?.217.1122.1171 .320.1079.741.691.864 in a state to undertake anything 40.2.1111.920.267.862.753.168.711.58. 467. 132.13.1388 in such a way 2.906.238.617. 691.906. 51.1214.164.2. 906.891.907.290"*

Using the codes already discovered by Scovell, this became:

> *"I do not believe I should have attacked yesterday without knowing the results and my observations convinced me as long as I do not have forces at least e 53 es to theirs, I must play for time awaiting the arrival of the forces of the North that 1252 promised and that if 74?. arrive 1079 will put me in a state to undertake anything 40. at that moment 862.753. rai around Salamanca in such a way as to get the English army moving and to 891 iter"*

The first unknown construction *e* 53 *es* is not that difficult to guess, the code 53 stands for *gal* and forms the word *equal* in English. Similarly 1252 seems to be the commander of the Army of the North. Although the last sentence contains some unknowns, the sense of this passage emerges: Marmont was telling his superiors that he would avoid battle until he was reinforced. The fragmentary nature of these partial decipherings may have irked Wellington, but he was sufficiently confident of what had been discovered to tell London on 30 June, "I know from intercepted letters that Marshal Marmont expects to be joined by a division of the Army of the North."

The stalemate between Marmont and Wellington was broken on the twenty-seventh when the defenders of the San Vicente convent finally capitulated. The British had started firing red-hot shot at the roof of the massive building and succeeded in setting it on fire. Even though they had survived one attempted storm and the British siege guns were making little impact on their walls, the defenders had no choice but to surrender. With the forts fallen, the Army of Portugal no longer had any reason to be lingering in such a dangerous and exposed location as the plains of the Tormes, particularly as Wellington would now be free to bring his entire armament into action.

So Marmont ordered a withdrawal about forty miles north to the line of the River Douro (which, in this higher part of its course is called Duero by the Spanish). Wellington's troops swiftly followed them.

The landscape, with its tall fields of billowing corn, vineyards and orchards, seemed lush and wonderful to British soldiers who knew only the barren moorland of the Beira Baixa frontier. There were other pleasant surprises too. The local Villa Verde wine, made from a green grape rather like the whites of northern Portugal, was most refreshing. Officers riding to and fro with dispatches or on reconnaissance discovered that most villages had a café where they could buy a bottle of wine and soothe their parched mouths with lemon ice cream.

For the rank and file, unable to fall out of their column of march to go in search of such delicacies, the heat became a severe trial. Most men felt the backs of their necks, their noses and foreheads burn and blister. The hot dry breeze chapped and broke their lips. In order to try to save his men from the effects of marching all day in this heat, Wellington set predawn reveille even earlier. Major William Warre wrote to his father about the consequences:

> "Our mode of life has been latterly extremely harassing. On the march up we turned out at 3am and only marched part of the day . . . we usually rise at 1am and often, after either riding all day or broiling in the

sun, on a position, which has not a twig to defend us
from the sun, or a drop of water but at a distance, we
do not get anything to eat or home till 9 or 10 at
night, and rise again at one, so that we are all com-
pletely tired, and our faces so burnt that we cannot
bear to touch them."

The Army of Portugal's staff noticed a new energy about their commander as they fell back to the Duero line. While it was evident that this
great natural barrier would give his army a measure of security, many
also assumed he knew something about possible reinforcements. General Foy had a different explanation: he believed the strain on his commander was becoming increasingly obvious. While close to Wellington,
the marshal had been "cold and apathetic," but as soon as they put
some distance between the two armies he was once more "ardent and
enterprising." The divisional commander wrote of Marmont, "He did
not want to deal with problems and always looked for ways around
them." The marshal's tendency to switch between introspection and
bravado had its reflection in the way he ciphered his letters: proud defi-
ance was broadcast *en clair*, real insights into his strategy were locked in
code.

As he fell back toward his new field headquarters on the north bank
of the Duero at Tordesillas, Marmont fired off letters to King Joseph
and General Louis Marie Caffarelli, the new commander of the Army of
the North (Dorsenne, his health broken, had gone home to France,
where he died of tetanus). Marmont stressed the absolute need for reinforcements, particularly of cavalry. One of these messages, from Marmont to Joseph and dated 1 July, was captured. In taking up his new
defensive line, Marmont explained:

"It is from here that I will manoeuvre 68. 85. 1215.
131. 69 I will take the offensive 817. 1009. 318.
33.1168. 1015. 922. 311.215.601.968. 1153 . 122.
879. 1188. 1157. 692. 811. 465. 1345. 210. 1019.
617. 135. 692. 1102. 249. 441. 13. 23. 502 . be able
to operate 868. 497. 1122 .424. 62.1085.44. 1030.
1216. 533. the likelihood of success."

Looking at this message with Scovell's discoveries about the *Grand Chiffre* :

> *"It is from here that I will manoeuvre to defend the Duero or that I will take the offensive as soon as the forces 33.1168.1015.922.* ont *meet up. I need an additional 1157 one thousand five hundred 1345 and 1019 or six thousand infantry men 502 be able to operate 868 on 497 left bank of the Duero with the likelihood of success."*

The first passage of code makes up *reinforcements* and the code 922 that eluded Scovell stood for *au* which joined to the next code (311, which he appears to have known) made *auront,* or *will.* It is quite likely that this context would have allowed a good guess at 1345, which meant *cavalry.* Marmont had in fact also asked for five or six thousand infantry, but this is where a previous deduction led Scovell into a mistake, albeit not one of enormous significance. The information sent to London on 25 June showed he thought the code number 135 meant *six,* when in fact it meant *seven.*

Notwithstanding the gaps in the decipherer's knowledge, this message would have given Wellington a clear sense of what kind of reinforcement Marmont needed to receive before he resumed the offensive. It was not entirely obvious from the letter whether by thousands of extra infantry he meant Bonnet's long-expected division, but this was the assumption in headquarters.

There were two other most important pieces of information in the letter. The first was a complaint by Marmont that not one soldier of the Army of the North's promised reinforcement had arrived in Valladolid, to his rear, by 28 June. The other was this humble sentence: "I dare to beseech your Majesty if you can, send me your cavalry from the Tagus." This was most significant because it allowed Wellington to begin unlocking the secret of where both Joseph's Army of the Center and D'Erlon's corps to the south might be, and what their orders were. If Marmont succeeded in drawing up the former to unite with his troops, then D'Erlon would be left too weak to mount a major strike against central Portugal.

Marmont's letter of 1 July also presented almost comically the

French commander's desire to say one thing to the British who read his mail and another to his masters in Madrid. It contained the passage:

> *"I am not anxious about the future and am confident*
> *of   a   glorious   outcome   81.918.215.74.713.*
> *413.1055.1168.607.711.1100.280."*

Scovell's grasp of the cipher revealed the coded passage to mean "if I receive the reinforcements that I have asked for."

By 5 July, Wellington's headquarters had settled into Rueda, a pleasant town in the wine country a few miles south of the Duero. The British put scouts close to the river but kept their divisions a few miles back from it, denying the French a chance to study their deployment. Marmont's forces, on the other hand, were deployed in strength, ready to receive anyone who attempted to cross this watery line.

Once again, Scovell had a chance to stay put for a few days and set his mind to attacking the cipher. His every waking hour consisted of trying to please his commander and he knew that if he could deliver some breakthrough in deciphering, Wellington would be gratitude itself.

Mulling over the information extracted from Marmont's coded letter of 1 July, the general must indeed have been satisfied, because it had given him new insight into French dispositions. Marmont's complaint about the nonappearance of any troops from the Army of the North helped convince Wellington, along with other reconnaissance reports, that there would not be any substantial reinforcement from this quarter. Some cavalry had been sent off by Caffarelli, and some intercepted uncoded messages helped the British keep track of its progress. Since Marshal Soult would not help either, this left only the force under Madrid's direct control, the Army of the Center, to provide substantial succor to Marmont. Although Wellington had received reports that some of these troops had started marching, he did not know where. They might be intended to join with the Count D'Erlon in some diversionary raid. Now he had clear evidence of Marmont trying to draw the Army of the Center's cavalry into his own field of operations in front of the British main army.

As the hot July days passed on the Duero line, the outposts kept a vigilant watch on French positions and one false alarm followed another of an impending French assault. Wellington could only hope that the guerrillas operating on the other side of the river would warn him of the arrival of any new French forces. Better still they might bring him some dispatch that might tell him how long he had to bring Marmont to battle before that marshal's constant pleas for help finally produced an army that was larger than his own and he would have to turn back toward the Portuguese frontier.

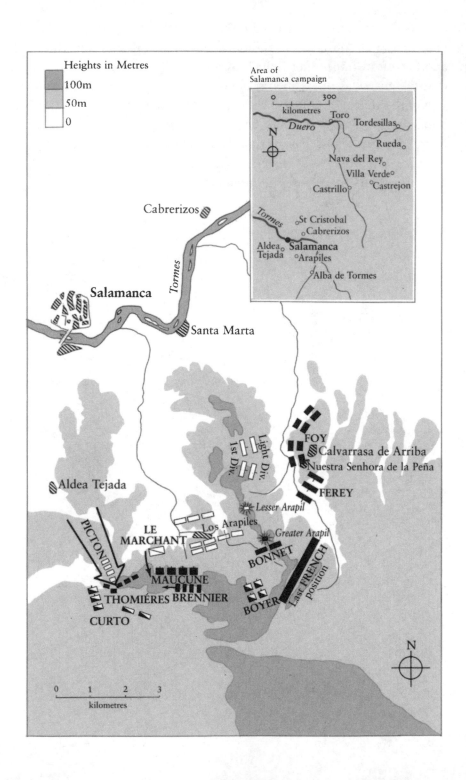

Heights in Metres
100m
50m
0

Area of
Salamanca campaign

kilometres
300

Toro
Duero
Tordesillas
Rueda

Nava del Rey
Villa Verde
Castrejon
Castrillo

Tormes
St Cristobal
Cabrerizos

Aldea
Tejada
Salamanca
Arapiles

Alba de Tormes

Cabrerizos

Salamanca
Tormes

Santa Marta

1st Div.
Light Div.

FOY
Calvarrasa de Arriba
Nuestra Senhora de la Peña

FEREY

Aldea Tejada

Lesser Arapil

PICTON
LE
MARCHANT
Los Arapiles
Greater Arapil

BONNET
Last FRENCH position

MAUCUNE
THOMIÉRES BRENNIER
BOYER

CURTO

0   1   2   3
kilometres

CHAPTER FOURTEEN

*I. dont. 1082. 365. eve. we. we. 669. ev. 398. 326.
deceived. 481. t. 980. 985. 186. t. 843. 688. and.
1297. 536. 174. o. 1024 . . . is. t. 980. 854. e.
326. 536. 700. w. 171. made. t. 980. 1015. 131. t.*

TRIUMPH OVER THE GREAT CIPHER, JULY 1812

*A*fter the campaign's furious start, nobody knew what to make of the long pause on the Duero. The British kept their forces back from the riverbank but allowed lookouts and staff officers to conduct their surveillance there. The river presented a formidable barrier, dissuading the British commander from launching an attack. Day by day the enemy became a little more relaxed and finally began to approach their side at the same time as Wellington's men. Major William Warre, in a letter to his father, described the scene:

> "The French are on one side of the river, and we are
> on the other. Both parties are very civil to each other,
> and both seem on the qui vive for fear the other
> should cross and attack him. It is comical enough to
> see hostile troops quietly watering their horses, or
> washing within 30 or 40 yards of each other, like

> *perfect good friends. We are forbid to talk to them*
> *for fear of spoiling our French, and are therefore*
> *highly profuse in bows and dumbshow. I hate the*
> *very sight of the villains, but it is no use for either*
> *party to annoy the other when nothing is to be*
> *gained by it."*

In Medina del Campo, young Guards officers took advantage of the hiatus in operations to entertain the local gentry. For eight successive evenings, they held dances in their impromptu mess, lavishing champagne and compliments on any half-respectable dancing partner they could find.

While this surreal impasse went on, the more junior members of both armies found themselves at a loss trying to understand their commanders' plans. On 7 July, General Bonnet finally marched into Marmont's camp, bringing sixty-five hundred infantry, a battery of guns and a hundred horse with him. This brought the marshal's infantry and artillery strength to the sort of numbers he felt were a prerequisite for offensive action. He still felt weak in cavalry, having about twelve hundred fewer than his enemy. He addressed this deficit in a remarkably resourceful, if unpopular, way: the Army of Portugal's officers had their personal mounts requisitioned. Troopers whose horses had died or gone lame suddenly found themselves astride some nag that had been carrying a colonel's camp kettle and cognac until the day before. Clearly these horses were untrained in the evolutions required for mounted warfare, and their new masters had but a few days to school them. By this expedient, Marmont had added about a thousand men to his cavalry formations and, if nothing else, that might look impressive through an enemy spyglass.

Marmont was still hoping to receive more cavalry from Caffarelli and King Joseph, but he felt that he was reaching the point where he must bring matters to some sort of conclusion. He had seen for himself at San Christoval that Wellington would not attack, even when he had superior numbers and the advantage of the ground. While he understood his generals' reservations, the time was approaching to disorient this British mediocrity with some brilliant maneuvers and then hit him hard on the open plains of León.

Once Bonnet's division had joined them, Marmont began marching and countermarching up and down the river. Feints were made, fords explored and alarms given. The British had to react to each movement in earnest as their outposts sent back reports. One day after another, divisions were stood to, cavalry formed up near some threatened ford and everyone scorched by the sun for a few hours before being sent back to their bivouacs. Inevitably, frustration began to build among the British officers, who knew that each of these responses had to be conducted with alacrity and precision lest they incur the wrath of their commander, or worse, allow the passage of the French van. One British major wrote home grumpily, "They have manouevred a great deal. In fact they seem to keep their people in constant motion . . . to what end all this marching and countermarching of theirs can be, I cannot guess."

If Marmont's maneuvers were succeeding in their aim of confusing the lesser officers, what of their captain? Wellington, by mid-July, had lost the initiative. He understood that each day's inactivity played into the Army of Portugal's hands. Sooner or later the French would build to a strength where he could not face them in this open country, and then it would be a matter of clapping spurs to his exhausted beast of an army and driving it back toward the Portuguese border.

At his table, Wellington was withdrawn. The staff were perplexed that he had not given battle on the San Christoval position, when the superiority of British numbers was so evident. He understood their inferences and he did not care one jot for their opinions. He had ignored the siren calls of those around him before on at least a dozen occasions during these years of Peninsular campaigning. No, he alone was responsible for the fate of this precious British army and he alone would decide.

And London? That was a more delicate question. He had told them he was seeking a general action with Marmont, an affair that might end with the church bells ringing across Old England, Eagles laid at the Prince Regent's feet and handsome promotions for one and all. If he produced nothing there was bound to be criticism and scorn from the usual voices in the Commons. He might even become the victim of popular lampoon, like the duke of York following his fruitless expedition to Holland. Wellington after all had marched fifty thousand men to the "top of the hill" and was about to march them back again without result. He had lost his earlier opportunity of smashing Marmont while the balance of forces was really favorable. Wellington would have to ready the ministry, through the agency of Earl Bathurst, his new master as secretary of war, for the disappointment of a withdrawal to Portugal.

On 3 July he wrote to Lieutenant General Graham, commanding the army's left wing (who was about to return home sick), "It appears certain that Marmont will not risk an action unless he should have an advantage; and I shall not risk one unless I should have an advantage." The next day, in a letter to Bathurst: "I hope that I am strong enough for Marmont at present," Wellington explained, "but your lordship must see that so much depends on the Spanish forces to the north, if they cannot match our advance and move up to the Duero line, well, then, we may be obliged to fall back." On 13 July, he wrote in a note to Lieutenant General Hill, commanding the force detached to the south in Estremadura, "I am apprehensive that, after all, the enemy will be too strong for me; but we shall see."

By 14 July, with spies' reports coming in that Joseph's Army of the Center was collecting in readiness to march, it was time to tell Bathurst in London that hope for a large battle was disappearing: "It is obvious that we could not cross the river without sustaining great loss, and could not fight a general action under circumstances of greater disadvantage than those which would attend an attack of the enemy's position on the Duero." Another piece of bad news made Wellington's mood even gloomier. A planned landing by several thousand British, Spanish and Sicilian troops under the command of General Lord William Bentinck on the Mediterranean side of Spain, in Catalonia, had been postponed. Wellington wrote to his brother (in Cadiz) on 15 July, "Lord W. Bentinck's decision is fatal to the campaign, at least at present."

At the outset, one month before, it had seemed clear to everyone on the staff and at home in Horse Guards that the key criteria for Wellington's efforts would be the balance of forces with Marmont and the availability of the right fighting position. When both of these had been favorable, at San Christoval on 20 and 21 June, Wellington's confidence had faltered. Now that the initiative was passing to the French, he had to explain himself to the politicians in London, and indeed those running the Spanish war in Cadiz. In his disappointment and frustration, Wellington placed the operations of the Spanish forces in Galicia and Lord Bentinck's Catalonian expeditionary force at the center of the picture, even though he had never expected them to produce anything more than diversions. Good manners, and his unfailing political instinct, dictated that he blame the Spanish in his letter to Bathurst, and the British commander, Lord Bentinck, in the version that would be passed to the Spanish authorities.

Having warned his political masters, Wellington began to worry about the military practicalities of getting away from the Duero line without mishaps. The reports that the Army of the Center was about to march concerned him greatly, for if they attacked his right flank or moved directly on Salamanca rather than joining Marmont, he could be in serious difficulty. It was at this delicate juncture that the guerrillas delivered another clutch of intercepted mail.

The most interesting of the dispatches was written on a tiny slither of paper hidden in a riding crop. It was largely in the *Grand Chiffre*, but it was clear that it was from King Joseph to Marmont. This highly important piece of information, sent from Madrid on 9 July, reached Wellington late in the afternoon of the sixteenth and its contents might well reveal exactly what the king was planning to do with the armament he had collected. Just as the staff began their study of this important document, urgent reports of movements along the Duero began to arrive.

During the day, Foy and Bonnet's divisions had begun crossing the River Duero at Toro, on Wellington's left. Since he had kept the main body of his force a little way back from the river, the French crossed without opposition. On the evening of the sixteenth, the British commander confidently expected this breakout at Toro to build into Marmont's general attack, and he ordered a leftward movement of all his forces. Headquarters joined in the shift westward.

The men of the two armies got little rest that night, as the sixteenth became the seventeenth. The British moved into defensive position, ready to face an eruption of French troops from Foy and Bonnet's bridgehead.

Marmont, however, had deceived his opponent. In the darkness, those two divisions crossed back over the river, destroyed the bridge and started moving eastwards. At the other end of the French line, divisions under Maucune and Clausel moved over the Duero at first light on the seventeenth, accompanied by a brigade of light cavalry under General Curto. Within a few hours they had occupied Rueda, which was to the right of Wellington's line and which the British general had laid open as a result of Marmont's feint the previous day. The first stage of Marmont's maneuver had succeeded brilliantly. He had fooled Wellington into moving left, only to reappear on his right. The Army of Portugal was across the river virtually without loss and Wellington had missed his opportunity of using it as a defensive barrier. During the next few days the marshal used the same tactic repeatedly, marching southward around the British right in order to outflank it. These maneuvers served his higher purpose: if Wellington was not fast on his feet, the French would get between him and the Portuguese frontier, cutting off his line of withdrawal.

Scovell reflected on the events of the seventeenth with little sentimentality: "On the evening of this day it was discovered that we have been outmaneuverd and that the Enemy had actually crossed in great force at the Bridge of Tordesillas and the Fort of Pollos. Marmont deserves great credit for the way in which he carried on the deception."

The British fell back about twelve miles, taking up a new defensive position along the line of a small river, the Guarena. Before dawn on the eighteenth, Captain William Tomkinson, attached to the staff of the army's cavalry commander Lieutenant General Stapleton Cotton, went out to inspect the outposts on this new defensive line.

"I had scarcely got beyond our picquets when I met a squadron of the enemy's cavalry. More were coming up, and in half an hour the picquets were driven back on Castrejon, and from the number of squadrons showed by the enemy, it was evident they were in force, and advancing," he recorded. The French cavalry were accompanied by a powerful company of horse artillery, armed with sixteen cannon. These men, riding on their limbers or on horses so they could keep up with the cavalry, were soon bringing their guns into action against some squadrons that General Cotton had drawn up in their way. Tomkinson fell back in front of the French, only to find a troop of the 16th Light Dragoons (with which he had been serving until a few weeks before) standing ready to charge. The effects of the French artillery were immediate. Trooper Stone, whose mount stood in line with the squadron, was hit, and "the shot, round shot, hit him on the belly, and sent pieces of his insides all over the troop—a piece was on Lieutenant Lloyd's shoulder, the first time he was ever in action," Tomkinson later recalled. Within an hour Lieutenant Lloyd, who had only joined the regiment the previous day, was dead too. A desperate cavalry battle was joined as Cotton's brigades protected the rear guard of the army.

Marmont had begun the march south on the eighteenth with the intention of repeating his previous day's feat, moving down toward

Salamanca so quickly that he would oblige the British to do the same. Since he knew the celebrated marching power of the French *fantassin*, he was confident that he would either outstrip the British, threatening their line back to Portugal, or cause them to become disordered by these efforts. He had not however reckoned on the hunger for battle among his subordinates at Castrejon. The commander of the column nearest the British, General Clausel, saw an opportunity to attack.

Fairly soon, the French onslaught had forced the British cavalry back. A troop of Royal Horse Artillery came under attack as it retreated. The French horsemen tried to slash at the reins and traces of the teams pulling the guns, but failed to stop them. The British brigades fell back for ten miles, with Clausel's troops trying to catch up with them. The heat was oppressive and the dust thrown up by these deperate maneuvers began clogging the mouths of horses and men alike, making them desperately thirsty. On crossing the half-dry bed of the Guarena many threw themselves down on their bellies to lap up the tepid, dirty water.

At last, British infantry of the 4th and Light Divisions drew itself up and prepared to meet the onslaught, but at this point the French cavalry did not press their advance, since they would have had little chance of riding down these veterans. Instead they busied themselves with a continued bombardment from their horse batteries and called up a division of infantry. The French moved forward, drums beating the *pas de charge,** but were repulsed by the 4th Division, who gave them a volley and then advanced with bayonets fixed. The light was failing after several hours of continuous maneuvering; Clausel knew his time, like his men, was exhausted.

During the fighting on the eighteenth more than five hundred men of the British and Allied armies were killed and wounded—the French lost even more. At the end of it, Wellington knew that he would have to fall back again. The French were showing considerable aggression and a desire to bring on a decisive encounter. Wellington could not see any suitable killing ground on the flat land between where that day's action had been fought and where he had stood on 20 and 21 June, at San Christoval a few miles north of the River Tormes. On the nineteenth, therefore, the British continued to march south, relinquishing the remainder of the territory they had occupied for the previous month.

---

*"Charge pace," a faster march used when approaching the target of an assault.

With each side's infantry marching across the parched León plains, the two armies sent dust billowing into the skies. Their paths moved closer and closer until they were marching along beside one another at a distance of only five hundred or six hundred yards. The British looked over their left shoulders at the French, who looked back over their right. Each side watched its opponent marching along all day waiting for the least irregularity in its formation or drill to attack. Major Warre wrote to his father, "There never was a more interesting or beautiful sight than that of two hostile armies of upwards of 35,000 men each moving parallel within a mile and a half of each other and often within cannon range." One young Guards officer said in his letter home, "We have amused ourselves with plenty of marching lately, very little fighting but a good deal of chess playing with the enemy."

This contest was testing the mettle of every player. Wellington and Marmont knew that any slight mistake on their part might precipitate an onslaught that would break their army and their reputation in one hideous battle. For the superior officers, there was a sense that every order from their chiefs had to be attended to swiftly and properly or they might be held responsible for disaster. Those lower down in the ranks wondered about their own fate: would the campaign end without the general engagement they had expected for the past month or might there still be some great fight that would claim their lives?

Riding along, Captain Tomkinson turned from watching the parallel march of the French and looked aloft, where vultures and other birds of prey were circling. The blood and suffering of the previous day's combat were fresh in Tomkinson's mind. Watching the birds as they awaited their carrion, he was unable to stop himself thinking about "the horror of being wounded without the power to keep them off."

During the two days since the march had begun, Scovell had been riding with the army trying to snatch a few moments to decipher Joseph's message to Marmont on 9 July. It began:

> "I received your letter of _ July: it is unfortunate that
> you were not able to attack 1214. 609. 656. 803.
> occupied 58. 850. 112. 1168. 13. 1388. 1153. 820. I
> have received a letter 1030. 1252. 989. 1241. 112.
> 56. 1019. 315. 10. He has counter manded 752. 722.

> *890. 44. 566. 134. who he told you 929. 858. 490.*
> *631. 670. 313. 285. 413. 51. 1178. 1196. 518. 473.*
> *and of some bands. I am very 835. 531. 1178. 673.*
> *891. 1095. 649. 1016. 304. 274. 139. 498. 561. 666.*
> *He has done very little to look 13. 521. 110. 874.*
> *761. 409. feints 164. 413. 549. 1089. partial, wanted*
> *to 521. 512. 890. 1178. 577. 238. 2. 1105. 858."*

Inserting what he knew, Scovell could decipher this to a considerable extent:

> *"I received your letter of _ July: it is unfortunate that you were not able to attack the English army while they were occupied with the siege 1168 of Salamanca. I have received a letter from General Caffarelli in Burgos of the twenty 1019 of 315. He has counter manded the march of the troops who he told you would help 490. 631. 670. on the movements of the English army and of some bands. I am very far from happy with the change of orders he has issued. He has done very little to look for the enemy, who, by feints and partial attacks wanted to prevent him sending you help."*

This deciphering is not without fault, though the error is not particularly significant: 1241, General Caffarelli's location, was not Burgos, as Scovell thought, but Vitoria, somewhat farther north, in the Basque country. Joseph went on to explain how Marshal Soult and General Count D'Erlon had overestimated the strength of Allied forces in front of them (and of the guerrillas) to justify their own failure to act in support of Marmont: nothing could be expected of them either. For Wellington this was definitive proof that there was nothing farther to be feared from the Army of the North. Joseph's dispatch also provided that uniquely satisfying species of intelligence: that a strategy of his own, namely the use of the Spanish to tie down troops north and south of Marmont, had worked.

The real nub of the letter came toward its end. Wellington had been aware for many days that units of the Army of the Center were leaving their usual positions and concentrating. He was unsure however where they were heading. It might be that their concentration was purely defensive in case he, Wellington, pushed toward Madrid. It might be that they were meant to join D'Erlon in an offensive against his exposed right or the central Portuguese frontier. While allowing for the possibility that he might have to fall back in defense of his capital, Joseph expressed his wishes for the coming days as follows:

> *"I really would like to be able 643. 1148. 398. 112. 858. above all since I learned that you could no longer count 285. 846. 544. 1238. so I have given the order to General Treillard 1178. 7. the valley 112. 1383. 906. 86. 942. 323. 69. 708. 1377. 13. 1265. 1003. 1269. 164. 989. 670. 1148. 398. 31? (pour). 1016. remainder 285. 981. 1070. 86. 794. prior to marching 498. 642."*

This became:

> *"I would really like to be able to support you, above all since I learned that you could no longer count on the support of the Army of the North. So I have given the order to General Treillard to evacuate the valley of the Tagus only leaving 708 regiment of cavalry in 1269 and to move with the rest to Naval 1070 nero prior to marching toward you."*

Thus, Wellington had the confirmation that much of the Army of the Center was marching to unite with Marmont. The phrase "Naval 1070 *nero*" was obviously Naval Carnero, which gave the British a good sense of Treillard's route of march. Joseph then described how he had removed his troops from different centers around the capital. This information allowed Wellington and the staff to conclude various factors central to their strategy for the coming days: that the Army of the Center would unite with Marmont; its strength (adding the figures they already knew of its composition and subtracting those of the various detachments diverted by Joseph); and its likely route of march.

This was intelligence of the very highest order, especially since Wellington was a general who defined so much of what he *did* do by setting out the limits of what he would *not* do. He would not fight Marmont once he had made his junction with Joseph, that was clear. But spies' reports of 20 July (two days old) suggested that the Army of the Center was not yet moving. Wellington could therefore calculate that he must bring on a general action in the next four days or else give up the game. He also knew from the 9 July letter that he could seek this battle without worrying about the French armies north and south of him.

There was one small reinforcement that might reach the marshal at any moment, but Wellington knew it would not be large enough to alter radically the balance of forces. An unciphered dispatch hidden in a Spaniard's clothing and dated 12 July showed him that the only hopes still entertained by Marmont of a reinforcement by the Army of the North were a column of cavalry with one battery of guns (less than one thousand men and six cannon) that might still get through. In his uncoded missive to the commander of that column, Marmont had revealed a certain desperation: "the valor of the army and the glory of French arms do not allow you to spare a single day in setting out."

After a tiring day with the two armies completing their parallel march down to the line of the River Tormes and Salamanca, Wellington wrote to Earl Bathurst in London: "I am quite certain that Marshal Marmont's army is to be joined by the King's, which will be 10,000 or 12,000 men, with a large proportion of cavalry." The general was therefore quite confirmed in his resolution "to cross the Tormes, if the enemy should; to cover Salamanca as long as I can; and above all, not to give up our communication with Ciudad Rodrigo; and not to fight an action, unless under very advantageous circumstances, or it should become absolutely necessary."

The commander of forces did allude to one advantage he enjoyed over Marmont, namely in the matter of communications: "The Army of Portugal has been surrounded for the last six weeks, and scarcely even a letter reaches its commander," he told the secretary of war. Given the effectiveness of the guerrilla screen, it was quite likely that the marshal was unaware of Joseph's letter of 9 July (and indeed, it became clear several days later that none of the copies sent by His Catholic Majesty had got through to Marmont). Consequently Wellington understood more about the situation of the French armies than did the marshal himself, a state of affairs that presented obvious dangers for Marmont. If he was unaware that the king was marching to his help, he might seek precipitate action against his retreating enemy, fearing they would escape him, rather than waiting for this substantial reinforcement.

British headquarters had evidently been impressed by the aggressive spirit shown by the French during their crossing of the Duero and attack on the Castrejon line on 18 July. Wellington had every reason to believe that Marmont would try to bring on a battle between 21 and 24 July. He had already chosen two suitable defensive positions where the British might fight such an engagement. One was the familiar ridge of San Christoval, a few miles north of the city. The other was south of the Tormes, near the village of Arapiles, where the topography would allow him to observe the approach of an enemy force while concealing the bulk of his own.

Early on 21 July, Wellington drew up his army in battle array on the San Christoval ridge. Marmont chose as he had done one month before, not to oblige him by assaulting this formidable position. Instead, the French advanced guard went to the south and east, finding fords across the Tormes that would allow them to continue their march and perhaps, by veering west after they had crossed, draw a great arc around the south of Salamanca, thus cutting Wellington off from his route back to Portugal.

With reports of Marmont's movements coming in during the afternoon, Wellington realized that his first chosen battle position was becoming useless and he would have to order the army to cross the river as well and take up the second. Since the distance upriver to the British fords was less than that to the French ones, his divisions were able to make up for the lost time of occupying their morning position and begin assembling south of the Tormes during the afternoon.

Wellington had already had the opportunity of looking over the ground on that side of the river during his advance through Salamanca several weeks before. The geography there was particularly favorable to his purposes. Any army heading back to the Portuguese frontier had to travel southwest from the Spanish town. Two chains of features would help the general cover that movement. One ran south from the Tormes, a gully a couple of hundred feet deep carved by a tributary of that river.

The other salient natural position was a ridge running more or less west-ward from the first. At the "elbow" of these two chains of high ground were a pair of rocky tors, the Greater and Lesser Arapil hills. As night fell on 21 July, Wellington's army occupied the first line, presenting a barrier several miles in length running south from the Tormes. Ahead of it was a screen of light cavalry, observing the French divisions as they formed after their own crossing and went into their bivouacs.

That night, the open plains south and west of Salamanca were stud-ded with the fires that soldiers of both sides built to dry their clothes and cook supper. Most of the troops were exhausted and famished after marching fifty miles in a few days. Their officers had played their parts as pawns in Wellington and Marmont's gigantic game of chess and were suffering from a profound mental as well as physical fatigue. There was still a sense of expectation that action might be joined and these listless feelings of nervous excitement charged the conversation in the bivouacs just as the heat and dust had charged the atmosphere above.

Long after most men had fallen into a deep sleep on the dusty earth, the pealing of thunder announced a torrential downpour. Many a soldier's blanket was soon awash with rain and mud. Lightning bolts plunged from the sky, cavalry horses reared, neighed, broke their teth-ering and careered about, trampling somnolent dragoons under hoof. It was not the rest that these tired men would have hoped for. What was more, for thousands of them, this disturbed, crazy night was to be their last.

CHAPTER FIFTEEN

*I. dont. 1082. 365. eve. we. we. 669. ev. 898.
r. deceived. 481. the. 985. 186. t. 843. 688.
and. 1297. 536. 174. o. 1024 . . . is. t. 980.
854. er 536. on. w. 171. made. them. 131. t.*

THE BATTLE OF SALAMANCA, 22 JULY 1812

*I*t was still morning on 22 July when Pakenham's division went splashing through the ford at Cabrerizos. The previous night's rain had brought the river up above its usual July depth and many of the men found the cold water soaking them all the way up to the chest. They held their muskets above their heads, anxious to keep their weapons dry and ready for action.

By one of Wellington's characteristic dictates the deputy adjutant general (and his brother-in-law) Edward Pakenham had been placed in command of the 3rd Division. Its usual commander, Picton, had fallen ill. The chosen man, for Pakenham was most decidedly among the inner circle of the staff, had thus found himself leading one of the most formidable formations in the army, nearly six thousand veterans with the nickname Fighting Division. With them was the small Portuguese cavalry brigade under D'Urban that had been detached on intelligence-gathering duties earlier in the campaign. As their horses came dripping out of the Tormes, the last Allied presence north of that river had been called in. These troops marked the tail end of the British redeployment back toward the Portuguese frontier.

With the evacuation of Salamanca, Wellington had ordered his supply train down the Ciudad Rodrigo road at dawn. A great column of wagons, pack mules, camp followers and other livestock was making its way back toward the border. Although the thunderstorm of the previous night had thoroughly soaked the soil, it did not take long for its top to be dried by the sun and for the movements of men and beasts to send its characteristic dusty smudges across the azure morning sky.

Marmont's staff officers and cavalry vedettes were out early trying to form an idea of their enemy's movements. In crossing the river, both armies had turned through a right angle. For days they had been marching south, with the French trying to get around Wellington's right flank and cut off his withdrawal. Now the British general occupied a line that extended south from the Tormes. Marmont's game, turning the British right, remained the same, but that now meant pushing his people around the southern end of a British line rather than an eastern one.

As the French divisions got under arms, General Foy, occupying the end of the French deployment closest to the river, set out to survey the enemy lines. The British had occupied the ridge opposite, a move by Wellington that denied the enemy any knowledge of what lay beyond the feature. Foy could see them drawn up, half a mile away across the gully that ran from south to north, carved by a tributary of the Tormes. Foy knew that the few battalions he could see probably represented a small portion of the enemy army's deployment. At times, glancing through his telescope, Foy could spot Wellington and his staff on the flat-topped tor to his front. He decided to press forward a little to see if he could get a better idea of the British position while he awaited his marshal's orders. Somewhat to his surprise, Foy discovered British and Portuguese light infantry on his side of the ravine, around a ruined chapel known as Nuestra Senhora de la Peña.

He decided to deal with these outposts as usual, sending his own

---

*Names given to the light infantry or sharpshooters of the French infantry battalions.

voltigeurs and *tirailleurs** forward to drive them in. The French light infantry set off with alacrity, skirmishing up to the rocky edge of the ridge, alternately firing, running forward and dropping into cover behind a boulder or in a fold of the ground while they reloaded. As this exchange of fire picked up, Wellington sent more light troops forward. Dark-green-clad marksmen of the 95th Rifles reinforced the defenders of Nuestra Senhora de la Peña. With more than a thousand men on each side stubbornly exchanging shots, Foy realized that this was something more than the usual nighttime picket just waiting for its orders to move out.

Wellington was determined to maintain the position around the ruined chapel a little longer so that he could keep his own main body out of sight while trying to force Marmont into showing his. That way the British general would allow the baggage to get well under way and see whether the day might present an opportunity to offer battle while the numbers were still advantageous. Just a couple of hundred yards behind the battalions spotted by Foy early that morning, but shielded by the lie of the land, were no less than five divisions of British infantry standing in closed column, ready to march.

The British commander jotted his first orders of the day. Major General Pakenham and the cavalry marching in his company were to make a long trek, ten miles or so, all the way behind the army (and for most of their journey, invisible to the French). Having started the day as his left flank, on the river, they would eventually become the right and be ready to check Marmont's usual game of trying to get around that side of the British line. Meanwhile the men that Foy had seen early that day were being pulled back off their ridge and replaced with a rather more formidable looking assembly, Wellington's main infantry reserve, the 1st and Light Divisions. Four divisions still remained hidden. For Wellington's intention in posting the 1st and Light was to act as a strong rear guard if he continued his withdrawal or as a temptation to the French commander to fall upon what he would see as a manageable portion of the British army.

As the British commander surveyed the ridge on the opposite side, studying Marmont's reactions, he was accompanied by a large entorage. At first sight this assembly might have seemed an unruly riot of color, but each man had been assigned a place in the great scheme of things: there were his boys, like March, Somerset and the prince of Orange, ready to drive their thoroughbreds across the Spanish fields in the delivery of some pencil-scribbled note; Cotton with his glittering entourage of young cavalry officers; Beresford in a blue Portuguese coat, surrounded by his own retinue (Majors Warre and Hardinge among them); and there were those dedicated to the efficiency of the staff rather than its decoration, Lieutenant Colonel De Lancey, Major Scovell and others of the quarter master general's staff.

Two miles away, Marmont was surrounded by his own people. Even though it was only 9 A.M., the armies had already been in motion for hours. When the Army of Portugal's commander heard reports about the fighting around Nuestra Senhora de la Peña, he drew precisely the conclusion that Wellington would have wanted. It was clear the British were moving off again. Vedettes had seen the baggage heading back toward Portugal. If most of the British force could not be seen, it was probably because they too had joined the march. The troops across from the chapel were no more than a rear guard. Should he attack?

Marmont's best hope had always been to catch a British division or two without proper support and hammer it; but if Wellington was returning to the frontier, the French would soon lose the opportunity. Foy, the marshal's onetime classmate from the artillery academy, worried about his chief's judgment. "He is a good man, estimable and respectable," wrote Foy, "but he and others are entirely deluded about the nature of his talents. He was not born to be a field general. His face too easily reveals the hesitancy of his spirit and the anxiety of his soul; thus the army enters into his secret. He asks advice too often, too publicly and from too many people."

On the morning of 22 July, Marmont's uncertainty revealed itself once more in orders that would keep his options open. Artillery was to be brought up, ready to open a cannonade on the British divisions in front. Meanwhile, Thomières and Maucune's infantry divisions, accompanied by light cavalry, were to make their way south and turn Wellington's flank there.

As the morning wore on, the front began to turn through a great arc. It became obvious that the French were crossing the 1st and Light Divisions' feature about one mile to the south. Wellington's attention suddenly turned to this advance, near the larger of the two flat-topped

(Arapil) hills that the locals call *los hermanitos*, the little brothers. Seeing French troops appearing near this rocky tor, he ordered some Portuguese infantry to take it, but they failed. At this point, Wellington resolved to throw the 1st and Light Divisions south, to decide the fate of this singular feature and perhaps draw Marmont into the open in its defense.

But indecision that morning was not only evident in the French camp. Almost as soon as he had set his men in motion, Wellington changed his mind. Scovell, among several staff officers, watched it happen and recorded, "Lord Wellington was more than once about to attack, but was prevented by the insinuations of those about him." Another officer of that group, Captain William Tomkinson, watched the general confer with his old confederate Beresford before canceling the attack on the Greater Arapil, and noted rather more candidly:

> "Marshal Beresford, no doubt, was the cause of the alteration from what he urged. Yet, at the same time, Lord Wellington was so little influenced, or, indeed, allows any person to say a word, that his attending to the marshal was considered singular. From all I could collect and observe The Peer was a little nervous. It was the first time he had ever attacked."

Instead of precipitating battle, the British general fell back once more on that which he knew best: a defensive posture that challenged his opponent to bring on the fight. He was doubtless aware of the murmurings of his staff, for once more, just as he had done on 20 June, the general had faltered at precisely the moment when battle seemed desirable. Major FitzRoy Somerset, ever loyal to his master, detected the insinuations and wrote somewhat defensively that Wellington "was fully as anxious as the youngest *fire eater* in the army to avail himself of any favorable opportunity to attack the French" (emphasis in original). Having halted the attack on the Greater Arapil, the general busied himself positioning several divisions along a new line, a step made necessary by Marmont's maneuvers to the southeast. The 1st and Light would remain in their north-south arrangement, whereas the new positions would stretch back from the east to west, the whole British deployment forming a right angle or L shape.

Wellington and his staff galloped up the Teso de San Miguel, a hillock that rose behind the village of Los Arapiles, close to the bend in this new line. Although this vantage point was not as high as the "little brothers" to its left and front, it was an extremely good place to study the field. If he looked over his right shoulder, more or less behind him, Wellington could follow the progress of Pakenham and his light cavalry as they moved along, following the orders he had given them that morning. Ahead, behind a ridge topped with dwarf oaks, he could see plumes of dust that revealed the passage of French forces to his right. Atop the bigger of those fraternal features, the Greater Arapil, he could see Marmont and his suite. Between himself and his adversary, Wellington's sharp eye could discern a dip in the ground where he could hide many of his troops from the marshal's gaze. Wellington ordered the 4th and 5th Divisions, with Le Marchant's heavy cavalry brigade, to occupy that ground.

At about 3 P.M., Wellington's servants brought him a picnic lunch on the Teso San Miguel. Munching some chicken, he watched French teams setting up their cannon on the ridge opposite him, and beyond Los Arapiles, the tree-topped Monte de Azan, apparently with the intention of bombarding the center of his new line. He looked to his right. The dust still showed the progress of a French force at least a mile away. He totted up the Army of Portugal's constituent parts. Foy's division remained where it had been that morning. There was another atop and around the Greater Arapil hill. There were two or three more deploying on the ridge to his south, with the cannon. Elsewhere he could see the columns of dust kicked up by marching feet. Scouts brought further reports of the French division and cavalry marching farthest to his right. Why were they still moving, if everyone else was establishing a new line in front of the village of Los Arapiles? Wellington knew how many divisions there were in the Army of Portugal and he could account for all of them. Scovell's deciphering had told him very clearly that there were no reinforcements yet from the Armies of the North and Center. What were those people doing on the French right, moving farther and farther away from support? Marmont's maneuvers were creating precisely the sort of threat to his own army that he had been hoping for the past five weeks to cause the British. Wellington threw aside his half-munched chicken and announced, "By God! That will do!"

The briefest of instructions to the QMG staff on top of the hill followed. Wellington then clapped heels to his charger and galloped off the back of the Teso San Miguel in search of Pakenham. Within minutes he was outpacing those who tried to follow (De Lancey among them). Soon the single figure of the British commander came galloping across the scrub to meet his brother-in-law at the head of his column. "Edward, move on with the 3rd Division, take those heights in your front and drive everything before you." Wellington directed Pakenham to move up the end of a ridge just south of the village of Los Arapiles and strike the unsupported French division moving northwest across it. "I will, My Lord," the divisional commander replied, and the two men shook hands. And with this simple exchange, Wellington had lit the fuse under the bomb intended to destroy Marmont. The British commander turned about and began galloping back to Los Arapiles. Meanwhile, the staff had flown to each corner of the army relaying messages so that everyone would know their part in the battle about to happen.

Major Scovell took his horse closer to the French down the front of the Teso San Miguel, and behind Los Arapiles to a hollow beyond where Le Marchant's brigade was waiting. His old teacher and mentor, now in command, was nowhere to be found. Scovell surveyed the brigade of heavy cavalry: more than one thousand horsemen of the 3rd Dragoons, 4th Dragoons and 5th Dragoon Guards. Almost every officer there would have been known to him, for the heavies were a tight-knit brotherhood. The 4th, after all, was his old regiment, the source of so much pride when he was commissioned into it and of so much regret when he had been forced to sell up and exchange with Oliver of the 57th. His old commanding officer, Lord Edward Somerset, was at the head of the 4th that day, as was another acquaintance, Colonel Dalbiac, the second in command. Scovell's misgivings at being unable to join them can only be guessed at, but he knew he had Wellington's business to attend to that afternoon. These tough men in their patched red coats, overall trousers and watering caps watched the familiar staff officer moving among them. Some of the veterans bore the livid scars of past combat on their countenances. They were a superior kind of soldier, paid more than the footsloggers and brighter with it. Tall men on big mounts, dubbed *les messieurs en rouge* by their enemy, the heavies had been waiting in reserve more or less throughout Wellington's entire campaigns until that day.

At about 4 P.M., the French batteries on the ridge only about 750 yards away opened fire, but the brigade had been sent to their fold in the ground precisely to make them invulnerable from such shot. To be double sure, the troopers had dismounted and stood next to their horses holding them by the reins. Scovell weaved through until he found his brother-in-law, Major Leigh Clowes, who was in command of the 3rd Dragoons. They greeted one another cordially and Scovell delivered his message. "You should expect the immediate advance of the 3rd Division to your right," he said, their conversation punctuated by French round shot ripping through the air a few feet above them. Be prepared to support them, for Lord W plans to use Pakenham's men to hit the French on their flank.

Not long after Scovell's visit, Wellington appeared and found Le Marchant. He told the brigade commander to be prepared to move forward and hazard everything on a charge should the opportunity present itself. Le Marchant may well have said a silent prayer, his habit before battle, and looked about for his son, Captain Carey Le Marchant, who had joined his father's personal staff despite every insistence that no special favors would be shown.

The 4th and 5th Divisions of infantry then began moving forward to take position south of Los Arapiles. They drove out some French light troops and found themselves under fire from dozens of guns on the Azan ridge opposite. Their metal began biting into British ranks, flipping men over in crazy somersaults or sending an arm or head on its own yawing into the sky. Batteries of Royal Artillery six-pounders began answering the French cannonade. Soon shot was crisscrossing the land, a pounding of guns and musketry that began to fill the air with a dense smoke, blotting out the bright blue dome above.

Marmont too had realized that something was wrong with the division on his flank. He looked out from atop the Greater Arapil, straining his eyes to see through gaps in the pall. What was Thomières doing? Was he trying to bring on a battle all by himself, just as Clausel had four days before? Why was he getting so far ahead of Maucune on the ridge? Marmont knew he had to stop it at once. He scrambled down the rocks just below the summit, mounted his horse and set off toward Thomières.

At around 4:30, Thomières discovered the terrible consequences of his headlong advance. His 101st Regiment marching at the head of the column had been spotted by D'Urban and two of his Portuguese cavalry scouts. They turned, bringing up two hundred Portuguese horse, and swiftly charged the French infantry. Such was the unexpected nature of this attack, the horsemen bursting through the trees just a few hundred yards in front, that the leading battalion of the 101st had no time to form square or even bring its men together in closed column. They broke and fled. The bloodied routers came running into his main body of troops, and out of the oaks in front of him, the 3rd Division appeared in two columns. Barely missing a step of their march, the British troops deployed into battle line. He had seconds in which to respond. Desperately, he tried to order his men out of their column of march and into some sort of formation. His artillery battery came swiftly into action, and Curto at the head of the cavalry on his left reacted instinctively to the danger that had suddenly appeared. Shells began to fall into the British ranks. Pakenham's men, however, were already moving in a line just two men deep, so the shot did them far less damage than the 3rd Division's own guns, smacking into the deep files of deploying French.

It probably took no more than fifteen minutes for Thomières division to be defeated. D'Urban, and some squadrons of the 14th Light Dragoons under Colonel Hervey, soon drove off the French horse and the 3rd Division continued its advance up onto the Azan ridge. The two leading French regiments had lost all formation and were trying to defend themselves as a clump of individuals. One of the 3rd Division's brigades advanced up to them in a kind of crescent, the two ends of its firing line curving around the dazed mass. After receiving two French volleys, the redcoats, with the Irish of the 88th at their center, shouted a couple of hurrahs and went in with the bayonet. In moments the 101st's colonel and its eagle, the gilded symbol that the emperor had urged them to defend to the death, had both been captured.

As this had been going on, the 4th and 5th Divisions had also advanced into the trough that separated them from the French and up the other side toward Maucune's division. The British battalions began a heavy fire of musketry, which was returned by the defenders.

For a moment the French held the ridge, making the most of its natural strength, but then the 4th and 5th Divisions' batteries engaged them with howitzer fire. These artillery pieces were able to loft a shell on a higher trajectory than a normal cannon, and if the fuses of their shrapnel shells were set just right, they would explode over the heads of the

French ranks, showering them with hot metal. Scovell watched the howitzers open up from near Los Arapiles and noted, "A few shells most
judiciously thrown made the Enemy give way, and our light troops and
line hurried on and gained the Heights." The French, flinching from this
new source of death, dressed their ranks back a few yards from the top
of the ridge line. In the new position, enveloped in smoke, they could
not see that Le Marchant's heavies had mounted and were deploying
into line in front of Los Arapiles.

The 4th Dragoons and 5th Dragoon Guards emerged from their cover
and, one by one, troops fell into a solid line of horse. The 3rd Dragoons
followed on in reserve. With a chorus of trumpets, they all set off on a trot
past Los Arapiles and toward the ridge. At this point General Stapleton
Cotton appeared and ordered Le Marchant to charge, an instruction that
seemed entirely superfluous given Scovell's earlier warning and Wellington's personal commands. At that moment, however, Le Marchant could
not see beyond the ridge and much of the field was wreathed in thick
smoke. Cotton lost his temper with the brigade commander and strong
words were exchanged. Le Marchant continued on his way after this, trying to fulfill Wellington's original order to attack in support of the 3rd Division and leading his men into the uncertainty ahead.

The French artillery played on them ineffectually, for much of its fire
had been turned to the British infantry, which was closer at hand. Le
Marchant looked to his left and right, surveying the line of troopers that
moved forward, filling the air with the jingling of saddlery and the sweet
smell of horses. Here and there men pulled back on their stirrups, trying to
check the impetuosity of their steeds. Others spurred them on so they did
not fall behind. Regularity was everything in the business they were about
to conduct. They had been trained to ride almost stirrup to stirrup, forming a solid wall of flesh and metal. If the mere sight of this great armament
did not cause the French infantry to break and run, the matter would be
settled by the merciless application of the 1796 heavy cavalry saber.

Just a couple of minutes after they had set off, the heavies came cantering up the Azan ridge, directed by Le Marchant to move into a space
between the 5th Division on his left and the leading elements of Pakenham's 3rd on his right. At last, the trumpeters sounded the charge,
unleashing the torrent that had been kept in check until that moment
only by an iron discipline.

The footsloggers of the 66th and 15th *de ligne*, forming one of Maucune's brigades just behind the ridge, probably had no idea what was about
to hit them. They were enveloped in smoke and had moved back from the
ridge line to escape the British artillery fire, spirits shaken too by the sight
of Thomières's men who were flooding around them. Their hallooing and
shouting as they fled back over the ridge was an intimation of the arrival of
an enemy force on their flank at any moment. Fearing cavalry, their commanders had initially formed them in squares, but packing the men
together like this had only increased the effect of a hail of musketry by the
5th Division to their front. The British battalions were deployed in line, firing into the densely packed Frenchmen, who could only respond with volleys from one or two sides of their squares. The French commanders had
taken their companies out of square and were just moving them back again
to escape the withering fire when they heard the thundering of Le
Marchant's men. Many of the infantry were not even facing the right way
at that moment, but those who turned around became witness to a terrifying spectacle. When the *messieurs en rouge* erupted from the smoke, only
seconds remained in which to react.

The 66th were lost in moments. The point of each saber delivered a ton
of mass at the speed of the gallop. Where they connected with their targets,
hundreds were impaled. Those not run through by those sharp blades were
sent flying by horses' shoulders or trampled under thundering hooves. The
moment of contact between dragoon and *fantassin* was in most cases a fleet-
ing one, and having ridden down the 66th, Le Marchant's brigade maintained its forward momentum toward the 15th. With the advantage of a
few moments' warning, their officers had turned them about and managed
to fire off a volley. About a dozen dragoons dropped from their horses, but
then the 15th too disappeared under the flood of cavalry.

Le Marchant, who had led from the front cutting down many men
with his own hand, knew that his brigade was breaking up. Many
troopers were wild with triumph and had gone off in pursuit of little
groups of enemy soldiers who scattered into the oaks on the back side
of the ridge. The brigadier detailed a squadron to herd the prisoners
and then carried on rallying his regiments for a further charge. They
met the 22nd Regiment, the leading unit of another Army of Portugal
division, Taupin's, at the charge once more. These battalions had the
time, while the British heavies were reordering their ranks, to align

themselves in heavy columns and deliver a powerful volley when the British were only ten yards or so away, felling dozens of men of the 5th Dragoon Guards. This last-minute fire did not save them, though, and seeing that the galloping cavalry could not be checked, despair spread immediately in the ranks.

By now, the heavy brigade's charge had almost expended all of its immense energy. Eight battalions of French infantry had been ridden down. Colonel Somerset's 4th Dragoons had taken five pieces of artillery too. Watching from his vantage point behind Los Arapiles, Wellington turned to the commander of his cavalry and exulted, "By God, Cotton! I have never seen anything so beautiful in all my life!" The British commander knew that Pakenham's charge and the actions of Le Marchant's brigade had ruined two enemy divisions and that Marmont would need a miracle to recover from the loss of one-quarter of his men.

What Wellington did not appreciate was that Marmont had been wounded at least one hour before. He had fallen victim to one of the British artillery shells as he turned to mount his horse, trying to organize his forces against the British onslaught. Marmont had been hit in the arm and was evidently losing a lot of blood, for he was carried from the field. His place had been taken by his most senior divisional general, Bonnet, who had been similarly powerless to save the French left.

All across the ridge, the combat of two armies had degenerated into the brawling of individual groups. Bands of five or ten French infantry, many of them lacerated with dreadful sword wounds to the head or upper body, were meandering around, trying to find their bearings. British dragoons, meanwhile, were riding about, hacking as they passed. One young officer wrote home, "It was a fine sight to see those fellows running and, as we held our swords over their heads, fall down on their knees, drop their muskets and cry: *Prisonnier, Monsieur!*" As Le Marchant was trying to restore order and bring together one squadron for a final charge, he was shot. The ball broke his spine, killing him almost instantly. Like Moore and Craufurd before him, the torchbearer of scientific soldiering had been killed at this moment of triumph.

The shattered remnants of the 101st, 66th, 15th and 22nd infantry were either skulking in the trees or giving themselves up to British infantry. Some fifteen hundred surrendered to the 5th Division. Elsewhere, the 3rd Division met the French fugitives: "Hundreds of men frightfully disfigured, black with dust and worn out with fatigue and covered with saber cuts and blood threw themselves among us for safety," one diarist recalled.

Among the French casualties were several of their leaders. General Thomières had been shot during the fight with Pakenham; he was captured but would soon die. Colonel Jardet, the ADC whose ciphered letter from Paris had provided such good intelligence to the British earlier in the year, was also killed. Command of the Army of Portugal devolved at this critical moment onto General Bertrand Clausel, who, in the best style of his imperial master, resolved to meet this present emergency with an immediate attack of his own.

The British 4th Division had already been checked atop the ridge, and Clausel threw the three uncommitted French formations into a general advance in this cental sector, supported by a dragoon brigade. At first, Wellington's men were driven back toward Los Arapiles in disorder. Marshal Beresford, accompanied by his ADC Major William Warre, rode into the retreating columns, trying to rally them. Beresford was soon shot in the chest and fell from his horse (although he survived). Warre recorded, "I escaped very well with two shots on my sword scabbard, and one thro' my holster, which is as near as I ever wish to have them."

Although Clausel's counterattack initially made good progress, Wellington had more in reserve than his opponents and was able to throw three fresh divisions in their way. Wellington himself was now riding about the center, often on his own, firing off orders to the staff who somehow still managed to find him in the gloom and cacophony of battle. Clausel's attack had lost momentum, and for the British army there was one more great step to be taken to complete the victory. The French, meanwhile, had begun falling back to a position about half a mile behind the Greater Arapil hill, where they would make their final defense. Sensing the change in fortunes, Wellington sent the prince of Orange with an order to bring up the Light Division. He then ordered an assault on the Greater Arapil, which captured another French battery.

After 8 P.M., with darkness almost enveloping the battlefield, Scovell found Wellington and was issued with new orders: to bring the 5th and another division across from where they had been fighting earlier in the afternoon. He galloped off to his task, even taking it on his own initiative to redirect one of the divisions at one point on its march across.

By 10 P.M. the battle was almost at an end: elation spread among Wellington and his staff. When the officers of the adjutant general's department would eventually compile their returns, the loss of the Allied forces was around five thousand (including wounded), whereas that of the French probably exceeded fourteen thousand. Two eagles had been captured, a loss that always irritated the emperor, and twenty cannon.

Everything was set, late on 22 July, for an energetic pursuit the following morning. A couple of days before, Wellington had deployed a Spanish brigade to the main bridge on the French line of withdrawal over the Tormes. With any luck, thousands of men would be stuck on the Allied side of its channel. Two brigades of cavalry awaited the dawn keenly. They were fresh and had not been committed in the fight that the British would remember thereafter as Salamanca and the French as Los Arapiles.

On the battlefield, soldiers' wives went in search of their fallen husbands. Susannah Dalbiac was one, turning over the disfigured faces of one dragoon after another before hearing the joyous news that her husband was not dead. Scovell was relieved to find that his brother-in-law had also survived the great charge that had done so much to win the day. Clowes told Scovell that riding off the field he had encountered General Le Marchant's son, Carey. The young captain was quite ignorant of his father's fate and Clowes, who had led his regiment gallantly throughout the day, found that his courage had failed him at this dreadful moment and he could not bring himself to tell Carey that his father was dead and that he and his seven siblings were orphans.

The staff had a brief respite that night. They chattered excitedly in their bivouacs about a victory that had transformed every expectation of the war in Spain. Some wrote home, keen to break the news of the triumph to their loved ones. William Warre told his sister:

> *"You cannot think how beautiful it is to be cannonaded all day, being very tired and hungry, and at 5 p.m. instead of sitting down to eat a good dinner, to set to give the French a good beating in a very strong position, which, however, is the best part of the whole* divertissement, *and though Ld Welln. naturally got all the laurels, it was a most glorious business."*

The following morning the pursuit was resumed, and General Wellington made the painful discovery that the Spanish force he had intended to block the Tormes had relinquished its position even before the action of the twenty-second, allowing the French to escape across the river. His immense disappointment was tempered somewhat late in the morning of the twenty-third when Bock's brigade of heavy cavalry caught the French rear guard near Garcia Hernandez. The retreating troops belonged to Foy's division, the only one of the Army of Portugal that had escaped largely unscathed from the previous day's pounding. Scovell watched from a nearby ridge as the German Legion dragoons prepared to charge the French, noticing squadrons of French cavalry nearby who did nothing to intervene. Their spirit had been broken, he reflected, for they had ceased to risk their own lives in defense of their comrades.'

Faced with the imminent onslaught, the rearmost French battalion formed square, but this specific, usually infallible tactic, was to fail them this day. As the German dragoons charged the French, their commander and his horse were hit by a hail of musketry; man and beast fell together onto the firers' ranks. In that moment, the integrity of their defense was broken. Troopers rode into the breach and the battalion was finished. Once cavalry rode into a square, it dissolved in seconds, for the French found themselves attacked from behind and it became a matter of every man for himself. A little farther along, another regiment was mauled too. Foy's division thus suffered more than eleven hundred casualties and Wellington's heavies notched up their second triumph in as many days.

The events at Salamanca caused considerable eclat in the French command. Every previous assumption that Wellington was some sepoy general, an overrated mediocrity, had to be cast aside. Indeed General Foy himself was moved to compare his adversary to the greatest captains of the previous century: "The battle of Salamanca . . . put Wellington in almost the same class as Marlborough. We had the opportunity, until that moment, of knowing his prudence, his choice of positions, his skill at drawing things out; at Salamanca he showed himself to be a considerable manoeuvrer; he kept his dispositions hidden almost all day; he waited for our movements before revealing his own; he revealed little; he fought in an oblique order; it was a battle in the style of Frederick [the Great]."

Wellington's private verdict was given succinctly in a letter to Sir Thomas Graham: "After manoeuvring all morning in the usual French style, nobody knew with what object, [Marmont] at last pressed upon my right in such a manner, at the same time without engaging, that he would have either carried our Arapiles, or he would have confined us entirely to our position. This was not to be endured, and we fell upon him, turning his left flank; and I never saw an army receive such a beating."

On 24 July, Wellington halted the army and set about writing his victory dispatch. There was praise enough to go around; the ordinary soldiers were thanked, as were the many senior officers, several of whom had fallen wounded. Le Marchant's heavies did not get the credit that their pivotal role merited, and it seems that General Cotton, following his argument with their now-dead commander, had already gained his revenge in the way this record was written. For the more junior officers, any mention in this missive meant promotion. Most of his aristocratic favorites were there: De Lancey, the prince of Orange and FitzRoy Somerset. The honor of going home with the victory dispatch and laying the captured eagles at the Prince Regent's feet was given to a highborn ADC, Captain Lord Clinton.

While Wellington might have ignored Scovell on many an occasion, he knew a secret shared by only two or three officers in headquarters. Without confidence about the size of the enemy army, he would never have given battle. It was Scovell's deciphering of letters in the Great Paris Cipher that had given Wellington the pronounced advantage as the campaign had drawn toward its climax. They had told him first that Marmont's army would not be reinforced by large numbers from the north, and then had revealed exactly when he must take them on. For this achievement Scovell was mentioned in the Salamanca dispatch and made lieutenant colonel just fifteen months after getting his majority. If he had any regrets at not sharing in the glorious charge of Le Marchant's brigade, this must surely have swept them away. For Scovell had achieved another step of promotion, not by drawing blood but by the application of science and intellect.

CHAPTER SIXTEEN

I. dont. b. 365. eve. we. we. 669. ev. 398. r. deceived.
181. the. 985. 186. t. 843. 688. and. 1297. S. 174. o.
1024 . . . is. the. 851. erson. who. made. them. out.

THE MARCH TO BURGOS, SUMMER AND EARLY FALL 1812

*N*apoleon had decided that Marshal Soult, a onetime private in the royal army, was among his most brilliant generals. As a sergeant at the time of the revolution who had soon risen to divisional commander after that tumultuous event, Soult was completely confident of his master's approbation. Indeed, he believed that he was but a victory away from being made monarch of some unfortunate vassal state. Soult's pretensions seem to have been touched off by Napoleon's decision to give the throne of Naples to another of his favorite subordinates, Marshal Joachim Murat. Despite his aspirations, which had shown themselves in Oporto during the brief occupation of 1809 and led many officers in Spain to deride him as *Le Roi Nicolas* or the Sultan of Andalucia, a royal title had eluded Soult. Nevertheless, he could use the stewardship of Andalucia to outdo his peers in another area: amassing wealth.

The French system of imposing taxes on Spanish communities following victorious conquests or episodes of revolt often took the form of property simply being carted off by Napoleon's troops. Marshal Soult

freely exploited these powers to amass a personal fortune. Even following the French drubbing at Salamanca and despite the fact that Wellington's advance through the center of the country made it a very real
possibility that he would be cut off from France, Soult would not con-
template abandoning the lucrative vice-royalty he had carved for himself in Andalucia. Moreover he knew that the emperor had a weakness
for bullying the siblings he had placed on several of Europe's thrones,
among them King Joseph of Spain. The marshal believed he could play
on Napoleon's ill will toward his brother Joseph. The king had been
sending him fresh appeals to quit the south of Spain.

On 12 August, Soult tried an extraordinary gamble. He wrote to
Napoleon himself in an attempt to destroy the little credibility Joseph
had in the eyes of his own brother and dictate the strategy to be pursued
by the entire army in Spain, a letter upon which he believed his own fate
and that of his nation's arms in Spain would depend. The question was
how to get it to the emperor without it falling into the wrong hands?

In the aftermath of Salamanca, resentments between Napoleon's
marshals in Spain burned with fearsome intensity. Recriminations, accusations and rhetorical *rhodomontades* flew between them and their masters. While each sought to distance himself from the latest disaster and to
heap the blame on another, no member of the marshallate embodied the
spirit of recalcitrance more spectacularly than Nicolas Soult.

Since no message from Paris had reached his desk for more than
four months, Soult knew that sending an overland courier would be
risky. Even a squadron of dragoons could not protect such a messenger
from parties of insurgents. Although he trusted the cipher, in this specific case it would be equally disastrous for the secret missive to fall into
King Joseph's hands; even the strongest of escorts could not protect his
dispatch from some curious French officer also holding the key to the
Grand Chiffre.

Soult's solution was to give it to the captain of a French man-of-war
that was sailing from Malaga to Marseilles. Plenty of ships made the run
up the Catalan coast unmolested, but there was always the chance that
a Royal Navy frigate might intercept and board the vessel.

When it was no more than a few days out of Malaga, the ship carrying Soult's dispatch was sighted by a Royal Navy cruiser and a chase

began. The French captain evidently knew that he was carrying a letter for the emperor himself but was not aware of its contents. He decided to play it safe and make a run for one of the French-occupied Catalan ports. As soon as he landed, the captain saw to it that the letter was conveyed directly to the commander of the Army of Catalonia, Marshal Suchet. Suchet had done very well for himself in Spain, being the only general officer to receive his marshal's baton there. He had come by the same hard road as many of the other French commanders—the Italian campaign and the smashing of Austria and Russia in 1805. He was less senior than Soult and perhaps more nervous about remaining high in the emperor's esteem. Being in possession of the same deciphering table as Soult, a copy *en clair* was on his desk by 8 September.

Eloquently, and with many expressions of shocked disbelief, Soult informed the emperor that his brother Joseph was a traitor. According to the Soult, King Joseph had sent emissaries to negotiate with the Spanish government in Cadiz. The reason Joseph wanted him to quit Andalucia, Soult insinuated, was that his deal with the Spanish involved returning the south to their control in return for an accommodation in the rest of the country. The key passage of this scurrilous denunciation reads, "It is my duty to inform your Excellency that I have a fear that all the bad arrangements made [by Joseph] and all the intrigues that have been going on, have the object of forcing the Imperial armies to retreat." The marshal's letter showed his gift for melodrama, suggesting that "I have thought it necessary to lay my fears before six generals of my army, after having made them take an oath not to reveal what I told them save to the Emperor himself."

"Perhaps my suspicions are ill-founded," Soult concluded oleaginously, "but in such a delicate situation it is better to discuss even the worst things . . . my peace of mind depends on the well being and service of the Emperor and of the safety of the army confided to my command."

Quite what Suchet's reaction was at having such an extraordinarily compromising document fall into his hands, has not been recorded. Did Soult have such an intimate rapport with Napoleon that he could denigrate Joseph in this way? If so, perhaps Suchet should send the message on its way. On the other hand, as King of Spain, Joseph was his own nominal superior just as he was Soult's—Suchet knew that forwarding such a message could then make him an accessory to treason. He resolved to act quickly.

The day that Soult wrote his letter, Wellington's army entered Madrid. The British general was a little nervous about taking this portentous step because he knew that the French could still unite a field army large enough to drive him back to the borders of Portugal. The political consequences of leaving the Spanish capital to be reoccupied could be serious, but he felt the blow his advance to Madrid would deal to the entire French enterprise in Spain would justify the gamble. Meanwhile, the longer Soult refused to quit the south, the longer Wellington knew he had to hunt the force he had battered at Salamanca, the Army of Portugal.

Joseph's regime and the class of Spanish sympathizers that had served it did not await the Allies' arrival. The king's French secretary of state, part of the evacuation of 9 August, noted that "all of the French families and those of the compromised Spaniards, who were more worried about the vengeance of their compatriots than the maltreatment of the victors, were rushing to leave the city, and a great many of them, bereft of means of transport or the money to hire it, decided to make the journey by foot." This crowd, thousands strong, made its way southeast toward Valencia, the nearest city, where the king was setting up his temporary headquarters.

During the last two weeks of August 1812, the British commander was feted by *Madrileños*,* nearly hysterical over their liberation. The general was never entirely comfortable with displays of public emotion and civic flattery, but he bore it well enough in the line of duty. Everywhere, redcoats were greeted with enthusiastic *Vivas!*, in the churchs *Te Deums* were sung for the city's deliverance and Wellington was obliged to sit through numerous tedious panegyrics. The great Spanish master Francisco Goya decided he must paint the conquering hero. Knowing rapid brushwork was the order of the day, Goya took a portrait of King Joseph on horseback that he had already started and added the British commander in chief's head instead. Goya's painting was ready for public exhibition on 1 September—a day of rejoicing and thanksgiving for Madrid's deliverance. Wellington took an instant dislike to it, feeling

---

*Citizens of Madrid.

that the body of the figure in the painting was too heavy altogether while his own was lean and wiry.

To escape the metropolitan clamor, the general had moved Allied headquarters to the royal palace *El Escurial*. Scovell went in search of the palace's art treasures, only to discover that the royal residence had been "stripped of its jewels and ornaments by the French." Only frescoes, which even the most rapacious marshal could hardly have carried off, remained. Scovell always took any opportunity to visit the great cultural sights of Iberia and added the Escurial to his list of edifying excursions, along with the great library of the University of Coimbra, Lisbon's churches and Roman ruins of Merida.

Despite his reluctance to attend further noisy celebrations, on the first Wellington agreed to attend a bullfight in his honor in the amphitheater close to Madrid's Alcala gate. This was a most suitable way of greeting the liberation, since Joseph's Bonapartist state had banned this traditional sport. Major Scovell, among other staff officers, went with him. While Wellington's position ensured his invitation to far more functions than he would naturally have wished to attend, it was a rare opportunity for a more lowly officer like Scovell to spend a day enjoying himself, especially after a hard season's campaigning.

At 4:30 P.M., with the late summer's heat giving way to a cooler evening, the show began. Ten thousand people were crammed into the amphitheater, and Wellington's staff officer looked around at this acme of Spanish spectacles with relish. "After parading before Lord Wellington's box and having roses thrown at them by the ladies (for all the Spanish youth and beauty was there), two of the mounted men returned and the bull was let out amid the acclamations of the people," Scovell later jotted in his journal.

The first action of the contest consisted of mounted lancers taunting the bulls until the horned beasts charged, usually goring the riders' steeds. With his love of horses and innate sense of fair play, Scovell found this display revolting, noting that "two had their bowels let out, and the most cruel part of the business is that the Rider is not thought any thing of unless the poor animal dies under him." Matadors on foot then dispatched several more bulls by plunging swords into the shoulders of the swaying, bloodied beasts. Scovell was transfixed by it all and wrote, "I never saw a more cruel or a more interesting sight than this is altogether."

*   *   *

Wellington's attendance at the bullfight may well have been a deliberate ploy to ensure that he was publicly seen just as he was about to begin a bold strategic gamble. On either the same evening or early the next day, his headquarters was on its way again, heading north out of the city through the Guadarrama mountains and into the plains of northern Castille. The British drive northward would end around 135 miles north of the capital at Burgos. A corps under the trusty Rowland Hill was left to guard Madrid while the commander of forces was to try to use the bulk of his army to bring on another battle with the Army of Portugal. Wellington was racing against time; he had to hammer this French corps before it could be reinforced.

While Wellington's march to Burgos was based on a sound starting premise—that after Salamanca the thirty-five-thousand-stong Army of Portugal was still brittle and would collapse if seriously assaulted—it also involved considerable risk. The strategy relied, though, on Soult pigheadedly holding on in Andalucia, for if he abandoned the south, he would bring eighty thousand troops into play against the Allies and any move into northeast Spain, nullifying the Allied advantage in numbers and creating the risk that their supply lines back to Portugal might come under attack.

While Wellington's force pushed north, General Bertrand Clausel, the Army of Portugal's commander, despaired of the morale of his troops: "It is usual to see an army disheartened after a check: but it would be hard to find one whose discouragement is greater than that of these troops." Unfortunately for Wellington, Clausel kept falling back to avoid battle and as the British commander pursued him, the garrison of Burgos got in his way. He could not simply bypass it, since that would leave them free to threaten the rear of his army.

Almost one thousand years before the British general ever laid eyes on it, Burgos had been a bastion against the Moorish advance into northern Spain. Its castle, positioned at the end of a great spur of high terrain dominating the River Arlanzon, was surrounded on three sides by steep slopes. When Napoleon saw it in 1808, he had admired the natural strength of the spot and ordered its medieval center to be clad in all manner of modern defenses so that it was fit to face the age of gunpowder and breaching batteries. The one easy approach, along the tongue of land behind the citadel, had been blocked by a great redoubt bristling with guns, the Hornwork of San Miguel. A girdle of thick walls surrounded its old stone defenses and some two thousand picked men had been thrown into it by the French as they retreated.

From the outset it was apparent to many on the staff, including Scovell, with his experience of so many reconnaissance missions, that this fortress would not fall easily. And even if it could be taken, how would the Allied army be able to maintain this position so far into Spain, hundreds of miles from the safety of the Portuguese border? Certain doubts must have afflicted Wellington as well, but he committed himself to the siege operation.

After the horrors of Ciudad Rodrigo and Badajoz, it was asking a great deal of Wellington's tired army to attempt a third major operation of this kind in one campaigning season. Knowing well the feelings of the regiments that had suffered so horribly in the great breach of Badajoz, he decided to excuse the Light, 3rd and 4th Divisions from the work at Burgos. On 19 September the fortress was surrounded by troops of the 6th and 1st Divisions.

Wellington moved swiftly into attack, ordering the storm of the San Miguel Hornwork on the very first night of his siege. Troops of the 42nd Highlanders, the Black Watch, assaulted the position frontally, but took hundreds of casualties as they stalled in their approach. Only the intrepidity of the major placed in command of some light companies sent around the back of the work rescued the storming operation. He managed to break in and take it. It was none other than Edward Cocks, a onetime colleague of Scovell's in the intelligence department, who now led the storming parties of the 79th Highlanders, putting himself forward to lead these Forlorn Hopes under the gravest risks, driven by the desire to distinguish himself. On 27 September, Major Cocks heard a rumor going around the lines that he had been killed. He went into the trenches where British troops were burrowing their way toward the castle's walls asking for news, and received the ominous reply, " 'Nothing, Sir, but Major Cocks is killed.' One man actually argued the matter with me. A little further were my own men and some of my friends, condoling over my fate. The surprise on their faces was very whimsical and it was not a little gratifying to observe how one's death took."

As the siege progressed into attempts to batter the citadel itself, responsibility for directing this deadly work rested with the staff, and it was here that the British commander's old animosity toward the scientific soldiers was rekindled. Wellington's direction of the siege caused deep divisions, most importantly with his principal specialist adviser, Major John Burgoyne of the Royal Engineers. Siege warfare, with all its calculations about trajectories and the weight of shot needed to open breaches, was regarded by most officers of the time as the ultimate expression of scientific generalship. But following the great success at Ciudad Rodrigo nine months earlier, Wellington fancied that he had a pretty good idea of how to take a fortress more swiftly than the "experts." The stage was set for conflict.

Major Burgoyne's main criticism was that his commander's lack of confidence about success caused him to throw men away with a series of half measures. After one operation at Burgos, Burgoyne wrote home bitterly that failure was the result of "the miserable, doubting, unmilitary policy of small storming parties." During this row, Wellington did not apparently display the scorn that some witnessed on other occasions for low-bred officers of the technical arms. However, members of the staff who came from such backgrounds were well aware of the general's prejudices. Wellington believed the experience of France showed that artillery and engineer officers were potential revolutionaries, given that many came from bourgeois families and had, as he put it, "no connection with property." He distrusted them, as he distrusted some Wycombites, because intelligence and education had been the main criteria in granting them an officer's commission.

In the case of the general's assistant QMG and commander of the Guides, the tensions had been exacerbated by a rebuke on Wellington's part during their advance to Madrid. On the march, when communications with Lieutenant General Rowland Hill's detached corps had broken down for a single day, and despite his previous pleasure (notably the mention in dispatches), Scovell received a considerable dressing down. While relations between the AQMG and his master soon returned to their usual pitch of formal correctness, Scovell could not forget the incident, for it gave him an intimation that his devoted service to headquarters during three and a half dangerous years had not been enough to overcome Wellington's personal prejudices. In addition to the vital codebreaking work, Scovell's organizational skills had also made him quite indispensable in running the army's communications. Dozens of new messengers (most of them Don Julian's guerrillas) had been taken on to help cover the greater distances between the Portuguese frontier and Burgos. By late 1812 Scovell was directing hundreds of men in this task and, adhering to the principle that prompt payment was the best defense against treachery on the part of the messengers, spent £22,477 in little over one year on it. None of this, though, seemed to count as much as a noble pedigree in the eyes of his master.

Scovell's resentment, usually carefully kept off the pages of his journal, emerged openly during the bad-tempered conflict between science and intuition in headquarters at Burgos. When officers gathered in huddles to discuss the operation, Scovell was naturally inclined to take Burgoyne's part. In fact, he repeated his criticisms almost to the letter.

On 22 September, for example, he wrote in his journal after one attack, "It failed and the cause, in my humble opinion, was the taking of men by detachments instead of at once taking a regiment." Although the use of bands of volunteers from different units was common in storming operations, it evidently struck many of the staff as a bad idea at Burgos. Specifically, Burgoyne felt that any Forlorn Hope of picked volunteers needed to be backed by a full regiment acting in support: Wellington refused to commit men in this way. When the final assault failed on 19 October, Scovell wrote, "I have little doubt that a well supported attack would have carried the place."

It had soon become apparent that the small train of heavy guns marching with the main army was quite inadequate to the task of battering Burgos. More than once these eighteen-pounders were established in a battery, only to be overwhelmed by the fire coming from within the fortress. Gun carriages were smashed and men ripped apart by the fire of the garrison defenders. Wellington did not have the time to bring up the large train he had used earlier in the year and which, by an uncharacteristic oversight, he had neglected to call upon when he first meditated the siege of Burgos. One member of the staff suggested that they ask the Royal Navy for help. A messenger could reach the Biscayan littoral in just a few days and would then be able to ask Commodore Sir Home Popham, who commanded the squadron there, for the use of heavy naval guns. For ten days, Wellington did not accept this very wise advice, and when he finally acceded to it the guns could not be brought over the Cantabrian sierra fast enough to alter the issue.

While Wellington was tackling these myriad problems at Burgos, Scovell was trying to cope with some quite new difficulties of communication.

By August it had become clear that the army would march deeper into northern Spain, closer to the Biscayan coast, and that consequently there would be closer cooperation with Commodore Popham. This officer was a fire eater, a type that became famous in his service: in 1806 he had interpreted a vaguely worded set of orders from the admiralty so liberally that he launched an invasion of South America on his own initiative. He combined audacity in action with great diligence in matters of staff work and was something of a savant on the matter of codes. Indeed as far as the navy was concerned he had written *the* book on the subject. Popham's treatise, *Telegraphic Signals or Marine Vocabulary*, had made communications by flag between warships more efficient and secure. With this background, naturally Popham suggested that communications between them, across no-man's-land, ought to be protected by a cipher.

Wellington relied on Popham to coordinate actions by guerrillas on the coast and support them, but he did not feel that ciphers were justified. He wrote back to the commodore: "I beg to observe to you that I have no cipher in which I could correspond with you: and unless the Spaniards in the north are very different from those I have seen elsewhere, or the enemy opposed to you more active than those I have met with, you have no reason to apprehend that your letters will be intercepted. Those to whom they may be entrusted may not take the trouble of carrying them; but they would prefer death to delivering them to the enemy." In other words, he did not believe their communications were in jeopardy. This reply might be seen equally as a backhanded compliment to Scovell's efficient system of Spanish messengers, a poignant comment on the lack of a common code between the two services, or indeed an example of the kind of *froideur* that rendered professional intercourse between army and navy so unsatisfying to both partners.

When it came to communications with the army's expeditionary corps in eastern Spain (which had finally landed after Lord William Bentinck's procrastination earlier in the summer), Wellington took a different line: he was quite certain that he wished to encode his thoughts. In this case, messages going between the two armies could be sent either back into Portugal, thence by boat around to Catalonia, or by Spanish messengers across central Iberia; either way there was a risk of them falling into French hands.

Wellington's attempts to furnish the armies with a common cipher had initially been almost as badly managed as King Joseph's first experience with the *Grand Chiffre* in 1811. A diplomatic cipher had been sent out, but there had been problems initially with making sure both sides had the same table and later with words not contained in the tables.

Scovell's solution to the problem was most ingenious. He made sure that both headquarters had copies of the same edition of pocket dictionary and used this tome as the basis of his code. So, to quote an example given by him, the code 134A18 could be deciphered as follows: 134 was the page number; A is the column; 18 is the number of words or letters from the top. This type of code is extremely strong, and it successfully protected communications with the Catalonian expeditionary corps. It was his experience with breaking French ciphers that gave Scovell such a solid grounding in codes and helped him establish this "two book" system. The British need for such ciphers was obviously less than that of the French (with their need to coordinate operations across a bandit-infested country), but it is remarkable how the man in charge of Wellington's communications arrived so quickly at what was a virtually impregnable solution.

As the siege of Burgos progressed, it was becoming more and more apparent how difficult an undertaking it really was. The trenches needed to approach the walls under cover proved very hard to dig. The ground was rocky and the slope so steep that French sharpshooters on the ramparts more than one hundred feet above were often able to fire down on the working parties. Attempts to batter the walls with gunfire proved so ineffectual that Wellington and Burgoyne decided to try blowing them up instead. The first blast of this kind, on 29 September, hardly inspired confidence. As Scovell noted wearily, "Recourse was had to a mine which in my humble opinion was made at the opposite place to where it ought to have been formed."

One day of frustration followed another. Morale sank among the rank and file and tensions rose in the staff. For the general and his staff officers, Burgos was made all the harder by the loss of a trusted friend. Just twelve days after he had written home about the exaggerated rumors of his own demise, Edward Cocks was cut down during fighting in the trenches. Scovell noted simply in his journal, "My firm friend Cocks was finished in this business." Cocks's daring scouting missions in the early days of the war had made him a particular favorite of Wellington's, who wrote, "He is on every ground the greatest loss we have yet sustained."

After four weeks of grim struggle, Wellington ordered a storm at dusk on 18 October. It failed. A series of costly attacks brought the British close to the inner defenses but did not carry them. By the time Wellington gave up, 509 men had been killed and more than 1,500 injured, all in vain. The soldiers cursed the bloody place.

The failure at Burgos left Wellington horribly exposed. He was hundreds of miles from the Portuguese frontier and knew that the time when Joseph could assemble a large army was fast approaching. He had also discovered that Clausel's corps had been reinforced from France and was ready to advance against him. After stubbornly holding out for so long, Soult had, at last, evacuated the south and was in a position to combine forces with the others.

The decision on 21 October to fall back toward the frontier had important political consequences. British troops relinquished the Spanish capital to the taunts of its distraught citizenry. The army faced a long and arduous withdrawal back to the Portuguese borderlands. Inevitably opinion in London would see the failure at Burgos as a costly reverse and the campaign, with its glorious episodes of Ciudad Rodrigo, Badajoz and Salamanca, would end on a sour note. As Wellington's men began their march, the first driving rains of the fall lowered their spirits further.

With Wellington countered at Burgos, King Joseph found himself considering the consequences of Marshal Soult's scurrilous dispatch of 12 August. Soult's objective in writing it, namely his desire to hang on in Andalucia, had been superceded by events, but the reverberations caused by that ill-judged letter had been slowly gathering force in the French high command.

It had not taken Marshal Suchet, the French commander in southeast Spain, long to send Soult's treacherous letter on its way. Unfortunately for Soult, his habit of picking quarrels had also made him an enemy of Suchet. So Suchet took the king's visit to Valencia as a welcome opportunity for retribution. Soult's message was forwarded to the very man it had accused of treason.

The duke of Dalmatia's letter was an unhappy product of a system in which different commanders had maintained their own direct relations with the emperor. Even since March, when the right to direct strategy had at last been ceded, the recalcitrance among his commanders still rendered Joseph's job a grievous burden.

By the autumn of 1812, southern Spain had been evacuated, and almost everywhere the *guerrillas* were gaining strength after the French humiliation at Salamanca. What vexed Joseph the most was that he still carried all the responsibility but in fact had very little power. His response to reading Soult's letter therefore was to try to use it as a pretext to have him sacked.

Joseph picked his trusted staff officer Colonel Desprez to carry a letter to the emperor demanding Soult's dismissal. This officer set out from Valencia on 9 September on a journey that was to become something of an epic. Having traveled three hundred leagues to reach Paris on 21 September, he discovered that his imperial master was away in the midst of Russia and he had to ride a further eight hundred leagues across eastern Europe until he finally arrived at Napoleon's headquarters in Moscow on 18 October.

While Colonel Desprez was making his way to an emperor who insisted on maintaining the ultimate personal control over the Iberian struggle from the other end of Europe, Joseph was having to deal with Marshal Soult in person. Having quit Andalucia, Soult met Joseph, Suchet and Jourdan for a council of war in Cordoba on 3 October.

"The ruler's first interview with the marshal produced some lively arguments," according to Marshal Jourdan's understated account. "They were conducted face to face. At all times Joseph, always generous, appeased him and showed himself ready to forget what had happened." A new battle plan was proposed in which Soult would be given

command of a substantial column and move toward Wellington. Some
of his army of the South, however, would be needed by other commanders, a proposal that triggered an immediate outburst: "The Duke of
Dalmatia, having received his orders, instead of hastening to carry them
out, pressed the King to make changes, gave him advice and suggested
that he did not have the right to transfer from one army to another
troops that the Emperor had confided to his command . . . the King,
deeply unhappy with this obstinacy, directed him to carry out his written orders, or failing that to relinquish command of his army to the
Count d'Erlon."

Soult was cowed into cooperation; the king argued bygones should
be bygones: neither was sincere and both decided to bide their time.
Since Colonel Desprez was still on his odyssey along the highways of eastern Europe, Joseph knew that it would be some time before he received an
answer to his request for the marshal's dismissal, time in which it was
essential that they act to retake some of the ground lost in this disastrous campaign.

By 17 October Joseph had cajoled his marshals into launching a
new plan of war. Soult's Army of the South, and Joseph's own Army of
the Center, would attempt to link up with Clausel's force to the north. It
was exactly this movement that sent Wellington scurrying back from
Burgos to the comparative safety of the Portuguese border.

When Joseph finally received the emperor's response to his letter of
9 September, many weeks had passed. The missive itself must have been
a bitter disappointment to the king of Spain. His messenger, Colonel
Desprez, had reached Napoleon on the very day that the emperor's fortunes had turned. He had just resolved to abandon Moscow, having
realized that holding Russia's capital would not secure her capitulation.
The emperor's message was therefore terse, telling his brother to sort
out the problems with Soult by himself.

The final chapter in the saga of Soult's letter had not yet played itself out
as Wellington's army marched from Burgos back to winter quarters on
the Portuguese frontier. The straggling and desertion seen during Sir John
Moore's retreat to Corunna in 1808 or Wellington's march back from
Talavera the following year once more reappeared. The distances covered

were large and as the British army moved onward some of its members went in search of food, drink and plunder. Others, driven to distraction by the privations of campaigning, and perhaps the horrors of Burgos, risked death by deserting their colors. Between 23 October and 29 November, some forty-nine hundred men disappeared from the ranks.

Joseph's army tried to bring on a second battle near Salamanca, but pursued by the united armies of Portugal, the South and Center, there was no chance that Wellington would ever have fought them. It was in mid-November, just after it had passed the site of July's great victory, that the Peninsular army's supply system broke down completely.

The ensuing privations of the 1812 march shared by all ranks were brought home most poignantly by Rifleman Edward Costello of the 95th Rifles, who wrote in his memoirs, "On this retreat, Lord Charles Spencer, a youth of about 18 years of age, suffered dreadfully from hunger and fatigue. Trembling with cold and weakness, he stood . . . anxiously watching a few acorns which, to stay the pangs of hunger, he had placed in the embers to roast . . . the tears started silently from his eyes. He will not forget, I expect, how willingly the rough soldiers flew to offer him biscuits, which they could not withhold from one so tenderly and delicately reared . . . there are times when Lords find that they are men, and men that they are comrades."

The campaign was effectively over by the third week in November. Wellington and his staff settled once more into winter quarters in Frenada, the little village on Portugal's upland frontier. One of Wellington's first tasks on arriving was to pen an angry message, cursing the army for marauding and desertion: "From the moment the troops commenced their retreat from the neighborhood of Burgos on the one hand, and of Madrid on the other, the officers lost all control of their men. Irregularities and outrages were committed with impunity." It will come as no surprise that this bad-tempered outburst caused deep resentment in the army after a retreat in which men had dropped dead from exhaustion and officers of noble birth had been reduced to eating acorns.

Having vented his spleen, the commander of forces calmed himself with frequent fox hunts, galloping for miles over the Portuguese sierras. His spirits restored, Wellington would begin to use his time in winter quarters the way he liked best: in rooting out and eliminating the imperfections of his army.

Scovell's ingenuity however became so restless that during the shrinking days of November and December 1812 he used every opportunity to try to discover the few parts of the *Grand Chiffre* that still eluded him. It was as he worked away on this task that a copy of Soult's fatal August letter eventually found its way to Frenada.

PART IV

WINTER QUARTERS, THE VITORIA
CAMPAIGN AND AFTERWARD

CHAPTER SEVENTEEN

I. dont. believe. we. were. ever. deceived. 481. the. 985. 186. t. 843. 688. and. 1297. S. 174. vell . . . is. the. 854. erson. who. made. them. out.

FRENADA, DECEMBER 1812 TO MARCH 1813

*J*t was about midnight on a December evening and few people were
stirring in the bivouac. The two hundred members of the convoy
were mostly sleeping around faltering embers of the campfires they had
built earlier. They were a little north of Valladolid on their way back to
France and were doubtless tired from many hours in the saddle. Most
huddled under blankets, trying to shut out the cold and find a spot where
they could dream of home and sleep unmolested by stones or roots
beneath them. The security of this little convoy, it is clear, was lax.

The leader of that French caravan moreover had not reckoned on
the change that had befallen the country in the past few weeks, one that
made even the plains of Segovia a risky place. The British might have
relinquished Madrid and withdrawn toward Portugal, but the occupiers
were to discover that things had not been restored to the *status quo ante*
Salamanca.* On the contrary, everywhere in Spain guerrilla bands had

---

*The situation before Salamanca.

been inspired by the summer's events. They had finally seen the Bonpartist edifice in Spain shown up as a hollow façade and many entertained the hope that 1813 would see their country free of the French at last. In the hills, guerrilla chiefs like Longa ruled large tracts; collecting taxes and ruling the land like robber barons.

Down on the plains of Segovia, Joseph's convoy had been watched as it went into its bivouac in that December twilight by Jeronimo Saornil's guerrilla band. This chieftain was quite different from Don Julian Sanchez or Longa, who the British considered gentlemen. Saornil had been a common criminal imprisoned in his native Valladolid before the French invasion and the new authorities had unwisely released him. A British officer who had encountered Saornil's band in the summer of 1812 wrote, "They are complete *banditti*, two-thirds clothed in things taken from the enemy. The only pay they receive is from plunder." When Marmont had pulled the Army of Portugal back to the Douro line in July, Saornil had come to the attention of the British for being able to provide captured messages in territory that was unfamiliar to Don Julian's men. Naturally, Saornil had greatly appreciated the silver paid on the nail for these enemy papers.

That December evening, he timed his attack carefully. The few sentries placed by the French barely had time to shout an alarm as Saornil's horsemen burst out of the darkness. The element of surprise was so complete that even the guerrillas balked at murdering the enemy in their beds. Some 180 were taken prisoner and two British officers who had been under escort were set free. As his men started stripping the convoy's members of their valuables, Saornil surveyed his spoils.

An ornate saddle lying beside a svelte horse caught his attention. The owner seemed to be some kind of secretary to King Joseph. Saornil cross-examined him. Wearing a dark green hussar's jacket tied up with a red sash and a top hat bearing the skull-and-crossbones motif, the guerrilla chief must have struck terror into this prisoner. The king's servant took one look at this pirate's unshaven face and knew that his only choice was to cooperate or die. He handed over a tiny key and explained its use. Saornil examined the saddle and fiddled with a brass ornament on its side, sliding it back to reveal a keyhole. Turning it, a small compartment built into the thick leather under the pommel dropped open. Inside was a package of documents. Breaking the seal, Saornil tried to read one. Large amounts of text had been written in the king's *Grand Chiffre* and there were several such dispatches folded together. Saornil wagered that the British would pay a high price for this. He would take them to Lord Wellington in person.

Settling into the little farmhouse that would be his billet for the winter, Scovell at last had time to consider personal matters. Mary had been left behind in Lisbon all these months of campaigning. With little chance of the British army moving forward until late spring, she would now be safe in Frenada: it was time to send for her.

Meanwhile, the army moved into its winter quarters in frontier villages, and headquarters was set up in the same grindingly poor village that it had occupied the previous winter. The better sort of Frenada inhabitant had a two-level dwelling, with the ground floor reserved for livestock. The most a staff officer could hope for was a small room in one of the single-story farmhouses that formed most of the village. Only the commander's house, on Frenada's little square opposite the church, had a room large enough for Wellington to entertain fourteen or fifteen officers at dinner.

Those who had not wintered at this impoverished upland headquarters before, like Francis Larpent, thought it "wretched." Larpent was a London lawyer hired by Wellington as part of his plan to enforce some order on his unruly soldiery. The new judge advocate wrote of his own accommodation, "I am literally buried in papers, saddles, portmanteaus, bundles, bedding, panniers etc and have no room to give a visitor but by standing myself." Larpent soon discovered that George Scovell was one of the few men in Frenada capable of erudite conversation and they became firm friends. It was perhaps an indication of the narrow intellectual horizons of most of the army's officers that Scovell became such a valuable find to this highly educated outsider. In his journal, Larpent noted Scovell's impressive intellect and the administrative efficiency that he had brought to the Guides, post office and communications generally.

There was another attraction to seeing Scovell, of course—his wife. Somehow, he had obtained lodgings large enough for them both to live in comfort and to entertain four or five guests at their makeshift dinner table. Larpent wrote, "I have dined here with Major and Mrs Scobell [*sic*], the only lady here; I there for the first time (to the credit of the lady) got a tender fowl, and a piece of mutton, for even at headquarters they kill and eat wholesale."

Larpent and the other guests did not just eat well in this rude Portuguese cottage, but enjoyed games of cards afterward with George and Mary. What more agreeable way to follow the lady's roast than with a hand of loo, winner takes all? An invitation to one of these "very pleasant little dinners" became an ace in Scovell's hand during the long winter quarters, especially in helping to draw De Lancey or Somerset into the schemes Scovell began to hatch for the 1813 campaign.

As was usual, many of the better-connected sort went home for winter. One officer who had departed under a cloud was Colonel James Willoughby Gordon. He had served briefly as the army's quarter master general during the autumn and soon after his arrival had started sending indiscreet and often pessimistic accounts of the campaign to political friends, most of them Whigs fiercely critical of the Peninsular War. Wellington discovered this behavior when several details from one of his dispatches to the secretary of war appeared in the *Morning Chronicle* before the letter had even reached the minister's office.

Gordon's indiscretion annoyed Wellington all the more because following the setback at Burgos and the losses on the retreat, Wellington was extremely sensitive to the notion that his operations during 1812 might be considered a failure in London. The general's ADCs awaited the daily post from Lisbon with some trepidation, for if Wellington read a newspaper article critical of the war it was sure to sour his mood for the remains of the day. He wrote to the secretary of war, complaining, "From what I see in the newspapers I am afraid that the public will be much disappointed at the result of the last campaign, notwithstanding that it is in fact the most successful campaign in all its circumstances, and has produced more important results than any campaign in which a British army has been engaged for the last century." He trumpeted the capture of Ciudad Rodrigo and Badajoz as well as the victory of Salamanca before conceding, "the only occasion on which I have been seriously mistaken was at Burgos."

Whatever the newspapers might say, the victory at Salamanca had established the general's reputation both with the ministry and with the wider European public as an extremely successful commander. He now had the power to pick or discard those he worked with and no longer had to care a jot whether this might offend party interests. The Tory Major

General Charles Stewart, adjutant general for three years, had gone on a sort of unlimited leave from the army early in 1812. At the end of the campaign it had been the turn of the Whig Gordon. A plague on both their houses. Wellington could now choose his staff by his own criteria, not by those of the political patrons of Horse Guards. Men of good family and military merit, that was what was required. His victories also meant he was no longer as dependent on a narrow cabal of Tories to sustain his position. "As I have long ceased to think of home politics, it cannot be said that I am of a party different to that to which any other person belongs. I serve the country to the best of my ability abroad," the general told one member of Parliament in a letter from Frenada.

One more sacrifice was required to exorcise the demons of Burgos: the senior Royal Artillery officer at headquarters. This officer struck fair-minded observers as decent but somewhat ineffectual, and the failure to bring a strong train of siege guns to Burgos had been an important ingredient in the British reverse there. Wellington put this unfortunate colonel under such pressure that he resigned and the general sent him on his way home with these brutal words: "As you state that you don't feel yourself equal to the magnitude of your situation . . . I can feel no scruple . . . in pleading guilty to the charge of not placing confidence in you . . . I have found that you were not so capable as I had believed you for the arduous task which you had undertaken."

Wellington then asked London for the return of George Murray, his previous QMG, and this request was granted, and the Scot, who managed to combine zeal and charm in equal measure, appeared in Frenada early in 1813. Once back in charge of his old department, Murray returned to his office as quarter master general and became the second most important man in the army, in practice if not by seniority.

There were also many items in the newspapers crossing Wellington's desk at the end of 1812 that gave him satisfaction; the beginning of Napoleon's retreat from Moscow in October had especially caught the British popular imagination. Caricatures showed "General Frost Shaving Little Boney." A giant wielding a razor marked "Russian Steel" was shown trampling French armies and grappling with a tearful Bonaparte.

By the time the scale of Napoleon's defeat in the east was known, Wellington had set off for Cadiz. He left, accompanied by Colonel FitzRoy Somerset, on the twelfth. The Spanish regency had let him know it was willing to give him supreme command of all their armies for the coming campaign. The precise terms of this arrangement needed to be tied down face-to-face.

Those remaining at Frenada would have read the *Times* of 17 December with fascination. The paper published an "Extraordinary Gazette" devoted to Napoleon's failure in Russia, telling its readers:

> "Buonaparte is wholly defeated in Russia; he is con-
> quered and a fugitive. And what can we say more? We
> have seen his army pass from victory to victory; we
> have seen it overthrow kingdoms, and oppress peas-
> ants—violate every human right, and diffuse every
> species of human misery. And now where is it?"

As Christmas approached, the little square outside headquarters was abuzz with gossip about the latest events. Staff officers and generals up from their divisions strolled in greatcoats and fur-lined caps trading the latest rumors: Napoleon had fled his army; the entire host, 500,000 men, no less, had perished in the snows. If the French generals had grumbled the year before that they were stuck in Spain while others were going to win glories against Russia, now it was the British officers' turn to rue the fact that they were unable to witness the spectacle of a general *débandade** of Napoleon's mighty army. It was into this hubbub that the distinctive figure of Saornil and his bodyguards arrived, bearing their valuable cargo.

The guerrilla chieftain went to the door of headquarters only to be received by Colonel Campbell, the head of Wellington's household. That would not do, he had important French dispatches that could only be delivered into the hands of the general himself. The colonel answered that Lord Wellington was abroad and might not return for some considerable time. Saornil was implored to share his information. But the mustachioed guerrilla was quite firm: he had to see Wellington in person. These were letters from King Joseph to Napoleon himself, they could only be delivered to someone of the highest rank.

It took some hours to convince Saornil that he must hand over the

---

*A disbandment, the complete collapse of military order.

papers promptly if they were to be of any use at all. Eventually the Spaniard agreed, on the promise that Wellington would accord him every honor and civility once he returned to Frenada.

Scovell would have studied Saornil's package with some excitement. Since the end of the campaign there had been a dearth of information about what was going on inside the enemy camp, and before setting off for Cadiz, Wellington had complained to London, "I have not yet any intelligence upon which I can rely of the exact position of the enemy's armies."

The letters spread out in front of him were one from Joseph to the emperor, two from the king to the minister of war (General Clarke) in Paris and one from Marshal Jourdan to the same official. The letters had dates ranging from the last week of November to 10 December, this demonstrating the severe difficulties of French communications. They contained many passages in the now familiar *Grand Chiffre* and were written on fine parchment watermarked with the French Imperial Eagle.

Among the enclosures was an *en clair* return for the Army of the Center that detailed the location, even of its battalions, their strength and who was in command. This document alone would prove a most useful starting point for piecing together enemy dispositions prior to the next campaign.

Joseph's letter to Napoleon trumpeted his achievement in the latter part of the campaign, declaring, "The enemy's hopes since the 22nd July [Salamanca] are today vanished, people have been disabused about the power of a united army." Scovell's knowledge of the cipher was pretty much complete but his annotations on the letter revealed one or two remaining uncertainties. He underlined places where he had resorted to pure guesswork, one sentence reading, "I hope that the Army of the South will not delay in gathering *in Murcia, the whole country* will then soon be re-occupied." He was right about Murcia but the phrase "whole country" should actually have been deciphered "all centers."

This letter of Joseph's had been superceded by events, for in it the king had asked his brother for reinforcements as part of his plan to reestablish control over the country. What Joseph didn't yet know was that Napoleon, far from providing fresh cannon fodder for Iberia, would now be looking for the veterans serving in Spain to replace his fallen army.

Jourdan's letter to General Clarke in Paris, however, was much more up-to-date. The old marshal seems to have recognized that reinforcements were out of the question and therefore launched a sort of preemptive attack on the minister, laying out in detail the desperate situation in Spain. Instead of Joseph's empty boasts, this message painted a vivid picture of the miserable conditions prevailing in the French army.

Jourdan noted that Marshal Soult's Army of the South was occupying a line close to the British, and that "only Monsieur the Duke of Dalmatia can know the positions occupied by the English army, but since he had not made any report to the King on this subject, it is quite impossible for me to give Your Excellency any information." Jourdan also criticized Suchet for failing to send reports and noted that no mails from Paris had got through to Madrid for weeks. Clearly the situation in the Pancorbo and elsewhere on the route from France was most dangerous.

The marshal's tale of woe also showed that the Armies of the South and Center had almost run out of ammunition, most units had lost all their transport wagons, there was widespread guerrilla activity and the army's pay was months in arrears. Jourdan's letter left little doubt that the French armies in Spain would be unable to undertake offensive operations against the Allied field armies for months. The initiative therefore rested in the hands of Lord Wellington.

As to the particular direction of an Allied thrust, that would depend on further intelligence about French dispositions and a greater understanding of their scheme of operations, which was precisely the information contained in a further letter from Joseph to the emperor dated 22 December 1812. Scovell's knowledge of the *Grand Chiffre* had during many quiet hours of reflection in Frenada improved to the point where, in his own words, "I had it so complete at the end of the campaign of 1812 as to decypher a very long letter of Joseph to his brother of which the whole even to the date was in cypher."

Joseph's letter of 22 December, with its frank assessment of future operations, was perhaps the most important message that Scovell worked on. Certainly, like the king's dispatch to Marmont of 9 July 1812, it would have the greatest consequences for Wellington's overall strategy.

The king had positioned 100,000 troops along the lines of the Douro and Tagus Rivers. This deployment formed a sort of diagonal line from northwest to southeast, ending just south of Madrid. Since these troops were quite spread out, for reasons of supply, they had assumed their defensive line some way back from the Portuguese border. Outposts would be manned in places like Salamanca, well forward of the Douro-Tagus line, so that the main defensive cordon should have early warning of any British advance. Joseph believed that with such dispositions of the armies of the South and Center, he could "combine their divisions as events dictate." If things went wrong, this defensive line was at least positioned to shield the main line of communications back to France via Burgos.

In his letter Joseph also made some ambitious political proposals, for example, to "declare Burgos the royal seat until there's peace and take all archives and other attributes of the capital and establish my government there." This idea, which relegated Madrid to the status of a sparsely garrisoned outpost, was to find favor with the emperor, although the removal of government from the capital took far longer than anticipated.

When Wellington returned to Frenada on 25 January, little time was wasted in briefing him on the latest intelligence and handing him deciphered copies of the captured correspondence. The general found Joseph's bombast in his letter to the emperor of 21 November particularly amusing. Near the end, the king had written that the Spanish had formed a very negative opinion of the British during their brief occupation of Madrid and that "the inhabitants prefer the orders of a sovereign of your house to the theories of the *Cortes*."* The general was so pleased with this nugget of political intelligence (since he thought it displayed both Joseph's delusions and portrayed some of the wilder orators of that Spanish assembly in an unflattering light) that he shared it with Don Andes de la Vega, a prominent Spanish politician, in a letter of 29th January:

> *"I enclose an extract of a letter from King Joseph to Napoleon which was in cipher and which we have deciphered, which is well deserving of your attention and that of your friends in the* Cortes. *It is in few words but contains a text upon which much may be written. I am not an advocate for King Joseph's judgement or for his veracity; but, although we rarely find the truth in public reports of the French government or of their officers, I believe we may venture to depend upon the truth of what is written in cipher."*

*The Spanish parliament.

In his last remark, Wellington had given his strongest testimony to the value of deciphered French communications and thus, more or less explicitly, to Scovell's work. Messages in the broken Great Paris Cipher had become his most reliable source of strategic intelligence. The only curious thing was that he put this vital labor at risk by sharing with a Spanish politico that Joseph's cipher was being read at Frenada. Cadiz, after all, was a playground for all sorts of spies, charlatans and intriguers. In truth, matters of political intelligence sometimes excited Wellington so much that he let his guard down. It was just as well that he had been much more careful about mentioning the invaluable product of codebreaking since the summer of 1811 in his many dispatches to London.

The general had also eagerly consumed the military detail in Joseph's later missive. In a letter to Earl Bathurst on 10 February, he indicated for the first time that his plan of action for the 1813 campaign would involve defeating Joseph's river line by going around its northern extreme. Wellington began preparations to send his battering train of siege guns around to Corunna, where it would be kept while he decided where exactly in northern Spain it might be used in the coming campaign.

All this vital knowledge came at a price, and this time it meant that Wellington had to honor Colonel Campbell's promise and sit down to dinner with the notorious ruffian Saornil, who had been loitering about Frenada for weeks. Those invited to share this experience included Colonel Campbell, Francis Larpent and General O'Lalor, one of the Spanish staff that had grown around Wellington since his appointment as *generalissimo* of that country's armies.

This dinner began, as usual, at about 5 P.M., and Saornil arrived "looking like a dirty German private dragoon in a smart new cavalry jacket." Staring down at his place setting of silver cutlery and gleaming crystal he became quite confused. It was an awkward moment for this onetime convict. Larpent recorded that "the Spanish General O'Lalor treated [Saornil] like a child, told him what to do and eat; but he [Saornil] had, I concluded, dined long before, for he ate little or nothing."

Following Saornil's visit, more captured dispatches were received at Frenada that allowed Wellington to learn about the unedifying struggle between Soult and Joseph. On 8 January 1813, Joseph wrote to his brother, "It is an absolute impossibility for me to work with [Marshal Soult]; I demand his replacement."

A couple of weeks later, Joseph finally abandoned any restraint he had felt about spelling out in full the extent of Soult's disloyalty and scheming. For months, Joseph had kept the contents of Soult's letter to himself—probably because it was too humiliating to confess to his brother that an eminent marshal had been plotting against him in this way. But on 28 January he wrote to the emperor again, finally informing him of the marshal's indiscretions in all their painful detail. He included a copy of Soult's infamous letter of 12 August, accusing the king of treason.

Couriers running between Joseph and Paris had to make their way along the road from Burgos to Bayonne on the French side of the border. Although this route was referred to as a *chaussée*, one with a wide, well-drained surface, it ran through some particularly inhospitable territory. A day's ride beyond leaving Burgos, traffic had to climb into the Cantabrian hills toward the Pancorbo pass, a defile that had become infamous among the *bataillons de marche** and *estafettes* who used the road, for its jagged sides soared out of the ground and high into the sky. In many places, the guerrillas were able to hurl boulders from its ledges down onto the French below. It was in here that the guerrilla chieftain Juan Longa hunted the French and their collaborators.

Longa was a gunsmith from Rioja who had joined the patriotic insurrection in its early days. His band varied in strength between a few hundred and a few thousand. They had successfully evaded many attempts to wipe them out. They judiciously sought refuge in the high sierra whenever things got too bad. By late 1812 Longa's guerrilla band had evolved into a well-organized three-thousand-man force able to launch raids using either guerrilla skirmishing tactics or the kind of formal evolutions carried out by infantry of the line. Longa's skill at creating this force had been rewarded with a colonel's commission in the regular Spanish army and he had also evolved a close relationship with the British, through Commodore Sir Home Popham. The British supplied him with weapons and in return he began to relay intercepted documents or other more delectable trophies. In May 1812 he had captured a convoy of King Joseph's servants bearing a thousand bottles of fine claret, which he sent to Wellington, where it lubricated the headquarter's

---

*Route battalions, made up of detachments going to different units who marched together for some kind of security.

table for the remainder of the campaign. Although Longa's men were well disciplined by the standards of many bands, they remained ferocious in action; William Warre testified in July 1812 to an ambush where "an intercepted mail from Paris to Madrid which was taken by Longa, who killed 400 men who escorted it except 12, who, he says, did not show so strong an inclination to leave their bodies there."

It may well be possible that the courier bearing King Joseph's letter to his brother of 28 January had fallen into Longa's hands in the Pancorbo pass. The precise details of what happened are lost. Whether it was a Spanish collaborator or some French staff officer, and whether he was tortured or simply shot through the brain at point-blank range, the messenger and his precious cargo were separated.

The further details of how the papers made their way to British headquarters are also unclear. It seems likely that having been handed to the Royal Navy, the papers bearing the mysterious numbers of the Great Paris Cipher were then sent around to Portugal and headquarters at Frenada. Scovell would only have to have read the first line to see both the importance of the message and the fact that it was in the cipher he had already cracked: *Pour l'Empereur*—for the emperor.

Scovell would have folded out the deciphering table that he had attached to his copy of Conradus. Two other papers were enclosed with the king's dispatch, including the infamous Soult letter. It was copied onto cartridge paper bearing the Royal Navy watermark. The whole bilious correspondence documenting months of French cabal and intrigue thus ended up on Wellington's desk.

There can be little doubt that these letters provided Wellington a precious insight into the enmities of the Army of Spain command. There were always rumors and reports from spies, but it was laid out before him in two or three letters captured that winter in the same words that Joseph had intended for the emperor. The feud between Soult and the king would have harmed the morale of French forces; as always when subordinate officers were forced to choose sides in such intrigues, suspicion, hostility and division were natural. This climate was a further consideration in assessing how the king's forces might react to a British attack in 1813.

*   *   *

For King Joseph, the early months of that new year brought one ghastly revelation after another. His brother's public explanation of the Russian failure, the twenty-ninth *Bulletin*, published in Paris on 3 December, reached the English secretary of war's desk in London on the twenty-first and finally arrived in Madrid on 6 January 1813. Since so many sons of Picardy or the Languedoc lay dead in the Russian snows, this announcement required a certain amount of candor on the emperor's part: most of the *Grande Armée* was lost.

The *Bulletin* reported that the onset of heavy frosts after 6 November had killed thousands of horse. By the fourteenth, "the men seemed stunned, lost their gaiety, their good humor and dreamed only of misfortunes and calamities. The enemy seeing on the roads the traces of this terrible calamity that was striking the French army, tried to profit from it." Since the phrase "to lie like a *Bulletin*" had entered common currency in Paris years before, such admissions from a notorious propaganda sheet caused deep forebodings in Madrid.

Unofficial reports of what had happened began to circulate at King Joseph's court. The most important of these came from none other than Colonel Desprez, who, having ridden right across Europe to acquaint the Emperor with Marshal Soult's seditious letter writing, was then caught up in the retreat from Moscow. On his return to Paris, Desprez had written to Joseph: "We lost prisoners by the tens of thousands—but, however many the prisoners, the dead are many more. Every nightly bivouac left hundreds of frozen corpses behind. The situation may be summed up by saying that the army is *dead.*" Joseph, Jourdan and all other officials were deeply shocked by the estimate that of half a million men, only twenty thousand men had marched out of Russia alive.

As if all this were not bad enough, Desprez also shed some light on the emperor's views of the king's tiresome quarrel with Marshal Soult. Napoleon had celebrated the marshal as "the only military brain in the Peninsula," a clear insult to anybody else who presumed to direct the French armies there. It came as cold comfort to His Catholic Majesty that a letter from General Clarke received in the same mail finally recalled Soult to France, not of course for the reasons Joseph would have wanted but as part of the recall of fifteen thousand veterans needed to begin the reconstruction of the French army. He may have been relieved about the duke of Dalmatia's departure, but at the same time he could scarce afford to lose those experienced soldiers.

The emperor had also issued a screed of directives to his brother. The capital was to be made in Valladolid, rather than Burgos as Joseph had suggested, but the difference had little effect on defense plans; General Caffarelli was to be sacked for his failure to stamp out the guerrillas in the north and there was to be a major onslaught against those insurgents. The emperor seemed to have been reduced to a cold fury by the long interruptions in communications along the Bayonne *chaussée*, that arterial route that formed the main link with *la patrie*. Hearing of this further installment of trouble in the north must have delighted Wellington, who had been an enthusiastic advocate of sending more weapons to the guerrillas there.

For the staff in Frenada, February and March days dragged. They engaged in all their usual country pursuits. Officers armed with fowling pieces brought in plover and woodcock for Mary Scovell to roast to perfection. Often, usually every other day, Wellington rode one of his eight hunters to hounds. The principal object of the general's chase seems to have been maintaining his personal strength and skill at equitation, for in all these months it was said only one single unfortunate fox fell into the clutches of the Frenada hunt. On many a day officers scrambled down the rocky gorge behind the village with their fishing rods before casting into the inky waters of the Coa. This pursuit was perhaps more therapeutic than hunting, for the population of that river could provide them with intelligence as well as supper. For much of the year, very little swam up the rocky bed of that river, but the arrival of fish was linked by rain to the question of when they might march out of quarters and drive the French from Spain. It was only when the downpours of March and April had raised the level of the Coa that trout and the fish locals called *bogas* and *barbos* could migrate up from the Douro. Wellington was awaiting those same rains to nourish the fodder of Castille and Segovia. It had to be green and tall before he could set his brigades of cavalry on their trajectory to the northeast, and that year the seasons seemed a little late.

As in 1812, the officers of various regiments, notably in the Light Division, spent many a winter's day putting on theatricals. In January it had been *She Stoops to Conquer*, February's production was *The Rivals*. Captain Hobkirk of the 43rd had the honor of playing Mrs. Malaprop, with fresh-faced young lieutenants taking the younger female parts. "It is impossible to imagine anything more truly ludicrous than to see Lydia Languish and Julia . . . drinking punch and smoking behind the scenes at a furious rate between the acts," wrote one spectator. Wellington attended *The Rivals* at its makeshift playhouse in Gallegos, riding twenty miles there and twenty miles back to Frenada in the darkness. Officers of the Peninsular army went to great lengths to amuse themselves in those long winter weeks of 1813.

Of all the officers in Frenada, Scovell must have enjoyed the most pleasant evenings, for with Mary he had laughter, companionship and the pleasure of society. Having finally beaten the *Grand Chiffre*, however, he found himself with too much time on his hands. He began once again meditating a great new project, a scheme that might unite his own interest with that of Lord Wellington, Judge Advocate Francis Larpent and the good of the service: the formation of a Staff Cavalry Corps.

CHAPTER EIGHTEEN

J. dont. believe. we. were. ever. deceived. in. these. let. 843. 688. and. 1297. S. 174. vell . . . is. the. person. who. made. them. out.

THE VITORIA CAMPAIGN, APRIL TO JULY 1813

*I*n April 1813 each cavalry regiment in the Peninsular army received a request for volunteers. Men of good character and exemplary service were asked to come forward for the formation of a Staff Cavalry Corps, where they would be placed under a commandant and receive training in their new duties.

At Frenada, George Scovell threw himself into his new task with customary vigor. He had been appointed brevet lieutenant colonel and major commandant of the Staff Cavalry Corps.* A plan that he had first committed to paper in 1808 for an embryonic regiment of headquarters horsemen, able to turn their hands to a variety of duties, was finally coming to fruition.

---

*This must be distinguished from the Royal Staff Corps—an organization of field engineers and craftsmen (to which Sturgeon belonged) that had existed throughout the Peninsula campaign—and the Provost Marshal, the small force previously charged with organizing the army's law and order.

Their commandant had long understood that special troops were needed to maintain discipline, particularly during marches, and even in 1810 Scovell had written of the need for a *gendarmerie*. During Wellington's retreat from the frontier to the lines of Torres Vedras in that year, Scovell had ridden through a riot in the town of Leira, recording: "A most disgraceful scene of Plundering commenced chiefly from the Stragglers, the Portuguese soldiery and the Women. It was not stopped until the unfortunate men were hanged on the spot by the Provost, and more than 100 flogged. Safeguards should always be put on towns when an army has to pass through or near. A sort of *Gendarmerie* such as the French has is absolutely necessary in all large armies to superintend the Police, arrest stragglers etc." During the retreat from Burgos in 1812— some weeks prior to Wellington's angry General Order rebuking the army for its conduct—Scovell had again been scribbling ideas in his journal for how a new force of this type might work.

In April 1813 he had been given the task of making this plan a reality. Francis Larpent, the judge advocate and Scovell's frequent dinner companion, was an enthusiastic supporter of the new project. The men of the Staff Cavalry were all volunteers and many were veterans who knew well the tricks of stragglers and camp followers. By the end of the month parties of new recruits were arriving. Larpent recorded: "Officers do not take to it as yet, but very good-looking men have volunteered in general." Those who answered the call to Frenada were given a smart new uniform. They had a red cavalry jacket with dark blue lapels and an elegant shako. In all, about two hundred men joined the Staff Cavalry. Men of the Household Cavalry held back. They let it be known that since they had been police at home (by which they meant the king's final defense against the mob), they had no intention of being police in Spain.

The new corps would fulfill all of Scovell's dreams of commanding a regiment of British cavalry and at the same time create the kind of HQ troops that John Le Marchant had proposed in 1802. Wellington, it is clear, wanted the Staff Cavalry for one purpose above all: to police the bloody-backed rogues of his army. So Scovell added the title of "father of the British military police" to those of assistant QMG, forge designer, chief Guide, mapmaker, postmaster, code maker and code breaker.

Ambition and circumstance threw Scovell into the role of Wellington's truncheon, a duty that did not necessarily sit well either with his gentle temperament or his views on discipline. He certainly did not share Wellington's faith in generous amounts of flogging and hanging. Like many a reform-minded officer, though, the campaigns in Iberia had convinced Scovell that the British army contained a substantial element of criminals. Sir John Moore, a noted skeptic when it came to using the lash, had been shocked by the plundering and drunken criminality of his men during the Corunna campaign. Almost every officer who had witnessed the riot and rape in Badajoz in 1812 was repelled by it.

The British soldier was usually a volunteer and many fell into the hands of recruiters while penniless and longing for drink. When they sobered up in some garrison, many regretted their decision to join, but the gallows awaited any deserter who was caught. On the march, this army became a volatile assembly, one in which many men sought any opportunity to steal. Taking the possessions of a dead Frenchman was permitted, stealing from the peasants was not. Scovell was struck by the narrow section of British society dredged up by traditional recruiting methods and the higher quality of many French recruits who were products of the world's first properly organized conscription system. "It is quite wonderful to see the intelligence of these fellows when compared with our own," Scovell wrote after interrogating a French deserter in October 1812.

Evidently some senior officers must have asked whether Scovell was really the right man to impose order, since later in 1813 he wrote to a colleague at Horse Guards, "You need be under no apprehension on the score of my good nature when the good of the Service is placed in competition with it. I should be very sorry to be accused of cruelty, but I do not see the keeping up the discipline of any army in that light." Wellington at least had faith in Scovell to discharge his new responsibilities professionally and that was the key thing as they stood on the threshold of the 1813 campaign.

The word about headquarters was that Lord Wellington intended putting the army in motion on 1 May, so Scovell did not have long to turn the little detachments of five or six men who came from each regiment into an effective corps. It helped his task greatly, however, that all of these recruits were trained mounted troops, unlike the deserters he had introduced to horses when forming the Guides years before.

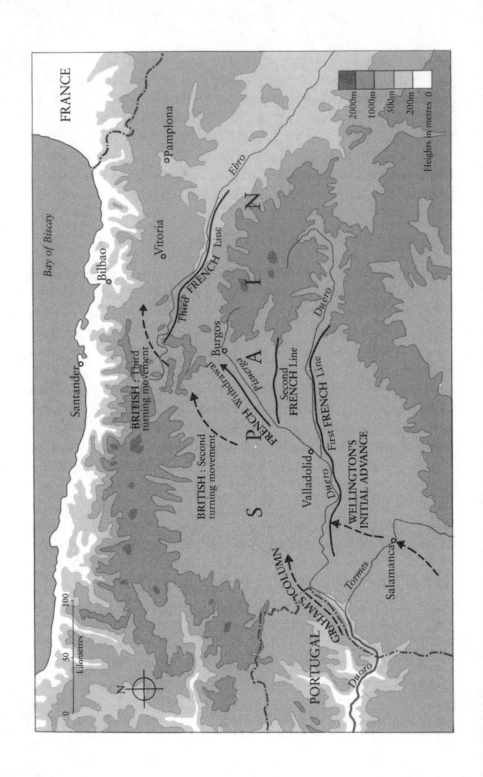

FRANCE

Bay of Biscay

Santander

Bilbao

Vitoria

Pamplona

Ebro

Third FRENCH Line

BRITISH : Third
turning movement

Burgos

Pisuerga

FRENCH Withdrawal

S P A I N

Second
FRENCH Line

Duero

BRITISH : Second
turning movement

First FRENCH Line

Valladolid

Duero

WELLINGTON'S
INITIAL ADVANCE

GRAHAM'S COLUMN

Tormes

Salamanca

PORTUGAL

Duero

N

0   50   100
kilometres

Heights in metres 0

2000m 1000m 500m 200m

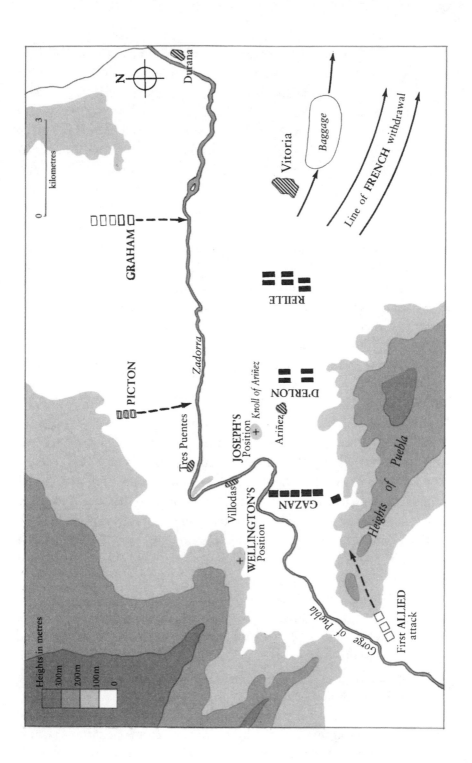

The first corps founded by Scovell, the Mounted Guides, was to continue in present form, and on 21 April he relinquished its command to Lieutenant Colonel Henry Sturgeon, an extremely capable officer with a background similar to his own.

These new developments did not excuse Scovell from his cipher work, though, and as Wellington made his final preparations for the 1813 campaign, some important new dispatches were captured. The most significant, dated 13 March, from King Joseph to General Charles Reille commanding the Army of Portugal, brought Wellington's understanding of the general scheme of French defensive operations up to date.

The new dispatch showed that a general offensive against guerrillas in northern Spain had begun, which was drawing half of the Army of Portugal north, a step that precipitated a redeployment of the armies of the South and Center. This was important news for British headquarters since the French were repeating their error of early 1812 in reducing their force opposite Wellington at precisely the moment that he was meditating an offensive. It meant those corps facing him would not be the 100,000 suggested in Joseph's letter of December, but more like 80,000. The king also informed General Reille, "I am counting on moving my headquarters to Valladolid at any moment."

Shortly afterward, guerrillas in northern Spain also provided the British with a letter from Colonel Lucotte, one of Joseph's staff officers, to Madrid sent on 16 March. Lucotte spoke with authority about Napoleon's view because he was on his way back to Madrid from Paris, where the emperor himself had directed him as to how the campaign in Iberia should best proceed. Lucotte was not important enough to use the *Grand Chiffre*, but had resorted instead to a very curious cipher of hieroglyphs. It was different from others Scovell had worked on, as its encoding table involved lines of letters that would suggest the next few substitutions, not just the conversion of single characters one by one. Notwithstanding the application of this new principle, Scovell seemed to have regarded this new code as something of an insult to his intelligence, scribbling on the bottom, "Decyphered at Frenada with ease in 6 hours and immediately sent home by L. W."

Lucotte described the collapse of security on the main road to France, noting, "Supplies are hardly guaranteed from one day to the next all along the line; and the Emperor believes it is of the most pressing importance to take urgent steps to secure communications." All of this confirmed the British general's view that the operations against Mina and Longa in the north would last for some time. Wellington passed the message on quickly to London, mainly because of its political content—Lucotte suggested that the emperor was expecting Austria to join the coalition against him at any moment. In forwarding this intelligence to Earl Bathurst, the general showed a caution absent from his own communication to Cadiz of 29 January, warning, "This letter was in cipher and it is desirable that its contents should not be published."

The colonel also made clear that the emperor's desperate struggle to raise a new army meant Joseph's constant demands for cash were falling on deaf ears in Paris: "Sire, it is absolutely necessary to replace the money that is not coming from France with forced contributions in Spain and by drawing it from Valencia—Napoleon's needs are enormous." The system of coercing localities to provide money for the army was a familiar feature of the occupation of Spain, but reports such as Lucotte's inspired a last great wave of formalized looting of cash and items of value from the locals. Lucotte told the king that he was hastening down as fast as he could, in company of Colonel Desprez. That officer, who had spent a few weeks in Paris restoring himself to health after the horrors of the retreat from Moscow, was showing admirable devotion to duty in returning at this juncture.

While Scovell was working on those latest intercepted messages, a letter that Wellington had sent to London eight months earlier finally received its reply. It was from Earl Bathurst and contained the report of the London government decipherers on the French correspondence that had been sent before the Battle of Salamanca. These experts in secret writing had taken all those months to add 164 new meanings (and they confessed their uncertainty even over some of these) out of the 1,400 numbers in the cipher. They added an exculpatory note: "With the few cyphers and consequently the slender materials which the decypherer had to work upon, it was scarcely possible to render this key more complete."

Wellington was evidently unimpressed with this tardy reply and its contents. Had headquarters been dependent on London to crack the code, none of the results so critical for the Salamanca campaign and indeed the one he was about to launch would ever have been achieved. He could not resist the temptation to send them back a copy of Scovell's deciphering table, which by that point had opened up pretty much the entire code. The general wrote back to London sarcastically:

"I am very much obliged to your Lordship for the key of the cipher as far as it had been discovered, which you transmitted to me on the 5th April last; I now enclose for your information such parts of it as have been made out by Lieutenant Colonel Scovell without reference to the key received through your Lordship."

It was significant that Wellington acknowledged Scovell's sole responsibility for this work in writing, for back in the summer of 1811 when simpler ciphers had first appeared on the Spanish border, other officers, such as Somerset and Hardinge, had also been involved in the decoding. The general's pleasure at reading his enemy's most secret correspondence was curtailed somewhat, however, during the early months of 1813. The flow of intercepted French messages had declined markedly. Those French divisions facing Wellington remained largely inactive, so there was little need for their commanders to communicate. The new French defensive line was more compact and some way back from the hunting grounds of that interceptor of mails par excellence Don Julian Sanchez, whose attentions were otherwise engaged, in any case. He was training his men to act as a regular force at the head or flanks of Wellington's column of march, leaving less time for long-range patrols in search of enemy messengers. The general's most reliable provider of reports from inside the enemy camp, Father Patrick Curtis, was also out of action. He had been banished from Salamanca by the French early in 1813, seeking refuge in Ciudad Rodrigo.

As the time neared to send his army into action, Wellington needed to be sure that his strategy of moving through the difficult country to the northwest of the French defensive line would work. To this end, several officers were sent out on reconnaissance during April. Among them was Lieutenant Colonel William Gomm, an assistant QMG, who had been campaigning, like Lieutenant Colonel Scovell, since Sir John Moore's expedition and had done equally well out of staff work. Unlike Scovell, he did not reside in the main headquarters but was attached to the 5th Division.

Gomm emulated the tactics of previous exploring officers, setting out with just a servant and a pair of horses to make sketches and check the levels of different water courses. Evading the cavalry patrols that the French sent into this no-man's-land, they made their way through the hilly country, crossing the Douro to the west of the main French line on the river. He worked his way up to the Esla, a tributary of the Douro that Wellington needed to cross if he were to bypass the French with his first great turning movement. During the last three days of April Gomm found himself getting drenched with rain. At last the downpours needed to nourish the fodder were doing their work.

The AQMG of the 5th Division returned unscathed and thrilled with the success of his mission, writing to his sister that "far from finding my employment irksome, I enjoyed it; and it became so much the more interesting from the probability of my being shortly called upon to lead my flock in the same direction." Luckily for Wellington, the explorations of Gomm and others were not detected. Similarly, a train of wagons bearing pontoons destined to be used to bridge the Esla was brought up to northern Portugal without the French finding out.

By early May the elements of a grand scheme to advance on the French by a large and unexpected maneuver were nearing completion. Furthermore, Wellington's quest to perfect his army had resulted in improvements in all areas. A firmer discipline had been imposed, resulting in dozens of court-martials. Judge Advocate Larpent pronounced with grim satisfaction, "We have flogged and hung people into better order here." Scovell's new Staff Cavalry Corps was ready to take to the field too.

All aspects of supply had been attended to. After years in the field, the troops had finally been issued tents. Their old, weighty, iron camp-kettles had been traded in for lightweight tin ones. Great magazines of supplies had been accumulated and were being brought upcountry by the mule trains. Many regiments had been issued with new uniforms. The old ones had literally become washed-out rags, held together by the locally procured cloth. For the heavy cavalry the new outfits were of quite a different style. The old bicorne that drooped on the head like a soggy croissant had been replaced with a handsome Romanesque brass helmet much like those worn by the French dragoons.

The army was also more numerous than ever before. Drafts and reinforcements had taken the total of the Anglo-Portuguese main army to more than eighty-one thousand men. Several divisions of Spanish troops were now placed under Wellington's direct command. His host was about to enter battle with a much stronger cavalry arm too, a brigade of hussars and the heavies of the Household Cavalry having joined the army.

Bringing this great force to bear would require a level of organization not seen before. Thomas Graham and Rowland Hill would each lead a column of several divisions, and at that level the troops would be officered by the likes of the dependable Picton, Pakenham and Lowry Cole. Perhaps Wellington's greatest comfort was that he would have Major General George Murray at his right hand once more as quarter master general. And it was to Murray that he looked to draft the complex orders directing these assembled divisions through the rough border country and into the place where they would discomfit all of King Joseph's calculations.

At last Wellington launched his army. One British body moved through Salamanca, and that seemed to position them to march in a great diagonal across northeast Spain toward Valladolid and Burgos. This was what Marshal Jourdan had planned on, and as Wellington knew from intercepted letters, it was the axis around which all of the French divisions could easily concentrate.

Just north of Salamanca, on 25 May, the British caught up with General Villatte's rear guard. Four guns of the Royal Horse Artillery opened on the French infantry regiment marching across open ground. The crack and whoosh of the British six-pounders did nothing to disconcert the French march and Scovell marveled at their steadiness. For a footslogger, it was an unpleasant business to be moving along with two brigades of enemy cavalry trotting behind and beside you. Any mistake in the alignment of companies or the execution of a turn might create the opening that the enemy horse were waiting for. If that happened, it would all be over in minutes and those *messieurs en rouge* would be carving you up with their sabers, as they had those wretched battalions at Arapiles the previous July.

As Scovell watched the French marching along he started to meditate on how the column could be attacked more effectively by the British cavalry. Every time the horse artillery stopped firing to allow an attempt at a charge, the French battalions slowed up a little, closed ranks and prepared to receive what they knew was coming. He saw a division of the Royals gallop forward. It was the same result again: faced with a steady phalanx of men presenting their muskets, the heavies had pulled up fifty yards away and turned about. What they *ought* to do, he thought, is deploy a small body of cavalry hovering about the French flank who could sweep in whenever they saw an irregularity of formation. Only when this charge was about to strike home should the horse artillery cease firing.

This game of cat and mouse continued across the plain for a couple of hours before the British broke it off; it had cost the French around 100 dead and 150 prisoners. Scovell admired them for escaping without greater losses. He felt for the conscripts, each struggling to keep up and turn on the right command, lest any mistake produce their ruin. And these feelings produced anger that their general should have put his men through this trial, Scovell writing, "General Villatte ought to be punished for keeping his Infantry in Salamanca so long." Scovell scribbled down these reflections on how the engagement might have been better managed in his journal as soon as he found a moment. That record had, by the summer of 1813, expanded into its third volume. At the head of a body of British horse, Scovell could not stop himself thinking like a cavalry commander. Little matter that he had left the 4th Dragoons seven years before. Now he had the Staff Cavalry formed up behind him and, unlike the Mounted Guides who were cast about the country in their small packets, these men had been prepared to act as a single unit if the need arose on the battlefield.

Wellington remained with the force advancing north of Salamanca for a couple more days. His presence was intended to deceive French spies. At the same time this column was marching precisely along the line that the enemy expected, General Thomas Graham's force of forty thousand was moving through hill country well to the northwest, making its way toward the Esla valley. Lieutenant Colonel Gomm was riding with Graham's column, containing five infantry divisions and two brigades of cavalry. Thus, Wellington made sure the French were pinned to the Douro River line; Graham's force was making that barrier irrelevant.

*   *   *

At French headquarters, there was the customary lack of good information. Marshal Jourdan had seen to it that silver was broadcast around the border region for months in advance hoping to attract some good spies, but he noted, "Despite the care taken by the Chief of Staff [himself] to the secret service, and despite the money put into this service, it always failed to obtain precise intelligence on the Anglo-Portuguese army. The reports received were so contradictory that instead of clarifying matters they increased uncertainty." Worst of all for the marshal, a patrol of dragoons in the Esla country failed to spot Graham's column at first, creating a false sense of security for some days.

On 28 May, with the advance continuing rapidly, Scovell received a most welcome order. He was to take the Staff Cavalry Corps and report to the Light Division to act as the light cavalry for that famous body. Lieutenant Colonel Scovell's dream of leading mounted troops in the advance guard was suddenly quite real.

For the next few days the Staff Cavalry performed as the reconnaissance screen of the Light Division. Its men moved forward in small numbers by day to scan the country for any sign of the enemy, and manned the outposts needed to warn of any surprise attack by night. Scovell's delight at this small but significant role was only exceeded by the pleasure of his commander in chief when it became clear that the French had abandoned their defensive line, beginning a headlong retreat from the Douro line on 2 June.

Everything at French headquarters was confusion and recrimination. Their attempts to concentrate forces were just taking too long. Breathless messengers arrived with reports of each new sighting by reconnaissance parties of Graham's column. There was a council of war in which Jourdan suggested advance rather than retreat, a notion that was immediately dismissed by King Joseph, who recited his brother's orders like a catechism: communications with Bayonne must be maintained at all costs; no conquered provinces should be given up; it would be dishonorable to concede to Wellington without offering to give battle.

But where could His Catholic Majesty rally his scattered host? A decision was made to collect at Burgos. Joseph still had not concentrated the divisions of the Army of Portugal that had been sent to fight guerrillas in the northern sierras. Without them, he had half as many men as Wellington and could not offer battle without inviting nemesis for himself and what remained of French rule in Spain.

By 10 June it was becoming clear to the king that his hopes of gathering all his forces around Burgos had been unrealistic. Wellington simply kept pushing his army forward around the French right. Again the British had moved around the flank of the enemy position and their choice was stark: retreat once more or be cut off from France. Joseph issued orders for a concentration behind the River Ebro near the Basque city of Vitoria.

Leaving Burgos, the French detonated mines around the ramparts, a procedure that went disastrously wrong, sending masonry crashing onto the heads of hundreds of French troops who were marching through the town. British troops were not immediately aware of this, but they did hear the distant boom of the mines going off. Veterans of the failed siege of Burgos were heartily glad: "We were all delighted to hear of its fate. What a thing it would have been if it had never been attempted! The army would probably have wintered near Salamanca and Cocks would now have been with us, half mad with delight at our rapid and successful advance," Captain Tomkinson commented.

As Wellington's troops marched into the hill country northwest of that city there was an intoxicating good humor about the army. The days were warm, but not oppressively so as they had been during the maneuvers around Salamanca the previous summer. The countryside was largely undisturbed by the war: "This enchanting valley is studded with picturesque hamlets, orchards of cherry trees, and fruitful gardens, producing every description of vegetation," one diarist recorded. Crossing a bridge, the Light Division saw its bands lined up and heard them playing "The Downfall of Paris." "We were much amused at their wit on this occasion," remarked one officer, "and we had it followed by a national tune or two to remind us of Old England."

The daily marches were a prodigious feat. Back in 1809, on the journey down from Oporto to Abrantes, even a stage of three leagues each day had left dozens of men straggling behind and committing every sort of outrage. In June 1813, the soldiers were frequently covering five leagues in a day and leaving few in their wake. Scovell, whose duties included collecting stragglers, noted, "Our Men are marching much

better than I ever saw them." The provision of tents had made a big difference, for fewer soldiers were sick. Each divisional commander had
also become adept at organizing his columns of march and Provost so as
to make it harder for the malingerer to fall out of the ranks.

On the fourteenth, Scovell found himself invited to a picnic lunch in
a nearby field. His hosts were the prince of Orange, General Alava (one
of Wellington's Spanish staff), Judge Advocate Larpent and Lord Fitz-
clarence, one of the young ADCs. Together they hacked pieces from a
cold ham, tasted the rough country bread and sipped champagne
brought by the prince's servants. It must all have been rather intoxicating to someone who had once believed his life held no more in store
than long hours at the engraver's bench.

The plain of Vitoria is surrounded on all sides by highlands with access
to low pasture afforded through a few passes. The city's position had
made it a crossroads for centuries and King Joseph as well chose it as
the place to rally his footsore army. They had been marching hard for
three weeks and needed rest. Their leaders also required time to adjust
to the fact that Wellington had just evicted them from a great slice of
Spain, including its most fertile lands and great cities like Madrid and
Valladolid, by maneuver alone.

It was a good place to rendezvous with the Army of Portugal's divisions that were straddling the main line of communications to Bayonne.
With the Salinas pass on the Bayonne road to their rear, the French
armies occupying the plain only had to plug the four other main routes
into the plain to defend themselves effectively. Better still, any attacker
wishing to use three of those passes—those to the east and north of the
Vitoria lowland—would have to divide his forces on long, roundabout
journeys through steep-sided valleys, thus opening themselves to defeat
in detail as each of these columns appeared at its destination. This left
just one obvious route into the city, the Puebla Gorge, where the main
chaussée from Burgos arrived at the southeast corner of the plain. Jourdan and Joseph hoped that geography would equalize the balance of
forces for them and allow them to fight to advantage.

Jourdan, it has to be said, did not expect a fight at Vitoria at all.
"Lord Wellington had shown himself, from the opening of the campaign,

more disposed to force the retreat of his adversaries, by manoeuvring on the right, than to confront them head on to give him battle, we believed that continuing with this method, he would head for Bilbao . . . to force us to fall back in haste on Mondragon so as not to lose our communications with France," the marshal noted. Prudence, however, dictated that Jourdan deploy the king's armies in earnest. General Gazan, Soult's successor in command of the Army of the South, was placed with twenty-six thousand men and fifty-four cannon to block the exit of the Puebla Gorge. Gazan's left was anchored on a steep-sided ridge, the Heights of Puebla, and his right on the River Zadorra. That stream curved around his position and stretched eastwards back across the plain. The position was less than three miles across Gazan's front, but the possibility that Wellington might use the three passes entering the plain from the north meant the French deployment had to be about seven miles deep, since any eruption from those northern gateways to the plain would leave Gazan with the enemy behind him. This curious characteristic of the French battleground, that it was deeper than it was wide at the front, led one British officer to observe caustically that the French position had two major defects, the first of which was that it was facing in the wrong direction!

Wellington's attack on the Vitoria position began on the morning of 21 June. An Allied column under Lieutenant General Hill was to make its way up the backside of the Heights of Puebla and onto the great ridge that commanded Gazan's left. Some Spanish troops led the way up the heights and were followed by Hill's 2nd Division. During their ascent they had one important factor in their favor: that the southern side of the ridge is a much easier climb than the scarp on Gazan's flank. As the French general saw the puffs of musket shots from his lookouts and heard the crackling of a fusillade, he was forced to send battalions up, almost on all fours (the gradient being one in one) to reinforce them. When they arrived at the top breathless, these Frenchmen found themselves being impaled on the bayonets of the 71st and 92nd Highlanders and 50th Foot.

Making their way to a knoll behind Gazan's position, Joseph and Jourdan regarded the fighting along the ridge line with foreboding. Their hopes of employing the natural strength of the terrain in their defense were crumbling. Moreover, they were acutely aware that they could not afford to lose, for at that moment just behind Vitoria were great columns of Spanish *afrancesado* refugees, wagons containing all the state papers removed from Madrid, the army's artillery park and numerous *fourgons** belonging to the army command. More troops were ordered onto the ridge to try to stop the British attack.

Watching this reinforcement move up at about 10:30 A.M. from the slope above a village called Villodas on the left bank of the Zadorra, Wellington was pleased. For him, Hill's attack was no more than a diversion designed to achieve precisely these results. Any reserve that the French committed south toward the ridge now was one less brigade to be used later against the two large Allied columns that he had set marching toward the passes at the north of the plain. Wellington's plan, if it succeeded, would be one of annihilation: General Graham had been sent around to the farthest east of those passes, to cut off most of the French army from its line of withdrawal.

Wellington allowed the fighting atop the ridge to go on for three hours to be sure that the other columns would be able to act in concert. While absolutely necessary for his overall plan to work, it meant that the troops on the Puebla Heights paid a very heavy price. The French threw more and more men into the attack. The 71st was forced back briefly, losing its commanding officer and leaving "not 300 of us on the heights able to do duty, out of above 1,000 who drew rations that morning." That Scottish narrator fired 108 rounds from his musket, rendering him unable "to touch my head with my right hand; my shoulder was black as coal."

Eventually, at around 12:30, Wellington ordered the 4th and Light Divisions to move forward toward Gazan's front. On 21 May his whole campaign had begun with a movement to pin the French to their river defense line. Now that its climax had been reached, the same idea was being used at the tactical level, on the field of Vitoria, for if Gazan was to be cut off from his retreat, he would have to be kept where he was.

The Light Division soon stormed two bridges over the Zadorra on the right of the French line. They ran up a steep slope behind the water and were soon under attack from the French. As the fighting intensified, the Light Division men were heartened to see the head of the 3rd

---

*A four-wheeled wagon reinforced with much ironwork enabling it to carry heavy loads.

Division appearing across the plain to their left. The first of the flanking columns came into action, and after a brief cannonade Picton's Fighting Division stormed the next bridge down the Zadorra.

With this event, Joseph's nerve seems to have faltered, for at about 2 P.M. he could, from his little knoll just two miles away, see that both of Gazan's flanks were in danger and that he would have to order a general withdrawal of his first line. The 3rd Division promptly deployed into line and began assaulting the village of Arinez, the second position of the French army, with cheers and great rolling volleys of musketry.

For the French it was now vitally important to fall back quickly, trying to extricate their guns and infantry, under the covering fire of their artillery. Around 4 P.M., with the battle was at its peak, the 2nd, 3rd, 4th and Light Divisions as well as a couple of brigades of cavalry were forcing the French eastward. They in turn responded with barrages of cannon fire. The whole floor of the valley was cloaked in dense smoke from the battle.

At last Graham's column began attacking at the back of the French position, trying to force a passage across the Zadorra. This he was unable to do, and with that failure the hope that the battle might see the destruction of the entire French army began to vanish. The rest of Wellington's host, however, continued to follow its original orders, pressing forward in other parts of the field.

With this ferocious British assault going on around them, Joseph and Jourdan realized that their hour of judgment was close and that, with the Bayonne road threatened, the only way out of the plain was due east, on small mountain roads to Pampluna, toward a remaining French garrison. Any hope of uniting with the other half of the Army of Portugal had been forgotten; all that mattered now was saving what remained of their force under their own hands.

A general retreat began, as one by one divisional commanders recognized that there was no way to extricate their artillery. Dozens of guns were falling into British hands. With brigades of infantry turning about and trying to flee to the east, holes appeared in the French line through which British cavalry began to flow.

Antoine Fée, a French conscript serving with the dragoons of the Army of the South, watched as this last line of cavalry tried to save the huge train of baggage that lay just to its rear:

"Our dragoons found themselves in an area dissected by many ditches and fences marking the many market gardens, and could not maintain their formation; the horses were brought down, their riders, having got them up again turned around and I found myself, like all the others, in the middle of a great rout, pursued by English hussars, who had nothing in front of them and threw themselves on the baggage, sabring many who were unable to offer resistance. To add to the terror of this unarmed mob, howitsers and shells began going off in the air, showering those below with splinters."

At twilight, hussars of Grant's recently landed brigade broke into the French rear. Their arrival caused a general panic and dissolved the last bonds of discipline that were still holding many French units together.

Surrounded by screams, gunfire and the thundering of horses' hooves, it became apparent at last to Joseph, Jourdan and those around them that their kingdom was forfeit and so might their lives be at any moment. One of the king's courtiers recorded:

> "[Joseph] was held up like the others and running the risk of being caught by English hussars. I saw a man hit by a musket shot falling at the feet of his horse. Luckily for the King, his regiment of Guard light horse remained within range of his group at all times and having pulled back slowly and in good order, arrived just at this moment."

Under this escort, Joseph fled the field. Jourdan was separated from him but also managed to make his way together with a couple of ADCs, swords drawn, off toward the east. Beyond the city of Vitoria the ground was naturally quite boggy, and as chaos set in wagons and gun limbers toppled into the deep ditches besides the road, blocking the way to those who tried to follow. In many places drivers or officers cut the traces of draft animals and leapt onto them so they could gallop away, but each escape of this kind just left another disabled engine of war obstructing the roads.

Realizing that the coaches and heavy *fourgons* belonged to none other than the king and his ministers themselves, the 18th Hussars began looting the convoy. The scene that presented itself to the soldiers of Wellington's army was to prove one of the most memorable of their years of campaigning:

> *"The road to Pampluna was choked up with many carriages filled up with imploring ladies, wagons loaded with specie, powder and ball, wounded soldiers, intermixed with droves of oxen, sheep, goats, mules, asses,* filles de chambre,* *and officers . . . it seemed as if all the domestic animals in the world had been brought to this spot, with all the utensils of husbandry and all the finery of palaces and mixed up in one heterogeneous mass."*

Rifleman Costello, running through the town, saw an ornate coach leaving under escort of a French officer: "A comrade had followed and we immediately fired. The officer fell and the carriage stopped. We rushed up to the vehicle, it contained two ladies, evidently of high rank." An officer of the 10th Hussars appeared and took the women, one of whom was General Gazan's wife, into custody. Costello went off in search of something else of value, arguing that "all who had the opportunity were employed in reaping some personal advantage from our victory, so I determined not to be backward." Costello eventually clapped hands on a portmanteau stuffed with silver doubloons to the value of £1,000. Elsewhere a private of the 87th made off with Marshal Jourdan's baton and a trooper of the 14th Light Dragoons with the king's solid silver chamber pot. Heavy wagons bearing the name of General Villatte were found to be crammed with silver plate, altar pieces and religious artifacts stripped from churches in southern Spain.

On the strictly military side of the ledger, the *débandade* of Joseph's army left 151 cannon and 415 ammunition wagons in British hands. Almost the entire artillery (field and siege) of his army was lost. One of the more sublime ironies of the day was that a treasure convoy carrying five million francs that Joseph had been demanding from Paris for

---

*Chambermaids.

months also fell into the hands of Wellington's soldiery. Only a small portion of this money was ever recovered; the rest disappeared through the agency of soldiers into the mouths of orphans, the pockets of whores and the tills of drink sellers. French troops scattered into the hills, leaving their pursuers to take only two thousand or so prisoners. Lieutenant Colonel FitzRoy Somerset wrote to his brother, "The only thing to be lamented is that the enemy ran away so fast that we could not in fact do much harm to them as far as taking prisoners and letting the cavalry loose upon them goes." The many ditches, walls and hedges of the market gardens and smallholders' plots surrounding the city had also made it very hard for the British cavalry to pursue their enemy, just as it had for the French dragoons to protect the fleeing host.

Any member of the staff who surveyed this almost biblical scene of pillage knew that it would send Wellington into transports of rage. They were not disappointed. He was naturally furious that his plan to trap the entire French army had failed, but he put much of the blame for this on thieving soldiers. "We started with the army in the highest order, and up to the day of the battle nothing could get on better; but that event has, as usual, totally annihilated all order and discipline," the general complained to Bathurst. He added, "We have in the Service the scum of the earth as common soldiers . . . the officers of the lower ranks will not perform the duty required of them to keep the soldiers in order. The non-commissioned officers are (as I have repeatedly stated) as bad as the men. It is really a disgrace to have anything to say to such men as some of our soldiers are."

On the evening of the twenty-first, Wellington was forced to send the Household Cavalry brigade into the streets of Vitoria to secure the place against any plundering by British soldiers. The Staff Cavalry, it is clear, were too small in number to prevent the stripping of Joseph's caravans and, in any case, most officers saw nothing wrong in it. Even Judge Advocate Larpent opined, "The understanding that this was all fair seems pretty general." French military possessions, after all, qualified as spoils of war. Every standard and convention of civilized behavior told the British soldier that this was quite different from robbing the Spanish populace.

Scovell picked his way through the baggage in search of something very particular, a thing that was priceless to him but quite useless to the pillaging mob who was cackling and laughing, trying on the finest Parisian dresses, emptying out drawers and scattering papers to the winds. The best place to find what he was looking for would be the king's coach or nearby in some private secretary's *calèche*.* These were among the few vehicles that had been placed under the guard of dependable cavalry when Wellington had discovered that there were priceless paintings stripped from Madrid and left rolled up in the king's coach.

He finally found the large document, folded up, with the words *Sa Majesté Catholique*† written on its outside, in the king's leather paper case. Lieutenant Colonel Scovell opened the *portefeuille* to reveal Joseph's personal copy of the Great Paris Cipher decoding table. He also discovered the little booklet for enciphering, with its alphabetical listing of words, letters and phrases. So it came to pass that on 21 June, both French power in Spain and the *Grand Chiffre* died together.

Six days after the disastrous battle, Joseph sat down in the little town of Vera to dictate letters to one of his secretaries. Most of his army had fallen back through the Pyrennees to France. Bereft of artillery, they were incapable of resisting the British further. He and some other troops were moving east, at the foot of the mountains marking the frontier, toward the Army of Catalonia, the only remaining French force of any size in the Iberian Peninsula. Joseph had confessed so many embarrassing details about the Battle of Vitoria, but one more remained, which the minister of war in Paris needed to know:

> *"My papers were mislaid on the 21st; the* portefeuille *bearing the cipher was lost. It may be that it has fallen into the hands of the enemy. You will doubtless think it prudent, Monsieur le duc, to order the creation and dispatch of a new cipher."*

The king never suspected that the British had already been reading his most sensitive letters the entire previous year and could not have seen

---

*An elegant type of carriage.
†His Catholic Majesty, i.e., the king of Spain.

the irony that the code sent to strengthen his hold on power had actually proven one of the principal mechanisms for its destruction.

Early in July, British headquarters received an intercepted dispatch from the French minister of war to Marshal Suchet, in command of the Army of Catalonia, intended to explain the disastrous campaign that had led up to Vitoria:

"The King judged it expedient to abandon his first line of defense," wrote General Clarke, "and to move to 730. 140. 377. 1007. 406. 19. 484. 520. 684. 219. 241. 315. 73. 775."

Scovell only had to look at the message to know. Any attempt to apply the Great Paris Cipher would be fruitless. The code had changed, and remarkably quickly at that. He began to attack the new cipher, scribbling possible meanings down in pencil. But Scovell and Wellington realized there was little point. Precious few messages would be captured in the future in any case. The Army of Catalonia was falling back slowly toward the frontier too. French communications were now being sent almost entirely through their own country. There they were quite safe from the Spanish guerrillas, whose raids had of course been vital to the business of obtaining ciphered dispatches in the first place.

The commandant of the Staff Cavalry Corps would have several months' tough campaigning ahead of him in southern France. From time to time divisional orders in some impudent *petit chiffre* fell into British hands and gave Scovell an amusing afternoon's labor, but the real business of code breaking was over.

At about the same time that Scovell surveyed Clarke's letter to Suchet, King Joseph received a final dispatch of his own: the emperor was recalling him to France. He was no longer king since it would be quite impossible for the army to be regrouped for the defense of southern France under somebody who had failed so manifestly and lost the confidence of all its generals. A new commander would be needed to galvanize the weary remnants of France's Spanish legions. On 15 July, none other than Marshal Soult was appointed to that task.

CHAPTER NINETEEN

*"I don't believe we were ever deceived in these letters and Colonel Schoo-
ell . . . is the person who made them out."*

WATERLOO, 18 JUNE 1815

*I*t was early afternoon as the small group of staff galloped across
the top of the Mont St. Jean ridge and down toward their vantage
point overlooking the French. Ahead of them, straight up the line of the
Charleroi road, was the farmhouse of La Haye Sainte. Behind them,
the village of Waterloo. A heavy bombardment of the British line atop
the high ground was beginning, with a great mass of French artillery
lined up beyond the buildings and pointing in their direction.

The sky was thick with the smoke of several hours' hard pounding
as Lieutentant Colonel Scovell, Colonel De Lancey and Lord March,
accompanied by an orderly dragoon, had gone together to try to make
out what was happening in this part of the battlefield. Wellington and
Napoleon had been at war for twenty years, but this was their first time
on the same ground. There, in these green Belgian fields, they were
going to fight their final battle, the deciding match in the long Anglo-
French struggle for domination of the Continent. There were familiar

faces everywhere that day, hardly a member of the Peninsular staff had been overlooked. Hardinge was with Prussian headquarters as Wellington's confidential representative. FitzRoy Somerset was beside his master almost throughout the day. Only Murray was absent; he had not been able to travel over to Belgium in time for the battle and his place as the army's quarter master general was taken instead by William De Lancey.

Scovell was proud to hear that his name was on a list Field Marshal Wellington had prepared of those essential to the smooth running of his staff. He had been placed in charge of the army's communications once more.

As they pushed forward Scovell and his comrades were riding toward death. They had just galloped past Ompteda's brigade of the king's German legion, closer to the enemy, and the smoke had blinded them to the presence of a powerful French battery not far ahead. In any case, the din of cannon was so deafening that had one of them realized and called out, the others would probably not have heard him. This was an intensity of fire they had never experienced in Iberia. Napoleon had positioned a grand battery of eighty-four cannon to smash the British center.

Suddenly, the whizzing and cracking of round shot and grape filled their ears, followed immediately by the ominous smack of metal striking flesh. In a few short moments, De Lancey was off his mount and so was March. A ricocheting cannonball had bounced off the ground and hit the QMG square in the upper body. The dragoon who'd accompanied them was killed instantly by another shot. Scovell reined his horse in and it reared up. He put his hand up to his hat to stop it from falling off and a cannonball shot through his cloak, just under his arm. Another ball whizzed across his horse's rump, leaving a six-inch strip of pink flesh shaved hairless. Then five pieces of grapeshot hit the animal and Scovell too was dismounted.

He picked himself up and scurried across to De Lancey. Wellington and some other officers who had been riding not far behind appeared on the scene. The colonel looked up at Scovell and said, "I am mortally wounded," and bid him to look after March. The young ADC had been hit in the arm by grape and was able to get to his feet. They called out for help. De Lancey was carried from the field and March taken to a surgeon. De Lancey's wound was so severe that those who survived would later marvel that he had been able to stand at all. The shock of the cannonball had separated several ribs on his left side from the spine and his internal organs suffered enormous damage. Scovell himself had somehow emerged from that cloud of hot metal unscathed. He found another mount and galloped off to do the duke's business in another part of the field.

Just as De Lancey received his mortal wound, the battle reached its crisis. The French took La Haye Sainte just before the approaching Prussians joined the British on the field. Early that evening, having failed to break the Allied center, Napoleon threw his Imperial Guard into the fray. The emperor's most precious reserve marched to the top of the St. Jean ridge, where its battalions tried to deploy into proper attack formation. But the British Guards and the 52nd Light Infantry, mostly Peninsular veterans, had suddenly appeared to the front and flanks of the French columns and poured in a heavy fire of musketry. Those redcoats who had survived several seasons' campaigning in Iberia had learned their lessons well: they kept up a relentless salvo at pitifully close range. The grenadiers of Napoleon's Old Guard swayed and stumbled under this onslaught for a few moments, their officers trying desperately to rally them so they might return fire and press home their attack. And then the unthinkable happened, the mustachioed old grumblers of the Guard began leaving the ranks, fleeing back in ones and twos. Sensing their moment, the British light troops charged the remainder and put them to flight. The emperor's last gambit had been foiled. The Battle of Waterloo was won.

The price paid by the staff for this triumph was high indeed. They all knew that theirs was a dangerous business, but, somehow, almost all of them had come through years of peninsula campaigning alive and largely unscathed. On the evening of 18 June, however, Scovell and Wellington himself were among the few of the old campaigners still in one piece. The prince of Orange's arm had been shattered, as had FitzRoy Somerset's, and Hardinge too had been similarly struck at Ligny the previous day. Alexander Gordon (a favorite young ADC) was mortally wounded.

Early that evening, Dr. Gunning, the surgeon, sawed away at Somerset's arm bone, taking it off right above the elbow. He was awake throughout this grisly procedure, propped up by Scovell on a blood-soaked kitchen table. As was Somerset's style, he made light of his calvary. As the orderly carried off his severed limb, its owner called out, "Hallo! don't carry away that arm until you've taken off my ring."

Somerset's wound was bound up and he was loaded together with the prince of Orange, General Alava (Wellington's Spanish ADC) and Dr. Gunning into the duke's carriage and packed off to Brussels.

Scovell did not rest the following day. He managed to find out that De Lancey had been taken to a little Belgian farmhouse in the village of Waterloo and brought a surgeon there to attend to him. He was also able to discover that De Lancey's wife, who was in Brussels, had been told that her husband was dead.

When Lady De Lancey was brought to the farmhouse, Scovell met her outside and warned her of her husband's condition, adding, "any agitation would be injurious. Now, we have not told him you had heard of his death; we thought it would afflict him; therefore do not appear to have heard it." The couple spent a few hours together. Their married life had begun only a few months before, after De Lancey's return from the peninsula, but it was destined to end here, in a small house near the field of Waterloo, the following day. The colonel's young widow never forgot her debt to Scovell, who had made that last meeting possible.

Exhausted after the brief but intense violence of the campaign, Scovell took part in its final scenes. Napoleon was pursued to the gates of Paris and abdicated. The peace of Europe had been restored for many years. Lieutenant Colonel Scovell remembered many things about the day of Waterloo itself. How could he forget that, on the day of the battle itself, at about 9 P.M. Wellington had declared it was time for supper and asked Scovell to join him at his quarters. "This is too bad, thus to lose our friends," the field marshal said as they ate. "I trust it will be the last action any of us see."

Scovell was joined in Paris by his wife, Mary, where they were billeted in a handsome house with the commander of the Austrian army. The onetime apprentice engraver and Lancashire landlord's daughter thus found themselves sitting down to dinner with Field Marshal Prince Karl Philip Schwarzenburg and partaking in discussions about the future of Europe. This was how seven years of almost continuous campaigning had changed the life of George Scovell. The army had transformed everything for George and Mary and there was every reason to assume his future within it was secure, or so he thought.

CHAPTER TWENTY

SCOVELL'S LATER LIFE, 1819 TO 1861

*A*s Scovell walked along Wimpole Street in a state of some agitation on a bitterly cold January morning in 1819, Waterloo was already evolving into a thing of national legend. Things had not gone at all to plan for him, for his hopes of a secure future in the army had been dashed. Surprisingly quickly he had found himself driven to ask for help, and that was not something he was happy about doing. Scovell had resolved to write to the duke of Wellington.

Immediately following the Battle of Waterloo, the Staff Cavalry had become part of an Army of Occupation in northern France. Scovell's little corps was well suited to its duties, keeping the soldiery, deprived of long marches and battles, in order lest they vex the French to the point of revolt. He and Mary lived very well, for a moderate outlay and his mastery of the language had assured an entrée into society. That had been helped by the one further sign of the duke's approbation he had received at the beginning of 1815, a knighthood. His work forming the Staff Cavalry and breaking codes had earned him that noble distinction. Scovell's gratitude could easily be appreciated.

Whatever debt his old master may have felt in the peninsula and immediately afterward, it all seemed to have been forgotten by December 1818. The Army of Occupation had been brought home and Horse Guards, immune to all reason, had decided to disband the Staff Cavalry. The duke did nothing to save Scovell's corps, even though a quiet word might possibly have done so.

In many corners of what had been the Peninsular army, officers felt the loss of Wellington's interest keenly. William Napier wrote that as the seven-year struggle for Iberia terminated, so did "all remembrances of the veterans' services." William Grattan, one of the men who had led the 88th Foot at Salamanca in the 3rd Division's key attack, noted bitterly, "In his parting General Order to the Peninsular Army he told us he would never cease to feel the warmest interest for our welfare and honour. How that promise has been kept, everybody knows . . . that he neglected the interests and feelings of his Peninsular Army, as a body, is beyond all question." Had Alexander Gordon survived Waterloo, he could have reminded his colleagues in Peninsular headquarters that his assessment of Wellington, written in 1811, that he "has no idea of gratitude, favour, or affection, and cares not for anyone however much he may owe to him or find him useful," had been fully vindicated by events.

It might seem that Scovell had no more cause to resent what had happened to him than hundreds of other officers. He had, after all, been able to make the vital steps to major and lieutenant colonel in quick succession while the duke had done little to advance the careers of many other fighting men who had won his victories. But what must have pained him was that after 1815, the favored members of the staff were very much remembered. Almost all of Scovell's old friends had been looked after.

On Christmas Day 1818, Scovell was placed on half pay. For a lieutenant colonel this was only about £150 per annum and being *Sir* George did not alter the harsh financial realities that would now ensue. After years of solving problems few others in the staff could be bothered with, and indeed years of living well from it, he could see himself slipping back to the state of penury.

The duke, meanwhile, had joined the cabinet and was engrossed in party politics. He helped other loyal members of the staff, but only in as far as they were suitable to do his bidding without question on a new battlefield: the House of Commons.

FitzRoy Somerset was found a seat in Truro, Henry Hardinge became MP for Durham, Lord March (before inheriting the dukedom of Richmond) sat for Chichester and George Murray would represent the Perthshire constituency of his family estates. Charles Vere (AQMG of the 4th) was also mobilized for this service, gaining a seat in Suffolk. Some of them traded on their status as "A Hero of Waterloo and the Peninsula" in handbills they gave out on the election trail. Those who remained in the army had been given prestigious commissions in the Guards.

Scovell, however, with his reform-mindedness, intellectual self-confidence and lowly social standing had once more become a figure on the periphery of Wellington's vision. He was evidently unsuitable as a Tory MP, and it seemed that even his military services were now of limited value. It was just as it had been in 1809. The golden-haired aristocrats like Somerset and March hogged center stage. The duke remained faithful to that gilded youth sketched in glorious color in his memory of the peninsula. And while expediency had dictated some others be allowed supporting parts in Wellington's great Iberian drama, those, including Scovell, came to the final realization that Wellington had only ever seen them in the dull gray shades of mezzotint.

There was every sign now that the hope Wellington had uttered to Scovell on the night of Waterloo, that it should be their last battle, was being fulfilled. In the new climate of European peace, party allegiance had become paramount once more, and military professionalism counted for little.

Sitting down to write his letter, Sir George Scovell knew he must cast aside any pride. He knew that the duke would appreciate brevity and abhor circumlocution. Scovell set pen to paper:

> *"You are aware of the reduction of my Corps on the*
> *25th of last month and that one of the greatest evils*

*of life has befallen me, namely want of employment after
an active life. Relying on the uniform kindness of your
Grace to me, I take the liberty of requesting that should
any situation civil or military not beyond my capacity
fall vacant, I may not be out of your recollection as
being willing to exert my talent (such as it is) in any way
which I may be useful to your Grace or to the public."*

There is no record of any reply from Wellington.

Three years had passed since writing that plea to Wellington as the
November darkness came on with its usual suddenness and Scovell sat at
his desk. There was a pile of French dispatches in front of him. For eight
years they had been stored at army headquarters, their secrets guarded by
George Murray, the former quarter master general of the Peninsular army.
He was looking at the Paris Cipher again, more than a decade since he
had sat in the mayor's house of Fuente Guinaldo and started working day
and night to break it. Going through those angry Peninsular letters by
Marmont and Soult was like meeting a long-lost acquaintance.

Perhaps he should look at another before he abandoned the task for
the day? The colonel glanced out of his office window and into the
gloom that was engulfing the drill square. The cavalry barracks in Croydon were a smart establishment, modern-built in the neoclassical style.

In 1820 Scovell had been appointed as colonel in command of the
Royal Wagon Train, based at Croydon, a post probably arranged by
Murray, who was now a general. From that time onward, any steps in
rank would be determined by age alone. Seniority would eventually
bring promotion to the colonel who lived long enough.

The Wagon Train, comprising the army's supply troops, was
another in the long line of worthwhile tasks that Scovell applied himself
to, but which the better-connected officers would have avoided like the
plague. Murray knew that a man of the colonel's intellect would soon
get bored watching the schooling of drivers and wagoneers round and
round the square at Croydon. Indeed Scovell found his new duties so
dull that he had been thinking once more of leaving the army, wondering whether he might become head of one of the new police forces being
established in the shires and colonies.

Thus, late in 1823, Murray asked Scovell to reexamine many of the intercepted French dispatches from the Peninsular campaigns and to make some recommendations about the use of ciphers in the British army. Not one to take on a task by halves, Scovell decided to reexamine many of the decipherings he had done in the field in Rueda, Guinaldo or Frenada.

He examined forty-four letters in the *Grand Chiffre*. In many places he made notes, often scribbling the word "correct" in pencil by some of his earlier suppositions. He found few errors. A number of the letters he had not seen before. They had fallen into the British army's hands at some stage of the campaign but had eluded him at the time. Now they provided little fragments of knowledge or explained the context of things that had puzzled him for years. Eventually he sent the package back to Whitehall, but a few originals remained in Scovell's possession.

Apart from stimulating the colonel's mind, Murray may have had one other motive in mind when asking Scovell to complete this task, for Wellington and a number of other senior officers had been irritated by the appearance of a history, *Narrative of the War in the Peninsula* by Southey. This work produced great dissatisfaction and Murray was considering writing his own narrative of these events. Had he ever done so, it is most unlikely that Scovell's role would have gone unsung. However, the former QMG of the Peninsular army lost the race to publish to William Napier's multivolume work.

For decades, Napier's *History of the War in the Peninsula and in the South of France* was to set the tone of subsequent writing. It began the mythologizing of those campaigns, identifying the steadfast British national character as a key to victory. Ideas of grit, fortitude and honesty were central to Napier's view of the British soldier, and indeed to the political image projected by Wellington. The author eulogized the duke as "a master spirit in war." Not only were matters of intelligence or code breaking covered sparsely and inaccurately, but there was nothing in the text to suggest Wellington and his circle ever made Napier fully aware of the spectacular successes capturing and decoding letters in the *Grand Chiffre*.

In 1835, the printing of tomes of Wellington's dispatches started. Later editions of "Dispatches" included many captured French messages sent *en clair* and some that had been deciphered, but curiously only those in the simple or Army of Portugal codes were revealed. The breaking of the *Grand Chiffre*, the Great Paris Cipher, was to remain a secret for years to come. A line was drawn: the breaking of less complex codes could be alluded to, but that of the toughest one used in Spain remained a more sensitive matter.

Wellington had become a political leader by this time. The legend of his great generalship might have been undermined, however subtly, by revelations that he had been reading his enemy's most sensitive mail. Matters of espionage were regarded as somewhat underhanded.

Given that he asked Scovell to review that priceless intelligence at Croydon, in late 1823, we can be quite sure that Murray had at least been reminded of the significance of the ciphered dispatches shortly before the compilation of Napier's history began. Those around Wellington, and presumably the duke himself, did not see fit to tell Napier the story of how they had been broken. Scovell, having checked his earlier workings, bundled up the papers and sent them back to headquarters, his work with French army ciphers finally ended.

Early in 1829, Major General Sir George Scovell was appointed lieutenant governor of the Royal Military College at Sandhurst. It can be imagined that he followed in the footsteps of his old teacher and mentor John Le Marchant with some pride. Evidently it had been a gift of Scovell's former Wycombe classmate Henry Hardinge, who had become secretary at war in Wellington's ministry (the duke had finally captured the prime ministership the year before). Hardinge and Murray had risen so high that they were able to help their old comrade and ensure the comfort of his twilight years.

As lieutenant governor, Scovell was to receive £1000 each year. His natural longevity took him up the Army List and he acquired the colonelcy of a cavalry regiment. First it was the 7th Dragoon Guards and later the 4th Dragoons. Becoming the titular head of the regiment he had been forced to sell out of decades before must have been a sweet experience indeed. But despite the fact that he and Mary prospered in their old age, Scovell was to prove listless and dissatisfied due to the influence of his old superior and now prime minister.

Wellington had never liked the Royal Military College. In particular its junior branch, which trained young men in their teens prior to their

first commission, seemed to him a hotbed of sedition and riot. The prime
minister was also alarmed by plans to teach ordinary soldiers to read and
write, telling one friend, "If there is mutiny in the Army . . . you'll see
that all of these new-fangled school masters are at the bottom of it."

It seems likely that Scovell was offered the lieutenant governorship
with the understanding that no great innovations of curriculum or
reforms of the cadets' spartan living arrangements would occur. In any
case, such matters would have to be referred to the Board of Governors,
which remained packed with Wellington's placemen. Consequently,
instead of becoming a reforming educator, Scovell slipped into his
dotage, hunting and entertaining well at his residence. Having the
superintendence of the college without any ability to overhaul its curriculum must have been purgatory for Scovell, and it seems that he
turned his back on professional matters and grew steadily wealthier
from his various sinecures.

With the passage of years, time began to take its toll on the "Heroes
of Waterloo," and Scovell found himself called upon to attend the
annual celebratory dinner at Apsley House in London. His exchanges
with Wellington remained brief and formal. Only one topic seems to
have united the old soldiers: their strong feelings, love one might even
say, for FitzRoy Somerset. When Scovell commissioned a portrait of
Somerset in 1841, he sent a print to Wellington, and this at least
received a reply, albeit of the briefest kind. The young military secretary
of the Peninsular headquarters rose up the army hierarchy to become
Lord Raglan and Field Marshal. His name was to live on in history as
the man who ordered the charge of the Light Brigade in the Crimean
War. When he died of dysentery the following year, Scovell was heart-
broken, feeling the loss of someone who was the closest thing he would
ever have to a son.

On 10 August 1836, the duke went to dine with friends at Mr. Rogers's
town house. His table companions often found him a witty raconteur
on the subject of his battles and affairs of state. As the silver cutlery
scurried back and forth across the porcelain and crystal glasses carried
fine wine to the lips of the highborn diners, the discussion moved to the
subject of ciphers and their use in protecting secrets.

Count Bourck, the Danish minister at Joseph's court in Madrid, was a singular case, the prime minister recalled. *En clair*, he would simply tell the true state of affairs, leaving nothing unsaid of each new ghastly reverse for the French, but avoided offending King Joseph's spies when they read his mail by adding, "but this is what the extreme side of the other party report." He had no need of a cipher. There were knowing smiles and polite laughter. Was your Grace ever deceived by the French ciphers?

The duke replied that the smaller codes had all been broken easily and those of a more complex nature were often made out as well. His audience was impressed, and he evidently detected their admiration of this intellectual feat. One of the diners had a further question on the subject: Surely a task of such a complexity would have to be undertaken by an expert in this arcane business. Had your Grace anybody with the army for the purpose of making out ciphers?

"No," replied the duke, nobody in particular. "I tried, everyone at headquarters tried, and between us we made it out."

The most generous explanation of Wellington's remark is that he was old and had simply forgotten Scovell's achievement, attributing the code-breaking successes of the Peninsular War to "everyone at headquarters." The less kind interpretation was that it was vanity that led Wellington to claim the credit for himself and his favorite, FitzRoy Somerset.

For decades, Britain's old Peninsular enemies remained ignorant of this distorted view. Charles Parquin, for example, a former cavalry officer who had been escorting Marmont at the Battle of Salamanca in 1812, wrote memoirs in which he testified that although the French had lost the engagement, "the enemy ought to have been happy that the Marshal, who had been waiting for seven days, did not wait one more day. For King Joseph and Marshal Soult [sic] would have arrived followed, by 40,000 men [sic]." In fact, in that particular situation, not only had deciphered letters kept Wellington perfectly acquainted with Joseph's plan to join up with Marmont, but the seizure of all messages announcing the impending arrival of this reinforcement had left the marshal himself in the dark.

In the decades following the Peninsular War, the magnitude of Scovell's code-breaking achievement slowly revealed itself. The participants in those campaigns died one after the other, leaving diaries or papers. Some officers working on the staff had been aware of what Scovell had done. When William Tomkinson's journal was finally published in 1894, it contained the following passage, written shortly after the Battle of Vitoria in 1813:

> *"The French in all their correspondence make use of a cipher which they constantly vary . . . there arises considerable difficulty in making out the meaning. I don't believe we were ever deceived in these letters and Colonel Schovel [sic] (Commandant of the Corps of Guides attached to Headquarters) is the person who made them out."*

Tomkinson had slightly exaggerated Scovell's achievement, for definitely there had been a period during the first half of 1812 when there had been difficulties in reading coded messages. However, Wellington's papers themselves contained official confirmation of Scovell's work. He had, when writing to Earl Bathurst, the secretary of war, in April 1813, identified Scovell alone as the person who had been working to break the Paris Cipher. After waiting months to see the disappointing progress made by the best decipherers in London, Wellington had written back to his political master enclosing the solutuons, "made out by Lieut Colonel Scovell without reference to the key received through your Lordship." Indeed, although the duke subsequently forgot the fact, Scovell was the only officer ever mentioned as a code breaker in the headquarters correspondence from the peninsula.

Scovell himself did not write memoirs, nor was his fascinating journal published. He and Mary lived to ripe old ages: she to her eightieth year and he to his eighty-seventh. When he expired, in January 1861, he was interred beside Mary in the grounds of the Royal Military Academy at Sandhurst, dying a prosperous general, leaving the handsome sum of £60,000 to his relations, servants and friends. His lifetime struggle to escape his lowly origins was a success. Even if Wellington ill used him in the years following the Peninsular War, the army had looked after Scovell well.

He did not just leave behind cash when he was buried, however. During his years in Iberia and, later, while reexamining the captured

French correspondence at Croydon in 1823, Scovell had kept many of the originals and copied other examples of the coded letters he had worked on. Dozens of them, together with his annotated little code-breaking crib, Conradus, remained in his papers. In his will, knowing the importance of the documents he had retained all those years, he made a specific note of his bequest to his nephew of "all my papers on the subject of the Great Paris Cypher."

So despite his obscurity in his later life, the legacy of Scovell's code breaking was not lost. Reviewing the documents available today, its influence on Wellington's strategy is obvious. At times it is explicitly stated in some of the general's dispatches; at others the precious thread of knowledge that the code breaker unwound for his commander in chief can only be followed by hints.

It must always be remembered that the essential prerequisite for gathering that vital intelligence was the ruthless campaign by the Spanish guerrillas against French communications. As for its use, that depended upon the flawless execution of orders on the battlefields of Salamanca or Vitoria. But it is safe to say that without someone to break the code, those French dispatches would have remained just useless, tantalizing paper, with streams of digits successfully concealing the writers' meanings.

Once unlocked by Scovell, however, they revealed so much knowledge that was priceless to the British general: the strength and plans of Marmont's Army of Portugal, as it maneuvered opposite Wellington just before Salamanca; and in 1813, when Joseph and his generals prepared to fight their final battle for Spain, the deciphered letters unlocked their preparations and strategy behind them; the quarrels between marshals, their faltering confidence and the poor condition of their armies.

These campaigns—Scovell's of the mind coinciding with Wellington's in the field—marked the turning point of the war in Spain. Even in 1811, the British still feared another Corunna, another evacuation. By late 1813 they were escorting the French across the Pyrennees and back into their own country. While there were a few great code breakers before Scovell and certainly legions of them afterward, it might justly be said that he was the father of this secret business, at least on the battlefields of modern Europe.

NOTES ON SOURCES

PRIMARY SOURCES

This book is based largely on eyewitness accounts and journals of those who fought in the Peninsular War. The main manuscript sources are:

Scovell Papers: in the Public Record Office, under the class number WO37.

Beaufort Papers: referred to below as BP.

Letters of FitzRoy and Edward Somerset, residing in the private collection of the duke of Beaufort and reproduced with his permission.

Wellington Papers: referred to below as WP. These are now held at the University of Southampton Library and reproduced with permission.

Le Marchant Papers: listed below as LMP, they are now in the Library of the Royal Military Academy at Sandhurst.

In addition to these archives, many eyewitness accounts in the form of letters or journals have been published. These are noted below, along with the specific file references for the manuscript collections mentioned above.

Chapter One: Retreat to Corunna, January 1809

3. "Scovell brought the glass to his eye and searched the horizon . . .": Scovell left us a journal as part of WO37 at the PRO that describes this scene.

4. "Its officers had already begun speculating what the next few years might hold for them as prisoners of war": this fear was expressed by William Warre of the staff. His journal and letters are published as *Letters from the Peninsula 1808-12*, published in 1909 and reprinted by Spellmount in 1988.

5. "Moore's soldiers had become euphoric at the sight of the sea": this is mentioned by several diarists of the Corunna campaign.

5. "One captain of the 10th Hussars kept a record": Captain Alexander Gordon of the 15th Light Dragoons (Hussars) published as *Cavalry Officer in the Corunna Campaign*, London, 1913.

6. "A commissary, one of the civilian supply officers accompanying the army, wrote in his journal": this was A. L. F. Schaumann in *On the Road with Wellington: The Diary of a War Commissary*, originally published in 1924 and by Greenhill Books in 1999.

8. "Another of the young DAQMGs had his own secret weapon in the advancement game": this was William Maynard Gomm. Details come from *Letters and Journals from 1799 to Waterloo*, London, 1881.

Chapter Two: The Battle of Corunna, January 1809

14. "He had his own private worry about the embarkation . . .": Scovell made this concern explicit in his journal.

19. "Hardinge later recorded . . .": Henry Hardinge's memo on the death of Moore is quoted in the biography of Hardinge by his son, the Second Viscount Hardinge.

20. "'recounting the day's events, and mourning comrades who had stood on the threshold of their careers . . .'": this comes from the memoirs of Louis-Florimond Fantin des Odoards of the (French) 31st Light Infantry.

21. "who had deserted the French and given good service to the British army . . .": details of the early Guides are contained in Scovell's papers.

21. "several officers (including the dashing Captain Warre) claimed in their journals and letters home the honor of being the last man to leave": evidence may be found in Warre's and Gomm's respective journals.

Chapter Three: Interlude in England, January to March 1809

24. "Stewart damned Moore several years later in one of the first histories of these events": his *History of the Peninsular War* is published under his title of Lord Londonderry.

25. "[Wellesley] wore his full dress uniform": this detail emerges from the account of his appearance in *Gentleman's Magazine* published that year.

26. "In replying to the vote of thanks, he thus told them": there must be various records of Wellesley's speech, but I found one in the Goodwood Papers (the duke and duchess of Richmond's papers) in Chichester Record Office. Wellesley had sent it to the duke, who was his most important godfather in the Tory hierarchy.

27. "Sprotborough Hall, a huge mansion . . .": the hall no longer stands; I found details of its layout and furnishings in *Sprotborough Hall* by Gordon Smith, a privately published mongraph made available to me by the local library in Sprotborough.

27. "He was 'the son of very respectable parents . . .'": Scovell's early life is something of a closed book. This quote and some other details come from the journal of Edward Healey, one of his servants, and was published in several parts in the *Journal for the Society of Army Historical Research* through 1987.

28. "he paid a vast sum, £3150, to buy a captain's commission in the 4th Dragoons": details of these transactions can be found in WO31/158.

28. "its officers were soon doing long hours in the salons and assembly rooms adorning the fashionable set surrounding the Prince of Wales": according to F. Scott Daniel in his history of the 4th.

30. "Mary, it seems, shared Jane Austen's view . .": the quote comes from *Mansfield Park*. "George and Mary were married in May 1805 in Manchester Cathedral": the record of this remains in the Register of Marriages at Chester Record Office.

30. "the extra pay received by a deputy assistant quarter master general, just over £172 per annum": details of pay from *The Regimental Companion* by Charles James, published in 1811.

30. "[Scovell] transferred from the 4th Dragoons into the 57th Foot": details of the transfer are in WO31/224.

30. "he spent the best part of two years working away at Wycombe on French, German, mathematics, trigonometry . . .": details of the syllabus are from RMC documents at the modern-day Royal Military Academy, Sandhurst, where they still keep a class of papers (WO99) relating to the college.

33. "He was . . . directed to make his way to Cork Harbor for embarkation": Scovell kept the letter from Brownrigg and it remains in the Scovell Papers.

Chapter Four: Northern Portugal, May 1809

35. "It was about 10 A.M. on a typically sleepy May morning . . .": this account is drawn from Scovell's journal, Wellington's official dispatch about the operation, personal observation at the place of the crossing and some other officers' journals. While looking at the Beaufort Papers I came across a fascinating letter of 13 May 1809 (FmM 4/1/4) from FitzRoy Somerset in which he wrote: "I believe Sir Arthur thought that the greater part of the French army had left Oporto and that as soon as our men entered into the town, they would send an officer to beg us to take care of their sick." This suggests that Wellesley's crossing of the Douro was not as bold an act as it is usually made out to be. Notwithstanding this, the army clearly did move

into Vila Nova gingerly, French pickets were spotted on the north shore and the first
wave of British troops crossed the Douro with great anxiety while a grand battery of
guns was deployed to cover them. All of this leaves me supposing FitzRoy Somerset
exaggerated his case a little and that his general was moving forward with justifiable
caution.

37. "The 16th had gone in and lost many men . . .": details of this bungled
engagement come from William Tomkinson (one of the officers injured) in *The
Diary of a Cavalry Officer in the Peninsular and Waterloo Campaigns 1809-15*
(published in 1894 in London and then again by Spellmount in 1999) and Edward
Cocks, an officer of the same regiment, whose letters and diaries were assembled
very expertly by Julia Page in her book *Intelligence Officer in the Peninsula*, published by Spellmount in 1986. My occasional references to Cocks's views all refer to
the original materials reproduced in her book.

38. "Marshal Soult was woken": the French side of this story comes from Captain
Fantin des Odoards, already mentioned, and General Maximilien Foy. Maurice Girod
de L'Ain published many of the general's letters and diary remarks as *Vie Militaire*.

40. "Scovell penned a letter to Colonel John Le Marchant . . .": this is in the Le
Marchant Papers at Sandhurst, dated 27th May 1809, LMP packet 13a, Letter 1.

44. "the Portuguese military commandant of Braga came to the headquarters
asking to see Wellesley": this incident is covered in Scovell's journal and the letter to
Le Marchant mentioned above.

50. "They saw any argument for reform . . .": Le Marchant's proposals for the
formation of a general staff, written in 1802, contained a proposal that the staff should
be chosen on the basis of ability. It was one of several reasons why this extraordinarily
forward-looking document (a copy of which is kept at the Sandhurst Library) was suppressed by the quarter master general at Horse Guards.

51. "'It is well understood by the Government . . .'": this letter from Le
Marchant to Colonel William Stewart, 18 June 1806, may be found in the letter
books of the RMC, part of the papers currently kept at Sandhurst.

51. "it had taken the experience of the Corunna campaign to convince him
finally of the army's deperate need for reform": Scovell said explicitly that he had
been converted to Le Marchant's views on reform "since I left Wycombe" in a letter
to Le Marchant of 23 November 1808, LMP Packet 12, Item 3.

52. "'These are in fact the description of officers who have revolutionised other
armies'": this quotation of Wellesley comes from a letter to Lieutenant General Sir
Herbert Taylor of 11 April 1821 contained in *Military Correspondence of the Duke
of Wellington*. Although written some time after the Peninsular campaigns, Wellington stressed in the letter that this is what he had "long thought." Certainly the general's disdain for low-bred officers from the scientific arms (artillery and engineers)
was remarked upon by a number of diarists at Peninsular headquarters, for example, Sir James McGrigor.

53. "Scovell had formed a scheme and lobbied for it . . .": his ideas for auxil-
iary cavalry are mentioned in the same letter to Le Marchant of 23 November 1808
mentioned above.

54. "Anxiously, Scovell went on to explain himself": he repeated the arguments he had made in the interview in his journal, in the letter to Le Marchant of 27 May, and years later (1854) in an interview with an unnamed officer who was tasked with forming a Corps of Guides for the Crimea. The memorandum prepared as a result of that interview is in the British Army Museum library manuscript collection. These sources state, for example, Scovell's belief that Murray promised him promotion in return for taking on the job.

Chapter Five: From Oporto to Abrantes, June to July 1809

57. "soldiers of the Guards, the Buffs and numerous other regiments were woken by the reveille of drums and bugles": details of how the army got under way are taken from the 1837 edition of Colonel Gurwood's *Selected General Orders* (and reproduced by Charles Oman in his *Wellington's Army*) and of the order of march from a General Order during the Oporto campaign, also in one of Gurwood's volumes.

59. "One captain in the Buffs, for example, confessed in his journal that he knew nothing . . .": this was T. Bunbury, in *Reminiscences of a Veteran*.

59. "Sergeant Cooper of the 7th Fusiliers . . .": his memoir, *Rough Notes of Seven Campaigns in Portugal Etc*, frequently undermines the official account.

60. "One officer of the 14th Light Dragoons . . .": Peter Hawker, *Journal of the Campaign of 1809*.

62. "One of Colonel Le Marchant's correspondents in the peninsula . . .": Captain Tryon Still, letter, LMP Packet 11, Letter 13.

63. "Colonel Murray had already made clear in writing the previous summer . . .": his letter is in the Scovell Papers, WO37, dated 26 September 1808.

63. "Wellesley refused a French émigré a commission in the Corps . . .": letter to Charles Stuart in Wellington's Dispatches, 13 March 1810.

65. "Stewart could not remove the general from their custody, although he left this account of their interview": in his *History of the Peninsular Wars*.

67. "One French general wrote, "I shall always remember how I was afflicted with great anxieties . . .'": this was General Matthieu Dumas (father of the novelist Roland).

67. "One Frenchman conscripted in the summer of 1809 and bound for Spain . . .": Antoine Fee, *Souvenirs de la Guerre d'Espagne*, Paris, 1856.

69. "In drawers of the foreign ministry there were still copies of the 1750 ciphering table . . ." And indeed, there still are. An example of the 1750 type was kindly copied for me by Jerome Cras at the Centre des Archives Diplomatiques in Nantes (catalogued as Boston, *consulat, serie A, carton 1*) as was a copy of the instructions for the use of the cipher drawn up in 1750 (Rome-Saint-Siege, *ambassade, 111*).

Chapter Six: From Talavera to the End Campaign, July to October 1809

72. "Captain Moyle Sherer of the 34th Foot . . .": Sherer, *Recollections of the Peninsula* (originally published in London in 1823 and then again by Spellmount in 1996), along with Sergeant Cooper, *Rough Notes on Seven Campaigns*, republished by Spellmount in 1996.

73. "'I am sorry to say that our officers are too much disposed to treat with contempt all foreigners'": this statement by Wellington was in a letter of 8 October 1811, proof that Wellington judged all his people by harsh standards, not just the rank and file.

73. "He had arranged uniforms for his men: brown jackets . . . with red collars and cuffs . . .": this is described both in the Scovell Papers and the memorandum of 1854 in the National Army Museum.

79. "'I was particularly struck by the style of [his] order . . .'": this eloquent description comes from Captain Moyle Sherer and actually relates to the Battle of Busaco, early in 1810. I hope the reader will forgive me taking this chronological liberty.

79. "Lord Wellington later gave this account of a furious row": this was related in John Wilson Croker's memoir of the duke of Wellington. Croker was one of several acquaintances who stepped in with their anecdotes when it became clear Wellington would never write memoirs of his own.

80. "'If there is to be any influence in the disposal of military patronage . . . ?'": this comes from Wellington's letter to Lieutenant Colonel Torrens, the military secretary at Horse Guards, a man with considerable influence in the business of promotion, of 4 August 1810.

82. "While serving as adjutant of the 4th, Scovell had gotten to know Edward and the Somerset family": it is quite possible that there was some earlier connection between the duke of Beaufort's family and that of Scovell, whose father hailed from Cirencester, just ten miles from the Badminton estate. Nevertheless, searches through the Beaufort family archives at that stately home by Mrs. Margaret Richards (the present duke's archivist) failed to turn up any link. Scovell senior was not a tenant of the Beaufort estate, neither does he seem to have been a member of the local gentry. Perhaps he was a tradesman who did business with the duke.

84. "Contact was made with Spanish civilians willing to relay reports and generous sums were promised": these details come from letters of 9 and 25 January 1810, in Dispatches.

85. "'it is most difficult to form any judgement from the Spanish and Portuguese accounts of the strength of any French corps . . .'": this quote from Wellington comes from a letter to Lieutenant General Hill on 20 February 1810, in Dispatches.

Chapter Seven: The Battle of Fuentes de Oñoro, May 1811—The Army of Portugal Cipher

89. "Before the first light . . .": the details of the cavalry battle of 5 May are drawn from Brotherton's memorandum in Hamilton's *Historical Record of the 14th (King's) Hussars*; Cocks's journal, edited and reproduced by Julia Page as *Intelligence Officer in the Peninsula; Letters and Diaries of Major The Hon Edward Charles Cocks*; Tomkinson, who was another officer of the 16th Light Dragoons and who bequeathed us *Diary of a Cavalry Officer 1809–1815*; and Scovell's account in his journal.

The attentive reader will notice that I have skipped Scovell's story throughout 1810 and early 1811 in order to move forward to Fuentes de Oñoro to see Scovell's brush with death, and even later in 1811, until the introduction of the first French ciphers in the campaign. I apologize to any reader who feels hard done by, but would stress that I am not setting out to write a biography of Scovell per se. The principal military event that I have left out was the Battle of Busaco on 27 September 1810. During this fight Marshal Masséna threw his troops against Wellington, who occupied a steep fronted ridge. The French came badly unstuck and the British continued falling back to the lines of Torres Vedras, having shaken the invaders' confidence badly. Late on the night before the battle Colonel Murray, the QMG (with Scovell) in company, detected a weak point in the British deployment and ordered some battalions to plug it. This stands as a rare example of one of Wellington's officers changing his orders without his master's approval and not being condemned for it. Murray had the satisfaction of being proved right on the day of the battle, when a French corps struck the British line precisely where he had predicted, and Wellington doubtless respected him for his initiative.

91. "'the only instance I ever met with of two bodies of cavalry coming in opposition, and both standing . . .'": Tomkinson.

92. "A cry of 'No quarter!' was going around the British cavalry . . .": this telling detail emerges in one of Cocks's letters, reproduced by Page.

92. "'There was a general, I might say, flight, but the disorder was really terrible'": Somerset's letter to his brother, the duke of Beaufort, 8 May 1811, BP FmM 4/1/6.

92. "Don Julian Sanchez's guerrillas were attached to Scovell's Corps of Guides . . .": this is a little-known but highly significant fact given the subsequent role of Sanchez's men in intercepting the mail that Scovell would decipher. The arrangement had been in effect since 25 August 1810, according to a letter from FitzRoy Somerset to Scovell dated 27 July 1811 and copied into the military secretary's letter book, reference WP 9/2/1/1.

95. "Masséna's headquarters found three soldiers who were willing to run the risks of trying to penetrate . . . and get the message to Brenier": the main source for this story is Baron de Marbot's memoirs. He was on Masséna's staff. Curiously, British sources make no reference to the execution of the two captured men, alleged by Marbot, or indeed of the discovery of any ciphered messages being found on them. Marbot is regarded as a charlatan by many British historians, but the French

evacuation made clear that a messenger got through. Personally, I find the idea that these brave men carried coded messages somewhat doubtful. Why not just memorize the message?

97. "the Anglo-Portuguese force operating to the south near Badajoz . . . had picked up a most interesting dispatch": *D'Urban's Peninsular Journal 1807–1817*, originally published in 1930 and then reissued by Greenhill Books in 1988.

98. "He and D'Urban discovered the meaning of the captured message on the same day they received it": that at least is the clear impression left by D'Urban's journal, which makes reference to the contents of the letter.

99. "On the twenty-first, Wellington left Elvas . . .": Scovell's journal.

100. "Among the staff officers milling about outside headquarters in Elvas the affair of the sixteenth generated much gossip": good sources for this are Tomkinson, Warre and D'Urban.

100. "Wellington's aristocratic young military secretary, FitzRoy Somerset, wrote home . . .": his letter of 23rd May 1811 is in BP, 4/1/6.

102. "Wellington had seen Scovell's Corps of Guides at work and had been impressed": this is actually a quote from a letter to Lord Bathurst in February 1813 and contained in Wellington's Dispatches.

102. "Later that summer, Scovell and the Guides were given the task of establishing a daily post between the two halves of the Anglo-Portuguese force": this post was formally established by Wellington's General Order of 14 August 1811, although in practice it had been running for some weeks beforehand.

102. "Scovell later said, with evident pride, 'There was no instance of any of these orderlies betraying his trust'": this comment appears in the interview with Scovell about the Guides conducted in 1854 by an anonymous staff officer who was putting together a similar unit for service in the Crimea, and is contained in his notebook held at the National Army Museum.

103. "the Portuguese had maintained links of signaling stations up to Elvas and Almeida on the frontier": details of the telegraphic system come from *Les Renseignements, La Reconnaissance et Les Transmissions Militaires du Temps du Napoleon, L'exemple de la troisieme invasion du Portugal 1810*, by Charles-Alphonse Raeuber. I am grateful to Rene Chartrand for providing me with a photocopy of his copy of this text.

103. "Once he became superintendent of military communications he was given extra pay of £50 per annum, which was soon increased to £80": the subject of pay and allowances in Wellington's army is labyrinthine. This increase was announced in a letter from George Murray to Scovell, copied in Somerset's letter book, WP 9/2/1/1. Further details of the extra pay and financial arrangements of the Guides can be found in the PRO, under AO 1/171/488.

103. "Scovell was handed a small notebook containing a handwritten copy of a most unusual text: *Cryptographia* . . .": thankfully this precious little tome survives as WO37/9.

104. "Among diplomats and royal princes ciphers had been growing in size and complexity . . .": see for example, *The Art of Decyphering* by John Davis, a very rare public offering on this subject published in London in 1737.

105. "His replacement was Marshal Auguste Frederic Marmont, duke of Ragusa": details of Marmont's career from his own *Memoires* and Girod de L'Ain's book on Foy, *Vie Militaire*.

105. "Marmont had one advantage over the others. He had used ciphers in the Balkans . . .": an example of his 1807 cipher is included in *Le Chiffre sous le Premier Empire* by Lieutenant Colonel J. Volcoq, *Revue Historique de L'Armée* No. 4, 1969.

106. "Before his own departure from Paris, Marmont had already discussed . . . with Marshal Berthier . . .": this seems clear from a letter Berthier wrote to Marmont on 10 July 1811 contained in Napoleon's *Correspondance*.

106. "he got his staff to prepare a new code table for use between himself and the Army of Portugal's six divisional commanders . . .": details of the Army of Portugal cipher are drawn from Scovell's Papers, WO37.

107. "One Army of Portugal staff officer recorded . . .": this quote comes from de Marbot's memoirs.

Chapter Eight: The Blockade of Ciudad Rodrigo, June to November 1811—The Great Cipher

110. "Joseph complained he had no authority . . .": details of Joseph's complaints are compiled from various letters of this period contained in Du Casse's *Correspondance du Roi Joseph*.

111. "he carried a note dated 17 May summarizing what had been agreed in the military sphere": the memorandum is reproduced in Du Casse.

113. "The arrival of Berthier's missive caused consternation at Joseph's palace": Joseph's response to Berthier's letter emerges from his letters reproduced in Du Casse.

114. " '[We] greatly pity the poor King Joseph . . .'": FitzRoy Somerset's letter to his brother of 18 July 1811, BP, FmM 4/1/6.

114. "Marmont's generals began cloaking their orders in the Army of Portugal cipher": its first appearance would seem to have been in a letter from Marmont to Dorsenne on 29 August. Since, however, I have been unable to find this in ciphered form, I cannot be completely sure.

115. "In the summer of 1810 his men surprised a company of about one hundred French dragoons": this anecdote (and the British officer's quote) are contained in the journal of John Fox Burgoyne, a Royal Engineer officer who was nearby, dated 30 June 1810.

115. "Sanchez had served as a noncommissioned officer . . .": details of his career from *Hazanas de unos Lanceros, Diarios de Julian Sanchez "El Charro"* by Emilio Becerra de Becerra, a collection of documents about the guerrilla leader published by the local authorities in Salamanca in 1999.

116. "one British officer drew this memorable pen portrait": Captain William Bragge, in the collection of his letters, *Peninsular Portrait 1811–14*.

116. "Sanchez had been brought under British pay in October 1810 . . .": this fact is contained in Cocks's journal. D'Urban suggests it may have been earlier than this, August 1810.

116, "one of the messages sent by Marmont's principal aides-de-camp . . .": this is a letter dated 6 March 1812 from Colonel Jardet to his chief. It is found in WO37/1. While I would have liked to find an early example of the Army of Portugal cipher (i.e., from August 1811), I did not succeed. Jardet's message is very long—much more than 711 characters—but I considered this sufficiently long a portion of it to analyze the cipher.

117. "A message from General Montbrun . . . provides a good sense of how Scovell attacked the cipher . . .": my vagueness here is deliberate, since I must confess that the original ciphered version of this message does not appear in Wellington's Dispatches, only the deciphered one, with passages in italics to show which words were ciphered. This French text was therefore enciphered by *me* in the year 2001 using an actual Army of Portugal cipher. It remains the case, of course, that the passage "HE Marshal the Duke of Ragusa" was in code, surrounded by uncoded words, just as it is shown in the chapter, hence the code-breaking technique would have been the same in 1811.

121. "One of them noted they had formed 'an extremely favourable notion of the judgement and good sense' of Marmont": this was Charles Stewart, writing as Lord Londonderry in his *History of the Peninsular War*. Perhaps it is wrong of me to quote Stewart's opinion of anything or anyone, but although I have generally condemned him as a dangerous fool, like all people of this kind he occasionally succumbed to outbursts of good judgment.

123. "Henry, aged twenty, had come out to fill a lowly civilian post, as a deputy assistant paymaster . . .": a record of Henry Scovell's service was passed to me by his descendant Martin Scovell and its principal points are confirmed in the Challis Index of Wellington's officers at the Royal United Services Institute.

123. "In Ciudad Rodrigo, the principal agent was a former member of the town *junta* . . .": this emerges in a letter from Wellington to his brother on 17 May 1812. The general says his Spanish spy performed service of "utmost importance to the cause."

123. "In Salamanca, Wellington's principal correspondent was an Irish priest . . .": quite a few contemporaries wrote about Curtis, including Tomkinson in his journal. There are also many references to him in Wellington's Dispatches. It is unclear exactly when he began his career as a spy, but it seems to have been in the summer of 1811.

124. "General Regnaud, the governor of Ciudad Rodrigo, had been captured by Don Julian Sanchez": this event was described in very different terms by General Dorsenne, writing to Paris, and in Wellington's Dispatches. The British general says Regnaud had an escort of twenty cavalry and was captured under the guns of the town. Dorsenne's version is that Regnaud only had three or four people with him and stupidly rode more than one league from the city.

124. "D'Espagne had first wanted to shoot Regnaud . . .": this detail and some others in this account come from two letters from FitzRoy Somerset to his brother, dated 16 October and 22 October 1811. Their Beaufort Paper references are FmM 4/1/6 and FmM 4/1/7 respectively.

125. "Wellington's table in the Frenada headquarters . . .": a delightful description of the general's dining arrangements in Frenada is contained in the journal of Captain Thomas Browne, an officer of the Staff, published by the Army Records Society in 1987.

126. "Wellington's spy in Ciudad Rodrigo immediately fled the city . . .": this is described in Wellington's letter of 17 May 1812, in Dispatches.

126. "Lieutenant Colonel John Grant . . . presented himself": his arrival at Frenada is recorded in Scovell's journal, WO37/7.

126. "At the end of October a ciphered message from Marmont to General Foy was captured . . .": it is reproduced in Wellington's Dispatches.

127. "When Regnaud's successor as governor of Ciudad Rodrigo arrived on 30 October (escorted by an entire division of infantry), he most likely brought new codes with him . . .": this is my deduction, since Scovell's journal talks about the meanness of the French cipher and the fact that he has just finished deciphering the message. If it had been one of the ciphers already known to him, making sense of it would have been light work. Scovell's papers contain a deciphering table for at least three different versions of the Army of Portugal code.

127. "Scovell had been doing it, but so had Somerset, and even Wellington himself . . .": Wellington told Ellesmere that Somerset had been good at deciphering and it is contained in Ellesmere's memoir of the duke. Scovell's papers never mention anyone else being involved in this work. Since he remained a lifelong friend of Somerset it is hard to imagine Scovell wanting to deny him any legitimate credit. On the other hand, Somerset, as military secretary, used ciphers in the course of managing Wellington's own correspondence with other potentates, so we may assume he was familiar with them and was probably involved in deciphering in its early stages.

Chapter Nine: The Attack on Ciudad Rodrigo, January 1812

131. "A gentleman could hardly hope for better sport": accounts of these activities are contained in Londonderry's *History* and several journals, including Larpent, Cocks and Tomkinson. Although Scovell was revealed in later life as a keen huntsman, his journal makes no mention of him hunting in Beira Baixa.

132. "One of Colonel Le Marchant's correspondents in the peninsula informed those back at Wycombe . . .": Captain Tryon Still, 10 May 1810, LMP Packet 2a, Item 4.

132. "On hearing of Orange's imminent arrival, FitzRoy Somerset had written home . . .": Somerset's letter to his brother of 14 July 1811, BP, FmM 4/1/6. Wellington's treatment of Orange provided one of the best examples of his favoritism toward blue bloods. Wellington mentioned the young ADC in his dispatch for the combat of El Bodon in September 1811, and in a letter of 12 June 1812 to Whitehall asked that the prince should be given a special medal, "although he is not exactly in the situation which would entitle him to it, he has rank, and certainly deserves it, and would be highly flattered at obtaining it." The contrast with his refusal to write similar testimonials to obscure officers who most definitely *were* in the situation to

receive the favor (for example, Captain Norman Ramsay of the Royal Horse Artillery, who saved his guns in the desperate fighting of 5 May 1811) is striking.

133. "You may suppose the Puff . . .": Lieutenant Colonel Alexander Gordon in a letter to his brother, 27 November 1811. It is reprinted in *At Wellington's Right Hand*, a book of Gordon's letters edited by Rory Muir and published by the Army Records Society.

133. "The officers in the lower branches of the Staff are sharp-set . . .": this quote comes from Francis Larpent, later judge advocate in Wellington's HQ. Although he is referring to the atmosphere during the staff's second winter in Frenada (1812–1813), this passage beautifully sums up a situation that study of journals and letters shows was apparent long before.

134. "On 19 November, Napoleon started dictating a series of terse orders": these are drawn from the official record of vol. 23 of his *Correspondance* and vol. 8 of Du Casse's *Correspondance du Roi Joseph*. In most cases they consist of his notes to Berthier to pass on to the relevant generals, which is why I have written the passage in this way.

135. "Berthier informed Joseph . . .": this message is reproduced in Du Casse.

136. "Jourdan's arrival seemed to turn this volatile assembly . . .": the evidence for this will become clear in following chapters. Jourdan in his *Memoires* said he believed Soult, his most implacable enemy, never got over the snub of not being appointed himself to this top job.

137. "The enciphering table arranged words, syllables, phrases or letters alphabetically": Scovell copied out the enciphering table in WO37/9.

137. "the person deciphering would use the other table, one in which the codes were listed in numeric order, each followed by its meaning": King Joseph's personal deciphering table can be found in the Wellington Papers, WP 9/4/1/6. Close examination of the document reveals the way the last two columns (giving ciphers 1201–1400) have just been glued on to a standard 1750 table.

138. "It was a code of such strength that Napoleon considered it safe to send letters about matters of the utmost importance in the hands of some local peasant": I am paraphrasing the emperor's actual words in a letter to the duke of Taranto during the 1812 Russian campaign and contained in vol. 24 of the *Correspondance*.

139. "In sending out the tables, Marshal Berthier urged the recipients . . .": this comes in a letter from Berthier to Marshal Davout written 18 March 1812. I found it on the Russian State Military Historical Archive in Moscow in Fol 440/1/348. Berthier's letter and the instructions for the use of the *Grand Chiffre* had been captured by Russian troops when they seized Marshal Davout's baggage at Krasnoie in November 1812, during the retreat from Moscow.

141. "'During this march,' one of its young officers recorded . . .": this was John Cook of the 43rd Light Infantry.

141. "That night the infantrymen had worked away feverishly in the darkness with picks and shovels . . .": the account of the Ciudad Rodrigo siege is based largely on the testimony of three eyewitnesses: Private Edward Costello of the 95th, Lieutenant John Cook of the 43rd, and Sergeant William Lawrence of the 40th. Happily for the modern reader, all three of these valuable journals have been reproduced by Eileen

Hathaway's Shinglepicker Press (28 Bonfields Avenue, Swanage, Dorset BH19 1PL). Mrs. Hathaway has done an invaluable service in collating the accounts of other eyewitnesses and using them to confirm or amplify details given by these three soldiers. The result is a very strong historical record in each case. Some additional details (e.g., the number of siege guns opening up on the fifteenth) come from Scovell's journal.

145. "In a private letter to the Duke of Richmond . . .": see Wellington's Dispatches.

147. "After a few days in Paris, Jardet wrote a twenty-eight-page letter back to his commander in Spain . . .": happily this original document survives in WO37/1. Although it is clear that Scovell deciphered messages before March 1812, it is only those after this date that (mostly) survive in his papers in the Public Record Office.

Chapter Ten: The Storm of Badajoz, March 1812

153. "On 17th March, the bands struck up . . .": according to Lieutenant Cook of the 43rd.

153. "One young officer of the 95th Rifles hoped that . . .": this was Harry Smith in his autobiography, first published in 1903.

155. "This vague instruction had been superceded by further orders . . . from Napoleon on 18 and 20 February . . .": these details are drawn from Du Casse (vol. 8) and the French correspondence produced as an appendix to Wellington's Dispatches.

156. "Napoleon had scribbled a most important order to Berthier in Paris": contained in Du Casse.

157. "Even in the symbolic act of passing the cipher to General Clarke . . .": this order was actually only given on 4 May 1812 and is contained in a letter from the emperor to Berthier, reproduced in Napoleon's *Correspondance*, item no. 18685, vol. 23.

158. "The fickle nature of many messengers in French pay": this account is pieced together from Scovell's journal (alas, he does not say whether *he* was the man who negotiated with the Spaniard) and that of Edward Cocks.

159. "he would continue his journey to Seville with every incentive . . .": neither Cocks nor Scovell suggests the messenger was executed or sent back into Badajoz. Whether the man decided to undertake more of these lucrative missions or whether he confined himself to less hazardous business, we can only speculate.

159. "One young officer recorded, 'It required every man to be actually in the trenches . . .' ": Lieutenant John Kincaid in his memoir *Random Shots* (reprinted by Spellmount in 1998).

162. "one diner recalled: 'There was little conversation . . .'": McGrigor in his most perceptive memoir, *The Autobiography and Services of Sir Jas McGrigor*, London, 1861.

163. "Sergeant William Lawrence of the 40th had volunteered . . .": these details are all taken from the excellent Shinglepicker Press reprint of Lawrence's memoirs, *A Dorset Soldier*.

163. "the thought struck me forcibly—you will be in hell before daylight!":

this was William Green, another diarist of the 95th. So memorable is this phrase
that it has provided the title for a recent book on Peninsular sieges.

163. "Rifleman Costello of the 95th was one of a team . . .": Costello's memoirs, like Lawrence's, are reprinted by the Shinglepicker Press.

166. "One eyewitness saw: 'General Philippon . . .'": McGrigor again.

167. "Scovell's friends Somerset and Hardinge were both promoted lieutenant
colonel . . .": to be strict, this emerged not in the victory dispatch but in subsequent
correspondence.

167. "Many surviving soldiers and officers profited . . .": the interesting, if
somewhat discreditable, detail that officers were involved in this stealing emerges
from the journal of E. W. Buckham, a commissary who encountered the gentlemen
in question selling their spoils in Oporto.

Chapter Eleven: From Lisbon to Fuente Guinaldo, April to June 1812

170. "'The streets of Lisbon glittered with uniforms . . .'": this detail, and
much else in this description of Lisbon, comes from *Recollection of the Peninsula* by
Moyle Sherer. This officer was an unusual diarist, confining his accounts of battles
to a page or two and devoting great passages of descriptive writing to the country
and people, providing details which it is hard to pick up elsewhere.

170. "Major Scovell's leave had only been possible because the main army
would take a week or ten days to make its way back . . .": Scovell's own journal
(WO37/3) makes clear he was only allowed to go under these terms.

171. "Marmont's guest was none other than Lieutenant Colonel Colquhoun
Grant, Wellington's intelligence officer": Grant related these details to Sir James
McGrigor, his brother-in-law and Wellington's chief surgeon, who left his own
Peninsular memoir, mentioned above.

172. "militiamen and Don Julian Sanchez's guerrillas had swarmed about the
French rear": we are now entering the phase of this story where Scovell's papers at
the Public Record Office, WO37, contain most of the relevant original documents.

172. "The way the English conducted themselves . . .": Soult's letter to Berthier
of 17 April 1812, in WO37.

173. "it took him just three days to travel from the Portuguese capital to
Fuente Guinaldo . . .": Scovell's journal again.

173. "Wellington remained in the handsome mayor's house in Fuente
Guinaldo's plaza": the building is still there. Alas, when I visited, the lady who owns
the part of the building that Wellington had used as his office was out.

173. "Wellington did not feel free to make his next move . . .": Wellington's
Dispatches make clear that he had not finally made up his mind which way to attack
until mid-May.

173. "Further study also allowed certain deductions to be drawn . . .": these
observations about the pattern of the cipher are mine. Scovell's notebooks give a
general sense of how he attacked the codes but are not so specific as to tell us, for

example, which code number he worked out first. Having worked on the French originals for months I can say, though, that once familiar with the patterns of these letters, the recurrence of numbers like 13 or 210 pretty much leaps out at you. It becomes the fastest way of checking quickly whether the letter in question is in Joseph's *Grand Chiffre* or some other code.

177. "Since Marmont was assuming many of his messages would fall into British hands . . .": in a letter of 6 July 1812 to Jourdan (it is in the Scovell Papers), Marmont says explicitly that pretty much everything he writes ends up in enemy hands. He was just hoping that one of the duplicate or triplicate messages would actually reach its addressee as well.

178. "There was hardly a general in Spain who had not reflected on the emperor's imminent departure for Poland . . . and what it meant for their own expectations": this is apparent, for example, in Jardet's letter to Marmont cited in the previous chapter. The expectation of the Russian war was so widespread that cleverer British officers were reflecting on it in their journals of spring 1812 too— Cocks and D'Urban being two examples.

179. "The harvest came a little later in the north, which bought him a week or two more to fight the Army of Portugal . . . on more favorable terms": Wellington discusses the question in these terms in a letter to Lieutenant General Graham on 24 May 1812, reproduced in Dispatches.

180. "On the last day of April, one of Marmont's messengers was seized by Don Julian Sanchez's lancers . . .": that they were responsible for the coup emerges in McGrigor's journal.

Chapter Twelve: The Salamanca Campaign Opens, May 1812

183. "Early on the morning of 19 May, soldiers of the 71st and 92nd Highlanders . . .": my account draws extensively on *A Soldier of the Seventy First*, originally published in 1819. Some controversy surrounds the identity of the author, or indeed whether the experiences related were actually those of more than one man.

185. "Wellington dwelt long on Major General Lumley's panic . . .": see Wellington's letter of 28 May to Liverpool, in Dispatches.

185. "Wellington, behind his customary mask of inscrutibility, awaited the outcome of this new campaign at Westminster . . .": that he discussed London politics is clear from the letters of FitzRoy Somerset that mention these topics (e.g., Perceval's assassination). Somerset was also part of a big Tory family, but it is apparent reading these missives (in the Beaufort Papers, FmM 4/1/7 and FmM 4/1/8) that Wellington was careful about expressing strong personal opinions.

185. "an altogether safer topic for table talk than London politics": Cocks's and D'Urban's journals.

186. "A further package of captured letters, dated 1 May . . .": preserved in the Scovell Papers, WO37/1.

188. "By the end of May 1812, Scovell was beginning to get a real toehold on the slippery precipice of the code": the key evidence of this is the report of some

London decipherers who later attacked the code. Their results reside in the Wellington Papers, as WP 9/4/1/5. These careful men noted on their chart which codes had already been cracked by Wellington's staff before work began in London. Since we know they were asked to help on 25 June 1812, this record of what had been achieved up until that date is critical to understanding Scovell's early results. Scovell's own table is part of WO37/9 and seems to represent his achievement up until late 1812.

189. "Wellington was impatient . . .": his impatience on this point emerges in several letters in his Dispatches; for example, on 7, 18 and 25 June 1812.

189. "There was also the little office in London, off Abchurch Street, where the foreign secretary and prime minister retained a few fellows . . .": see Ellis, *History of the Post Office*, Oxford University Press, 1958, for an account of these decipherers.

190. "Jourdan had drawn up a memorandum at the end of May outlining what needed to be done to defend French interests in Spain": which he helpfully printed in his *Memoires*, also quoting from Clarke's fatuous reply.

191. "Antoine Fee, the young pharmacist to a dragoon regiment . . .": who left us the memoirs referred to previously.

193. "Marshal Beresford had been sent out to examine this inhospitable country . . .": on 24 May, according to Scovell's journal.

194. "On the evening of 12 June, the soldiers of Wellington's army rested around their bivouacs . . .": our old Light Division companions, Lieutenant Cook and Rifleman Costello, are the source of these details.

Chapter Thirteen: The Great Cipher Under Attack, June and July 1812

197. "shouts of *Viva!*; cups of local wine; petals scattered from upstairs windows . . .": these scenes come from Tomkinson, Warre and Scovell's journals.

198. "an intercepted letter the following day that contained, *en clair*, nothing less than the Army of Portugal's Morning State . . .": referred to in Wellington's Dispatches, 14 June 1812.

200. "Among the rank and file, Marmont was a popular leader": the descriptions of Marmont come from Robert Christophe's *Les Amours et Les Guerres du Marechal Marmont*, a rather purple text, giving much space to the notion that Napoleon was sleeping with Marmont's wife while the marshal was on campaign. The unnamed officer is Captain Charles Parquin in his *Les Souvenirs du Capitaine Parquin*, an account considered unreliable by the historian Charles Oman, but containing some good color nevertheless.

201. "I will maneuver about Salamanca . . .": Marmont's letter of 22 June is in the Scovell Papers.

202. "a round shot, eight pounds, went very near Major Lawrie who stands in my way for promotion!" : the ambitious officer in question was Edward Cocks.

202. "'Very little confusion was occasioned,' noted one of those present . . .": this was Tomkinson, who was acting as an ADC to General Stapleton Cotton at the time.

203. "The British troops had slept on beds of flattened corn . . .": details of the scene atop the San Christoval ridge from our indefatigable Light Division diarists Lieutenant Cook and Rifleman Costello.

204. "For the general, there was an opportunity to receive his secret correspondent, Father Patrick Curtis . . .": Tomkinson tells us they met at this juncture, also that the open way Curtis was received might pose problems for him in the future, an accurate prophecy.

205. "Wellington resolved that he must obtain the services of the best decipherers in Britain . . .": Wellington's letter to Bathurst is in Dispatches; the above-mentioned document, WP 9/4/1/5, tells us what Scovell knew by 25 June.

207. "The British had started firing red-hot shot at the roof of the massive building and succeeded in setting it on fire": this was the idea of Major Sturgeon, another Wycombite who was a source of almost as many good ideas as Scovell.

207. "The landscape, with its tall fields of billowing corn, vineyards and orchards, seemed lush and wonderful . . .": details from our reliable guides to this campaign, Tomkinson, Warre and Scovell himself.

Chapter Fourteen: Triumph Over the Great Cipher, July 1812

214. "young Guards officers took advantage of the hiatus . . .": according to a letter from Charles Cocks (Edward's brother), who was serving with them. It is reprinted in Julia Page's book.

215. "One British major wrote home grumpily . . .": William Warre, who I will quote a good deal on the Salamanca campaign, since his description of these events is both insightful and often funny, unlike some of his earlier ramblings.

215. "The staff were perplexed that he had not given battle on the San Christoval position . . .": all of our usual informants in the British officer corps (Warre, Tomkinson, Cocks, and Scovell himself) commented in their journals on how puzzled they were that Wellington had not given battle. In their polite, understated way it is clear that many of them thought their commander had missed his golden opportunity.

215. "he did not care one jot for their opinions": the operative quote from Wellington being, "the staff officers of the army are attached to me to enable me to communicate my orders to my inferiors, and otherwise to assist me in the performance of my duty," Dispatches, 14 October 1812.

217. "The most interesting of the dispatches was written on a tiny slither of paper . . .": it resides in WO37/1.

218. "Scovell reflected on the events of the seventeenth with little sentimentality . . .": in his journal, WO37/7b.

219. "A troop of Royal Horse Artillery came under attack as it retreated . . .": several interesting details in this account of Castrejon come from Lieutenant John Cook of the 43rd Light Infantry.

220. "One young Guards officer said in his letter . . .": this is Charles Cocks again.

223. "After a tiring day with the two armies completing their parallel march down to the line of the River Tormes and Salamanca, Wellington wrote to Earl Bathurst in London": this letter is actually from 21 July, Dispatches.

Chapter Fifteen: The Battle of Salamanca, 22 July 1812

228. "General Foy, occupying the end of the French deployment closest to the river, set out to survey the enemy lines": Vie Militaire, a biography of Foy by Girod de L'Ain, includes long passages of direct quotation from the general's letters and diaries, a vital source on the French side of the battle. Other information on their perspective comes from Du Casse's collection of Joseph's documents, Marmont's *Memoires* and Jourdan's memoirs. I have also referred to Souvenirs *du Capitaine Parquin* by Charles Parquin. Many authorities consider the last unreliable but he is good for color.

229. "Pakenham and the cavalry marching in his company were to make a long trek . . .": the British sources on the battle differ on when Pakenham got his orders and where exactly they were in the early part of the day. One thing is clear, though they had moved far enough by 3 P.M. that their orders *must* have been given early on.

230. "Foy . . . worried about his chief's judgement . . .": these damming meditations by Foy came from a letter to a friend in France on 16 July 1812 and are quoted by Girod de l'Ain. The fact that these reflections were contemporary to the campaign is important, for Foy later became one of the many officers to villify Marmont for his defection from the imperial cause in 1814.

230. "Marmont's uncertainty revealed itself once more in orders that kept his options open": all of Marmont's rather sad attempts to explain what happened suggest he had not resolved to attack Wellington with his full strength.

231. "Scovell, among several staff officers, watched it happen . . .": the journal once more. Scovell was often so careful about what he wrote concerning his master that his remarks might be taken to be the equivalent of rolling his eyes skyward when the orders to attack were canceled.

231. "Major FitzRoy Somerset, ever loyal to his master, detected the insinuations . . .": in a letter to his brother on 27 July 1812, BP FmM 4/1/8.

232. "He looked to his right. The dust still showed the progress of a French force at least a mile away": standing atop the Teso San Miguel it is clear that Wellington could not actually see the men of Thomières's division moving up, as some writers suggest.

233. "the single figure of the British commander came galloping across the scrub . . .": according to William Grattan of the 88th in his *Adventures with the Connaught Rangers*. D'Urban suggests DeLancey and Sturgeon did keep up with Wellington. The two men are the main sources for what happened at this end of the battlefield.

234. "Scovell . . . found his brother-in-law, Major Leigh Clowes . . .": there is an account of their conversation in Le Marchant's papers. It is a letter from Clowes

to Scovell some years later (LMP Packet 17a, Item 5). Scovell copied Clowes's letter, added an account of his own and sent them to Le Marchant's son Denis.

236. "Le Marchant's heavies had mounted and were deploying into line . . .": my account is drawn together from Denis Le Marchant's life of his father, the Le Marchant Papers and R. H. Thoumine's superb but rather rare biography of the general, *Scientific Soldier*, Oxford University Press, 1968.

236. "Cotton lost his temper with the brigade commander and strong words were exchanged": this was revealed in the biography of Cotton, *Memoirs and Correspondence of Field Marshal Viscount Combermere*, penned by his widow, Mary. It was obliquely confirmed by Tomkinson. I am very grateful to Rory Muir for bringing this curious episode to my attention.

238. "One young officer wrote home, 'It was a fine sight . . .'": Lieutenant Norcliffe of the 4th Dragoons, reproduced by Rory Muir in *Salamanca 1812*. He kindly showed me sections of the manuscript before its publication.

240. "Clowes . . . could not bring himself to tell Carey that his father was dead . . .": this touching scene was brought out of the Le Marchant Papers by Thoumine.

242. "Wellington's private verdict . . .": Dispatches, 25 July 1812.

242. "For this achievement Scovell was mentioned in the Salamanca dispatch . . .": I see no other explanation for the mention than his codebreaking. His activities on 22 July were admirable and risky, but no more so than his actions beside Wellington at half a dozen other major battles, none of which earned him a similar distinction. Clearly there was no sense that the honor was being used to make a long-overdue promotion (as was often the case), since Scovell had received his majority just the previous spring. Given the difficulties of moving from major to lieutenant colonel, we can safely assume Scovell would have waited years for it had Wellington not been extremely grateful for his work during the Salamanca campaign.

Chapter Sixteen: The March to Burgos, Summer and Early Fall 1812

244. "On 12 August, Soult tried an extraordinary gamble": a copy of his letter resides in the Public Record Office in the WO37 class. Unfortunately for us, this is one of the messages for which the ciphered original is unavailable. Napier suggests that the Soult letter was only read after being captured in Joseph's baggage at Vitoria in June 1813, but I do not believe this to be the case.

244. "no message from Paris had reached his desk for more than four months . . .": this fact, along with the details of how it was being sent, were contained in the letter itself.

246. "The king's French secretary of state, part of the evacuation . . .": Miot de Melito; the quote is from his memoirs.

247. "on the first, Wellington agreed to attend a bullfight in his honor . . .": some sources say the last day of August; I have gone with this date because it is

in Scovell's journal, WO37/7b, which also provides the colorful passages that follow.

248. "General Bertrand Clausel, the Army of Portugal's commander, despaired of the morale of his troops": this letter was not intercepted by the Allies. It is reproduced in Du Casse, *Correspondance du Roi Joseph.*

249. "On 27 September, Major Cocks heard a rumor . . .": this comes from the very excellent book based on his papers by Julia Page.

250. "After one operation, Burgoyne wrote home bitterly . . .": Burgoyne's published journal is an anodyne work. The letters were obtained later by Sir Charles Oman and used in his great work.

250. "the tensions had been exacerbated by a rebuke on Wellington's part during their advance to Madrid": this unusual evidence of an open clash between the general and Scovell emerges from an addendum (probably added months or even years after the event) to his journal. I have not quoted verbatim, since the writing is bad even by the standards of Scovell's often atrocious hieroglyphics.

251. "Scovell was directing hundreds of men in this task and . . . spent £22,477 in little over one year on it": details from accounts found at AO 1/171/488.

252. "He wrote back to the commodore . . .": Wellington's Dispatches, 11 August 1812.

253. "A diplomatic cipher had been sent out, but there had been problems . . ." these emerge in Wellington's dispatches of 29 August and 2 September 1812.

253. "to quote an example given by him, the code 134A18 could be deciphered as follows . . .": it is among his remarks on codes in his Conradus notebook, WO37/9.

255. "'The ruler's first interview with the Marshal produced some lively arguments'": Jourdan's *Memoires.*

Chapter Seventeen: Frenada, December 1812 to March 1813

261. "It was about midnight on a December evening and few people were stirring in the bivouac": details of Saornil's raid are gleaned from Francis Larpent's journal, *The Private Journal of Judge Advocate F. S. Larpent.* This is an excellent book, full of the sort of detail most officers at headquarters considered irrelevant. It also includes recollections of George and Mary Scovell.

262. "A British officer who had encountered Saornil's band in the summer of 1812 . . .": Captain William Tomkinson.

265. "general sent him on his way home with these brutal words . . .": Wellington's letter to Colonel Framingham, in Dispatches, 6 May 1813.

265. "Murray . . . became the second most important man in the Army, in practice if not by seniority": for reasons of brevity, I have not told the story of London's attempts to foist a second in command on Wellington. Farcically, their candidate, General Sir Edward Paget, was captured by the French in November 1813, just one week after coming out to the army. In a letter to Earl Bathurst in Dispatches 26 December 1813 (during a further round of pressure from London for a second in

command), Wellington expressed his views pungently, calling an officer in such a post "a person without defined duties, excepting to give flying opinions, from which he may depart at pleasure, must be a nuisance in moments of decision; and whether I have a second in command or not, I am determined always to act according to the dictates of my own judgement."

267. "before setting off for Cadiz, Wellington had complained to London 'I have not yet any intelligence . . .'": letter to Bathurst, 2 December 1812.

267. "The letters spread out in front of him were one from Joseph to the emperor . . .": Saornil's prizes are a significant example of intercepted correspondence *not* found in the Scovell Papers. They are in the Wellington Papers, WP 1/361 Fol. 2, and when placed together reveal the original folds of the courier's packet.

268. "a further letter from Joseph to the emperor and dated 22 December 1812 . . .": in the Scovell Papers, WO37/2.

271. "For months, Joseph had kept the contents of Soult's letter to himself—probably because it was too humiliating to confess to his brother that an eminent marshal had been plotting in this way": this is my interpretation. There are suggestions in Joseph's later letters that the king may have copied Soult's 12 August message before to the emperor. It may be that he assumed the papers had been lost in Napoleon's baggage in Russia and therefore sent another copy in January 1813.

273. "On his return to Paris, Desprez had written to Joseph . . .": his letter, dated 3 January, is in Du Casse's *Correspondance du Roi Joseph*. I must confess a certain fascination with Desprez, in some sense an unsung hero of the French staff system, and someone whose knack of being in the wrong place at the wrong time allowed him to witness all of the great moments in the collapse of Napoleon's power. He was also in the Waterloo campaign!

274. "It was only when the downpours of March and April had raised the level of the Coa that trout and the fish locals called *bogas* and *barbos* could migrate up from the Douro": I am no fisherman; this knowledge was derived from a restaurateur in Almeida who proved a mine of useful local detail.

275. "It is impossible to imagine anything more truly ludicrous than to see Lydia Languish . . .": according to Leach of the 95th.

Chapter Eighteen: The Vitoria Campaign, April to July 1813

277. "In April 1813 each cavalry regiment in the Peninsular army received a request for volunteers": by an order of Wellington, 13 April 1813, Dispatches. The authority to raise them was given by the duke of York in a letter of January 1813.

277. "A plan that he had first committed to paper in 1808 . . .": this emerges in his letter to Le Marchant of 23 November 1808, reference given above. Alas, I have not found the plan itself.

278. "By the end of the month parties of new recruits were arriving": the quote comes from Larpent's memoirs, as does the intriguing information about the reluctance of the Household Cavalry men to serve—an early example of the special

pleading by these regiments that anyone who has served in a subsequent British army will find all too familiar.

278. "Those who answered the call to Frenada were given a smart new uniform": it was sketched by the artist Charles Hamilton Smith and published in a book of British uniforms in 1813.

279. "You need be under no apprehension on the score of my good nature . . .": this comes from Scovell's letter to James Willoughby Gordon, the quarter master general at Horse Guards, of 4 July 1813. It now resides in the British Library Manuscript collection as Add. 49506. It is clear from the letter that the charges against Scovell must have emerged into the open following the pillage of French baggage at Vitoria in June 1813, an outbreak of general thieving so large that Scovell's two hundred men could hardly have stopped it.

282. "The most significant dated 13 March, from King Joseph to General Charles Reille . . .": another original dispatch preserved in the Scovell Papers, and also in Lucotte's.

283. "It was from Earl Bathurst and contained the report of the London government decipherers . . .": this is the table referred to in previous chapters, WP 9/4/1/5. Earl Bathurst's covering letter of 5 April 1813 is also in the Wellington Papers.

284. "The general wrote back to London sarcastically": his letter of 24 May 1813. I am convinced that it was sarcasm since the knowledge of the Great Cipher was sufficiently good by early 1813 for the general freely to be quoting chunks of ciphered French dispatches to Spanish politicians (see above) and the secretary of war. Scovell's own papers state the cipher was to all intents and purposes completely broken by the end of 1812.

284. "He had been banished from Salamanca by the French early in 1813, seeking refuge in Ciudad Rodrigo": Curtis's fate emerges in a letter he wrote to Wellington and which survives in his papers at Southampton University.

285. "Gomm emulated the tactics of previous exploring officers . . .": details of his mission emerge from Sir William Gomm, *His Letters and Journals from 1799 to Waterloo*, London, 1881.

285. "All aspects of supply had been attended to": details gleaned from various journals by our regular informants, Lieutenant Cook, Rifleman Costello, and Captain Tomkinson.

286. "Just north of Salamanca, on 25 May, the British caught up with General Villatte's rear guard": Scovell describes the action and his thoughts in his journal, WO37/7b.

288. "Marshal Jourdan had seen to it that silver was broadcast around the border . . ." : see his *Memoires*.

289. "The countryside was largely undisturbed by the war": the first quote comes from Cook, the one about the band from G. Simmons, *A British Rifleman*, London, 1899.

290. "On the fourteenth, Scovell found himself invited to a picnic lunch in a field": this bucolic vignette was sketched for us by Larpent in his journal.

290. "Jourdan, it has to be said, did not expect a fight at Vitoria at all": the quote is from his *Memoires* again.

292. "The 71st was forced back briefly": details from the journal *A Soldier of the Seventy First*. Most of those lost Highlanders had actually been captured and were free the following day.

294. "One of the king's courtiers recorded . . .": Miot de Melito in his memoirs.

295. "The road to Pampluna was choked up with many carriages filled up with imploring ladies . . .'": this rather literary description came from Lieutenant Cook. This panorama of destruction and pillage reminds me of the Mutla Ridge, where I saw the remnants of Iraq's army following the liberation of Kuwait in 1991.

296. "FitzRoy Somerset wrote to his brother, 'The only thing . . .'": letter to the duke of Beaufort of 26 June 1813, BP FmM 4/1/9.

296. "The many ditches, walls and hedges of the market gardens and small-holders' plots surrounding the city had also made it very hard for the British cavalry to pursue . . .": this was the view of FitzRoy's brother Lord Edward, the cavalry commander, in his letter home of June 1813, also in the Beaufort Papers.

297. "He finally found the large document, folded up, with the words *Sa Majeste Catholique* written on its outside . . .": Joseph's table resides in the Wellington Papers, WP 9/4/1/6.

297. "the minister of war in Paris needed to know": Joseph's letter of 27 June to Clarke is in Du Casse.

297. "The king never suspected that the British had been reading . . . for the previous year . . .": this seems obvious, given his letter to Clarke. A French researcher, Cyril Canet, while helping me, uncovered a letter in the Army of Catalonia's carton (File 295, item 17 at the French army archives at Vincennes) suggesting that they were aware that their ciphers had been compromised in 1813. This letter to Marshal Suchet is dated 15 February. We must assume that the author was referring to the simple *chiffres* used only in that army area. If not there is a possibility that headquarters never reacted properly to this alarming news.

298. "an intercepted dispatch from the French minister of war to Marshal Suchet, in command of the Army of Catalonia . . .": Scovell Papers, WO37/3.

Chapter Nineteen: Waterloo, 18 June 1815

299. "It was early afternoon as the small group of staff galloped across the top of the Mont St. Jean ridge . . .": this account is based on Scovell's later memorandum on the battle (in WO37), a manuscript account left by his servant Edward Healey (residing in the National Army Museum Library), and *A Week at Waterloo*, edited by Major B. R. Ward, London, 1906, which contains the account of Lady De Lancey, Colonel William's widow.

Once again, I have skipped in the narrative here. Scovell's campaigns in Spain and France during the latter part of 1813 and early 1814 tell us little or nothing about code breaking or indeed the relations in headquarters. Scovell's conduct following the fighting at St. Pierre d'Irrube in December is worth mentioning, though. During this action Captain Carey Le Marchant, son of the late general, was mortally wounded. It is clear from the accounts of others that Scovell did everything to help the young officer in his final days, which were spent in Scovell's billet. This humane side of the man is rarely visible in his journal and emerged again following Waterloo. When the Peninsula War ended, George and Mary rode back across France to the Channel coast. They evidently had an enjoyable time, taking in Paris and visiting many other cultural sites.

Chapter Twenty: Scovell's Later Life, 1819 to 1861

305. "FitzRoy Somerset was found a seat in Truro . . .": details of these Parliamentary arrangements can be found in the *Dictionary of National Biography* entry for each man.

305. "Some of them traded on their status as 'A Hero of Waterloo and the Peninsula' . . .": one of Charles Vere's handbills is preserved in the British Library as *Biographical Sketch of His Military Services*.

305. "Scovell set pen to paper": the letter is in the Wellington Papers, WP 1/613/30.

306. "There is no record of any reply from Wellington": not in the Wellington Papers, which have been very thoroughly indexed as part of an on-line project. This means it is most unlikely even that a letter to another correspondent of the "find that chap Scovell something to do" variety exists. The Scovell Papers contain no reply, and given some of the materials included in that collection it seems impossible that any courteous letter from the duke would not have been kept.

306. "wondering whether he might become head of one of the new police forces . . .": a letter from Somerset to Scovell asking him whether he is interested in becoming head of the New Zealand police survives in the Scovell Papers.

307. "Thus, late in 1823, Murray asked Scovell to reexamine many of the intercepted French dispatches from the Peninsular campaigns . . .": there are many fascinating jottings from this exercise in WO37/10, including lists of all messages examined.

308. That it was Hardinge's doing emerges in a letter in WO99/24, part of the papers kept at Sandhurst. In it, Scovell complains that he is not receiving all of the allowances promised to him by Hardinge when they agreed to terms for the job.

309. "The prime minister . . . telling one friend, 'If there is mutiny in the Army . . .'": Wellington wrote this to the Rev. Gleig, his biographer. It is quoted in Hugh Thomas's *The Story of Sandhurst*.

309. "When Scovell commissioned a portrait of Somerset in 1841, he sent a print to Wellington . . ." : a copy of Scovell's accompanying letter of 20 September 1841 remains in the possession of Martin Scovell, his descendant, who showed it to me. John Sweetman, in his biography of Raglan, also mentions the portrait: Somerset (Raglan) wrote complaining that his friend Scovell had gone to the trouble and expense of having the painting done, whereas his own son was not interested in hav-

ing a copy. This is one of the reasons why I do not think it is too strong to speak of Scovell's friendship as love.

309. "When he died of dysentery later the same year, Scovell was heart-broken . . .": this is evident from several letters in the Scovell Papers, as was his desire to protect Raglan's reputation.

309. "On 10 August 1836, the duke went to dine with friends at Mr. Rogers's town house": this anecdote, complete with the final quote, comes from Stanhope's *Conversations with the Duke of Wellington*.

SECONDARY SOURCES

Throughout the writing of this book I have been using *A History of the Peninsular War* by Sir Charles Oman. He has been used as the decider on such issues as casualty numbers. These seven thick volumes, despite their occasional faults, are one of the greatest works of military history ever written. Certainly no journey into the past has ever given me such pleasure as beginning Oman's series and reading it through to its conclusion. It is a case, I think, of the reward derived by the reader being commensurate with the time put in. *Wellington's Army 1809–1814*, also by Oman, is a valuable reference for details such as the brigading of units and changes of command, as well as a very good synthesis of the soldiers' journals. *Wellington's Headquarters*, a classic study by S.G.P. Ward , London, 1957, was also valuable to me in gaining an initial understanding of how it all worked.

I have also drawn on Elizabeth Longford's biography of Wellington (in two volumes: *The Years of the Sword* and *The Years of State*). She is very good both on his Tory connections and her insights into his brilliant if unforgiving psychology.

A last word of praise belongs to the *Dictionnaire Biographique des Generaux et Amiraux françaises de La Revolution et de l'Empire* by Georges Six. This research on the lives of Napoleon's senior officers is fantastically useful when searching for details about some of the French Peninsular letter writers. It is only a shame that no work of the same comprehensiveness exists for British officers of the period.

INDEX

Wellington, General Arthur (*cont.*)
  military colleges and, 308–9
  Murray and, 55
  Oporto and, 35–42, 58–60
  papers of, reveal Scovell's skill, 311,
    312
  Popham and, 252
  Portugal defended by, 83–84
  Regnaud capture and, 124–25
  Russian campaign and, 265–66
  Salamanca and, 193–95, 197–204,
    206–7, 209–11, 215–20, 222–24,
    227–34, 236, 238–42, 264–65
  Scovell oversees communications of, 54,
    55, 102–3, 63, 252–53
  Scovell's deciphering and, 188–89, 193,
    205–7, 242, 283–84, 311–12
  Scovell's relationship with, after war,
    303–6, 309–10
  Scovell's relationship with, during war,
    51, 250–51
  Soult's escape from Portugal and,
    44–49
  Spanish allies and, xvii, 66–67, 75,
    77
  staff and, xiv–xvii, 79–81, 132–33,
    265, 301–2
  Staff Cavalry and, 278–79
  suppresses publicizing of breaking
    French code, 307–10
  Talavera and, 75–77
  Vimeiro and, 25–26
  Vitoria and, 282–93, 295,
    296
  wife and, 81
  Waterloo and, 299–302
Wellington, Kitty (wife), 81
Whigs, 9, 24, 94, 264, 265
William, prince of Orange, 132, 133, 229,
  239, 242, 290, 301, 302
Wycombites ("scientific soldiers"), 50–51,
  53, 83, 94

York, duke of, 8
  army reforms and, 50, 61
  Clarke affair and, 31–32